'[James Stern] is one of the world's best s...
MALCOLM COWLEY

'I've never been able to forget your stor...
ignorant I tell them as my ow...
ARTHUR MILLER

'The one man who might *just* persuade Wystan to alter *one* word
in a poem, my dear, is Jimmy Stern.'
BRIAN HOWARD TO MICHAEL WISHART

'You have only begun to do the great work as a novelist that it lies
within you to do: there is no one writing in either America or
England today that you need fear comparison with.'
LEWIS MUMFORD

'A miracle of understanding . . . overpoweringly impressive . . . What
Mr Hersey did for the single bombing of Hiroshima, Mr Stern has
succeeded in doing for the whole aftermath of the German war and for
the allied occupation – nor could even Tolstoy have done better.'
ANNE FREMANTLE on *The Hidden Damage*

The Hidden Damage is 'one of the very best books of imaginative
interpretation that has been done in our time'.
LEWIS MUMFORD

' . . . all that Jimmy was, his independent mind, his life-long passion
for writing of the highest standards, and his gift for friendship. I think
of him as one of the few truly unique people I've known in my life and
always remember how, from him, came some of my earliest encouragement as a writer. His own title could be used by us to describe him: the
man who was loved – and sometimes even a little feared, because he
was so uncompromising in his integrity, but that was part of his value.'
NADINE GORDIMER on 3 December 1993 to
James Stern's widow, Tania

JAMES STERN

For Elizabeth
very dear friend
for more than
half a century
from Miles
June 2006

JAMES STERN

A Life in Letters

1904–1993

MILES HUDDLESTON

MICHAEL RUSSELL

THIS BOOK IS FOR
MAGGIE
AND IN MEMORY OF
GRACE MILDRED
1903–1981

The right of Miles Huddleston to be identified
as the author of this work has been asserted by him
in accordance with the Copyright, Designs
and Patents Act, 1988

First published in Great Britain 2002
By Michael Russell (Publishing) Ltd
Wilby Hall, Wilby, Norwich NR16 2JP

Typeset in Sabon by Waveney Typesetters
Wymondham, Norfolk
Printed and bound in Great Britain
by Biddles Ltd, Guildford and King's Lynn

ISBN 0 85955 272 1

Contents

Illustrations

Acknowledgements

The first person to thank is David Hughes who in the beginning suggested that I write about Jimmy Stern. Subsequently he has helped me a great deal, as has John Byrne, Stern's literary executor, who besides allowing me to quote from Jimmy's letters – and from one of his own – has provided a vivid glimpse of the Sterns in their last days. Chris Fletcher of the British Library has also given me invaluable help in the Stern archive.

Three close friends, Anne Chisholm (who has provided a pen-portrait of Jimmy and Tania Stern later in the book), Imogen Olsen and the late Nora Sayre, have been tireless, unselfish and professional with their editorial suggestions. My wife, Maggie, has shown much forbearance, patience and endless practical assistance, not least with the vagaries of my word-processor. Gill and Peter Stern have given me hours of their time and unstinting help in matters of family history, photographs and the loan of books. Simon Stern, Jimmy's nephew, too, has helped me considerably. I am particularly grateful to Julian Fane and Alston Purvis for their contributions to this portrait of Jimmy.

I am indebted to the following for their impressions, stories and other material and for practical aid: Sybille Bedford, Gordon Bowker, Katherine Bucknell, Joan Crowell, Beatrice Dennis, Teresa Donovan, Lila Duckworth, Peggy Elting, Magouche Fielding, Christian Geissler, Anthony Hobson, Pixie Holford, Elizabeth Hughes (Royal Society of Literature), Sean Wyse Jackson, Gerard Long (National Library of Ireland), David Marr, Edward Mendelson, Michael Meredith (Eton College Library), Laura Mitchell, Andrew Orgill (Royal Military Academy, Sandhurst), Peter Parker, Frances Partridge, Vita Petersen, Elaine Robson-Scott, Jeffrey Rosenheim (Metropolitan Museum of Art, New York), the late Alan Ross, Jane Rye, Pauline Rumbold, Anthony Sampson, Sally Sampson, Tom Sawyer, Virginia Scholte, Rivers Scott, Alan L. Shrimpton (Bourneville Village Trust), James Slavin, Maeve Slavin, Humphrey Spender, Tina Staples (HSBC Holdings plc), Chantal Stokeley, Humphrey Stone, Solveig Stone, Isabelle Storey, Robert Sykes, Frank Tait, Kitty West, Pamela Wilson (*Time*).

For permission to quote from various sources, I thank the following: Michael Mallon for three passages from Harold Acton's memoirs; the Estate of W. H. Auden for two letters of W. H. Auden; the Special Collections of the University of Maryland Libraries and The Authors League Fund for five letters of Djuna Barnes; the Harry Ransom Humanities Research Center, the University of Texas at Austin, for a letter of Sybille Bedford; William Boyd for the extract from his Foreword to the stories of James Stern (unpublished); Southern Illinois University at Carbondale for two letters of Kay Boyle; the Rare Book and Manuscript Library at the University of Pennsylvania for two letters of Van Wyck Brooks; Anna Calder-Marshall for a letter of Arthur Calder-Marshall; Humphrey Carpenter for extracts from his biography of W. H. Auden; Robert Cowley for three letters of Malcolm Cowley; Roger Davenport for ten letters of John Davenport; the Harry Ransom Humanities Research Center, the University of Texas at Austin and David Higham Associates for four letters of Constantine FitzGibbon; Richard Garnett for one letter of David Garnett; David Gascoyne for the extract from his Journal; Nadine Gordimer for four letters; Don Bachardy for two letters of Christopher Isherwood, two extracts from *Lost Years: A Memoir 1945–51* and two from *Christopher and His Kind*; Nicholas Jenkins for extracts from 'Selves, Joined in Friendship' (*Auden Studies 3*); Sally Phipps for a letter of Molly Keane; the University of British Columbia, the Estate of Malcolm Lowry and Sterling Lord Literistic, Inc., for five letters of Malcolm Lowry; the Watkins Loomis Agency for an extract from *Being Geniuses Together* by Robert McAlmon and Kay Boyle; the Rare Book, Manuscript, and Special Collections Library of Duke University for three letters of Carson McCullers; Arthur Miller for extracts from four letters; the Rare Book and Manuscript Library of the University of Pennsylvania for four letters from Lewis Mumford; the Estate of Sonia Orwell for seven letters of Sonia Orwell; Peter Parker for a letter of Diana Petre; the Special Collections of the University of Maryland Libraries and Barbara Thompson Davis for eight letters of Katherine Anne Porter; Duff Hart-Davis and the Estate of William Plomer for eighteen letters of William Plomer; David Pryce-Jones for two letters of Alan Pryce-Jones and an extract from the latter's description of the *London Mercury* office in the *London Magazine*; Tom Rosenthal for a letter; Nora Sayre for four letters and her description of John Davenport; Humphrey Spender for a letter of Pauline Spender; Isabelle Storey for her letter; Barbara Mobbs for two letters of Patrick White;

Francis Wyndham for an extract from his collection of stories *Mrs Henderson*.

I have been unable to contact the estates or families of Pat Bogue (four letters), Nina Conarain (one letter), Brian Howard (two letters), Robert McAlmon (one letter), Sir J. C. Squire (two letters) and Bridget Tisdall (one letter), but would like to extend my thanks to them and/or their copyright holders *in absentia*.

Introduction

James Stern was born in 1904 in southern Ireland of a military, fox-hunting family. He was educated at Eton, failed to pass out of Sandhurst, worked on a cattle ranch in Rhodesia, and was apprenticed to the Stern family bank in Frankfurt and to another in Berlin, from which he escaped to become the assistant editor of Sir John Squire's *London Mercury* in 1929.

In 1932, a year after he had begun a nine-year European sojourn, mostly spent in Paris as a freelance writer, Stern published his first collection of stories, *The Heartless Land,* a direct result of his African experience. Seven years later, before leaving for America, where he was to remain for seventeen years, acquiring US citizenship, he published his second collection, *Something Wrong.*

The war and post-war years in New York were busy, productive and successful: he contributed stories and literary criticism to many of the leading magazines both in England and in America as well as the *New York Times* and the *New York Herald Tribune*; he became art critic for *Time* magazine; mostly with his wife Tania he translated books and plays by Bertolt Brecht, Franz Kafka, Hugo von Hofmannsthal, Erich Maria Remarque and Stefan Zweig; he edited and translated an edition of *Grimm's Fairy Tales*; he published *The Hidden Damage*, an autobiographical account of life in Germany before and immediately after Hitler; and he received a $1,000 Award from the American Academy of Arts and Letters. On that occasion, the novelist Glenway Wescott in his citation said: 'In recognition of his long, devoted and faultless practice of the art of the short story according to its great tradition: in strict prose without trickeries or exaggerations, nevertheless communicating a most constant intelligence and intense feeling.'

On his return in 1956 to live permanently in England, it appeared that his muse had all but abandoned him, although a third collection of stories, *The Man Who Was Loved* (1952), had contained some new work alongside reprinted material. In 1966, recommended by V. S. Pritchett, he was awarded the first Arts Council prize (£1,000) for the short story. Two years later a selected *Stories of James Stern* followed.

The last twenty-five years of his life were devoted to translation, mainly with Tania, of works by Mann, Kafka and Freud, to published tributes and profiles (W. H. Auden, Lawrence Durrell, Walker Evans, James Joyce, Malcolm Lowry), to an immense body of correspondence with eminent friends (Harold Acton, W. H. Auden, Samuel Beckett, Sybille Bedford, Lawrence Durrell, Constantine FitzGibbon, Nadine Gordimer, Arthur Miller, Patrick White *et al*), and to a protracted and fragmented attempt at an autobiography embodied in a series of vignettes, several of which appeared in Alan Ross's *London Magazine*.

A fastidious, modest and sometimes melancholy perfectionist, James Stern will be remembered for a handful of near-perfect stories, as an influential critic, as a scrupulous translator, as a generous, sensitive and affectionate friend, and as a writer of letters *par excellence*.

I first met Jimmy in 1950 when I was twenty and in a junior position with a firm of London publishers. He was a year younger than my mother, of whom he had been a dancing partner in their youth at hunt balls in the West Country. My mother and his, the redoubtable Connie Stern, would gallop to hounds over the Blackmoor Vale in Dorset. Thus, in some ways, we came from the same background, a world from which both of us had turned.

Jimmy and Tania were about to leave New York, where they had spent the last twelve years, on one of their extended visits to England, before deciding to settle for good near his parents in Wiltshire. Two years later, Secker & Warburg published Jimmy's selection of twelve stories, *The Man Who Was Loved*. Fred Warburg had asked Jimmy to write his own book jacket 'blurb', but Jimmy turned the task over to me. The four brief paragraphs were the first words of my own to appear in print. My signed copy bears the inscription 'For Miles the Magician (see Blurb) with the gratitude of the author'.

His attempt to persuade Warburg to employ me in his publishing house failed, but over the ensuing decades Jimmy, who had become my friend and literary mentor, generously introduced me to many of his eminent contemporaries: W. H. Auden, Alexander Calder, Walker Evans, John Lehmann, Henry Miller, Raymond Mortimer, S. J. Perelman, and Edward Sackville-West. It was a heady roll-call for a young publisher.

In 1968, when Jimmy was sixty-four, with fallow years as a writer behind him and the prospect of more ahead, his greatest friend, W. H.

Auden, wrote to him: 'I am convinced that what you should do now is write a straightforward and truthful autobiography ... Some people like myself have an uninteresting family background and, from a reader's point of view, an uninteresting life ... In your case both are of the utmost interest. I implore you, therefore, to write what I know will be a document of the greatest historical and, because of your talent, the greatest literary value.' Another close friend, William Plomer, had also written to him: 'You are perfectly equipped to write an idiosyncratic & brilliantly lucid & unforeseen kind of autobiography, & I shall be furious if it isn't printed in my lifetime.'

These pleas were partially answered, for Jimmy had been working on a projected volume of memoirs, but being a man of exceptional modesty he resolutely refused to accede to some publishers' demands for a 'name-dropping' autobiography. However, I make no apologies here for producing an account of his life, which of necessity includes the remarkable people with whom he became involved and of whom, in many cases, he became an intimate. For another friend, Malcolm Cowley, had written to Jimmy in 1977: 'My God, you've known everybody, his wife, his boyfriend, and his natural issue.'

In the beginning, having immersed myself in the British Library's James Stern archive, I planned to produce an edited selection of Jimmy's letters to and from his distinguished friends, many of which I have been privileged to reproduce here. Subsequently, having read the fragments of autobiography on which he had worked for many years, I realised that I could perhaps convey the essence of this extraordinary and complex man by reproducing many of the letters written by and to him and by linking passages from his own memoirs with words of my own. This may help to explain the unorthodox structure of the book which follows.

Christened James Andrew, he became known to everyone in later life as Jimmy (except that the younger of his two brothers, Peter, called him Jamie). It is as Jimmy that he appears in these pages.

2001 M. H.

I

Childhood and Youth
1903–1924

At the heart of a small village in County Meath, five miles equally from the market towns of Navan and Trim, stands Bective House, Jimmy Stern's boyhood home and the place to which his thoughts returned whenever Ireland was invoked. The beauty of Bective lies in its position, facing south over the Boyne to the distant hills of Skrene and Tara. The view from the wide gravel terrace, which runs beneath the well-proportioned windows to the tennis court and walled-in garden beyond, was, Jimmy maintained, as beautiful as the panorama of the Costa Divina from the Villa Cimbrone at Ravello; and even more romantic.

Today the house and its surroundings – the tennis court, the kitchen garden, the stable yard and outhouses – all exude an air of forlorn and faded glory, but in Jimmy's childhood a head gardener and his minions tended the slopes of mown grass and flower-beds which descend several hundred feet to the river. On the terrace stood ornamental stone vases filled with geraniums, and wide flights of stone steps, flanked with Irish yew, led through thick bushes to the water below.

Meath is hunting country and in that horsey world Bective was famous, because until his death in 1908 it had been the home of John Watson, the most renowned of all Masters of Foxhounds in Ireland's history of fox-hunting.

> … though he had died … and was buried in our cemetery [Jimmy wrote], his figure in pink coat, the features of his hairy face were as familiar to me as those of my father. For the same coloured reproduction of this man hung in the library or lavatory of every house I entered as a child. And it still hangs in many of those that have survived Time and the Troubles to this day.
>
> I talk of him, the Master, for his ghost still walked the corridors & my mother's voice fell audibly with equal awe whenever she pronounced either his name or that of Our Lord. For in the

hunting field – and for my parents there was no other field: it was life itself – this man was God ...

My family moved into Bective in the autumn of 1910, after a schoolroom and nursery had been built onto the house for us children, and the children to come. I was five years old and the eldest. Here in the great illusion of peace, in the blissful country silence (broken only by the occasional clatter of the Dublin train crossing the bridge over the Boyne), we learned to love the green land and its lore, to ride to hounds, milk a cow, to fish for trout and eel, and to know by name each tree, bird and flower. As well as the language of our parents, we learned the more vivid, poetic tongue of the people of Meath. Here, too, I learned the meaning of both personal and collective fear. For soon unforgettable things began to occur. One August afternoon our father appeared in the uniform of a British Army officer, to be driven away to war. It was five years before we saw him again. On the second Easter Monday after he'd gone, I heard thunder out of a clear blue sky. During that week the lodge gates of our home were locked and guarded by armed men, none of whom we knew. No one could get in; we couldn't get out. And a few weeks later I was in the yard one afternoon when Bolger, who drove the old Panhard car, came staggering through the door, his face and clothes covered in blood. He had run into an ambush on the Dublin road. Thereafter in the house we were bidden to talk in whispers ...

James Andrew Stern was born on Boxing Day 1904, not at Bective but at nearby Kilcairne Park, a forbidding, square nineteenth-century house, neither large nor small, also near Navan, standing in a field pretending to be a park. During that winter a plague of rats reached such proportions that his father used to retire to bed with his army revolver and take pot shots at 'the brutes' as they scampered about the room.

Jimmy was the first-born of an unlikely liaison. His mother's family, the Watts, were Protestants (her father was a whisky distiller) from Londonderry and County Kildare, his father's middle-class Jewish bankers from Berlin and Vienna.

People who knew my father and my mother from the time of their engagement maintain that the only interest they had in common was the pursuit of the fox. I have also heard it said that the marriage took place, even that it had been 'arranged', because of the large fortune on both sides. That there was some very tough bargaining between the two families I have proof, but the fact that the groom was a Jew and the bride a practising member of the Church of Ireland was surely not the ideal qualification for an early Edwardian *arrangement*. I believe what my parents had in common, the bond that not only drew them but kept them together until my father's death fifty-five years later, was their shyness, their unworldliness, their fear of life – of life, I mean, beyond their own limited horizons.

Jimmy's father, Henry Julius Joseph Stern, known as Harry, was a professional soldier stationed at Dundalk at the time of his engagement to his future wife,

a fact which explains [Jimmy wrote], how this young Jew from London came to meet the daughter of the whisky distiller from Londonderry. As a captain in a cavalry regiment [13th Hussars] it was my father's duty to go to wherever his regiment went. After my parents' marriage [15 April 1903], probably after my birth and possibly after Reggie's [Jimmy's younger brother] my father's regiment was posted to India. Now it seems that on hearing this news my grandfather, Andrew (known as 'Sovereign') Watt, put his foot down; he may even, after an argument with my father, have flown into a rage. What 'Sovereign' felt so strongly about was that no power, not even that of the British Army, should be allowed to carry off a daughter of his to such an unhealthy, outlandish region of the world as India. ... Faced with this choice my father, it seems, capitulated, resigned his commission, joined the 'Reserve', and for the first time in his life purchased a 'property'. Just how sad, how angry, my father felt at having his military career nipped in the bud by his father-in-law, I never heard. But knowing him as I did, I think that the day he resigned from his regiment must have been for him a very bitter day indeed.

Forced into 'retirement' as a country gentleman of very considerable means (at Bective he employed twelve servants in the house and twenty outside), Harry Stern appears now, nearly a century later, as a restless and socially ambitious young father in his early thirties. Between Kilcairne and Bective, he moved his family into another house, Somerville, where a second son, Reginald (Reggie) Herbert, was born, some fifteen months after Jimmy. Larger than Kilcairne Park,

Somerville was quite a mansion. It was here that the two boys learned to walk and, at the same time, to ride – Reggie

on a shaggy donkey, I on a brown Shetland pony ... I loved that pony. Deprived of human warmth, a child will at least offer its heart to animals, if animals there are. And of this lack Reggie and I had no cause to complain. Three dogs we had in the house: Cocker, pure black with a name explaining his breed; Cocker's son Raffles, with a tell-tale white 'waistcoat' and one white 'sock'; and Mack, a cream-coloured Highland terrier whom I secretly despised because (it is a profound and appalling confession) I realised that he, like me, knew the meaning of fear.

Mack, however, had no inhibitions about showing his fears, while mine I controlled until they would be controlled no longer. My mother despised that dog, too. 'Look at him,' she would jeer, when someone unexpectedly raised an arm. 'Just look at him – *running away*!' Poor Mack, I used to say to myself ...

You would think that boys brought up to ride and to hunt as we were would take to fox-hunting as the proverbial duck to water ... My brother Reggie did. But I did not. Had I possessed a small fraction of Reggie's 'nerve' (euphemism for fearlessness) on the back of a four-legged animal, I have no doubt that my life would have taken a different course. One of the rarest human beings I know is the man or woman who has hunted regularly at some time and will confess to having been 'frightened'. Even as a grown man I rarely mounted a horse and joined the field, the cavalcade, to draw a first covert without a sense of apprehension. As a child I was so terrified that my body would tremble in the saddle on the warmest day. Then why did I do it? What a question! Would any child of my parents have the heroic courage to admit to fear? Were they, my parents, aware of my condition, my predicament? My parents? What a question! My parents were the kind of people who would not have admitted to themselves, let alone to each other, that they had given birth to a child who could 'be afraid' – of *anything*. Had they been more honest, or possessed the courage of honesty, they would of course have used the word 'coward', but to have uttered that word in relation to one of their children would have been tantamount to admitting that somewhere within themselves there lurked a grain of fear.

Throughout his life Jimmy nursed an obsession with childhood. It manifested itself in his writing – his best stories deal with the subject – and in his fascination with children, though he never sired any of his own. 'I think my greatest pleasure is just sitting anywhere, at any time, just *watching* children – alone, or at play!' he wrote to Joan Lewisohn in the early '40s. 'I have a feeling that possibly the best thing about me is that I love children (it doesn't matter why); that is really where I feel deepest (possibly dangerously deep) ... Had I been a Father, I would have "spoiled" any son or daughter with sheer *love*.' In 1969 he told Isabelle Evans: 'T. always says of me that I cannot resist animals & children, & that I drive them both mad. (She means "mad with excitement").' These sentiments give rise to the subject of the Sterns' own childlessness. Jimmy and his wife Tania gave different reasons for their not having any family. One, an old chestnut, was that the world was too evil a place to bring a child into; another, which strikes a more genuine note, is that Tania wouldn't risk children with Jimmy because of his attitudes expressed above. It has also been suggested that the mumps he suffered as a young man had rendered him infertile.

He rated very highly the quality of innocence, which, he claimed, was only to be found in children. Yet some have thought that his sometimes over-eager, over-familiar approach to them – bending down to their level, with a poke in the stomach and a loud 'boo' – frightened children. Once, while visiting his neighbours in Wiltshire, he dismayed their small daughter by hooking the crook of his walking stick round his wife's neck and shouting 'Come on, woman!' On another occasion a mother complained about Jimmy's rudeness when her small son greeted him with 'I'm Adam.' To which Jimmy unkindly retorted: 'Well, I'm not Eve.'

His own childhood, to say the least, was an unhappy one ('the great hollow abyss that only a child can know'), principally because his aloof parents were unable to express their love for him. But were there compensations? From the evidence of his own words, it is obvious that Jimmy relished his privileged, moneyed, characterful and eccentric relations – especially on his mother's side – as well as appreciating the freedom and amenities which came with living in large houses. Being the eldest of five children, he may have felt that he was constantly being replaced – hence his special sense of the lack of affection. Yet there is a recurring note of self-pity in his preoccupation with his early lack of parental love.

My mother hated to be away from home, from her horses, her

dogs, her garden, above all her own *things*. She could not abide hotels, other people's houses, could not tolerate other women's tastes, their furniture, their beds, *their* things. And since she took no pleasure in reading and played no games, neither tennis nor bridge, neither golf nor croquet, what on earth was she to do for weeks on end in a hotel or a furnished villa, on beach or strand, beside the cold, hostile, frightening sea?

My father felt much the same, for similar reasons. And another. An army man accustomed to authority, to command and be commanded, my father felt lost, out of his depth, when he could not give orders, when there was no butler or footman, often not even a chauffeur, to shout for, or at. When he rang a bell in a hotel and an unknown youth, a strange woman or parlour-maid appeared, a look of desolation, almost of terror, would pass over his features. Afloat, so to speak, in the foreign surf, he would flounder, forget his reason for ringing, stutter, bluster, make a valiant effort to smile away his embarrassment, fail, then finally jerk himself to his feet and march upstairs to my mother.

'I say,' he would blurt out as though his dilemma were her doing, 'I can't stand this bally place any longer!' And, to everyone's relief, even my mother's, he would go for a 'beastly' walk. Or, better still, go *home*.

When Jimmy was thirty-eight and living in New York, he described his father to Joan Lewisohn: 'My father terrifies everyone, because he lives in mortal fear of everyone. His glowering bad-tempered face is nothing but a defence, concealing every known fear. He was all right in the Army because he was a number and had no responsibility. In private life his wife defends him against Women and the World. Poor man.'

Although Connie Stern's life centred solely on the horse, her husband was someone of a more inquiring mind. Apart from soldiering and fox-hunting, Harry Stern had two interests: the trees of Britain, of which he possessed considerable knowledge and had himself planted numerous specimens on estates he acquired; and the regimental uniforms of the British Army, a subject of which he knew as much as the recognised specialists in the field. The walls of his 'library' were covered in historical military prints, of cavalrymen mounted and unmounted, in full regimental dress. It was on account of this interest that he allowed himself to indulge his talent for drawing. Although his subjects –

sketched in pencil, then painted in watercolour – were limited to the chargers, officers and rank-and-file of cavalry regiments, every detail of harness and helmet, sabre and sabretache, every feature of a uniform down to the last badge and button, would be correct. On these pictures the Major toiled in secret while his children were away from home or at school. They never saw them nor heard any mention of their existence. When his children were around, the Major's artistic efforts and his paintbox were locked out of sight in a drawer.

An extension of Harry Stern's interest in regimental uniforms was his abstruse inquisitiveness about hunt buttons:

> He once (and I was beside him when he did and said it) [Jimmy told Pauline Wynn in 1974] saw a black-coated, top-hatted man among the field of the Portman Hounds with the initials MOBB on his Hunt button. I can see him now, leaning way off his horse, scrutinizing the man's backside button (on his coat). MOBB? He couldn't stand it any longer. 'I say, excuse me, but – well, I was just wondering – I was just wondering, I say, if you would mind – ha – to which Hunt your – your *buttons belong*?'
>
> An apoplectic face with a ginger moustache: 'Hunt? My buttons? Belong? Let me tell you, sir, these are *my own bloody buttons*!' ...
>
> We children, however [Jimmy wrote elsewhere], derived little conscious benefit or pleasure from our father's talent, his trained parade-ground eye. Indeed, the instant it caught sight of a loose shoelace, a stud visible above the knot of a tie, a ruckled stocking, a fly-button 'undone', or (a more heinous offence) the lowest button of a waistcoat 'done-up', he would pounce. '*You!*' he would bark. '*You'll* never get into Eton, y'know ...! Never make a soldier!'

Apart from those burgeoning fears that plagued Jimmy's childhood and which he so graphically dramatised later in stories such as 'The Broken Leg', there were experiences of natural beauty which fed his visual appetite:

> ... it was at Somerville that I first heard consciously what has been ever since, every spring I have spent in Western Europe, one of the wonders of the natural world: the call of the cuckoo. The first time I heard this miraculous sound I could not believe it; and to this day, each spring, whatever I happen to be doing, I hold my breath

in disbelief. At Somerville this miracle would come out of some bushes that grew along the sickle-shaped haha at the back of the house. Indoors or out, each time in my mind during the silence of a windless morning, I would stand stock still, while the magic was repeated and repeated and repeated.

A Lawrentian feeling for nature emerged later in his writing.

The Sterns lived at Somerville for four years until 1910, the year of the coronation of King George V and of the birth of their first daughter, Leila Mary, who died at the age of eighteen.

Thereafter, they moved to Bective. It was to be twelve years before the family, which by 1922 included a second daughter, Rosemary, born in 1913 and a third son, Peter Francis, in 1915, finally left Ireland forever. The break with Bective was a hard one. In 1978, while reviewing a book of stories, *Tales from Bective Bridge*, in the *Irish Press*, Jimmy wrote: 'I was seventeen and destined for the Army when I heard what was for me the gravest news yet: our Home was up for sale, had indeed been sold. We were leaving Ireland to live in England. A Mr Lavin had arrived from America to take care of the place while the new owner [Charles Sumner Bird, an American] was preparing to move in. Did it really happen, or did I dream that on the day we drove away I dared to look back, and there, framed in the front doorway, stood a girl of maybe ten?' The girl was the author of the stories, Mary Lavin.

> In my immediate family, as in the bloody history of my native land, 1922 is a memorable year. As soon as, if not before, the Treaty was signed and the country became known as a Free State, my father sold our home in County Meath [for £4,000. In 1976 it realised £400,000] and moved – with his wife, five children, Sumner the butler, Miss Magill the governess, Bond the chauffeur, Duncan the groom and family of ten children, seven horses and three dogs – to a pub in Blandford Forum in the county of Dorset. This cavalcade emigrated to the West Country so that my home-sick Irish mother could be within riding distance of her sister, our Aunt Eva Holford, who three years previously had also left Ireland with her family for her husband's home in that country.

They soon moved into Hanford, a sizeable Elizabethan house near Blandford, which, incidentally, is featured in Richard Hughes's novel *The Fox in the Attic* (1961).

After a few weeks in The Crown Hotel, Jimmy and Reggie, to

improve their French, were whisked off to spend their holidays in an Ecole Secondaire in the St Cloud district of Paris, overseen by their Stern relations. On the night ferry 'I remember feeling so excited that I crept out of our cabin and tramped the deck for what seemed hours rather than spend my impatience on a berth in total darkness to the sound of my brother's snoring.' Abruptly their French idyll was over before it had really started: Jimmy was rushed into hospital with typhoid. Eight years later he returned to Paris to write the stories contained in his first book and to remain in that city until 1939.

'Jimmy dear, *I* don't think Mummy and Daddy should have had any children *at all*. Not *one*!' was a remark once made by Eva Holford. Childbearing, after all, was a severe interruption to the main interest and activity of Connie Stern's life.

> ... there was nothing funny about my mother. Of all the human beings I have known I think her character was the most compli-cated, the most unpredictable, the most inconsistent, the most difficult to please. Except in the so-called moral and the hunting fields, the only thing that could be safely expected of my mother was the unexpected. In this respect she was the opposite of her husband. Whenever I heard anyone who worked for my father remark: 'Ah, you always know where you are with the Major', I assumed they were referring obliquely to his wife. Indeed, had he not 'worshipped the ground she trod on', I feel pretty sure I would not have seen the light.

With her delicate, china-like complexion, her gleaming auburn hair, and her fame in the hunting field, Connie Stern was not short of admir-ers. 'It was said in Ireland', Jimmy recalled, 'by all manner of people that no woman, and few men, had ever ridden across the green fields of Meath as "straight" as our mother.'

Many years later, in 1945, Jimmy wrote to Tania:

> Last night I had dinner alone with M at her Club. Her hair is white & rather becoming but she hates herself for looking 'old' ... It was pretty painful ... I felt absolutely nothing when I saw her. She has not changed an inch in any other way. She's as ignorant, as limited, & as much of a liar as she ever was. But after all, why should she change? Her lies were so outrageous that at first I

stared with an open mouth. Then I got acclimatized ... I was mighty glad when it was over. It was a nervous strain as it always is. You really have to talk a kind of baby talk to make her understand what you're talking about. Believe it or not, she actually does not understand what a word such as 'primitive' means. I look at her and cannot believe she is my mother. I feel I have more in common with any man or woman in the street.

A harsh judgement of a mother by her son, but that searing letter expresses the resentment and anger which had accumulated in him over forty years.

Jimmy described his father as a shy, reticent man.

It was this shyness, this inwardness and awkwardness that made his sudden bark, for a child, so frightening. Children embarrassed him. He did not 'like' them. Nor did my mother.

The bark was frightening because it would be accompanied by what we were too young to realise was an effort to smile: the massed brown needles of moustache would rise to reveal teeth normally invisible, so that for an instant he did not look like the man we knew, but like a fox at the moment of sniffing prey. No child could divine that the purpose of this grimace was to temper verbal punishment with mercy. A man incapable of expressing his feelings, of little humour and few words, who saw all things in terms of right and wrong, black and white, the world through the eyes of an old-fashioned professional soldier and every yesterday through the leading editorial of today's *Times*, my father instilled fear while attempting to fulfil what he considered to be a paternal duty.

Jimmy's school life began on 5 May 1914, before which his pre-prep-school education had been in the charge of a series of governesses. He was nine years old; his brother Reggie, aged eight, followed him to the same school, Wixenford, near Wokingham in Berkshire, in September of that year. Between these two dates the First World War broke out. On the morning after the Declaration, Harry Stern, in officer's uniform, was driven away from Bective to join his regiment, the South Irish Horse, in Limerick. Six months later he was on the Somme.

Those with homes in Ireland lived under the cloud of war for the following eight years. When Jimmy's father returned home from France in 1919, he said that in one important respect he would prefer the Somme – at least one could recognise the enemy.

Jimmy's views on his own emotional battlefields were similarly austere.

> I never could make up my mind (and never have) which I disliked the more – school or home. Especially in *winter*. School and home, remember, were always rather far apart, across the sea. Oh, the glory of the journey, however high the waves; the glory of being nowhere, being ungetatable, anon.
>
> As for arriving at school for the first time, I believe sheer curiosity outweighed any feelings of trepidation I may have had. I was the eldest child, after all; there was no one, thank God, or at least no one of my age, to feed me with forebodings. Going to school, moreover, as well as leaving it to return home continued to hold for us (or perhaps I should say for me) an element of adventure: not only did we travel on our own, unescorted, our journeys to and fro were long, complicated and, for the first four years, not without danger. (We missed being drowned on the *Leinster* by seven days.)

After many cold, cheerless, tummy-emptying hours on the Dublin to Holyhead ferry, which sometimes made frightening detours on account of German U-boats, the two brothers – Jimmy, 'thin small anaemic, what was known in the family as "nervy"', and Reggie, 'the Perfect Specimen of Boyhood' – arrived at Euston station to be met by Hutton, their grandmother's butler, 'munching his dentures above the thick woollen scarf – "'ere Master Jimmy, let me 'ave that Gladstone, oh I say isn't it 'eavy, books I'll be bound."' They were driven through the early dawn to a large house in Prince's Gate, overlooking Hyde Park.

Grandma, whom Jimmy came to love and admire more than any other relation of an older generation, had lived almost all her adult life in this Kensington mansion to which she and her husband had moved in 1874. Her father, Herr Biedermann, had been Court Jeweller to the Austrian Emperor Franz Joseph, and she had arrived in England from Vienna in 1867, as a girl of seventeen.

Her husband, James Stern, Jimmy's grandfather, after whom he was named, was a merchant banker with his own firm in the City. Although decidedly handsome, he must also have been rather dull, for neither Jimmy nor his brother Peter could ever recall hearing so much as an anecdote about him. He died at the age of sixty-six in the same week as

Queen Victoria. It seems that his main attribute was his wealth, for at his death he bequeathed his wife a net income of £8,000 (£430,480 today) a year. Each of his three sons inherited £275,000 (£14,797,750 today).

It was on a memorable day in the house in Prince's Gate that Jimmy at the age of forty learnt from his father that his maternal great-grand-father had been the Duke of Wellington.

'Your great-grandmother', Harry Stern told his son, 'was his mistress.' ...

'I was so astounded by my father's statement that I said nothing. What amazed me no less than the news was that my father, of all people, should have uttered it. Even "mistress", in this sense, was a word I had never heard him breathe aloud before. I was also surprised, and a little annoyed, that such a slice of family gossip should reach my ears for the first time so late in life.' Incidentally, the Iron Duke went to school in Trim, Co. Meath.

Eventually the two brothers were taken to the school train:

It was only then that the sense of adventure ceased, for here on the platform at Waterloo, crowded with porters and luggage, with fathers and mothers and sisters, we would see, to my horror and amazement, boys of our own age, and older, hang their heads – in tears!

Such scenes used to haunt me. Was I, were Reggie and I, so different? Was the prospect of school so dreadful for these boys? Or was the affection for their homes and families such that they could not bear to tear themselves away?

Wixenford, a preparatory school in which social snobbery abounded, boasted more than one scion of the nobility, but perhaps Lord Alfred Douglas was the most outstanding. However, it wasn't until the summer of 1929 that Jimmy 'spent an hour listening spell-bound to his stories of Oscar Wilde – or O.W., as he constantly referred to that courageous Irishman ... In his memoirs Bosie Douglas mentions having been for a short time, before entering Wixenford, at another school, which he describes as "very classy", in the sense that it was chiefly populated by "sprigs of nobility". If not in precisely those words, that is how I would have described the inhabitants of Wixen-ford.'

In 'A Sprig of Nobility', an early chapter of his unpublished volume of memoirs, Jimmy told the story of one of his schoolmates, Prince

Charles-Theodore, son of the King of the Belgians, whose groans and screams one night awoke his dormitory, if not the entire school. The Headmaster, in dressing-gown and pyjamas, was summoned by the distraught Matron. The Belgian Prince had swallowed a pin. '*Ma mère – je voudrais voir ma mère*,' he wailed. When Her Majesty, braving the threat of German U-boats in the Channel, arrived, her son bounced out of bed, flung his arms around her, and demanded to be taken away – to London – to see a play! This incident may well have provided the dreamy, diffident Jimmy with an example of what audacity and defiance of authority can accomplish.

Jimmy did not entirely avoid the habitual bullying endemic in such establishments: '... initially for my "Irishness" and after the Easter Rising of 1916, for denouncing the Black and Tans and defending The Rebels, I encountered open hostility and some physical abuse.' However, he escaped any anti-semitic animosity. Almost unbelievably, it was not until he was sixteen that his beloved grandmother let slip the enormous fact that the Sterns were Jews.

During my first year in the corner of that schoolroom at Wixenford two famous figures in embryo sat behind me.

Of the older boy I can offer but a sketch, for the best of reasons: I don't know him. From what I know *of* him it would seem characteristic that in that room he sat in lonely glory, without immediate neighbours, at a single desk. And on that desk he kept, of all things, a typewriter. I believe it was the first such machine I had seen at close range.

Its owner may have been twelve years old; but in my eyes he was a young man, and not so young at that. Short (for a man), with a head like a bearskin (secretly I always called him Busby) and a nose like the beak of a hawk, his immaculate figure exuded an air of such self-assurance and dignity that his presence, so close behind me, might have become alarming had he not tempered this sophisticated demeanour with the less adult habit of rolling bread-crumbs in the palms of his hands and tossing the pellets on to the back of my neck and head.

In contrast to the superior young man, who touched not even the periphery of my existence and almost certainly is unaware of my name, the other boy who sat behind me in that schoolroom not only entered my life, he had a definite influence on it.

Bino? Yes, such – almost since the beginning, since the early summer of 1914 – such was the name this delightful, generous, learned, much-loved man had given himself. [In fact, his nickname was 'Bambino'.]

A Venetian with North American blood, his jet-black hair, white skin and cupid's bow of a mouth would have drawn attention in any English establishment even had those red lips never uttered a word. As if to emphasise his strangeness, his roly-poly figure, he chose (or had been given) to wear grey Norfolk jackets with knickerbockers and black stockings. This plump, exotic little body in grey would sit behind me in the furthermost corner – not, like the rest of us, on a chair but on a bench …

The first of these two fellow pupils was Kenneth Clark (1903– 83), the art historian whose television series *Civilisation* reached a large audience, and the second was Harold Acton (1904–94), writer of historical studies, novelist and aesthete who spent some years in Peking in the '30s but returned to live at his family estate, La Pietra, in Florence, for the remainder of his long life.

Jimmy and Harold Acton pursued their friendship at Eton, to which they both went in 1918, joining the same house, Hugh de Haviland's. They were Oppidans (students who board in the town) and shared the same tutor, A. M. McNeile. The Headmaster was Dr C. A. Alington.

As for the 'beaks', Harold Acton in the first of his volumes of autobiography, *Memoirs of an Aesthete* (1948), describes one prominent eccentric:

Among the young masters was one who stood out a mile. Walking along the Eton High like a somnambulist, or like a juvenile giraffe that had escaped from a zoo, he wore a conspicuous orange scarf which trailed behind him … Were I to draw his caricature, I should portray him dangling over a dangling shoe-lace, which seemed his most characteristic posture. His eyes, of which one was opaque, roved distantly, and he always looked uncomfortable … I do not think Huxley had yet published any prose, but his experiences at this time were obviously incorporated in the beginning of *Antic Hay*.

Jimmy, in a letter to his brother Peter in 1979, wrote:

I'll never forget being 'taught' French at Eton by 'Satan' Ford, who came from Chicago, & always arrived in plus fours & a huge bag of golf clubs. Since he could not pronounce the King's English let alone a word of French, he used to point down at me as soon as he mounted his podium: 'Stoin! Yep, you there! Come right up here & take the class!' – the last word pronounced, needless to say, as in ass!

The year which heralded the end of the Kaiser's War saw a rich influx of talented boys who later became household names in the literary world and beyond. Some were Jimmy's friends throughout his life. Besides Harold Acton, there were Cyril Connolly, David Cecil, Anthony Powell, Robert Byron, Eric Blair (George Orwell), Henry Yorke (Henry Green), Oliver Messel – and Brian Howard. In a phrase appropriated from Lady Caroline Lamb's diary entry on her first meeting with Lord Byron, Evelyn Waugh, who modelled on Howard both Ambrose Silk in *Put out More Flags* (1942) and Anthony Blanche in *Brideshead Revisited* (1945), described him as 'mad, bad and dangerous to know'. Although he was born and brought up in England, Howard's parents both came from America. At sixteen, with the help of Acton, his close friend and rival, he edited the *Eton Candle*, a magazine to which established writers, mostly Old Etonians, such as the Sitwells, Maurice Baring and Aldous Huxley, contributed prose and verse. Harold Acton, in his *Memoirs*, provides a vivid description of Howard:

> His big brown eyes with their long curved lashes were brazen with self-assurance; already his personality seemed chiseled and polished, and his vocabulary was as ornate as his diction ... 'I am said to be the image of Max Beerbohm when he was beautiful as well as brilliant,' my new friend Brian confided to me ... At the age of thirteen he was definitely a dandy.
>
> Our friendship was an endless series of bickerings, but his company was so stimulating that it soon became a necessity to both of us. Brian could be very old and very young at the same time and his mischievousness was far more than the ebullience of youth. When one got the better of him in argument he would resort to crude mockery and personal invective, which often turned to violence. Once I had to push him into a shop window in self-defence. He had an intuitive gift for the malice that could stab and fester beneath the skin.

W. H. Auden described Howard as 'the most desperately unhappy person I have ever known'. His father loathed him and his mother ruined him with her smothering possessiveness. V. S. Pritchett has remarked that Brian Howard 'was one of those dangerous, brilliant and seminal nuisances, a plaguing character of wasted talent ...'

It is difficult to discover how close Jimmy and Brian Howard were at Eton, but this paragraph from Jimmy's diary for 24 April 1922 is revealing: 'If anyone knew anything about the psychology of B and myself he would know that it was precisely because I made *no* effort at all to attract B that he became infatuated with me. It is the same the world over. How seldom realized!' Four years later their friendship was to become a passionate one, especially for Howard.

Of another distinguished contemporary, Cyril Connolly, Jimmy sketched an acute pen-portrait in the *New Republic* in 1948 while reviewing the American edition of Connolly's *Enemies of Promise* (1938):

Like most schoolboys, we used to gaze at our contemporaries and wonder what they would be doing – ten, twenty, thirty years hence. What would have happened to the Witty One, the Athlete, the Esthete, the Bookworm, the Bore? What, we wondered, would have become of that thin, pale, pug-nosed Scholar whose ears alone prevented the derelict top hat from falling over the sly, humorous eyes? He was an oddity, whom the College toughs used to call 'Ugly' and 'Flinchface'. Craving affection, he bore insults bravely. Perhaps, like Swift, he already knew that 'nothing can render them popular but some degree of persecution'. At fifteen, by his own admission, he was 'dirty, inky, miserable, untidy, a bad fag, a coward at games, lazy at work, unpopular with my masters and superiors, anxious to curry favour and yet to bully whom I dared'.

Perhaps we should not have been surprised at anything he might do in later life, for at eighteen, by constantly 'trying to be funny', by flattery and appeasement, arrogance and wit, by emulating Machiavelli and practising the art of mixing 'enthusiasm with moral cowardice and social sense', he achieved a feat hardly more surprising than if today the editor of *Horizon* were to be invited by the Politburo to join that body in the Kremlin. Without a single athletic distinction, with not so much as a 'stick-up' collar to prove that he was in Sixth Form, he got himself elected to 'Pop' (The Eton Society ... an oligarchy of two dozen boys who were self-elected and could wear coloured waistcoats and cane boys of any house). Unbelievable! The triumph of the Funny Man. The Conquering Clown.

But he was a very clever clown – a learned apolaustic buffoon who loved good food and wine only less than he loved literature and love. All through the thirties he could be seen, his figure a quivering affirmation of his tastes, sitting under the plane trees of Southern France and Spain – talking, reading, eating, writing ... The ugly boy who craved recognition thirty years ago is recognized today as Cyril Connolly wherever the criticism of English literature is read.

Although Jimmy maintained all his life that his time at the famous school wasn't a happy one, there is little record of his state of mind and spirit whilst he was there. His lack of physical size – he was condemned to wear a 'bum-freezer' longer than his contemporaries, who had graduated to 'tails' – must have embarrassed him and may have given his peers an opportunity for bullying and abuse. It is true, however, that his strong familial connection with the 'horsey world' continued to influence him. With the connivance of his closest friend, Rory (Roderick) More-O'Ferrall, significantly a boy from Ireland, both horsey and not of an artistic or literary bent, he ran a sweepstake on the Derby – dramatised in 'The Pleasure is Great' – and was well known among the boys as well as some of the burghers of Eton as a 'betting man'. He became good at golf as well, a sport he enjoyed because it can be played alone, 'aloneness' being a state which Jimmy always enjoyed. 'Petty larceny' he also listed as an occupation of that time: 'When I was sixteen I had read almost nothing worth reading. In my home, books were more or less taboo. For this reason I stole books from bookshops. From a petty thief I became a crook & at sixteen made a fortune. I am still trying to write that story. I have failed because I lack the power of invention.' This admission will be seen to have a crucial bearing on Jimmy's development as a writer.

If we accept that his unpublished novel, 'The Pleasure is Great', is autobiographical, this description of a clandestine meeting between two boys, one older than the other, illustrates Jimmy's need for love:

Behind the mown grass and the cabins of Heron's Brook there runs a sandy lane dividing in half a large field, unkempt, uncultivated, high with ragweed and loosestrife and pitted like an overgrown battlefield with holes, some as wide and deep as bomb-craters ...

Alone in his crater, David took one of three Gold Flakes from his tweed-coat pocket, lighted it and, placing the towel across his chest so that he could pull it over his face at a moment's notice, lay back among the weeds with a sigh of what sounded like content.

Contentment, however, is strange to adolescence. His sigh was rather the inexpressible expression of the confusion and perplexity, the loneliness and the longing of that age. In it there fought – undeniable, fierce – a craving for love against the sense of sin this love involved. If the weeds the boy lay among could be called symbolic of his innocence, even more so was the cigarette burning his fingers the index of his sin. As well as the challenge to authority, it was his desperately determined farewell to childhood – to those lonely, thwarted years that clung to him with all the ferocity that he used in his struggle to force them away. He smoked as though by pulling on the tobacco and inhaling deep he could anaesthetise his guilt, could render himself insensible to conflicting allegiances, to his profound distrust and fear of human beings – to the fear, above all, of accepting as well as of offering affection. So great, so passionate was this desire to overcome his inhibitions that by the time the cigarette was smoked and its butt stubbed out, he had almost hypnotised himself into a state of passivity, into a condition that permitted him to utter aloud: 'What's it matter? What does anything matter?'

'Nothing matters! Nothing!' breathed a deep voice in his ear. Instantly he felt his body being enveloped in arms to which, shutting his eyes, banishing thought, he clung with all the longing of a child who, having been lost for hours, suddenly finds its mother.

For two full minutes not a sound was heard in the crater.

At length: 'Darling Dave', came the voice charged with parental concern, 'don't cry. We're together, Dave. I'll – I'll look after you ...'

At the sound of these words, he felt his whole body give a convulsive shudder. 'Oh, Steve,' he was amazed to hear himself murmur, 'why are you so good to me?

'Because I love you.'

The simple words fell on the air in a tone as soft, as tender as a mother's or a lover's. They drew from the shuddering boy a short cry, as of a child no longer able to endure in silence exquisite pain.

His hand went out and gripped the other's shoulder as though it would never let go.

This scene conveys the development of what Jimmy, when confiding to Nora Sayre many decades later, called 'my queer years', which extended into his twenties. It also alludes to another remark made to the same confidante to the effect that he had always longed to get married. When asked why, he said: 'In order to receive affection.'

Jimmy's father did not encourage further education. 'You'll be in the Army Class soon. Only another year. Then Sandhurst, of course.' The words must have reverberated in young Jimmy's ears. And it is saddening to discover a curt, printed card from H. J. White, Dean of Christ Church, Oxford, dated 28 April 1923, which reads: 'Dear Sir, I regret to inform you that you have been unsuccessful in the recent Entrance Examination.' This failure, it might be supposed, quite apart from the threat of a life in the Army, was disappointing since both Harold Acton and Brian Howard had gone up to Christ Church in 1922. It is, however, doubtful that Jimmy would have enjoyed more years of higher education, despite the prospect of sharing them with close friends. His mind was set on escape, as this passage from an unpublished story confirms:

> It was less than twelve months since I had left school in England where I had spent some four years of boredom punctuated by rare moments of horrible fear and delirious happiness ... ultimately I had left both school and England with two predominating thoughts semi-clear above all the others in my mind. Uppermost of these two was the desire to leave England – to disappear, to get right away from school and home, and to forget that either had ever existed or need ever exist for me again.

But a pig farm in Dorset was to be his immediate, short-term fate. 'It's easier to lose your temper over a pig than over any other animal. Unlike sheep, they're intelligent, go their own way which is never yours.' His boyhood fear of horses conquered, he was galloping over stiff thorn fences in the local point-to-point races during this brief period before the Army loomed.

The Royal Military College, as it was then called, at Sandhurst in Camberley, Berkshire: large, self-important buildings and grey, chillingly clean parade grounds surrounded by acres of parkland – the prospect must have daunted the eighteen-year-old Jimmy. He was to spend ten months there. On 12 July 1924, a relation on his mother's side, Constance Holford, recorded a meeting with Harry Stern at Lord's cricket ground. He was in a thunderous mood: Jimmy had been sacked from Sandhurst for smoking on parade 'as a dare'. Because Jimmy was frank and unevasive about his personal life, particularly to his trusted female friends, it has been suggested by one that, because he never broached the subject of his Sandhurst days to her, his departure was due to a sexual transgression. But a more convincing explanation is that he failed his examinations – intentionally.

Yet the end of his 'military career' was a watershed. Life could now begin – and it did, with a startling departure. In the year 1925 the writer he became began to emerge.

2

Africa, the Banks, and
'The London Mercury'
1925–1930

In December 1924, Uncle Bertie, a younger brother of Jimmy's father, took control of his nephew's life, arranging for him to travel to Southern Rhodèsia to be taught farming by a Scot called H. H. Phillips. Sir Albert Stern, a banker of great wealth, was known in the City as The Holy Terror and was knighted for his work as secretary of the 1915 Landships Committee which invented that 'monstrous war machine', the tank.

This banishment by the family of a difficult if not overtly 'bolshie failure' followed a classic pattern in that era of 'the remittance man'. What are we going to do with Jimmy? The Army won't have him; send him to one of the colonies; he knows a bit about farming ...

But Africa for Jimmy was a liberation. It didn't last long, but it conditioned his whole life.

Waved farewell by his father, Jimmy sailed on the *Arundel* to Cape Town. He danced to a gramophone on the top deck, played the ukulele, and met a girl two years younger than himself, Pat Bogue, who called him Paddy and to whom subsequently he wrote long letters every week. She was a strange, prickly girl: 'I am very reserved and quiet and have little or no conversation, and I always feel I'm being intensely boring to those poor creatures who are doing their level best to entertain me & sometimes wish they'd go to "blazes" (!) & leave me to myself, but they never do!!'

And this, three months after their shipboard meeting: 'I don't know whether to be angry or just take no notice, but who gave you permission to call me endearing names? "My dearest" indeed. I don't feel like anyone's dearest at the moment, let alone yours! Cruel, aren't I?' But a month later she had relented: 'Good Lord, Paddy, I didn't know I hurt you so much as all that, about you calling me "my dearest", certainly it is "damned" funny! But dear I'm sorry, I didn't mean you to take it so seriously, & as for forgiving you, why I do with all my heart though there is nothing to forgive really ...' In November she wrote: 'I corresponded with 4 or 5 of the Arundel passengers, four of which I don't care two hoots about, & have gradually dropped them altogether without saying a word, until one remains & that one I'll *never*, as long as I live, give up, & that Paddy my dear is yourself ... Oh Lord Paddy what can I do to get a glimpse of you, & I want to see you so.' He retained more than a certain *tendresse* for her: when in 1932 his first book of stories, *The Heartless Land*, was published the dedication page read 'To Pat Bogue of Natal, S.A.'. She died in March 1933 of blood poisoning from an infected boil on her chin. 'My own First Great Adult Love I never even kissed,' Jimmy told Isabelle Evans in 1969. 'We met on a ship in mid-Atlantic en route to Africa, and met once again a year later for a day, then never again. Very romantic.'

Work at Paddy's Valley, Phillips's Hereford cattle ranch forty miles north of Bulawayo, was hard. Although a repeated reading of Melville's *Moby Dick* was some consolation, loneliness was a constant companion, and having acquired a hatred of colonisation and racial intolerance, he found that the months passed slowly until his return to London in May 1926. However, as the following extract from a journal shows, Jimmy had begun to develop his gift for limpid description.

In the winter of 1925 he trekked with two other white men and a black servant across the country which lies between Nyamandhlovu and the River Shangani, on whose northern shore Major Allan Wilson and his men met their death in the Matabele Rebellion of 1896. The primary object of the expedition was to collect the annual Hut-and-Wife tax from the native Africans. At that time the region was entirely uninhabited by white men.

> Took the back seat out of the Overland, and filled half the space with shot-guns, rifles, ammunition, tinned food, blankets, flea-bags, a saucepan, a cooker, four water sacks, whisky, socks, two pairs of boots, two axes, two spades, a bundle of ropes, and two cameras. Petrol for six hundred miles.
>
> Denver's boy, Zidubi, sits in the space alongside, holding Dal, Denver's liver-and-white pointer, who lives on the summit of the paraphernalia, his muzzle on the crown of my sun-helmet.
>
> Zidubi's eyes dart here and there in his coal-black face. He is wearing a faded white woollen vest of mine, the buttons of which he keeps doing up, then undoing them again, all the time bursting

into little ripples of laughter, thrilled beyond concealment at the notion of driving in a car, at leaving the farm and kraal he has known all his life. He holds Dal by the collar and at intervals claps his hands, like an excited child. I'd say he is in his early thirties, but he doesn't know his age.

... It is good to be alive. Motion thrills me; I like being propelled along; I like being on a horse, in a tram, a train, best of all a ship. I hate speed. I like to sit, and see, and wonder, while indulging in the luxury of effortless travel. I like early morning sunshine wherever it may be; I love the sea at all times; I like the earth in the evenings and to be in a metropolis when darkness falls. And I dislike afternoons, except to lie about and do nothing in. If I had my way!

... The bush has been cut down ... But it has grown again – thin, stunted, wiry, dust-covered bushes already struck with the appearance of age, which has no meaning here. What is older than Africa? Or more indestructible? The West has only ruined its ancient face, a face like that of a man eaten with disease, a man once possessed of an austere, rugged beauty. Which has gone now, the beauty ravished. And the name of the disease is Greed.

Bashed in corrugated-iron huts, their roofs brown with rust, holes like eyeless sockets for windows, lie decaying along the way. It is as if an army had rushed the land, plundered it, ravaged it, slaughtered the men, women and children, and swept on. The Last Day of Creation might leave the world like this ...

Then the straight road ends, and we plunge down into an abyss of rocklike ruts where wagons have sunk in deep during the rains, leaving in their wake the empty arteries of their wheels. We bump and sway along over the cracked, sunburned earth, and at each bump the springs of the car give a grunt: Zidubi is shot from his seat and hits his head against the bar of the hood. Dal whimpers with fright on his perilous perch, while many parts of the car creak ominously beneath us ...

Denver says you can buy this land for between one and two shillings an acre. It is flat as a table, no hills, high grass, stretches of thin mopani bush. Very few kraals. Should be good bird country, but we see nothing move. The road is little more than a broad native footpath, just wide enough for one car. But the ground is hard, while sandy, and beyond the world of wagons.

Colburner leads the way. For two hours we average ten mph.

Denver says from now on we won't travel any faster, that soon the state of the 'road' will make us weep. Cheery little devil, Denver. But I like his nut-brown face and white hair. When Denver is being 'depressing' he watches you till he has forced you into despair, then roars with laughter and calls you a bloody fool for 'taking on so gloomy'! Though I've known him for some time, I know very little about him. He's like a chunk of Africa, guarding his mystery. One feels a mystery, just as one feels the mystery in the air round Zimbabwe. But I would never ask Denver to tell me of himself. I respect his reserve. Africa is full of Denvers, but their skins are rarely white.

... The country looks curiously fresh, the bush high, each bush a tree, some larger than others. I am not used to trees. These are tall enough to give shade. The face of Africa is changing. The sun shines through them and dapples the leaf-covered path with patches of shadow. I think of beech woods in Ireland. There is a curious sense of peace, and I imagine that if the cars came to a halt a great silence would envelop the world.

... only the men from the crowd approach us. The women, babies strapped to their backs, naked potbellied piccaninnys, and girls with half-formed breasts like inverted cups – they remain within the shade of the trees, peeping out, the eyes of the women wide with the suspicion of foxes surprised above ground. The naked children dart from tree to tree, like cubs at play over their earth. And they stare at us, at the cars, mouths agape, making birdlike noises of wonder in their throats.

Four months after his twenty-first birthday Jimmy developed a high fever and was eventually transported by oxen and ambulance to a hospital in Bulawayo. His illness was diagnosed as a combination of malaria and blackwater fever. (An attack of mumps, which he thought was syphilis, a year earlier, had also laid him low.) When asked by the doctor what he was doing in Southern Rhodesia, Jimmy replied: 'Learning to farm.' He refrained from saying that he was attempting to escape from the fate which would await him if he returned to England: namely serving an apprenticeship in the family bank. This prospect may well have been mooted by his father and uncle before his departure for Africa.

Later the doctor told Jimmy that despite his age, he was not yet fully grown (perhaps a delayed diagnosis of his physical underdevelopment while at Eton?) and that if he were to remain in Africa he would not be responsible for a repetition of his serious condition, a second attack of which might well prove fatal.

His father sent him one hundred pounds for the seventeen-day journey back to England.

> Thoughts of the immediate future were almost drowned by my love of the sea, by succeeding in making friends with passengers of both sexes on board and, with the few pounds that remained after paying my passage, gambling on the ship's daily 'run'. On the final day of the voyage, by a miraculous stroke of luck, when down to near my last pound, I won a small fortune.
>
> Just as well, for I hadn't been home an hour when my father calmly asked for the 'change' from the hundred pounds he had sent me! I took a certain pleasure in handing him half of my previous day's winnings!
>
> Before the week was out he [Jimmy's father] had braced himself to deliver the long-dreaded news. Standing facing me by his desk in the library, 'Uncle Bertie', he began, 'informs me that he has kindly arranged for you to have an interview with the Manager of the Old Broad Street branch of the Midland Bank. This is to take place on Monday of next week, the 14th of June. Meanwhile Grandma has been generous enough to offer to put you up at Prince's Gate. She is expecting you for luncheon tomorrow.'

To Jimmy, comfortably ensconced in his grandmother's house in Prince's Gate, the temperature of the early summer of 1926 was in pleasant contrast to the oven of Southern Rhodesia. In a nostalgic passage in *The Hidden Damage*, his book about post-war Germany published in 1947, Jimmy remembered the great Knightsbridge house:

> Hutton, ever-smiling in eternal tails, opening the door into the cool marble hall. The space. The flowers. The silence. On the wide, generous stairs the soft plum-coloured carpet with never a sign of wear. The Canalettos and the ormolu French clock. In the enormous dining-room the sideboard under which you hid and all alone travelled the Seven Seas [an allusion to a childhood game]. The womb of Wealth and Security, the World that could never end. The morning-room. The cyclamen and the roses. The Matriarch always wise and always old. The Dresden-china tea at five; the circular egg-and-anchovy sandwiches; and Robert Browning

who [said his grandmother] 'used to walk over from Wimpole Street on Sundays. He was a very charming old man.'

To shatter this picture of wealth and tranquillity came the General Strike, a nine-day stoppage called by the Trades Union Congress in support of the coal miners. Jimmy became a garbage collector in the Harley Street area, to the taunts of his socialist girl-friend whose father was a letter-sorter in an East London post office.

But the fate he knew would await him had arrived that summer of 1926 for the boy from Bective, the mongrel from Meath, the ex-officer cadet, African farmhand and budding writer.

Although Jimmy's allowance from his father was minimal and the wage of a humble Midland Bank clerk was a mere £160 per annum, if not exactly 'eligible', he was nevertheless a handsome twenty-one-year-old bachelor. His physical features were striking; with his finely shaped head, smooth dark hair and high wide forehead, not unlike his compatriot James Joyce, this well-mannered Old Etonian was surely on the invitation lists of many London hostesses. In fact, his grandmother had lined up one Miriam Rothschild as a prospective wife – 'she secretly hoped (prayed?) that I would propose to that dear girl.'

Nearly half a century later, in a letter on his seventieth birthday, Bridget Tisdall, an Anglo-Irish friend of those days, wrote:

I remember we met in the late Twenties, but where? Was it in some gold and white Belgravia ballroom? Or was it with Brian Howard, in a wine-red polo-necked jersey cutting a graceful figure on the Holland Park skating-rink? It is more likely the latter. I don't even remember dancing with you, though I do distinctly remember you in a white tie ... Unless my memory fails me, you, James, were intended for the family Bank. 'I refuse to be another pearl on the Stern necklace,' you muttered, and then gave an infectious cackle of laughter. We were lying on the bed together, fully dressed, in your grandmother's spacious Queensgate house. I was sex-shy and ignorant; our relationship never proceeded further, although you felt the urge to pat me on the head with what I felt was a touch of condescension, stroking my hair, and telling me I was like a spaniel ... I still have a snapshot of you as a young man, in an expensive hand-made shirt, sitting at a table, looking pensive, with a lock of curly hair falling over your eyes ...

After all, the Roaring Twenties were in full swing; Cecil Beaton,

Jimmy's contemporary, who in later years would become a close neighbour in Wiltshire, found that 'it was quite usual for him never to put on ordinary [ie. daytime, not evening or 'party'] clothes for a week or ten days at a stretch'. Brian Howard had come down from Oxford without a degree at the end of the summer of 1926 and it was at this time that the two friends' close attachment began to flower. While Oxford social life revolved around 'the horse', the Bloomsbury Group flourished in London and at Garsington Manor, Lady Ottoline Morrell's house in Oxfordshire. Jimmy was to be a guest – along with Julian Huxley, David Cecil and Raymond Mortimer – in her Gower Street home in London four years later.

In May 1927 Jimmy quit the Broad Street bank, and after a few weeks, at his parents' insistence, was on his way to further purgatory as an apprentice to the Bankhaus Jacob S. H. Stern in Frankfurt am Main. It was at this time that Brian Howard's passion for Jimmy appeared to be at its height:

It's a perfect nuisance the way I can't get you out of my mind, darling. And really, don't you think it's *extraordinary* of me to wait until I'd been with you in Frankfurt for three months before I – to put it blankly – fell in love with you? (I can never say any of these things to your face). I'm sorry if you find this sort of thing tiresome and embarrassing – but really I'm so much in love I don't know what to do ... It is simply that I'm thinking of you *ceaselessly*. Partly because Fabian produced a marvellous photograph of you in your African clothes – a tiny one – (upon which, by the way, you had written an *extremely* camp note) – which he gave me. You've got that blasted pipe in your mouth, but you're smiling in a way that's 'not at all nice' – in fact it almost makes me cry, I love it so. *Why* have you suddenly done this to me? ... My sweet, *let* me say all these awful, shaming things now – in a letter, since it's impossible to say them any other way. I want to write just one letter to you simply packed with what I feel. Let myself go ... I miss you so. I miss your grunt, particularly. And I miss your cool, solemn face. And the way you look at me when I say something like this – 'I met a very nice looking young gentleman last night.' ...

This is a very important letter. At least, from my point of view. It represents what I hope will mark an important development for the good in my character. I want you, as a favour, to keep it

... I'm having a rather extraordinary day with myself today. I think I'm beginning to realize things about myself ... I'm *such* an egotist that I *cannot* be objective. I think, in other words, practically entirely in terms of myself ... In my self-examination I began to analyse my love for you, and I discovered – this will surprise you – that, in a way, I don't love you as much as I make out. Now, this needs explaining. All I mean by it is that I think I must *change* the *sort* of love I have for you, if I can, into something greater and more *noble*. At present, to be ruthless, I have a rather *confused, selfish* passion for you. Vague and a little silly, though deep ... Now, you deserve – anyone deserves – and I should give – anyone should give anyone – something better than a misty, howling, formless, gloomy, aimless passion. Let me hastily add that my passion for you is not physical, as it was with Charles. It is, I fear, to a certain extent. But I have that, as you know, under control. So this passion for you I speak of is not so ordinary as all that. (I think physical passion is rather ordinary, really). But it is *formless*. It is too much, if you see what I mean, part of my egotism. Grief at your departure is too much grief at the departure of *my pleasure*. If I am to love you as I should, as you deserve, and in the way that will keep, strengthen and increase your love for me, I must change this. I must fight this thing in myself – this egotism.

In future, when I ask too much of you – refuse it. Remind me that I must change myself. You, who are good, and unselfish, will help me to do this, I know. I beg it of you ...

Jimmy, I think I must become mad, really mad, when I'm in London. I become a stranger to myself. I cannot come to grips with fundamentals at all. Then, again, my sexual side is so strong. It's really horrible ... you are *in part* responsible for the fact that my sexual side is, as it is, to a certain extent out of control. If you were different, and sex between us was possible (now, I'm not making suggestions – we've settled all that – I'm merely explaining something) and we lived together – *probably* things would be all right with me in that respect. Sex with you (I have had just enough experience with you in this way to know that what I'm saying is true) could never be injurious to my character ... I am determined, by changing this foggy passion for you into a clear, creative, considerable love – to keep it, and your love for me, which I haven't yet spoiled, for ever. If you can, please help me, and I ask you this in all humility, my sweet one – Now this is enough. Good-night and bless you.

Another letter ends: 'How nice it is going to be when we "marry and settle down".'

Yet, a remark to his mother, Lura, from Frankfurt in late November, disingenuously strikes a different note: 'The Stern boy who I see quite often is not in the least "queer-looking and conceited". He is a very ordinary, typically English type, who's been to Eton and Sandhurst, plays golf, smokes a pipe, and is really quite nice. He reads and I like him.'

Several diary entries for January 1928 indicate Jimmy's mental and physical state during those early months in Germany:

> I had a letter from B [Brian Howard had gone to Frankfurt to see 'a doctor about his lungs', he said, but really to be psychoanalysed by a Dr Prinzhorn] this morning but he really didn't say anything and seemed on the whole rather miserable which I must remember. I must endeavour to cure – it's stupid: thinks too much ... Later I went into Schatzi's ... I found myself leaving with *An American Tragedy* [by Theodore Dreiser (1925)], one of those books that one has heard so much about that one doesn't read it. They told me there, after having kindly asked after his health, that B owed them 80 marks. I think I shall be wary in future of going into shops that he used to frequent for fear of being made responsible for his debts!
>
> [Next day]: A vast, unnatural wave of depression has flooded my senses during the last 2 or 3 days ... Among the many things that have tended, during the last 30 hours, to make things decidedly worse for me, is the fact that I am now compelled to rise at the hour of 7 and to be in the office at 8. On my way to work I compared my present state of feelings to those I used to have when going for the first time to a New Department in the Midland and I discovered that I would have preferred to be back in that vile place again rather than in my present state.

Day after day at the Bank, he sat in his corner staring

> at the commercial section of the *Frankfurter Zeitung*, pages I could not have understood in my own language. I doodled and I dreamed. Now and again I fell asleep. I read the story or serial *unter dem Strich* on the front page, and I began but never finished

stories of my own. I planned tremendous novels. I made drawings of the vacant, sometimes vicious faces of the potential Nazis in the room. And I made drawings of the dark, sad, serious faces of the Jews … When the door opened and one of the directors passed through, everyone fell silent and pretended to be busy with papers on his desk. Punctually at eleven o'clock, out of table drawers appeared paper packages of bread, wurst, and ham. *Der verruckte Irlander* – the mad Irishman in the corner – was the only one without his thick mid-morning *Brotchen*, his *zweite Fruhstuck*, his second breakfast.

During the lunch hour in the summer I used to try to wash away the atmosphere of this airless office by bathing from a dock in the muddy water of the Main. Sitting in the sun, eating frankfurters and potato salad from a cardboard plate, I tried in vain not to stare at the world's biggest bellies lying out on the boards …

At six o'clock, after nine hours of wasted life, I would go off in search of friends, or I might start on a slow pub-crawl … Once these pub-crawls got under way, they might last anywhere from two to ten hours. Having traversed half the city via a succession of bars and beer halls, I seldom failed to land up on a stool at the 'Manhattan', [which] was run by Tommy Frohlich and his wife, Louise … My custom at the Manhattan was so regular, my visits so protracted, it was inevitable that Tommy, Louise, their employees, and I should become friends. It also seemed quite natural, when Tommy went off for the night or away on vacation, that I should take his place behind the bar. In this position, faced by an unusually complex clientele, in a small room invariably so packed that you had to shout to hear your own voice, I learned to speak an ungrammatical German with a German accent, how to mix a dozen different kinds of cocktails, how to drink without getting drunk, and how to behave towards others who had not learned that art.

Later, he recorded: 'I went to a bad film last night with K – she was most amusing about things in a curious, rather embarrassing flirtatious way, and I enjoyed it.' Three days later: 'K's passion for me is really extraordinary – it seems to increase instead of abating – I can't understand it at all; considering she knows probably more people in Frankfurt than anyone else. However, she is very kind … Women *are* useful sometimes I find – always married ones too – but it has always been so now I come to think.'

Back in England on holiday in August his sensibility was assaulted by a literary sensation:

All those troubles that have lately appeared to swamp my misty senses; all those personal grievances against fate which lately seemed to have dealt me so hard a blow – yea, all those and other personal things that have been weighing upon my floating mind, have been swept away out to sea as if they were so much sea-weed by this terrible crime, a ghastly crime, this suppression, this ban on that beautiful book – *The Well of Loneliness* [by Radclyffe Hall (1928)]. When I read the fact on the front page of the *Express* – that foul rag that I have now come to deem it – I felt almost as if some vile person had grossly insulted *oneself* – I felt as if someone had paid *me* the grossest insult – almost as if I myself had been done a great wrong – irreparable damage – an everlasting, unforgettable part of 'myself' taken from within me.

I wrote a long & rather good letter to B last night ... But I didn't send it – it lies now in a Book [*The Well of Loneliness*]. I wonder how long it will lie ... Pride, arrogance, stubbornness – I don't know what it was – I had thought about it all day & I found that it's not fair to *myself* to write that letter. I don't know the extent of my powers alone but I do know that with him my literary powers seem to disappear into oblivion. Superiority always kills me, though I verily believe my inferiority inspires him – and now that I find that I am preventing myself sending this letter, for the sake of purely selfish motives ...

I keep thinking of myself in Berlin – alone – & I shudder – I never shuddered in the past – alone in Africa, alone in France, alone in Germany – I very seldom, if ever, shuddered there or even at the thought of it before I went. And then I discover the only decipherable reason. Him. I had never known friendship – I had seldom, if ever, known real love – and now that I have tasted at any rate one, & perhaps both – I'm – well not as I was. I'm no longer alone as I was. In former days, I was alone and complete; granted the 'completeness' was a small 'whole'. But now I am no longer the 'whole' when I'm alone ... 'They', he, at least, says I have the talent for description, the talent to write, the power to reveal things on paper but the fact remains that those few scraps that he has seen & approved of have been written when I was more alone than at any other time ... There seems nothing but tragedy in this friendship, whichever way I placidly, normally look at it ... Does he realise that I can never write while he is near me; that the little I have written was accomplished when hundreds of miles separated us?

The ban on the Book, the night after I had finished it, exulting in its genius & overjoyed that something at last had been written to enlighten 'fools' & defy English chaste snobbery, has left me, after the first 'hell-fire' anger that went through me, limp, sad & entirely without hope for that which somehow appears to closely concern myself. What will happen? Will it always go on like that – that ghastly struggle against overwhelming odds in order to – merely in order to *exist*? I am strangely troubled: it has had such a queer effect on me: I had no idea I lived in the Book so much. I believe it was that which gave me the impulse to write that letter. Had I not justified it then perhaps I should have sent it. Who knows? Maddening that the Reading of a Book should be left to decide the fate of a Person, if not two people! And it's thus that Great Questions are answered, I suppose.

Today it seems surprising that a turgid bestseller should have had such an effect on him. His indignation may be explained by the fact that homosexuality was a subject which preoccupied him; Brian Howard's letter offers some indication of the depth and intensity of their relationship – 'Sex with you (I have had just enough experience with you in this way to know that what I'm saying is true) ...' – as does the confusion expressed in Jimmy's journal entry regarding the letter to Howard which he never sent. Even his grandmother feared that he might be or become homosexual. It is obvious that while still in his early twenties he had not yet emerged with his sexual orientation established, and it is obvious that because of this, he identified with the homosexual protagonist of the novel. Phrases from the journal entry above bear this out.

As has been said, Jimmy would later speak of his 'queer' period, which after all was commonplace in single-sex institutions like Eton. Yet at twenty-four this period had become an extended one. Not many years hence, however, his heterosexuality would be plainly apparent.

Once, a close woman friend of Jimmy's, while walking with him across Green Park to the Ritz for lunch, was touched and surprised to be shown a photograph of Brian Howard which he took from his wallet with the whispered confidence: 'The only man I ever loved.' But in an undated letter written in the '60s, when he had become a friend of Sonia Orwell, he wrote to her:

'An affair' with B.H. is most misleading. Only a handful of people still alive believe that it was a platonic, sometimes 'beautiful friendship'. At other times, needless to say, perfectly hideous. From 1926 to 1930 – in London, Provence, Devon and Berlin, but mostly in Frankfurt – we were constantly together, until his money ran out, whereupon he would return to Mom. In a strange way we *needed* each other; hélas – sooner or later – he needed an audience more. Which no doubt was just as well for me.

No letters from Jimmy to Brian Howard have survived.

In January 1968 he wrote to Pauline Wynn: 'I am surprised that I ever mentioned B. H.'s letters – because I would not like the fact of their existence to get back to Certain People. And I am even more surprised that you ask why I "refuse" to have these letters published. I'll tell you one day, if you still want to know.'

'Yes, people – individual human beings – are what matter to me,' he wrote to Isabelle Evans on 14 March 1969. 'And nature. I could not live without trees. And silence. Men *and* women, I love both sexes – provided they are lovable. But I suppose I love children more than adults. Innocence overwhelms me.'

At the end of her life Tania Stern told Lila Duckworth that Brian Howard was the only person in Jimmy's past of whom she was jealous.

Jimmy arrived in Berlin in October 1928. His job at the banking firm of S. Schoenberger & Co was compensated for by the legendary delights of the café and night-life of the city.

But that month his young sister, only eighteen, died. A sore throat had been diagnosed incorrectly as 'flu, but Leila had succumbed to a fatal attack of polio, although Jimmy in 1976 incorrectly attributed her death to sleeping sickness. The family were naturally distraught. Jimmy, returning to the Sterns' Dorset home, Hanford, seemed close to despair: at midnight on Christmas Day, only hours before his twenty-fourth birthday, he recorded in his journal: 'Crying has become a habit – eternal weeping – oh God my unhappiness is too much to bear some-times – there is now *no* one to turn to – no one to tell ... When my heart is seeming to break & my thoughts are with you darling, beloved, Leila – Leila Leila Leila, my own, oh Christ ...' Some months later he had privately printed and bound at Hatchards in Piccadilly a tribute to his sister, dedicated to his mother, and including encomiums from family and friends. Such altruism fits unexpectedly with the image of Jimmy as a man struggling to escape the bonds of family.

His younger sister, Rose, was irreparably damaged by the death of her sibling. Such was the shock that for the rest of her life she appeared to have been arrested in her 'teens. For many years she suffered from nervous collapses, could never be left alone, and had to be confined to various 'homes'. To make matters worse, her mother hated her, a hatred which, in Jimmy's words, she returned 'with a morbid, guilty, sentimental love – for which there ought to be another word'.

That December a second watershed had been reached. The black sheep no-hoper – in the eyes of his family – had resolved to try for a French university whilst attempting to have published what he trusted was in him to write. It was a desperate attempt to escape the yoke of the powerful men in the family, the successful bankers who had little or no tolerance of any other aspiration than the making of money. He was again hauled up in front of his uncle Sir Albert, now a figure of pure hatred in Jimmy's eyes.

> *Never, Never,* shall I ever forget that interview [he wrote in his journal], '… if you write you will never be able to say that by a certain date you will have so much money & that you will be able to do this, or that, be here, or there …' From the first moment I saw that it would be more hopeless than I had expected. There was no sympathy, in fact it was mostly sarcasm & ridicule … 'I cannot see anything more useless than frittering away your life in Paris – why you want to go there, God knows. Aren't there such things as English universities? If you had shown any instinctive urge to write when you were younger, or in your schooldays, then there would be more hope in contemplating it at this late date. Even if you had any talent there would be some point.' It was just as I had imagined – long ago – and every day since – only worse, much worse. Just an attack, venomous with ridicule – he is void of understanding, he is inhuman. He is forever bubbling over with the word 'Friendship' & yet he hasn't the faintest idea how to treat a sane & ambitious youth without making an enemy of him.

The authoritative figure of his childhood and youth, his father, had abdicated the decision about his eldest son's future to his brother, Bertie. A day later Jimmy wrote: 'The greatest milestone of my life ... Tonight I fought my life-battle, and won.' The lesson of the Belgian Prince had been learned. The French university never materialised; his future was on the doorstep.

The last weeks of 1928 [were] a time of great distress. They were also weeks in which I made a momentous decision – if any event of my youth deserves so extravagant an adjective. I suppose it could be said that it was during these weeks that I 'grew up'. By which I mean that I resolved at last to take no more orders from anyone. Henceforth I would not even do what was expected of me. With an almighty heave (from which I do not think I have ever quite recovered), I determined to shake from my shoulders the shackles of my family. Although far from sure what I intended to do with my life, and totally unsure of what I was capable of doing, I decided that the future, unlike the past and present, should be of my own making ... Now this was not quite so admirable or independent as it may sound. The intentions were there all right, but in turning them into decisions I was assisted first by Fate, then encouraged by a friend ...

One afternoon in the spring of 1929, a time of the lowest ebb in my life, I had been mooching to nowhere for an hour or more from my bed-sitter near Marble Arch [even the comfortable confines of Prince's Gate had been abandoned], when I was suddenly stopped in my tracks by that amusing and most talented of friends, Alan Pryce-Jones [then aged twenty, he subsequently married Jimmy's cousin, Thérèse 'Poppy' Fould-Springer, later became a distinguished editor of *The Times Literary Supplement*, and died in 2000]. 'You look horribly depressed!' he said. 'I feel it,' I replied.

Within days of this life-saving encounter in the Strand, entirely owing to Alan's generosity, I found myself sitting opposite J. C. Squire, Founder and Editor of that literary monthly, *The London Mercury* (1919–1934). The Editor's office was so small that without rising from my chair I could have leaned over the table between us and shaken Jack Squire's hand with my right and opened the door with my left. While he chain-smoked Gold Flakes, flipped through the pages of one book after another, or

scribbled his Editorial Notes for the magazine, I would read the
morning's manuscripts, totally unaware that I was learning how
not to write!

Around noon almost every day there came a knock on the door
and a young member of staff, a Mr Pink, would inform his boss
that a Mr So-&-So had called to see him and would be waiting
next door – the *Mercury*'s name for the Temple Bar, a famous
Strand-and-Fleet pub.

As soon as Jack had heard Mr Pink's announcement he
would nod towards the door, then glance at me. 'Oh Jimmy, just
run down and look after him will you!' And promptly continue
his scribbling, flipping pages or, in a desperate last-minute
attempt, dashing off his weekly review for the *Observer*, which
often had to be rushed by taxi to that Sunday newspaper's literary
editor.

The Temple Bar next door consisted of a long line of marble-
top tables for meals on the left as you entered, and a shorter bar
opposite on the right. Here it became my duty to 'look after'
anyone desiring an interview with the Editor until such time as
Squire chose to appear. Looking after such visitors meant intro-
ducing myself as a so-called assistant-editor of the *Mercury*, offering them drinks, and attempting to make them feel 'at home' at a
bar which, by the time the Editor joined us, was usually packed
three deep with garrulous men, most of whom followed, in one
form or another, the writer's trade. ...

[One day] I had eaten a snack with a friend in back of the
restaurant Next Door, and was on my way out, had in fact almost
reached the exit onto the Strand, when I was stopped in my tracks
by peals of hilarious mirth. Glancing round I saw, a few tables
away, the unmistakeable, unforgettable sight of G. K. Chesterton
and Hilaire Belloc, a chair for each buttock and, sandwiched
between these two huge men, a thin youth with a couple of
slightly protruding teeth, in a spate of talk!

I had already met this young man, attached at this time to the
Architectural Review, and who was soon to become both a good
friend – and laughing companion – to near the end of his illustrious life. His name was John Betjeman.

Pryce-Jones has this description, published in the *London Magazine*
(October 1956), of the *London Mercury* office which stood just

opposite the Law Courts in one of two houses which survived the Great Fire of London:

> [The office] was not like other offices ... In fact, it was more like a house party than an office ... I associate the small room with the physical presence of Squire, with MSS, and with visitors. First, the presence. It was to me, at the opposite side of the table, absorbing. Squire used to come up the dark passage at a running walk; he used to slump back into his chair, and he used to start a conversation at once. It was extremely good conversation – so good that it is his voice I remember, to the exclusion of everything else, except a pair of thick spectacles, and a fuzz of hair set on brown, wind-tanned skin. There would be ash about, and an eruption of paper. But the small details vanish in a general impression of vivacity, of kind candour, of a sort of obstinate manliness. The time I speak of is 1928 – the end, that is, of a soaring, stamping period in English letters. The writers of my generation brushed their hair carefully, drank cocktails, liked lifts in cars, read German, smoked Russian cigarettes rolled in black paper, and generally affected a very delicate approach to the art of living. By contrast, the writers of Squire's generation looked considerably blown about by the wind; they drank beer, walked like Meredith, they hated German, and their curtains reeked of pipe-smoke. Squire, therefore, although he was still a youngish man, seemed to me to possess a dinosaur quality: a dinosaur of rare tact, discrimination, and bounty. He must have thought me and my friends, with our talk of Rilke and Buchner, ridiculous in the extreme. But he never betrayed the fact by so much as an inflection. And when, at the earliest possible moment, we went off together to the Temple Bar, the pub next door, I almost felt myself capable of rising to the occasion while our visitors came streaming in: Belloc in flowing cape, and Beachcomber and sometimes Edmund Blunden; Hugh Mackintosh and Moray McLaren, my predecessor; perhaps, too, some guarded young man, feeling his way, like Stephen Spender or Wystan Auden.

Alan Pryce-Jones remembered how handsome Jimmy was at that time – 'All the girls in the office were after him!' One in particular, Helen Moran, declared herself: 'You stooped low to smell a flower. And suddenly I knew you; knew that I loved you, and would always love you.' Pryce-Jones, too, appears to have been strongly attracted to his contemporary, writing in June 1929 from Valence on the Rhone: 'You know that there are lots of things I have to say to you that I won't put down on paper and probably shouldn't tell you if you were here with me. But that is not because I do not think them, but because I hope you know already all that I could ever tell you. In fact, I have only two things to say, don't forget that I think of you rather a great deal, and don't leave this letter lying about! All my love, my dear, from A.'

While bibulous visits to Somerset Maugham 'and his odious Gerald Haxton' occupied much of Alan's time, as did a nineteen-hour party at Cannes 'during almost all of which I had to make conversation to Arnold Bennett', he wrote again that summer to Jimmy saying that

> I am exceedingly lonely without you ... I am thankful you are not going to the Leeward Islands, especially as either giving your favours to that old person or withholding them would have been equally painful ... Do you find the *Mercury* bearable? ... I hope you are enjoying yourself: I am certain J. C. S. and that tremendous Grace Chapman are enjoying you. The extraordinary respectability of Squire and his universal affection for queers will continue to make him adore you ... All my love, dear dear Jimmy.

Forty years later, in 1969, Alan Pryce-Jones wrote: 'One doesn't care for so very many people in life: but you have been very emphatically one of them. Your presence cast a glow over the Mercurial years we shared.'

After several happy months at 229 Strand, under Squire's benevolent eye, a new friend, introduced to him by Harold Acton, made Jimmy an unrefusable offer.

> A director of his family business, a highly successful advertising firm, Charlie Bevan [whose real name was Geoffrey Allen] was one of those men who could not be persuaded that the most expensive is not necessarily the best. Much the same age as myself, he was a swarthy, flabby, greedy, lugubrious, suspicious, yet fundamentally goodnatured soul with too much money and a mother. I still think Mum was the greater trouble. She lived somewhere in Surrey, too far for Charlie to drive his Rolls each day for his midday meal. So he waddled very slowly, on flat feet, to the Ritz, where he could telephone to Mum, and I would meet him, on Tuesdays. As a contrast to the smoke and beer of the crowded

pubs in the Strand, I looked forward to these weekly outings. They also allowed me to indulge my delight in the atmosphere of hotels.

That Charlie was not exactly an exciting companion I found restful after the literary gossip among minds so much quicker, brows so much higher, than mine. And he was almost pathetically appreciative of one's company.

The offer was to accompany Charlie on the SS *Olympic* to New York and Chicago, the two best suites on the ship – all free ('The firm will pay' said Charlie. '... you could help me with phone calls. And cables. Then there's the lerggage –').

I was still too unaccustomed to freedom to begin seriously considering how a trip across the Atlantic could be managed. Yet the seed had been sown. And ships to me were as chocolates to a child.

A full week passed before I dared mention the subject again in the presence of my Editor ... I waited until I saw Jack clutching his third whisky before luncheon in the midst of a story to a group of cronies downstairs in the Temple Bar. And even then I found myself mentioning the subject first to a mutual friend who, when the story came to its end, asked Jack if he still knew anyone in New York.

'Know anyone in New York,' snorted the Editor. 'My dear fellow, some of my best friends –' He stopped suddenly, glanced round, spotted me, thrust out an arm, pointed a finger. 'Jimmy, don't you dare cross the Atlantic without a letter from me to John Livingston Lowes!' ...

A letter from Squire written on 14 October 1929 shows the benevolent and paternal attitude his Editor had towards him: 'I hadn't realized the American thing was definitely settled. In that case you *must* go ... When you return come back here & we'll really settle down to things. I can give you a good deal now, old thing, & help you be yourself, I think – which is the beginning of writing – or one of the beginnings ... Try not to let anxiety & sorrow, even about your brother, overmaster you: that makes one incapable of doing things.'

Reggie Stern, it appeared, had suffered a breakdown. When Jimmy visited him at a doctor's house where he was being cared for, it was apparent that a return to the parental home was the last thing to be considered and that, in fact, family life had brought on a temporary illness. Escape for yet another Stern sibling had become essential.

Jimmy and Charlie sailed from Southampton on 13 November, 'I with a couple of suitcases and a few letters of introduction (including one to J. L. Lowes), Charlie with no fewer than fourteen pieces of "lerggage".'

(It is a matter of legend that on arrival at the New York docks, during the first month of the Depression, an immigration official asked Jimmy what his occupation was. 'I write. I'm a writer,' said Jimmy. 'Oh, what do you write?' asked the man. 'I write letters,' Jimmy replied.)

While Charlie had reserved a suite for himself and a single room for Jimmy at the Ritz-Carlton, his first evening in the city was spent with the photographer Berenice Abbott (1898–1991).[1]

I still think of the following two weeks as among the most exciting of my life. What do I (brought up in the British Isles) remember most vividly of that time and city? First, and without hesitation, the sensation of well-being. I have never felt so healthy, and seldom led a less healthy life. The sense of exhilaration gave one the feeling of dancing on air a few inches above the ground. I had heard rumours of the 'electricity' in the winter climate of New York. Well, that was no myth. I am not likely to forget the sparks that flew out and crackled as I pulled the vest over my head when changing my clothes. Or the severe shock the fingers received as they switched on a light or opened and closed a door.

And after the sense of well-being the friendliness and good temper of the population (including the cops), the lack of convention, the total absence of gentility, the toughness, and the humour. I have hesitated to mention the most important aspect of all, because it has long ago become a commonplace and is far from confined to the city or state of New York. However, on the

---

1 Abbott had arrived in New York in 1918 and four years later went to Paris to become a sculptor, joining a group of Americans among whom were Man Ray, Edna St Vincent Millay and Sinclair Lewis, who gathered at the Café Rotonde. She was a rival in love of Djuna Barnes, eventually becoming Man Ray's pupil and assistant and a highly distinguished photographer, who like Walker Evans took pictures of the impoverished before the Depression. Between 1939 and 1958 she produced arresting photographs, both aesthetically compelling and scientifically valid, which demonstrated the laws of physics.

assumption that virtues can never be too often emphasized, and as one who has lived in other lands and many years in the United States, let me join all those who believe that as a nation Americans are the world's most hospitable people …

At twenty-four I had formed no opinions, felt certain of nothing, had confidence in no one, least of all myself. With good reason. I had nothing to feel confident about. A few things I could do: I could listen. I could observe. And I could act. I still consider that I could conceal behind a mask of comparative calm, even from those who might have claimed to know me, the nervous tension of the potential introvert.

And yet looking back, I now believe that it was in America among Americans, in that gay, reckless, optimistic atmosphere, above all in the company of the Negro intelligentsia, that I began at last to break through the cement-like crust of my bourgeois British upbringing, to learn at last sometimes to utter an unhesitating Yes, where hitherto I would have withdrawn behind that cautious, instinctive, notorious No …

I led, not unnaturally, a highly disorganized, hectic existence, each day both ending and beginning almost invariably in Harlem, where I soon acquired the nickname of White Boy, and where instead of dancing (I never could dance), I used to sit by the hour talking, drinking, laughing, but above all watching, at one hall or club after another, the world's most elegant dancers dance.

His companion in those early New York days was Olivia Wyndham, who had travelled over with him on the SS *Olympic*, a photographer and upper-crust English lesbian, who fell in love with a black actress ten years her senior and lived with her and her husband in Harlem and Brooklyn for the rest of their lives. 'For a "well-brought-up" English woman', her relation, Francis Wyndham, wrote in his collection of stories, *Mrs Henderson* (1985), 'to vanish for good, apparently acting on a sudden whim, into a remote Negro ghetto confusedly associated in the ignorant British mind with drugs, drink, crimes of violence and embarrassing excesses of childish religious fervour … appeared to many of [her friends] a baffling enormity … while the less narrow-minded, though applauding the courage and characteristic lack of caution manifested by her pioneer spirit, feared that she had taken a final step into unexplored territory where it would be too dangerous for them to follow.' Jimmy, however, did, for this 'lost lady' of legend, social outcast, rebel and eccentric, who always showed him extreme kindness, was just the kind of person to appeal to Jimmy.

Over fifty years later, in answer to Nora Sayre's suggestion that he write about his experiences with Blacks in Africa, London, Paris and Manhattan, he wrote to her in 1984:

> ... I must have told you about my youthful, ridiculously naïve ambition [obviously encouraged by Olivia] on managing to reach the USA in 1929: nothing less than somehow making my way South, wandering about there for months (just what I was to live on, of course, I hadn't bothered to think!) doing research on just how Blacks had come to be there, where they had originally come from etc., and then returning, presumably to West Africa, living there for a while until I felt I had acquired sufficient knowledge to write a history of the Slave Trade in so far as it had concerned the USA ...!! What it is, or rather, was to be young!

But this fantasy of youth was never realised. Instead, accompanied by the enigmatic Geoffrey Allen, he travelled west by train: Chicago, the Grand Canyon, Hollywood, Beverly Hills, San Francisco – the journey must have intoxicated him. They drove north up the coastal highway; Jimmy played golf on several of the beautiful links which border the route, and among the first things he ever published were self-illustrated articles on Californian golf courses for a magazine implausibly called *Die Dame*. In the last week of 1929 he passed his American driving test. 'On New Year's Day 1930 I woke up in a kind of empty swimming bath', he wrote thirty years later to Isabelle Evans, 'surrounded by, almost *underneath*, a mass of non-white, not very gentle men, mostly (I think) Chinese and Japanese, in SF gaol. Offense? Need you ask! Known in the UK as "drunk and disorderly". All I remember (prior to the swimming pool) is taking their hats off, very slowly & soberly, a long line of wealthy businessmen coming out of the Big Hotel, putting their hats for a split second onto my own bare head, then popping them back on theirs.'

He resolved to travel home around the world via Russia, but in Honolulu adversity ruined his plans. Often in delicate health from childhood, he became seriously ill with psittacosis, a respiratory disease caught from parrots, with influenza-like symptoms – fever, chills and headache – which can result in fatal pneumonia. He was rescued by relations of his school friend, Harold Acton. It wasn't until six months later that he reached London via New York, where Olivia Wyndham

met him off his ship in a blizzard. 'Next Door to Death', a story
collected in *The Man Who Was Loved* (1952), gives a good description
of what Jimmy went through on that faraway Pacific island.

Written in the first person, the story is of a man's brief confinement
in a hospital on Oahu, one of the Hawaiian Islands. Suffering with a
wasting fever from an undiagnosed illness, he drifts in and out of consciousness, a hallucinatory state relieved by the tender and intimate
attentions of the young native and white American nurses. One
evening he overhears a doctor anticipating his imminent demise:

> ... a few minutes later, I heard footsteps on the veranda, more
> footsteps of someone approaching, and then greetings as of two
> men well acquainted. The voices dropped a little, and, straining to
> listen, I heard one man saying, 'Well, when can I have that bed?'
>
> And the other voice answered, 'Oh, that's all right – free tomor-
> row night.'
>
> 'Tomorrow – sure?'
>
> 'Yes – he'll be gone by then.'

True to his word, Squire at the *The London Mercury* welcomed him
back but, Jimmy recalled, understandably he was in a less patient
mood:

> Did I expect to sit here reading manuscripts for the rest of my life?
> Was I ever going to put pen to paper? That evening I took a deep
> breath, went back to my lodgings, wrote a few pages describing
> an African veldt fire and, in fear and trembling, handed them to
> Squire. 'Finish it,' he growled, 'and I'll print it!' I think it took me
> a month to 'finish it' – that is, to create a couple of characters and
> write a story around the fire. When I saw 'my story' ['The Cloud']
> in print, sandwiched between the work of Chesterton and Dame
> Ethel Smyth in the hallowed pages of the *Mercury*, the lonely lanes
> of Meath had never seemed so remote.

The story became one of the eight in his first published book, *The
Heartless Land* (1932).

Within a few months his confidence had taken hold and he left the
Mercury and London to settle in Paris. Most of his first collection of
stories was composed in what was the Hôtel d'Alsace, in the room
where, three decades earlier, Oscar Wilde had lived and died. He even

ate his meals alone either where Wilde, too, had eaten his, or round the corner at a bistro table which he often shared with a man for weeks before he learned that his name was Le Corbusier. The stories were written in a bedroom overlooking a narrow, noisy street, but 'in my imagination all were composed in the silence of a room overlooking the Boyne'. Thus Bective's atmospheric influence persisted; '... above all', he wrote years later, 'in reveries and dreams, Ireland is still home.'

He still received encouraging letters from Squire: 'How is your book getting on – if you can get the quality of your letters into it you'll be all right.'

Two years later Macmillan published *The Heartless Land* in London and a year later in New York. The novelist H. E. Bates (1905–74) wrote of the book:

> The country in *The Heartless Land* ... is Africa, and these eight stories deal solely with the lives in that country of English settlers, their wives, and the Kaffirs who work for them. With one or two exceptions they are stories of men without women, of the conflict of men against the everlasting heat, solitude, and monotony of African life and against themselves and the pain of living alone with one another; Mr Stern emphasizes above all the conflict of black against white, Kaffir against Briton, the primitive against the civilized, of darkness against light. In every story he shows us the littleness, pain, unhappiness, and cruelty that comes of one kind of life seeking to oppress another and one race another. In his analysis of these emotions, his understanding of his fellow-men, both black and white, and in the few glimpses he gives us of women, Mr Stern shows a wonderfully balanced sympathy and detachment, a fine tenderness and irony. He is a writer of both solid power and great delicacy, getting his effect by subtle contrasts of light and shade in feeling and atmosphere. In all of his stories there is something good; and in one or two ... where the grimness of life is softened by feminine influences, there is something melancholy, haunting and painful.

L. A. G. Strong, in *The Spectator*, found the stories 'vivid and powerful ... Mr Stern writes admirably ... his scenes, grim and terrible, are burnt into the reader's mind.'

The reviewer of *The London Mercury*, Jimmy's *alma mater*, as it were, wrote: 'There is acute observation and description intensely vivid and often beautiful. "The Man Who Was Loved" rises to almost magnificent heights of horror.'

Ethel Mannin, who became Jimmy's lover in 1930, wrote in the leading English socialist newspaper of the day, the *New Leader*: '... the author can write; he can feel, and that passionately, sensitively; he can observe, and that truthfully; he can think. Emphatically this is a book not to miss.'

The unsigned *New York Times* review was favourable, as were others in less important newspapers, but several found the stories too 'grim and terrible', whilst *The Times Literary Supplement*, also unsigned, divined 'a certain narrowness in the author's vision'.

Given the beneficial perspective of some six decades later, the Auden scholar, Nicholas Jenkins, has these perceptive words to say of the stories:

> ... their unifying theme is hatred: the hatred of the white settlers for each other, and their terrified and contemptuous hatred of the Africans – a feeling that in its turn is amply repaid. Although the stories are set in Africa, *The Heartless Land* is mainly about the Europeans, specifically the dregs of the British imperial culture in its most provincial and soulless manifestations. The book dwells on the moral corruption of the older settlers and their families in their Spartan outposts, and, repeatedly, on the agonized loneliness of the younger, single men in 'this wilderness'. The volume as a whole conveys a deep sense of bitterness; there are frequent eruptions of melodramatic violence and many of the stories end in a sense of encirclement and futility. This feeling is only partially offset by Stern's mordant social observation; the mood of barely suppressed rage is exacerbated by the fact that, underlying the African setting, are analogies with the embattled situation of the Anglo-Irish gentry amongst whom Stern had grown up. This quasi-symbolic dimension gives *The Heartless Land* something of the quality of a dream-sequence, as if readers of the book found themselves in a huge, unfamiliar terrain suffused with some urgent but obscure message ... The dominant literary influences, looming presences in much Thirties writing, are the stories of Maugham and Lawrence, but the racial situation gives a new twist to the familiar theme of the struggle to transcend the prison of social class ... the story in *The Heartless Land* most frequently mentioned by critics is 'The Man Who Was Loved', a piece with

strong Oedipal undercurrents. It is the most inventive story formally – in it two narrative methods are contrasted within a single frame ...

Jimmy was later to claim that for the art of brevity he was indebted to Hemingway, for story-telling to Maugham, to Lawrence and Liam O'Flaherty for their evocation of nature, and to Firbank for his dialogue.

He based Major Carter, the protagonist of the story 'The Man Who Was Loved', on a certain Major Robert 'Boomerang' Gordon of the Southern Rhodesia police who, years after Jimmy had last seen him in 1926, actually died in a manner uncannily similar to that which he had described in the story.

In 1965, in a letter to William Plomer, Jimmy had this to say about his first book: 'Though it is more than 30 years since I read it, I have always thought that its *interiors* were good, its prophetic quality not bad, but that it was spoiled by youthful self-pity.'

Today, seventy years after the publication of *The Heartless Land*, the stories convey a very strong sense of injustice. There's little room for humour or levity in the harsh reality of their setting. But a striking talent for descriptive writing together with a moving empathy with his characters, both white and black, make for an impression that persists. The integrity and seriousness with which Jimmy confronted the facts and dramas of daily life in Africa make one realise what an exceptional debut the book presented.

3
Paris, Marriage and 1939
1931–1939

The '30s in Paris was a time of cultural ferment; the city was abuzz with a shifting population of writers and artists from the New World as well as from its European neighbours. The previous decade had seen a similar activity when, like moths to a flame, English and American writers and painters like Djuna Barnes, Ford Madox Ford, Nina Hamnett, Ernest Hemingway, the Irishman James Joyce, Wyndham Lewis, John Dos Passos, Ezra Pound and Gertrude Stein flocked to the French capital. It was also a period of crises: Hitler's rise to power in 1933, the beginning of the Spanish Civil War in 1936, and the Munich Crisis of 1939 leading to the Second World War.

'1931–9 Lived (mostly in Paris, France) and travelled on the continent, as free lance writer, contributing stories, articles etc to English literary journals.' So runs an entry in Jimmy's *curriculum vitae* written in New York in the early '40s.

Jimmy wrote in 1984 to the Irish-American journalist, Maeve Slavin: 'Talk to Corbusier in Paris? Perish the thought: I talked to no one. I wrote. And when I'd published that book [*The Heartless Land*] in the UK and U.S.A. (in 1932) & was asked what I was writing *now*? I said "What? Write *another* book?" I was horrified: What? Go through all that *again*? So I have been writing letters ever since.' There is evidence that as early as 1935 he had written the twelve stories that were eventually to be collected three years later in *Something Wrong* – which he originally called *Boys* – a title which at the time may have failed to raise eyebrows. But 'talked to no one' was not strictly accurate.

He became a close friend of Gregori Michonze, a Russian painter, originally from Bessarabia, who arrived in Paris at the same time as Max Ernst. Michonze was one of the world's great bums: he spent three and a half years of the First World War in a German prison camp, which ruined his stomach forever but failed to kill his sense of humour. Max Ernst, who would later marry Peggy Guggenheim, was one of the best-looking men Jimmy had ever known, while his friend Man Ray was a fuzzy-haired, dark-skinned roly-poly. Ten years later in New York he would see a lot of Ernst who, with Guggenheim, lived on almost the same block as the Sterns.

Sybille Bedford, the novelist and biographer of Aldous Huxley, who first met Jimmy in the spring of 1937 in the company of Brian Howard and the antiquarian bookseller and bibliographer Percy Muir, remembers Jimmy's proclivity for speedy cross-dressing, a party trick which he played with great aplomb, lipstick immaculately applied, implying frequent practice. His diaries, too, show that he had a busy social life: 'Called on K. A. Porter [Katherine Anne Porter, the American short story writer and novelist] but she's not yet back from USA. Called on Sylvia Beach [who first published Joyce's *Ulysses* in 1922, owner of the English-language bookshop, Shakespeare & Co, and friend to many well-known writers]; she talked some American pseudo-literary twaddle ... saw the Surrealist crowd coming out of their Place Clichy café – Man Ray, André Breton & Co ... met Alan Pryce-Jones ...'

A rather more momentous meeting was with James Joyce. This was arranged by Joyce's old friend and sometime secretary Robert McAlmon, a writer and publisher (Contact Editions) of Gertrude Stein, William Carlos Williams and Ernest Hemingway, and husband of the English novelist Bryher, who was one of the '20s generation of expatriate writers in Paris. They were accompanied by the American painter and expert on costume, Hilaire Hiler.

In *The Listener* in 1961, Jimmy wrote:

At this time, the fall of that grim year 1934, Norah and James Joyce were living in a furnished apartment on the rue Galilee, a residential district a couple of blocks from the Etoile. In the *metro* from the Left Bank I remember feeling slightly nervous. The day was cold, sunless, the time the fearful hour of four ... The Joyces' apartment, if I'm not mistaken, was on the fourth floor. At our ring a door opened slowly, and there he stood. At first glance he struck me as smaller, frailer, than I had imagined. Dressed in a peacock-blue velvet jacket and dark trousers, he held himself in the position of the blind – chin raised, head tilted slightly back.

... Raised barely above a whisper, his voice – that tenor to which as a young man he considered devoting his life – sounded excessively tired, the voice of a sufferer in whose presence, as in hospitals, one feels instinctively all sounds should be muffled. His hand, too, suggested the hand of a recluse, an invalid – bony yet soft to the touch, conveying on the instant a marvellous gentleness. As it lay for a moment in one's own, the silken skin of the fingers softly closing, one forbore to do more than carefully close over them one's own.

In my mind's eye I can see but one book in that dim, depressing, impersonal sitting-room. (I remember wishing that we had brought a flower: must not his sense of smell be unusually acute? Then it occurred to me that maybe this very sense might explain the lack of flowers.) It was to the single book, which lay alone on a grand piano, that he – while Hiler and I seated ourselves on the sofa, and Bob on a chair – slowly, his hands out, fingering the furniture, soundlessly in slippers, made his way. The volume was large, of many pages and clearly new, possibly unopened. Joyce leaned over it, touched it with his long fingers, lifted it as though it were beyond price, then laid it down.

'Is that the American edition?' asked Bob, getting up.

Joyce said nothing, simply turned and handed the book to his friend with the faintest, barely perceptible, sign of a smile.

They talked, presently, of Ireland, fox-hunting, horse-racing, and, among others, of Sir Francis Becher, in real life Lord Dunsany, a neighbour of the Stern family in Meath. 'Wasn't he a very gruff kind of man?' asked Joyce.

In September 1957, while staying with the painter Katherine Church, who had married Anthony West, the son of Rebecca West and H. G. Wells, Frances Partridge, the Bloomsbury centenarian and diarist, asked Jimmy whether Joyce was a good talker. 'He didn't talk much; he only asked questions,' he replied. 'When I first met him he asked me questions for a whole hour about my childhood in Ireland. He was only interested in two things: Ireland and his own writing.'

Bob McAlmon was to have a hand in the composition of Joyce's great work, as he told Jimmy in his letter of 20 December 1949:

Certainly I typed the last pages of *Ulysses* but by urgent request after a late night and many drinks. He handed me the hen[*sic*]-scrawled script and 8 note books with markings in various coloured pencils and I was to insert new thought of Molly's where he had marked in colours in the various note books. Even drunk I knew that my eyes were to be taxed and that he would notice that I got some of the thoughts out of his mystic order. He detected that but agreed with me that Molly's thoughts might be irregular anyway. An English typist had typed the same passage for him, but her husband in a rage at its 'filth' had torn her typed copy and his original script to shreds. He had to rewrite it, and without asking outright he said several times during the course of the many nights 'you tell me you are a very fast typist, McAlmon. And surely you understand what I am doing more than that lady typist.' It was decidedly not temerity when I finally said, 'Oh, well, give me the script. I'll do it as quick as I can.'

Jimmy's love affair with the thirty-year-old novelist and travel writer Ethel Mannin began in 1930 and lasted four years. She had been married to John Porteous with whom she had one daughter, Jean, but was parted from her husband. The facts that she was of Irish ancestry and that among her literary influences was Olive Schreiner's *The Story of an African Farm* (1929) may have accounted for their mutual attraction. Ethel was a socialist and admired the writing of Bertrand Russell and the educational theories of A. S. Neill, the controversial founder of Summerhill School, of whom Jimmy became an admirer and with whom he corresponded.

Ethel Mannin wrote from five to six hours a day and, at the height of her career, vowed that she would publish two books a year, one fiction and the other non-fiction. Her long list of over a hundred publications is proof of her dedication.

They travelled together all over Europe. In 1982, Jimmy wrote to his brother Peter:

Re Austria: my time there, Vienna & Salzburg, was 1930–33 – just 50 years ago. I am almost sure that I stayed, always alone or more often with E. M. (now pushing 82!) at the Hotel Stein, in a lovely room on the top floor with a balcony overlooking the River Salzach, which runs (gallops) through the town. While in Salzburg do try to walk out of town – past a gorgeous swimming bath, where I bathed every day in summer – to a splendid country pub called Gasthaus Steinlechner near the village of Parsch. I don't remember this village at all, and am only aware of its existence by a letter from Kay Boyle in Col-de-Villefranche addressed to me on June 11, 1933 to Steinlechner's Gasthaus, Parsch, Salzburg. (I am constantly blessing myself for keeping letters!) As I think I've told you, I wrote 'The Broken Leg' [one of the stories in *Something Wrong*] in that pub, with E. M. banging away at one of her 97 books next door.

Ethel and Jimmy kept in touch until her death in 1984. One affectionate letter from her written in 1977 recalls the occasion of their first meeting: 'Alec Waugh … brother of the quite horrible Evelyn – whom I met that historic evening I met you. Ralph Straus had told me, "I have two young ones for you!" One was you, the other E.W. – who was quite studiously rude to me …'

The affair cannot have run smoothly, as Jimmy wrote to his wife Tania in the '40s: '… both E and I were so utterly ill-matched. She behaved towards someone younger than herself, in some very important ways, disgracefully; and I, in one very important way, was very stupid indeed – namely, I should have realized sooner what was happening, and gone. By staying all that time I realize, long ago, I did myself a great deal of harm.'

A close friend of Jimmy's, with whom he corresponded over many years, the American novelist Kay Boyle, recalled in a festschrift for his seventieth birthday a meeting with him and Ethel:

Another explicit memory is of Vienna at the wrong time of the year, at the wrong time of the century. It was the winter of 1933, and the streets were either covered with ice or damp with the suicidal *Fohn*. Mothers and fathers and their young children stood barefoot on the fierce ice, shivering in doorways, their hands out, saying nothing, silently dying of hunger before our eyes. And we – Ethel Mannin, Laurence Vail, you, I – took refuge in *Weinstubes* so as not to see these people too clearly. We were in a place and a season where people lived in hell … and our typewriters were silent as we looked the other way.

In the same birthday letter to him she remembered an earlier time:

The first memory is still bright with the colours of the Mediterranean hillside. You came to see Laurence Vail and me on the Col-de-Villefranche, and that was the first time we met. It was 1930 or 1931, when writers of short stories were seeking one another out all over Europe. I had read a story a few days before that Whit Burnett had published in his *Story Magazine*, and I can still see the yellow cover of the magazine, and the way the words looked on the page. It was a fine story, very simple, very moving, about the loneliness of a young Englishman living in isolation in Africa. I spoke about that story when we were having supper on the terrace of a hillside restaurant above Nice. So impressed I was by the story that I hadn't noticed the name of the author, and after I'd talked about it, you laughed your dry, witty, almost evil laughter, in which your whole face takes part, and you told me you'd written the story. And it was true.

Jimmy had been living alone at the Welcome Hotel in Villefranche, carrying on a lively correspondence with H. E. Bates about the placing of their short stories. Nearby, at the Villa Mauresque on Cap Ferrat, as Jimmy told Alan Ross in 1987, 'Willy Maugham used to sit alone, scowling at nothing day after day!' Visiting Kay Boyle and her husband Laurence Vail, he met Emma Goldman, the sixty-year-old Russian-born American anarchist, who was dressed appropriately in red.

In August 1933, Jimmy received the first of many letters from Katherine Anne Porter, another American incumbent of Paris in the '20s. In a review of Joan Givner's biography of her, Jimmy wrote:

I knew this extraordinary woman for more than half of her ninety years. I have thought that perhaps her life is the greatest literary success story of the twentieth century. Today I am convinced of it. All the more remarkable considering her relatively small output: some twenty stories, three short novels, a large volume of [Collected] Essays and Occasional Writings [1970], and finally the long work of fiction [Ship of Fools (1962)] American critics have hailed (mistakenly in my opinion) as one of the great novels of the past hundred years ...

I do not believe, however, that it was literature alone that made Porter's name all over North America a legend in her lifetime. As well as write she could also talk. Indeed, while she found the process of creation was mostly agony, the gift of the gab gave her continuous pleasure. Should someone apologise for interrupting her: 'Honey!' she'd crack, 'that's the only way you'll get a word in!' With this gift Porter talked, taught, lectured, and gave readings for years not only throughout much of her native land, but as far afield as Mexico, France and Belgium.

When I first met her in Paris in the Spring of 1933 I saw an aristocratic Southern Belle of infinite charm and as young as the century. Yet she had to die 47 years later before I learned that she had been born in a Texas log-cabin in 1890, lost her mother at the age of two, developed tuberculosis in her teens, and that the husband with her in Paris was not only her third, he was sixteen years her junior and not her last.

Christopher Isherwood, in his journal for 1946 (*Lost Years: A Memoir 1945–51*, 2000), has this waspish description of K. A. P.: 'The image she presented was that of a senior southern belle (she would have been fifty-two), extremely gracious and rather ridiculously ladylike – her "beauty" and her "breeding" were qualities to which she firmly laid claim and you had to accept them as real if you wanted to associate with her. Beneath these airs and graces [was seen] a tough coarse frontier woman, pushy, ambitious, fairly good-natured if handled with proper deference.'

K. A. P. wrote from Montparnasse:

Dear Jimmy Stern: I think your short stories are magnificent, and the several persons to whom I have given the book [*The Heartless Land*] to read think so too. My husband [Eugene Pressly] I think is a good judge, and so are Glenway Wescott and Lincoln Kirstein [editor of *Hound and Horn*] ... I should hardly know where to begin choosing my favorite, for every story is worth reading several times over and each has its own quality ... in all your stories I like the way you have taken the trouble to say what you wanted to say. I know you have, for only tough work will bring one to such ease of expression with directness and concentration of intensity.

Jimmy first met Malcolm Lowry in 1933 at a New Year's Eve party in Julian Trevelyan's studio which the latter shared with Max Ernst and Joan Miro. On that occasion Lowry punched Jimmy in the stomach during a jealous outburst involving his future wife Jan. Jimmy's second encounter with the author of *Under the Volcano*, one of the great literary 'drunks' of all time, was on a wintry night in Paris, in the most bizarre of circumstances.

It was pelting with rain ... So I ducked into a *bistro* [he wrote twenty-eight years later]. To me one of the many glories of Paris is that its inhabitants are practically immune to human eccentricity. Neither to the *patron* behind the bar, nor to the customer sitting alone at one of four small tables, did it seem in the least surprising that between them on the sawdust-covered floor there lay stretched, flat on his back, evidently asleep, a robust-looking fellow with a week of stiff red stubble on his face, and across his stomach a guitar.

After becoming acquainted, the two men repaired to the party to which Jimmy was on his way when this memorable night began. *Much* later they progressed to the Café Dome;

> [Lowry] then embarked upon a story about a *bordello* he claimed to have known in the port of Zanzibar. By the time the story ended the waiters of the Dome had started piling the chairs on to the terrace tables, the great shutters came rolling down, and over the city the night-sky began slowly giving way to a steel-grey dawn. It was then, without plan or pre-arrangement, that we set out upon the first of what Malcolm called 'little walks' ... I know where we walked *to*, and, more surprising perhaps, the hour at which we finally landed up in my flat ... Not far as the crow flies. But we were not crows. Moreover, when we stopped for what Malcolm called a 'breather', it was not on a branch. This, the first, but not the longest of our 'little walks', lasted twenty-eight hours ... .

Years later, in a BBC interview, Jimmy gave this description of Lowry:

> He had a Nordic look. Straight fair hair brushed back, sharp nose, deepset sky-blue eyes in a round face. And he wore a small moustache and tweed coats, which gave him an almost military air. But he was too short for the army type. Five foot eight, I believe. And his hands and feet were small. But this, like most things about Malc, was deceptive. To hold his forearm was like holding an iron bar. And his chest was the proverbial barrel. Kicking him up the backside, as I once felt compelled to do, was like kicking the stern of a hulk ... He spoke mostly in monologues. They would last for 5 or 10 minutes, or half a mile. If seated, he would lower his head, and peer at you from under his brows. The substance of his talk was dreamlike, often madly funny, but I found it impossible to memorize or reproduce. Among several people he would remain silent – then suddenly snort, a kind of guffaw, through his nose, presumably at his own thoughts. Which may suggest that he was a bad listener. On the contrary. He was the most prodigious listener I have ever known. As I learned to my cost. Though it took many years.

The two writers had read each other's first books; Lowry inscribed the copy of *Ultramarine* (1933) which he gave to Jimmy: 'To the heartless land from the heartless sea'. They did not communicate with each other again until 1940, although they remained 'old boozing companions ... until his alcoholic death in 1957'.

Extracts from a journal written in October 1934 reveal the extent of Jimmy's complicated involvement with various women:

E [Ethel Mannin] writes me letters, saying one from me would give her a heart-beat (!); tho' she's living with AA, it does certainly seem she'd rather be back with me. I wrote her a fortnight ago & said she was to do one of two things. 1: wire 'coming' stating time of the aeroplane's arrival, or 2: wire 'can't'. She did what I expressly asked her not to do: wrote me an immense letter, seeking explanations: I couldn't answer: a week passed: she wrote me another: a week has passed: I can't answer. To tell the naked truth: I really don't want her, unless under extreme strain.

G writes me letters from Warsaw, revealing her snobbery & her cowardice. 'I just want you to know', she says, 'how anxious I am tonight about *you* – (your health, your work etc) I wish you could be well' & ends: 'May I kiss you?' Bitch. 'I cannot face the idea of your being alone in Paris,' she says. God, *she* not 'facing'! This woman wants a lover, before it's too late: she 33. And she's a demi-vierge! Christ, how I hate 'em. But she's terrified of me. And she worships herself. She's like a masturbating man, but she's a woman – what's worse? I met her thro her 'desire' to translate *The Heartless Land*.

And now, after a month's celibacy, MU is here: she whom I met on a Channel Crossing, seduced in Dieppe, & lived with in London: she for whom I've waited & prayed for the last month; she's here – and I don't want her: chiefly, it seems, because I fell in love with P about a week ago. And P lives in the next street! P is one of the most beautiful creatures I've ever seen; and we want each other, too – so far as I can see... Oh, I wonder what P would be like as a mistress! I wouldn't mind marrying her; I wonder, tho', if there ain't a catch somewhere. There *would* be! Anyhow I know my heart hasn't beaten that way on sight of anyone for 5 years.

It is perhaps fortunate that the identities of these three women cannot be traced.

'God, what a time that was! The intrigues, the subterfuges, the lying, disappearing, excuses' – a sentence from his story, 'Solitaire', about a doctor meeting an 'old flame' eleven years after he ended their affair.

Jimmy, approaching thirty, was extremely handsome and obviously attractive to women, as the evidence of his philandering shows. But his wild oats had been sown and marriage was on the horizon. Henceforth he was to 'receive affection' to last a lifetime – give or take some serious setbacks.

A month later, on 7 November 1934, the woman with whom he was to spend the next fifty-eight years appeared in his life. Small and dark, with a perfectly proportioned figure and penetrating brown eyes set wide apart in a classically moulded face, she had a vital, arresting personality. They met at the flat of the singer Hedli Anderson – she eventually married the poet Louis MacNeice – with whom Jimmy had been living. 'He looked like a ragged tramp,' Tania remembered many years later. Jimmy wrote in the same journal: 'Tania Korella [*sic*] & Eda Lord dined here last night. Nice pair. The former should not be Lesbian … I understood that her name was Gorilla.' Tania and Eda were an 'item'. Eda Lord, whose harsh American upbringing was evoked in her first novel *Childsplay* (1961), after a disastrous marriage, came to Berlin to live in 1932. During the Second World War she suffered severely under the German occupation of southern France. In 1956 she set up house with Sybille Bedford, a life-long friend of the Sterns.

Tania (her real names were Constanze Marie Matilde) Kurella (1904–95) was born in Breslau (now Wroclaw), Poland, of German-Polish origin, the daughter of a psychiatrist. During a seven-year engagement to Tania's mother, he sailed twice round the world as a ship's doctor while in letters educating his fiancée in the philosophy, art and science of the time. When Tania was ten, her father's body was sent home from the war. She never found out whether he was killed or whether he committed suicide, but Tania believed that he was overwhelmed by the effort to support a large family. Tania's mother killed herself six years later, following cancer of the uterus. The family consisted of two girls and three boys, one of whom became a Soviet arts administrator and East German Communist *apparatchik*. Tania's lust for independence at the early age of sixteen – through sex – was pronounced. At one point she joined a Buddhist-Communist community.

In Berlin, where she and her younger brother Heini were brought as children, with its cult of physical fitness – not unlike that of the present day – Tania became a pupil of the physical therapist Else Gindler, who had perfected a method to develop 'bodily consciousness'. Its aim was to create 'a harmony between mind, body and soul'. A promotional leaflet sent out by Tania in New York during the 1940s stated that 'Awareness and conscious control of such vital psycho-physical functions as Relaxation, Breathing, Concentration, Posture and Poise improve good co-ordination of mind and body, thereby increasing and preserving our creative energies'. Subsequently, she started teaching pupils of her own in this technique.

In Berlin, Eda Lord and Tania became friends with the journalist Darsie Gillie and, after the two women's flight to France from the Nazi threat, they renewed their friendship when Gillie became the *Manchester Guardian*'s correspondent in Paris. Years later, Jimmy would tease Tania that he had beaten Gillie to the altar.

One evening, with Hedli and Eda, on the dance floor of the Bal Musette in Montparnasse, Jimmy kissed Tania Kurella and their life together began.

'Beloved Boy,' Jimmy addressed Tania, surprisingly, that April. 'Darling, I've suddenly decided to call you "Boy" from henceforth – with your permission ! – on the condition you don't retaliate by calling me girl!! ... I love my little oriental boy.'

During the summer of 1935 Jimmy and Tania were in Caparica, Portugal, from where he wrote to Alan Pryce-Jones:

> I'm with one Tania Kurella, a German; have been for three or four months; we get on remarkably well; she possesses the somewhat enviable quality of arriving in a strange country, learning its language in a few weeks and then making a quite substantial livelihood by teaching its wealthy folk a weird kind of Kultur-Gymnastik, for the good of their 'ealth. She's now thinking of attacking London or Lisbon; at present we've not decided which. She's the same age as myself and speaks rather better English than I do ... Splendid to hear of someone who likes being married; I wish it myself, and perhaps before so very long it may be possible ...

A year later, Jimmy and Tania were introduced by William Robson-Scott, a German scholar then teaching English at Berlin University, to Christopher Isherwood, with whom they were soon to share a house in Sintra, Portugal. Isherwood wrote of Tania in *Christopher and His Kind* (1977): '[She was] one of the most unaffected, straightforward, sensible, and warmhearted women Christopher had ever encountered.

She was also one of the most beautiful: small, dark-haired, dark-eyed, and with a body as beautiful as her face ... When she looked at you, she seemed aware of all the faults of posture which betrayed your inner tensions; but you never felt that she found them repulsive or even absurd. She was ready to help you correct them, if you wanted her to.'

After the initial shock at the prospect of a foreign daughter-in-law – and a gentile at that – Jimmy's parents accepted the inevitable. His grandmother, on the other hand, immediately welcomed Tania; she had feared that Jimmy was or would become 'queer'.

Reluctantly, the engaged couple agreed to a London wedding. They moved into one of the few rooms of the famous Charlotte Street restaurant, L'Etoile, and on 9 November 1935 were married in the church of the Holy Trinity, Prince Consort Road, Kensington Gore. The bride was given away by a childhood friend, Ernst Freud, son of Sigmund and father of Lucian and Clement. The vicar was the Revd J. O. Hannay, who wrote detective fiction under the pen-name George A. Birmingham. The reception was at 25 Prince's Gate, Jimmy's grandmother's house. They honeymooned in Windsor:

> We lived very grandly [Jimmy wrote in November 1965 to Pauline Wynn], in a huge gilt bed and golden private bath with red plush carpet. It was a Club where we were the only guests; there were about 6 servants, a first class chef & wine cellar, & a Russian billiards table on which we played through the foggy winter evenings. The place was run by a middle-aged Queer who was what my Father called a Bounder, & later was 'deported'. Actually he bounded off to Mallorca where I met him again living happily (& no doubt somewhat crookedly) with an enormous dog. He was that kind of chap.

Thereafter they returned with relief to their small flat in the Quai de l'Horloge, Paris, with its splendid view over the Seine. From the window they looked straight down, through immensely high poplars, onto the river and the *pêcheurs* below the Pont Neuf. Jimmy found it difficult to resist waving to the barges floating by. Their friend Anais Nin, diarist, novelist and critic, lived on a barge on the other side of the bridge. Not far away Henry Miller, the colossus of Big Sur, was experiencing the fleshly delights of the French capital.

> Dear old 'Hen' [Jimmy wrote to Pauline Wynn in November 1966], not a bad chap really, as Yanks go. I wish I had kept his

letters, the early ones, when we were both writing. Even then I thought he was a trifle naïve, he was discovering prostitutes with what he would probably have called a Capital Pee – in Pee-aris (Paris). Then he made a Pee-acket out of Pee-ornography, & like his old chum has been impotent ever since. C'est la vie. But he has a heart. And he has the generosity of the best Americans.

Jimmy's diary in April records how difficult he found it to write: 'Sat in front of work & felt my hands were made of lead & my head a vacuum. By mid-day choking with suppressed tears of rage and despair. But I must sit here *every* morning for at least 3 hours & concentrate. If I can't concentrate when T [Tania] is out of the house when *can* I? Got to be done. *Two stories must be finished by the end of May.*'
On a lighter note he wrote to Pauline Wynn in 1966:

Did I ever tell you that in Paris, among the 'rank and file', I was always known as Jimmy Kurella? Not a soul ever knew my 'pen name'. I say 'pen name', for in those days I used to write [!]. Even so, you'd expect someone to wonder about the real name of the husband of Tania Kurella. As a matter of fact I didn't: I never had any professional jealousy. Au contraire, I thought it was marvellous that the Woman could earn money. Above all, at what seemed to me to be hours spent in smacking people's bottoms. A quid an hour for a good whack. Think of that, I used to think. And have marvelled ever since.

Yet three years later that sombre note was sounded again in another letter to Pauline:

Not by any means everyone (I honestly don't think anyone who has not 'aspired' at some time to be a *writer*) knows what it means to be confronted with nothing but oneself. For me this confrontation is particularly frightening (so I believe) because I have known it since 1929. It was in that year that I experienced for the first time what I have just been experiencing *not* (alas) for the second time. It is something akin to facing Death 3 times. Death is the *End*. But this ridiculous thing a *Writer* faces, especially if he is 'getting on', is: Good God, here I am, in this blessed room, table chair light heat silence (what *more* do you want?) – v. good, *but* – look – supposing – for the next five months – five months of what may be the *last months* of my life – supposing I sit here every day as I sat this afternoon & not only *don't* write, just cannot think of any point in writing, anything, ever, at all! – Voilà. Then the awful thing is – if you are me – you get *ill* – in despair you drink too much, eat too much, walk too little – and have a(nother) heart attack. Et voilà le mort.

In the early spring of 1936 he had a letter from a new friend, Arthur Calder-Marshall, to whom he had been introduced by Kay Boyle, asking for a synopsis of a novel for the publishers, Harrap. Calder-Marshall had shown them *Boys*, the collection of stories which in 1938 was published under the title *Something Wrong*, but Harrap wouldn't even look at it without the prospect of a novel to follow.

Foot-loose and adventurous, the young couple sailed south to the sun, again to Sintra, in 1936. They arrived with William Robson-Scott on 11 July. 'At last', Jimmy's diary relates, 'Isherwood-Stern household. Move into two rooms and look like becoming settled. Read Connolly's *The Rock Pool* [1936] – French edition, & was horrified that an intelligent person should have filled 250 pages with such trash!'

Christopher Isherwood, who with W. H. Auden that March in Sintra had begun the collaborative writing of their play *The Ascent of F6*, was there with his German friend Heinz Neddermeyer. But the Sterns were yet to meet Auden, who had left in April.

> Isherwood I found nice [Jimmy wrote]. He's small and insignificant to look at. A clear open face with rather staring blue-grey eyes. ['Your squat spruce body and enormous head' – 'Birthday Poem' by W. H. Auden] Very much of the ascetic about him, and incredibly English ... For my likes, Christopher is a little too much like an old, decent, dutiful, worrying, English school-master. He gets tight on a glass of wine which doesn't suit my tastes at all. About a week ago we all went into Lisbon and had a beano of a lunch – half way through which, after about a half of a bottle of wine each, C was violently sick where he sat and remained sick, with T holding his head, for a good five hours. I was sorry for him, as I know what sickness is, but if one can't hold one's drink one shouldn't take it.

This strikes a prudish, hypocritical note; by some accounts Jimmy was on the way to becoming a world-class imbiber by the age of thirty-three.

In *The Hidden Damage* Jimmy remembered that one day

with a burst of boyish laughter Christopher had begun telling us stories of Brussels in the company of 'Mr Norris'. In the midst of them the radio had been turned on, and in the small Sintra house which we'd shared during that faraway, fearful summer of 1936, we listened to the first news of the civil war across the border, to reports of murder and rape in Seville. [The Spanish Civil War began on 18 July.]

'This is the beginning, only the beginning,' Christopher said, expressing my thoughts, and we glanced at one another, then away, as though to conceal our certain knowledge that at last Europe's armistice had ended ...

In Isherwood's 1977 slice of autobiography he wrote:

Christopher found Jimmy Stern sympathetic because he was a hypochondriac like himself (though with far more reason); because he grumbled and was humorous and skinny and Irish; because his brainy worried face was strangely appealing; because he had been a steeplechase rider in Ireland, a bartender in Germany and a cattle farmer on the South African veldt; because he was terrified of snakes and had been bitten by one (he implied that it had followed him around patiently until his attention was distracted by watching a rare bird); because he had written a book of extraordinary short stories, called *The Heartless Land* ...
Sometimes Jimmy would shut himself up in his room for a whole day or more, seeing nobody but Tania. But his sensitive nerves and spells of melancholy created no tension in the household. Christopher wrote in his diary: 'Jimmy's jumpiness is quite without venom towards the outside world. He is much too busy hating his father to have any malice left over for us.' And Tania took everything in her stride. She devoted herself to Jimmy yet found sufficient time to be with Christopher and Heinz and also very efficiently managed the housekeeping. This seemed – in the short run at least – a perfectly workable arrangement and I believe that – had the run been long – they might all have lived together in harmony for months or even years.

The 'arrangement' must indeed have proved satisfactory, for the prospect of the four friends going to live in Mexico was discussed. 'Darling Tania and Jimmy ... Thank God, you still meditate Mexico. We simply can't bear the prospect of living without you for much longer. But perhaps our passion is not returned,' wrote Isherwood on

24 October 1936. And: 'No one could have been nearer going to Mexico,' Jimmy wrote to Arthur Calder-Marshall in December 1938. But it wasn't to be. The political situation and Jimmy's hankering for New York were subjects never far from their minds during the next three years.

Jimmy and Isherwood kept in touch with each other about where to send their work. The latter wrote in October 1936, saying he had sent Jimmy's 'articles' to John Lehmann, who had recently launched *New Writing*. He added: '"Sally Bowles", the story you didn't much care for, is coming out in *New Writing* probably. John seemed to like it, and so I said yes; but I agree with you in my heart.'

In January 1937, at the Café Flore in Saint-Germain-des-Pres, the favourite hang-out of the expatriate literati, the Sterns met for the first time a man to whom they would be closer than any other individual and with whom they would remain intimate for the next thirty-seven years. W. H. Auden was on his way to or from the civil war in Spain.

Christopher Isherwood and Heinz, the Sterns, and Auden, made up the group. Cyril and Jean Connolly may well have been there, too. The poet was deep in a book. 'Needless to say,' Jimmy wrote thirty-seven years later in 'The Indispensable Presence', a tribute to Auden, 'all five or six of us had drinks. He didn't. He had a coffee. And should someone suggest a drink, he would shake his head and grunt. Pale, smooth-skinned, full-lipped, with a large brown mole on each cheek, he sat there, bent over, oblivious, absorbed. For one who found concentration difficult, it was an envy-making sight.' The Sterns were not to see him again for three years.

> Looking back [the tribute begins] over the past three and a half decades, almost all of our married life, we see him everywhere: in New York and Brooklyn, in Amenia and on the Main Line, in the shack we shared on Fire Island, in Bavaria and Berlin, in Oxford, in London. And here, in 'Wiltshire's witching countryside' – where we celebrated his last Christmas.
>
> The emphasis on the 'we' is deliberate, for Tania and I had the good fortune to share the friendship in about equal portions. Preferring to live with his own sex, yet hankering after the atmosphere of a family, of what he called a 'nest', he gravitated increasingly towards married couples – not always with the happiest results …
>
> How to describe, in a few pages, his uniqueness? What he

meant to us? What we have lost? I think we both feel, as never before, that part of ourselves has gone. For he was more than a friend, more than a personality: to us he was an indispensable presence. To many he was an intellect, an oracle. To us, above all, he was fun. He was so alive. So gay. And his heart was large.

In exile, alone and lonely, in grief and the gloom of war, in deep depression (whether his or ours), under personal attack ('Letters from home are beginning to take a sharper tone about my absence. And my bunion hurts!'), his curiosity, his fundamental optimism, his boundless sense of the absurd, never deserted him. His departures were a sadness, and his arrivals more eagerly anticipated, more welcomed, I think, than those of any other man we have known.

... he was so imaginatively indulgent of one's own weaknesses. He could express in a sentence that combination of affection, authority and encouragement, which he knew the child for years had craved in vain. From upstate New York: 'You owe it to us all to get on with what you are good at. If I hear another word about you not being able to write that story, I'll come thundering down disguised as your father, and beat you up!'

In 1942 Jimmy wrote to Joan Lewisohn: '... I rather doubt you would understand my feelings for him [Auden] ... there's nothing very extraordinary about our relationship; peculiar, perhaps for me, & very deep. I like so very few people – only 1 or 2 enough to like their faults. T. likes him equally, so that it often occurs to me that we are like 3 children together. Yesterday we chased each other round the house with hosepipes ...'

In the early months of 1937, Jimmy was hard at work preparing the twelve stories, dedicated to Brian Howard, which had been offered to Harrap and which were to be published by Secker & Warburg the following year.

In May, whilst the bombardment of Guernica by German aeroplanes was metaphorically pounding in his ears, Jimmy recorded a great day in their lives: 'We sailed away in a car of our own – became Vile People of Viler Property. I personally feel it's all wrong, until we are zooming through the Bois, without the expense of any energy, under the chestnut trees, then it seems perfectly all right.'

That summer, they took off for an extended tour of France, mainly in the south. On 10 July they arrived in Megève, near Mont Blanc, to stay with Kay Boyle and Laurence Vail.[2] Besides the children, the historian and publisher Milton Waldman and his wife Peggy were also visiting. Jimmy's brother Peter[3], who was at Lloyd's in London and living at his grandmother's Prince's Gate house, joined them there.

The three Sterns, the Waldmans, with Kay Boyle, her mother and Laurence Vail, all drove into Italy. In Aosta on 29 July Jimmy and Tania had their first recorded 'tiff':

> Had drinks in the Piazza, & later dinner at the Hotel Suisse, where we eventually slept ... Good dinner. After it, T decided 'something was wrong' & proceeded to walk out of Aosta, me following steadily in the shadows. Eventually we landed up in a dark suburb where we spoke despairingly, tipsily, of divorce etc ... Bed about 12.30. On pushing my bed nearer to that of T – not yet fully reconciled – it, the bed, collapsed with a violent crash to the floor.

There ensued much toing and froing from startled hotel guests and a row with the infuriated manager who, retreating through the door after restoring the bed, remarked: 'If you must do it, do it *quietly*, for the sake of the other guests!'

The Sterns moved on south and in eight weeks or so, with Jimmy recording in his journal the meals they ate and their prices, the state of the weather, and the cost of petrol, they visited Geneva, Grenoble, Toulon, Aix-les-Bains ('Main street most beautiful I've ever seen'),

2 Jimmy first met the Vails in 1930 or 1931 in the south of France shortly before their marriage. Born in Paris of American parentage, Vail after Oxford wrote for magazines. His surrealist play *What Do You Want?* was performed in 1920 by the Provincetown Players of Cape Cod. He also wrote a novel, *Murder! Murder!* but is principally remembered for his painting and sculpture. In her biography of Kay Boyle, Joan Mellen describes him as 'a red-faced man, slender, and of medium height with streaky yellow hair and a beak-like Roman nose ... [He] was a veritable soul of wit. Constantly amazed at life's contradictions, he was forever alert to the absurd. He was worldly, ironic, sophisticated, mischievous, and no fool, although utterly impractical about money.' Kay Boyle, the fecund bearer of the Vails' five children, led a long, prolific life as a novelist and short story writer which spanned virtually the whole of the last century. She opposed fascism in Austria, Nazism in France, McCarthyism in America, and in her seventies went to gaol for her opposition to the Vietnam war. 'Kay Boyle was prickly, exasperating, opinionated, and tough,' the biographer Deirdre Bair has written, and 'her role in twentieth century literature and culture is an important one.'

3 Peter Stern at that time was enthusiastically engaged with the St Pancras People's Theatre in Camden Town, north London. In 1938 he joined the Middlesex Yeomanry and served in Egypt and Italy. After demobilisation he ran a bookshop in Mexico, while pursuing his love for amateur dramatics there. The last decades of his working life were spent in the sales department of Secker & Warburg, his brother's publisher. He has twice married and has four children.

Cannes, Nice, St Tropez, Nîmes, Les Baux, Aigues-Mortes in the Camargue, Montpellier, and many places in between. En route they caught up with friends: Joan Black and Eda Lord, Brian Howard, Eddie Gathorne-Hardy, Desmond Ryan, and the Waldmans.

On 11 September Jimmy had a prophetic dream: 'Frightful dream, half-forgotten ... Joss [the name he called his brother Peter] & the Declaration of War. German-speaking friend of Joss tells secret he knows about German plans to invade England in June 1938. Scene of Declaration of War same day with T and Brian [Howard] – each one weeps silently, & all walk slowly away into painful sunshine, saying nothing, each one alone, head bowed.'

At the end of that month they were back in Megève before returning to Paris on 5 October. In spite of the threat of war, the daily round of Parisian life began again: drinks and meals with friends, visits to exhibitions, and some desultory translation to keep the wolf from the door.

That Christmas, according to James Knowlson in his *Life of Samuel Beckett* (1996), Jimmy was introduced by the poet Laz Aaronson to his famous fellow countryman. The two formed a great bond to be cemented over the years by meetings, meals and theatre-goings. Jimmy told Frances Partridge that Beckett was absolutely charming, but a very lazy man; he put off work as long as possible. His excuse was: 'Ah, but you see I'm inarticulate.' Jimmy told him how much he liked the silences in *Waiting for Godot*, to which Beckett replied: 'Aren't they lovely?'

Jimmy said that he invariably felt more at home with 'Le Grand Sam' than with any other human being. After seeing him, the world seemed a better place than it had two hours previously. Their conversations ranged from cricket to Moderne Deutsche Kunst, and – once – the subject of prize-fighters they admired, starting with Jimmy Wilde and Carpentier. The occasion was one of the very few on which Tania, whom Beckett adored for her beauty, sympathy and intelligence, seemed tongue-tied. To her talk was the one great stimulation life had to offer.

From the '70s and early '80s there are numerous slanting handwritten notes from Beckett arranging to meet the Sterns and bewailing the financial plight of their mutual friend, Djuna Barnes (whose welfare was supplemented by Beckett and Peggy Guggenheim, of whom Beckett had been briefly enamoured in Paris in the late '30s).

Jimmy's diaries for 1938 and 1939 are missing, if they ever existed, but a letter written from Paris on 5 December 1938 – a month after the

Nazis' infamous '*Kristallnacht*' – to Arthur Calder-Marshall gives a revealing description of the gloom and tension the Sterns experienced during that summer while touring the South of France:

> I knew the crisis was coming then; after what had been happening all summer it was inevitable; terrible those things that went on all summer – the German mobilization, the Italians even, over the hills behind us. And the French knew. That there wasn't a war, then, at the first moment in September, or that there wasn't at least an ultimatum from our side, is now too foul to think of … .
>
> We were in a small place in Toulon when it began. It poured with rain incessantly every day. About the 26th there were only four of thirty left in the hotel. Next day the Post Office closed, then the one bistrot. No waiters were left, and the waitresses had to go to their homes to look after aged relatives who'd been kicked out of their homes to make way for the Military. All cars under six years old had been requisitioned … I was all for remaining where we were until dismissed by the hotel people. Which is practically what happened. The four of us left on the Wednesday, the 28th, after having listened in horror to that most frightful of all speeches I've ever heard on the wireless, by Chamberlain the night before. We headed for Paris, travelling over 300 miles through floods and hailstorms … That journey was certainly the worst I ever did … We spent the next night without petrol, all the pumps had been shut down, in Avallon with Augustus John, who had the jitters good and proper. We arrived in Paris an hour after the news of 'Peace' being declared over the wireless. It was pitch dark, nearly all the lights being out or 90% dimmed. No one smiled. People looked even grimmer than they do now. But apparently all through those days Paris had been completely normal, that is to say there was no panic of any kind. Two million are supposed to have been evacuated, but the next day one didn't notice a dearth of human beings. But certainly over a million went. So far as being calm is concerned, the French, especially the Parisians, were magnificent.

Perhaps the lead up to the publication on 20 October 1938 in London of his second book and the acceleration of the Nazi threat, leading to the declaration of war in September 1939, prevented him keeping a journal. There were more pressing matters to fill his time, not least the rescue of refugees. In December a group of English residents in

Paris, including the Sterns, started a fund of money to be spent on food, during the Christmas week, for 750 Viennese refugees living under appalling conditions in Chelles, a town some twenty kilometres due east of Paris. They had been threatened with expulsion by the Department of Seine-et-Marne. Jimmy publicised their plight by writing to the *New Statesman,* which published his piece on 11 February 1939.

His grim childhood and adolescence, which haunted and tormented him all his life, pervade the stories in *Something Wrong.* H. E. Bates found the book 'full of the recaptured and reconstructed pain of childhood ... the strangeness of grown-up behaviour as seen by a child ... All Mr Stern's stories have their roots in reality, all his writing has the honesty, sincerity, and powerful earnestness of a man burrowing down into essentials ... In writing of childhood it is necessary to write with the heart of a child. As far as is humanly possible, Mr Stern does that.'

Stephen Spender (1909–98) wrote to Jimmy in November: 'I enjoyed the book very much, and it seems to me to contain some of the best stories I have ever read ... there is almost too much virtuosity in your invention of dialects, etc. The reader rather quails before your flights of realism into different countries, situations and languages.'

Ralph Straus in *The Sunday Times* wrote that

> Mr Stern cares nothing for the demands of the magazine reader wanting to be 'taken out of himself'. There is, it is true, no lack of design in his stories, but few, if any of them follow a conventional course or are neatly rounded off, to leave you with a comfortable conviction that all is right with the world.
>
> He knows well enough what ghastly tragedies may confront the sensitive child, and how few are the weapons at his command. So here you have stories of bravery and cowardice, stories of calf love, either cruel or ironic, stories of comradeship and misunderstandings, stories of birth and death and hypocrisy and fine feeling. And they are good stories, the work of a man who really does understand youth and its difficulties.

But the most remarkable review appeared in the most modest of papers, the short-lived Birmingham *Town Crier,* on 18 November 1938:

> *Something Wrong* is a cycle of stories about the experiences of children and adolescents (childhood is usually a better field for the short story than it is for the novel), about the terror and ecstasies,

the jealousies and unconscious cruelty of the immature, and about the shadow, now tragic, now horrible, now comic of the adult world.

Parents are inclined to regard their children as dream extensions of their personality; the strong-willed child reacts to this by doing the opposite of what is expected of him, often at great damage to himself; while the sensitive child is tortured only too often by the feeling that he is unworthy of his father or mother. 'The Broken Leg' is a terrifying study of this common situation.

'Travellers' Tears', perhaps the finest story in the book, is a description of the sudden awakening of a twelve-year-old American boy to a consciousness of beauty and love, an experience which happens to us all but which few can remember clearly. As in a poem, the properties of the story like the South Sea island night and the boy's American accent are determined by the dominating emotion, instead of being determined by the action or as they would have to be in a novel.

The reviewer then goes on 'to illustrate Mr Stern's method of approach', quoting from the story called 'The Holiday'. He ends his review: 'I recommend Mr Stern as one of the most moving and original short story writers who has appeared for a long time.' It is signed W. H. Auden.

Jimmy only heard of his friend's review after the latter's death. He wrote to Humphrey Carpenter, one of Auden's biographers: 'I nearly wept: I never thanked him!'

Something Wrong was shortlisted for the 1939–40 Stock Femina Vie Heureuse Prize, but the Chairman, Rebecca West, persuaded her committee not to consider it for long. Jimmy was, nevertheless, in good company; the other candidates were Elizabeth Bowen, David Cecil, Suzan Goodyear, R. C. Hutchinson, Rex Warner, and T. H. White.

Auden paid his friend a further compliment the following year: in the 15 August 1939 issue of American *Vogue*, in an article entitled 'Young British Writers on the Way Up – Ten authors discussed by two of their brilliant contemporaries', W. H. Auden and Christopher Isherwood wrote:

James Stern may reasonably claim to be the best of the younger short-story writers. A book of short stories is a bad proposition in publishing today, and magazines have printed far more of Stern's work than has yet appeared in book form. *The Heartless Land*, the first of his two volumes, deals entirely with Africa. *Something Wrong* is a series of stories about adolescents and children. Stern's wealth of subject-matter is astonishing. He can write with equal power about horses, old ladies, poisonous snakes, English drawing-rooms, South Sea islands, fishermen, governesses, little girls. He is equally at home when describing complicated mental processes and scenes of violent physical action. He seems to have no formula, no pattern; each story is a fresh surprise. If the English public could recognize genuine, solid talent, undecorated by the tricks which make for notoriety, Stern's name would be famous in England today.

4
New York
1939–1954

Although no written account of the Sterns' move from war-threatened Paris to the haven of New York in 1939 has survived, either in letter form or in a journal, a line from Christopher Isherwood, who had emigrated with W. H. Auden to the USA that January, marks their arrival in May ('So you've joined the Pilgrim Fathers') as did a postcard to Peter Stern on the 2nd: 'Arrived safe & sound yesterday 4pm – all well. NY magnificent as ever. Sun shining. Trees green, all OK at mo. Staying in this Parisy Pub [Café Lafayette, 9th Street & University Place] for moment.'

The fear of Tania's probable incarceration as an enemy alien if they returned to England must have been the crucial factor in their decision to go, but Auden and Isherwood's much publicised departure for America could also have added to their resolve. There is no evidence that Jimmy was the object of the same critical barrage which was directed at his two friends nor that his escape to the sanctuary of America weighed upon his conscience. One can only guess at the sentiments and reservations of his immediate family, but Harry Stern, in particular, who was both a staunch patriot and of a fiercely militaristic frame of mind, must surely have deplored the decision of his eldest son, already a drop-out from Sandhurst, to leave the beleaguered shores of Britain for the safety of the New World.

More mindful than ever of the urgent need to earn a living, Jimmy had sent an outline of his Eton novel, variously entitled 'The Pleasure Is Great' and 'The Sweepstake', to Christopher Isherwood in Santa Monica, California, who responded encouragingly early in 1940: 'I like it enormously ... it would become a classic among school stories ... here you have a real, unique story which not only keeps you in suspense right through but really illuminates its own setting ...' Reading it some sixty years later, there seems little justification for such praise, and for all Isherwood's encouragement, the script appears to have resided resolutely in Jimmy's bottom drawer, while stories (and letters!) and various journalistic projects occupied him more. Two years later he wrote a cryptic explanation to Joan Lewisohn, a young woman who later became very close to him, of what he was trying to do in the novel: 'Before I grew up I was two almost distinct people (this is one of the things I wanted most to reveal in my novel of Eton). At a certain moment in my life – on a warm spring day in London, meeting a certain friend – I decided which person I was going to be. I said Goodbye to the other, the other life I could have lived. I knew it had to be a choice, that I had to make a decision, I mean.'

In the early '40s Jimmy began to keep the letters of his many correspondents, a practice of which he was proud. Indeed, posterity may be grateful, too. But at least three – W. H. Auden, Arthur Miller, Patrick White – did not keep his to them; inexplicable in the case of Auden.

In a letter to his brother Peter from the Hotel Brevoort on 11th Avenue Jimmy wrote: 'Both still find NYC the best & liveliest town on earth ... Everything so exciting we're permanently exhausted.' From July 1939 they lived at 13 West 9th Street until they settled permanently into 207 East 52nd Street in 1941, an apartment found for them by Sybille Bedford and Allanah Harper.[4]

That month, Jimmy wrote to Katherine Anne Porter:

> ... I have always meant, by the way, to ask you not to read, or if you have, to try and forget, the unforgiveable pages entitled 'Travellers' Tears' [one of the stories in *Something Wrong*]. It was never meant to go into the book, nor be printed anywhere, and I blindly let it go through. If the book is ever published in this country [it wasn't] I'll see it's deleted ...
>
> ... I'd a card from Auden the other day, from New Orleans ... I have an enormous admiration for that English oddity, and I feel he's going through a bad time with himself – as, I suppose, we all are. If only he wouldn't insist not only that each one of us is born Good, but that we go on being Good.

Auden that year had joined the classes of relaxation and breathing which Tania was conducting from an apartment on East 68th Street. He decided that they were '*most* painful, but illuminating'. As Humphrey Carpenter writes in his biography of Auden (1981): 'Tania Stern soon found that Auden, though a keen pupil, was too clumsy and

---

4 In her magazine *Echange*, she published the work of Djuna Barnes, Edith Sitwell, André Gide, Thomas Mann and Norman Douglas.

impatient to benefit from what she had to teach; she felt that he was dismissing his body as quite unimportant to him.'

I did read 'Travellers' Tears' [K. A. P. replied from Baton Rouge on 13 August], since I read the whole book, and the idea struck me as quite all right; the only thing wrong was the American idiom, which was not well done because it was much too mixed ... There are about half a dozen (more perhaps) regional accents, besides the various argots of the cities, besides the drift of slang which changes from place to place and time to time rapidly, and it is devilish difficult even for an American who listens sharply as I do to keep them all straight ...

The following April, Jimmy heard from Malcolm Lowry, his nocturnal walking companion and drinking buddy, whom he had not seen since their memorable meeting seven years previously in Paris:

What the hell? So you are in New York. The other day I was taking a stroll up Little Mountain here [Lowry was writing from Vancouver], and noticing a boy climbing down a quarry I thought of your excellent story called, I think, 'A Sunday Morning' [actually 'On the Sabbath'], where the boy climbs down the cliff instead of going with 'them girls', and then can't get back again. Two days later, in a dentist's waiting room, I read again 'The Man Who Was Loved', in *Esquire*, and even took the copy away with me to read it yet again, when I learned you were in America. Well, and how are you? Damn it all, it's really good to hear news of you. I would give much to see your face again. I heard you were married, happily I hope. For myself, I have been happily divorced. A long, gay story. And hope to be married again next October.

To which Jimmy replied a month later: 'I arrived in this town (NY) from Paris a year ago this minute, and I've been on my hands and knees in every bar in town since then, searching your likeness under every stool and table.'

On 7 May, Lowry wrote from Vancouver again:

Jeeze, it was certainly good to hear from you and to think you've been in this hemisphere a year without my knowing it! I really caracoled on receiving your letter and am truly glad you made a happy marriage. You are one of the best short-story writers we have so I know you will never stop writing so long as you have a pen. I sympathize with you about novel writing, though. There is no, as it were, satisfactory design-governing posture for a true short-story writer, and I can understand how, difficult to please as to form, you kick at the amorphousness of the thing. So the short-story writer (like Chekhov) wanders around graveyards thinking it is no go. It is probably not that you can't write a good novel but that no novel suggests to you that you want to go and do likewise. Nevertheless it seems to me that a writer like you would produce the best kind of novel, that is the shortish one perfect in itself, and without being full of inventories (like Joyce) or poems (like Faulkner) or conjunctions (like Hemingway), or quotations from quotations from other novels (like me, 7 years ago). It is possible to compose a satisfactory work of art by the simple process of writing a series of good short stories, complete in themselves, with the same characters, interrelated, correlated, good if held up to the light, watertight if held upside down, but full of effects and dissonances that are impossible in a short story, but nevertheless having its purity of form, a purity that can only be achieved by the born short-story writer. Well, all that is as may be. (And I don't mean the kind of novel, written by not quite true poets, such as *The Hospital*, by Kenneth Fearing [1939], or *The Seven Who Fled* by [Frederic] Prokosch [1937], in which the preoccupation with form vitiates the substance, that is by a writer whose inability to find a satisfactory form for his poems drives him to find an outlet for it in a novel. No. The thing that I mean can only be done by a good short-story writer, who is generally the better kind of poet, the one who only does not write poetry because life does not frame itself kindly for him in iambic pentameters and to whom disjunct experimental forms are abhorrent; such a man probably will end up anyhow by being a poet, in the manner of the later Yeats, but meantime, my thesis is that he is capable of writing the best kind of novel, something that is bald and winnowed, like Sibelius, and that makes an odd but splendid din, like Bix Beiderbecke. But that is all by the way and my God what brackish bilge is this on a cold posthumous Monday anyhow!)

Jimmy answered on 27 May:

My God, Malcolm, there must be some conspiracy. I was on the point of writing you again, when I received your letter (postmarked 25th) an hour ago. I say conspiracy, Seventh Column, anything you like, because this morning the French Digest called me asking for my translation of André Siegfried which I posted them last Friday, after working like hell to get it done in time. And it hasn't arrived – just 20 blocks away. And now you write me that my letter written oh a good ten days ago hasn't reached you, either. What the hell?

Granted, it wasn't much of a letter; I remember feeling rather worse than usual that day; but it did tell you that I had posted your poems and a story of mine to Gingrich of *Esquire* that very morning. And they, booger 'em, not only arrived, but have returned with the following slip: 'Can't say that either the story or the poetry hits (or so this word seems) for us.' And initialled by some unknown reader. I'm very angry, for I have a feeling that although I wrote to Gingrich's secretary (he once told me to reach him direct that was the thing to do) he very possibly didn't read the things himself. It is possible, in fact, that he did not read the letter I wrote to him, in which I named you King and Genius and at the moment chewer of Columbian peanuts, which, I reminded him, was the lot of Geniuses until some such guy as himself was the first to recognize that even Geniuses occasionally need meat & taties. I even added that I thought him a lucky sod to get the chance to be the first. Well, that's that. I have the poems. What shall I do with 'em? The story I sent has also been refused by the *New Yorker*, so I suppose it will now go, among many others, under dust. But your poems, they ought to go on travelling, I think. I'm not in the least surprised they returned. Too good. Americans hate to have to think.

Yes, this state o' chassis wearin' me out. Did you ever know Francis [Stuart, a poet, novelist and quintessential outsider who courted ostracism, died at the age of ninety in 2000] or read his books? Did you see his wife, daughter of Maud Gonne, is in gaol for harbouring parachutes and German caps and British uniforms, if not parachutists themselves? And Francis, the evil bastard, in Berlin [where he spent the war years broadcasting to Ireland for the Nazis]. Yes, yes ... I don't know, don't know at all what's happened to 'one's other friends'. I hear of and from some, of one last week who joined up early on as he thought he'd be better off by doing that than waiting to be called, but oh poor shyte he's been regretting that impulse ever since; he's been all winter long in a damp hut with eight young (he's 34) blaspheming would-be bank clerks, the kind you know who breathe fuck on every foul breath and then retire, one by one, behind the nearest tree. Well, there he still was, a wet and weary and bitter Tommy, on some sodden field of Kent, until not long ago. I don't know, really don't know, and I have the German wife, and they are all being turned in now, and this country is just on the ghastly verge of hysteria.

Say, if you've changed your address, isn't my last letter lying there under the mat? Or maybe confiscated by the b-b-bailiff? I wrote it anyway, me boyo, and I sent it, just as I wrote and sent 40 bucks worth of translation which didn't arrive. Here's the slip to prove me words about the poems.

By the end of the summer, the Spingarns[5] had rented the Sterns their cottage in Amenia in upstate New York. From there on 17 September to Lowry, Jimmy became dismissive about his friend Djuna Barnes's most famous book:

You ask if I have ever read Djuna Barnes' *Nightwood* [1936]. Yes indeed, though I do not agree it's a 'terrific' book. I think it's a good deal of 'Hoky Poky', with a lot of reading up of 17th Century Engl Lit. Still, there are others, I know who agree with you, and I won't argue.

I also know the old gal, too – don't know whether you do or not. She's not so easy, unless you happen to be feeling that way, too. But she's a wonder in the right mood, which is seldom these days, and the last time I saw her, about two or three months ago, she was trying to get herself on to a train for the middle west, there to be sobered up and saved by an ancient gal friend, who, I suppose, must have forgotten...!

Well, what can I tell you? I guess I'll be conscripted right here very soon. The dates and years etc catch me by a few hours. Doctors providing, of course—for I'm not greatly strong after all these years, starting with malaria and black water and psittacosis before the age of 26. Funds, like yours, are running terribly near dry, and the Poor House – (I always want to go back to the one on the Dublin Road between Dunshauglin and Clonee, in the County Meath) looms larger every morn.

5 Joel Spingarn, a prominent officer of the National Association for the Advancement of Colored People, had a distinguished career in civil rights, and was the target of the anti-semitism of white supremacists. He was also on the staff of Harcourt Brace, who became Jimmy's publishers.

Today the September sun, the best of the year in this part of the world, is shining down on me through the caterpillar-laden trees. They, the caterpillars, come down like parachutists above my head, dangling slowly, falling, swept slowly towards me in mid-air on the faint breeze. And they land on the grass beside the table, where the kittens are ready to shake their fists in welcome, then pounce. And I'm reading a Life of Melville by a neighbour, Lewis Mumford, and thinking of the Writer and You, wondering a lot, then back to the caterpillars and the parachutists and shooters 3,000 miles away, where a few summers ago I sat under a cedar and typed out 'On the Sabbath', which strangely, to me, you seem to like. Yes, I do agree about 'Two Men'. I still think that was pretty good for my age. I wrote it more with the scissors than the pen. Like a cockney digging a garden in the country for the first time, I tried and failed and swore and tried again, and did what a countryman could have done in a day, in a couple of months. Yes, that was the time it took, and the *English Review* swallowed it whole a week later. Ethel [Mannin], I remember, was scarlet with envy. Little did she have to worry. I often wonder where she is.

I wish I could see some of your recent *Arbeit*. If possible, could you send me the June 30, 1934. I guess you probably could not. But I would like to see summat; it's such a hell of a long time since I saw you, and oh Lord, longer still since I sat reading *Ultramarine*. Would that I had a little of the silly vanity, or whatever it is that keeps people writing, that I had then. Though God knows it didn't help a hell of a lot. Still, I remember sitting alone in a kind of semi-ecstasy in the rue Cassini half of one summer, and getting through some 50,000 words of stories in under a month. I believe that's right. I guess the achievement once accomplished I simply didn't take any more interest, and I used up such a hell of a lot of material. Almost every story was, or could have been, with little addition, a miniature novel – and bang went the novels. A reviewer once said that about my child book (stories) – had never seen so many novels in a book of stories. I guess it's so long since I've had a chance to talk about myself in terms of writing that I'm boring you with this preamble. And as you may well never read it, I'll close here and pray you'll send me a word when and if you do.

In October the Sterns, as registered aliens, were about to be finger-printed and Jimmy was threatened with conscription under the draft.

Auden came on a short visit; Jimmy wrote in his diary: 'Reading between the lines, W was depressed. He seemed to be holding on to himself & his work – the little nervous looks towards, & openings of, his brown notebook – as a bulwark, & the only one, against internal despair of what he feels convinced the future must bring ...'

In 'Selves, Joined in Friendship', the title of his Introduction to 'Some Letters from Auden to James and Tania Stern' (*Auden Studies 3*, 1995), the editor, Nicholas Jenkins, wrote:

The Sterns never had children, and, perhaps because their nurturing energies were not diverted elsewhere, they functioned for Auden almost as an accepting surrogate family – a role that he was certainly aware of: he once begged Tania Stern to 'be my Big Sister always'. [In the same letter he wrote: 'And please, my dear, *never* hesitate to give or apologise for giving me advice. I am a great deal more dependent on you than you know or than I realize myself.'] His sexual nature was also acceptable to them, as it was not to his own family ... The Sterns were adaptable and uncensorious ... For their part, the Sterns found Auden to be immensely frank and direct, an arbiter, a seer, and, for all his idiosyncrasies, someone acutely sensitive to their own psychological needs. They often had the feeling that he secretly thought of himself as a doctor or a priest. Major Stern, like Auden, had structured his days by the implacable rigours of the clock, and Auden, who was often drawn to identify with and to protect people he perceived as weak or self-destructive, seems to have seized on such similarities to act out the role of a loving, stimulating father to Stern ...

But during his early years in the States, Auden was even closer to Tania Stern than he was to her husband, an intimacy that was partly rooted in her brief role as his physical trainer and partly in her personal warmth and intense, affectionate sympathy – qualities that she had radiated to many people including Spender and Isherwood.

In 1940 and the first part of 1941, Auden spent a lot of time out of New York ... The Sterns, though, tried to visit him wherever he was ... later that year [1940] they often saw him at 7 Middagh Street in Brooklyn, where he was living with George Davis [a writer, editor, novelist and wit], and Carson McCullers. James Stern recalled scenes of 'George naked at the piano with a cigarette in his mouth, Carson on the ground with half a gallon of sherry, and then Wystan bursting in like a headmaster, announcing: "Now then, dinner!"'

Generally Auden collaborated only with people whom he knew well; the works he undertook jointly were a way of furthering a personal bond ... Given his closeness to Stern, it was almost inevitable that they should begin to work together. Sometime during the early part of 1941 Auden asked him for help with a CBS radio dramatization of D. H. Lawrence's story 'The Rocking-Horse Winner'...

Jimmy was able to give him the know-how and jargon of the racing world. It was broadcast on 6 April 1941.

Also that year, Jimmy met Peggy Guggenheim, the wealthy, profligate and generous art collector. His connection with her was through Djuna Barnes and the latter's lifelong friend and sometime lover, Laurence Vail (1891-1968), who was Peggy Guggenheim's first husband and Kay Boyle's second.

Guggenheim wrote of Jimmy in her autobiography, *Out of This Century: Confessions of an Art Addict* (1980): 'He was a fascinating Irishman, a friend of Beckett and Laurence [Vail]. I had quite a *béguin* for him, but as our conversation was restricted to intellectual matters and to long talks about John Holms [her husband, a writer], whom he had never met, he did not suspect my feelings. He is a very good writer and surprisingly little known for one so talented.'

Jimmy dined with Nigel Dennis, another 'Pilgrim Father', and his wife Madeleine. They talked of jobs; Dennis was shortly to join the *New Republic* as assistant editor, but there was nothing immediately on offer for Jimmy. Whilst Tania was bringing home the bacon, having set up her soon-to-be-thriving 'sensory awareness' practice in a studio in Manhattan, where, according to Sybille Bedford, 'she received her lovers' (one of whom was the Australian Communist Alwyn Lee), Jimmy was translating – always a modest money-earner – two volumes of Stefan Zweig's *Brazil: Land of the Future* (1942) and contributing stories to various leading magazines: *Harper's Bazaar*, *Penguin New Writing*, *Penguin Parade*, and *Decision*. In a paragraph from an untitled, unpublished story, his attitude to 'jobs' is made obvious:

As a free-lance writer in New York, married to a painter, Derek Fordham often wondered how, on what, he and his wife managed to live. They lived chiefly, he often thought, on Hope. One day he might write a book that would earn for him more than his publisher's 'advance'. One day a slick magazine might (ha!) buy a story for a sum from which he could get a new suit of clothes, Frances a new dress. One day Hollywood might purchase the moving picture rights of a story. And one day Frances might meet – at a cocktail party, of course – a crackpot millionaire who liked, who bought paintings – *her* paintings. Such were the Hopes on which the Fordhams lived. But Derek also lived on Fear. His prime Fear was that one day, in the ever-present likelihood of his not being able to pay the rent, he might have to 'take a job'. Taking a job meant 'sitting in an office', being 'bossed around', taking to drink in order to forget what he was being made to do, in order to 'stand the pressure'. And to avoid this humiliation Derek was prepared to go – had, indeed, with Frances several times gone – hungry.

The '(ha!)' is a characteristic touch.

In a rather desperate note in his journal on 15 October, Jimmy wrote: 'T more than ever worried about the future ... wrote to Bernice B[6] telling her I find I can no longer afford to write, & if she ever hears of any kind of a job to let me know.'

Meanwhile a letter from Nina Conarain, who collaborated with Kay Boyle and Laurence Vail on their compendium entitled *365 Days* (1936), paints a strong impression of life on the other side of the Atlantic. She wrote from Maidenhead, Berkshire on 8 January 1941:

I'm sorry you're finding life a bit sticky in N.Y. It was awfully brave of you to go over there into the blue and I hope you'll strike oil again very soon. Indeed I didn't find your remarks about incomes and meals trivial – those things are far more important and far more wearing than any old war, war being an extraneous thing that goes on outside the realities like a thunderstorm or a particularly bad spell of foul weather. It isn't personal like struggling to get money or being scared over rent, or not having enough clothes. Hitler is far less important than any of that, though he may not think so. All he has done to us so far is to put an edge on to life, a sharpness to beauty, a zest unbelievable into ordinary things like a quiet firelit room and a half bombed B.B.C. transmitting Mozart. I wouldn't have missed being here near London for

---

6 Bernice Baumgarten, his literary agent, who was married to the novelist James Gould Cozzens.

anything just now. Those people in London – they are like something you would read about in a book, but the extraordinary fact
is that they are far more wonderful than even the newspaper men
can make them. You'd have to see them to believe it. They are
unshakeable. I try to work out where their heroism comes from
and it beats me. Maybe it is Englishness to the nth degree, the
unconscious arrogance of a Cockney working man saying [to]
himself as the bombs drop, 'Oh, well it's only them bloody
foreigners again. They always was a peculiar lot with their queer
lingo no-one can understand and their queerer ways.' If it is a
German bomb or an Italian bomb they can't take it seriously.
After all what else would you expect from a lot of dagoes. It MAY
be something like that – I don't know. But whatever it is it's
superb.

That February there came sad news from England: Jimmy's brother
Reggie, a professional jockey in Ireland, an owner of racehorses and the
husband of Joan Shepherd, a girl from Co. Cork, had joined up as a
subaltern in the Dorset and Somerset Yeomanry (Royal Artillery). One
of an anti-aircraft unit, he was killed during the blitz on Swansea, South
Wales. Although only two years younger than Jimmy, with whom he
had shared a room for years as a boy, they literally had nothing in
common but the blood in their veins. Reggie's continual humming, a no
doubt unconscious habit, was particularly irritating to his brother.
    It was decades later, in the winter of 1980, that Jimmy met the novel-
ist Molly Keane. 'I think I told you,' she wrote to him, 'I knew Reggie
quite well when he lived with Willie Hanley [in Tipperary]. He was
such a marred, unhappy character, but now and then broke surface &
talked, as when he told me about his brilliant (embarrassingly literary!)
brother & how the family totally failed in understanding ... He was a
wonderful rider, so quiet and modest.'
    The same year brought the Japanese attack on Pearl Harbor. 'Each
year', Jimmy wrote to Vita Petersen, an artist from Germany with
whom the Sterns became friends in New York, 'I unfailingly remember
the morning of December 7, 1941. It was a Sunday, and why I was out
before Opening Time I cannot imagine, but I know that Third Avenue
was deserted & between 52nd and 53rd, on Moriarty's Corner, I can
see as clearly as I can my fingers the huge headlines on the pile of papers
lying against the wall.'
    In the summer of 1942, Jimmy left the city for a two-week writers'

conference in Boulder, Colorado. He was the first winner of a scholarship sponsored by the publishers Doubleday Doran to enable an outstanding young writer to attend. There he met Richard Aldington, biographer of T. E. Lawrence, and Witter Bynner, the poet and intimate of D. H. Lawrence, whom Jimmy considered 'the most human example of she-men' when Bynner came to Jimmy's rescue after a mild attack of food poisoning. Katherine Anne Porter was also in the group.

There, too, he met a twenty-one-year-old undergraduate from Bennington, the rarefied East Coast seminary, who must surely have been the youngest member of the gathering. It was a fateful conjunction whose emotional charge would have an electrifying effect on her, on Jimmy and on Tania in the months and years that followed.

Joan Lewisohn, beautiful, open-faced, wide-eyed, with an abundance of dark hair, was the daughter of a wealthy collector of impressionist paintings with a mansion on 5th Avenue and a large house in Westchester County on Long Island Sound. She was majoring in English, her thesis being on the poetry of Gerard Manley Hopkins, though at this time she was studying the work of W. B. Yeats and William Blake. Besides writing poetry she had also come to the attention of Edmund Wilson and Katherine Anne Porter with a short story. Thus with her creative and intellectual aspirations she was open to the sympathetic attention which it was natural for Jimmy to provide. Having 'suffered', along with the luxuries, the limitations of an over-protected and privileged childhood and having had previously only one boyfriend, Terence, the son of the playwright Maxwell Anderson, Joan Lewisohn was a self-acknowledged novice in affairs of the heart. The thirty-two-year-old Jimmy's impact on her – and evidently hers on him – was volcanic.

Meanwhile, the close friendship which Tania and Wystan Auden already enjoyed appeared to be developing into something stronger. From the Pennsylvania house of Auden's benefactor, Caroline Newton, Tania wrote to her absent husband:

… the first night without you … for a moment I considered seriously to creep into Wystan's room for comfort and protection … I really think he is quite *the* most wonderful person I have ever known in my life – almost too good to be true. I think I have talked more to him this last week than I have ever done to anybody else in my life in such a short time – and I've so far not yet been disappointed or bored for a second. His understanding

and respect for life and love and everything connected with it and
his courage and sincerity almost takes my breath away – it only
breaks my heart to feel that one can't do anything for him to
relieve his loneliness.

Many years later she amused friends with an account of the great
poet's partial tumescence: in a conversation with Anthony Sampson in
1991, she implied that Auden had got into bed with her and 'the worm
wriggled'. She added that he was 'like a Viking' when young and fascinated many wives by his curiosity about heterosexual love, breaking up
marriages without ever going to bed. Kate Bucknell, joint editor of
Oxford University Press's *Auden Studies*, has claimed that Auden, his
sexual relationship with Chester Kallman having ceased after a couple
of years, 'wanted to sleep with Tania. But it was as much about Auden
wanting to acquire heterosexual traits along with everything he thought
went with a conventional relationship, such as a family.'

On their return east to New York and, in Auden's phrase, to 'the
world of work and money', Jimmy wrote the first of his fifty or more
letters to Joan – a letter of warning – which shows how far the affair
had progressed at the Boulder conference:

> Joannie: You know everything I have to say; I don't think there can
> be much between us left unsaid ... I'm simply acting seventeen &
> following, as usual, my instincts. I had no notion how to say good-
> bye to you [after the conference] ... I want horribly to telephone to
> you, but I know that would be fatal, & a crime ... There aren't any
> words, only my arms round you, angel, & a prayer of gratitude
> for you, for what we've had ... Whatever happens we shall both
> suffer, but none of us can get anything or anyone worth having
> without it. So 'Be Prepared' as the Boy Scouts say. My love, J.
> PS I scribbled a few words in the *back* of *The Heartless Land*, dar-
> ling; if they embarrass you, rub 'em out!

Thereafter Jimmy joined Tania and Auden in Berwyn, Pennsylvania,
from where, for the time being, the letters to and from Joan Lewisohn
flowed. They reflect his nervous concern both for her and for himself
and his passionate need to see more of her:

> When I know you are worried ... then I worry – and (this is
> egoism, but most important, since it concerns my nature, tempera-
> ment or whatever) I always have to be on guard against getting
> utterly upset: then I get ill. And I cannot afford illness – in all

senses of the word afford ... for days I've completely abandoned myself to a vision of a huge black mop of hair & a freckled face & brown eyes, above me, beside me, under me, all around me ... I see you in every place, in every position, in every dress; I see your extraordinarily strong arms & legs & feet, & I am astonished & almost frightened that I do not shut my eyes in agony at the thought that I do not know you more.

Jimmy had evidently confessed to Tania his involvement with Joan, but apparently not its depth. Both Tania and Auden were amused and indulgent at the influx of letters:

Probably it would be wise [Jimmy wrote to Joan], not to post me a letter *every day* ... simply for the sake of appearances ... I do believe one shouldn't try the Gods too high. Also one has *got* to have some consideration for other people. (T is really an *extraordinary* person: I believe she has actually grown very fond of you ...) I suggest that you write two or three times a week (not *once*!) ... Your letter arrived in its *envelope wide open* – came unstuck, I mean. W & T handed it me with broad smiles, both knowing, of course, from whom it came ... How naïve we were, weren't we, piggy, to consider, all those years ago, whether or not we should 'tell' all or nothing on our return! As a matter of fact, it's only because we both have such good relationships – you with your parents, & I with T – that we could ...

Jimmy's relationship with Tania was demonstrably good, but Joan's with her parents was less obviously so. In fact, they showed their disapproval of their daughter's affair with a married man ('He's an attractive, all right, weak, but very sensitive, intelligent man'), who did not intend leaving his wife, by employing a private detective to report on the lovers' movements.

Back in New York, in late August 1942, there is further evidence of Tania's awareness:

Odd things are happening between me and T. I have not tried to act very hard, to play the part of being exactly the same as I was. It required too much energy. And she has noticed it. She never said anything until last night, when I went into a reverie over a Spanish meal. 'I wonder what your thoughts are!' she said, half joking, but of course seriously meant. 'You've been quite different these last weeks. I suppose (knowing of course all the time) it's your girl friend.' I didn't bother to deny it ... 'Well,' she said, 'it's all right by me', in her comical accent.

What she really means is that however fond you may be of someone, however deep your love may be, you cannot treat them the same (and this excludes sex) when you've fallen in love with another. Of course she's right.

A few days later, after seeing Joan on to the train for Bennington and witnessing a kiss from the father of one of her class mates, he wrote jealously and disapprovingly: 'How dared that Papa of wotsername kiss you like that in the train. I never saw such impertinence. You wouldn't, and didn't, kiss *me* like that a few minutes after you'd met me!' And he goes on to lecture her:

Love, you see, when it's real is not public; it is something essentially private, secret; something for oneself alone, which no one can share, because no one knows it, has experienced it, but oneself; and for each one of us it is different – and always, when real, when right, sublime. It is only when not right, when not real, that it becomes public. You make it public because it is something not shared; it is simply an extension of yourself, a mirror, a flattering *photograph* of oneself as one would like others to think one to be ... Love, without secrecy, is a form of narcissistic prostitution, of airing one's wares, of exhibiting oneself not as one is, but as one would like others to think one to be.

He continues to berate her for not being 'a properly adult person' and vows not to discuss Blake and Yeats until she is, 'for the simple reason that those two dead gentlemen are your substitutes for living, the means by which you cling so tenaciously to your fantasy world, and the guard and fortress behind which you hide your over-prolonged adolescence.' He hopes that she won't take this diatribe too badly: 'If I can't write you a properly adult person, which somehow, soon, you've damn well got to be, then I can't write you at all.'

Far from objecting, Joan, who had recently read and admired *The Heartless Land*, continued to put Jimmy, the writer, the lover, on a pedestal:

For God's sake [he wrote] don't let yourself believe that I am anything but a very ordinary mortal; it is important that you shouldn't get to thinking of me as anything peculiar, because it's not fair on either of us. I don't want to have to live up to anything but what I know I am ... I have a feeling that possibly the best thing about me is that I love children (it doesn't matter why); that is really where I feel deepest (possibly dangerously deep), and why Wystan is always insisting that I teach.

Joan sent him her stories about which he was constructive and encouraging, but about her poems he was less helpful and inclined to be dismissive. She was hurt and disappointed by his criticism of them: 'Your poem ... the wind, the hurricane, the weather – why so much about the blasted elements?'

But he revealed more of himself to her than probably to any other person except Tania:

I'm really fascinated by everything ... Nothing really bores me – except regimentation etc. And even that makes me more violently angry than bored. I'm fascinated by human nature; and I'm interested in my own way in so many things that I'm capable of doing nothing, or rather no one thing, for any length of time. I was fascinated to see if I could write, and when it seemed that I could I really lost interest. Actually, my constitution, my vitality, is undermined. Sometimes I feel that I have experienced enough to die, that it is really my business to stop living. I cannot explain this, and I don't expect you to understand it; I don't really understand it myself.

In late November that year he was being brutally honest again: 'You're infernally selfish and self-centred (so am I, but I don't show it, because I've learned not to. I've suffered, and know what suffering can be, and therefore in some ways suffer more than ever because, while I sympathise with the suffering of others, I believe in a state of selfishness provided the all-important quality of Humility is not excluded) ... Your particular kind of selfishness is something which you can, will have to, grow out of – and it seems to me only a matter of time and suffering.'

By April 1943 Jimmy had started work in the offices of *Time* magazine – Tania insisted on him taking the job – and Joan, who had left Bennington in her last senior year to be with Jimmy, had persuaded her parents to rent an apartment for her, 7 Patchin Place, Manhattan, which Jimmy had engineered, no doubt with the help of Djuna Barnes who lived at No 5. Another neighbour was the poet e. e. cummings. The strains in his and Joan's relationship now began to show:

The fact is that to lead a double life & earn a difficult living all at

the same time is mighty hard. By double life I naturally don't mean
any part of it hidden, simply having to think of two people plus
all the daily thoughts without which life cannot go on ... by the
time I do see you I'm very often too tired to be anything but quar-
relsome & full of self-hatred. It's bad for me, & worse for you. I
don't quite know what to do about it. It's not, you see, as though I
could take all my time out with you and T, who in a sense gives a
blessing to the relationship, would not stand for that.

As you know, I shared a woman [Ethel Mannin] once with her
child. I waited for days and weeks for telephones to ring; I walked
to post boxes & post offices, followed and almost fell in love with
postmen over half of Europe, waiting, crying for pieces of paper
inside envelopes. The reason I kept it up was, I have since
supposed, because the tension blinded me. But it also killed my
love. I mention this only because I want to persuade you to believe
you have oceans of my sympathy which, because I'm by nature
undemonstrative, I feel I hardly ever show you. Last time I saw
you you unconsciously shot an arrow into me by saying something like: 'It's a good thing I haven't got an inferiority complex –
with you around.' Even if it were, as it probably was, meant partly
in fun, it struck home – and I have been thinking a lot about it (&
myself in relation to you) ever since.

In August 1943 Jimmy was fired from *Time*. That winter the depth
of his affair with Joan Lewisohn had been realised by Tania with devastating effect.

By the end of the year the two lovers had agreed to part. But their
correspondence continued until the autumn of 1945 when Jimmy's
extended visit to post-war Germany effectively terminated their relationship. From 207 East 52nd Street on 24 January 1944 Jimmy wrote:

Dear Just & Generous Joannie ... should I write at all? I am
absolutely determined not to phone. I know what that means for
both of us. I completely understand your attitude about not seeing
one another, & I am convinced that you are right ... T still wanted
to see you, partly I think, because she has learned your value & is
profoundly appreciative of your strength. And she wanted to
show her appreciation, & to talk things completely 'out' ... let me
tell you that you have given me, apart from all the happiness I
experienced simply by being with you, a shock that I badly
needed, a shock which made me see myself as I am, that made me

face certain realities which I dared not, that reconstructed my sense of values ...

Yes, the change of one's state of mind will take time, I know – for you, for me & for T – in fact, I think, especially for T. I don't think there's any doubt that she has suffered most. We suffered, each in our own way, all the time; but she suffered, she was completely shattered with suffering, twice in a month. And she's suffering still; she's still in a pretty bad conflict; and this is why her seeing you has not been *entirely* good. Before she saw you she could kid herself into thinking anything of you; since she has seen the kind of person you are, she can't kid herself any longer; she knows, & understands only too well. Consequently, it is all the more difficult for her to regain her equilibrium, to face life again as though nothing had happened ...

I know how difficult (& appreciate it all the more for that reason, naturally) it was for you to say that T 'needs me more'. Yes, I think she does, that she must ... That, you see, is what she still cannot get over, what pierces her mind in the darkness at night – that for 18 months I managed to live a double life unknown to her. The incredible thing to me was not that I managed to do it (lots of people do, after all) but that I really did feel convinced all the time that I was not (as she told you I was) so emotionally involved with you that I took anything away from her. I felt all the more certain about this when she noticed how much better she & I got on, how much nicer I was to her all these months. There were times, in fact, when you seemed happy & she seemed happy – when I began to think that what I was doing *could not* be sin in the eyes of anyone. At these times it got beyond wishful thinking & self-deception & because, so far as I allowed myself to see, a full life in which three people were happier than they could be under any other circumstances that I could imagine.

The sin I committed, of course, was not to allow you to talk. You did once, in the bedroom – I think it was the time you refer to as 'that awful night' – and I was speechless; I could say nothing: I couldn't help you. Should I have said: 'Well, in that case, I must leave you, for I only do you harm'? I suppose so, but I couldn't. I hadn't the courage & I felt, as I always have, responsible for you, & I loved you. If I *had* left you, I don't quite see how I could have squared it with my conscience. In other words, I was incapable of leaving you; I would have felt somehow as though I had killed you. So it had to come out in the classical way.

The only person to worry about is T, & that's my business. You see what's happened to her, don't you? She's fallen in love with you, via me – crudely speaking – and she's in a conflict ... I'm proud of you & terribly grateful to you & for every day & hour of your behaviour in a frightful position which I'm oh so glad I started, for it allowed me to know someone worth knowing.

Some months later, when Joan Lewisohn had begun work at *Partisan Review*, a job she acquired independently of Jimmy, they felt their continued deception of Tania had to stop. (A pregnancy scare may well have been crucial.) Although Jimmy wrote that the one thing he didn't want to face was to lose complete touch with Joan, he also felt 'exhausted by "us"; I grow less and less fond of ourselves'.

Finally, in September 1945, Jimmy asked Joan if she would go and see Tania in her studio. Joan was terrified – she imagined that Tania might be holding a gun – but she went. Their meeting elicited this generous and empathetic letter from Tania:

I want to thank you once more for having come to see me. I am very conscious of the fact that it wasn't quite fair to ask for your help – but apparently there are moments of despair and confusion in one's life when one has to be selfish and unfair! Anyhow, speaking to you helped me a lot and after you left me I suddenly felt at peace – the same way I had felt last winter both times after seeing you [at a party, but they exchanged no words], only more so. It comes perhaps from the fact that any tangible reality is better than the ghost of his and evasion – and also that I like you every time I see you!

There is only one thing that worries me now and this is that in speaking about J. I must have sounded awfully hard and disparaging and almost contemptuous. But I know that this was the result of the terrible shock and bitterness and disappointment and has nothing to do with what I really feel. Actually, after talking to you I found myself understanding both J. and you and the whole situation absolutely as if it had been my own. It is just that I seem to need clarity about some essential things in my life – a clarity which I have to pursue and protect at all costs.

I wish, Joan, that I could do something for you now in return – but I am afraid that I will have to leave that to life and other people.

Although Jimmy once talked to Joan about leaving Tania, he told her that he couldn't because she had been through so much horror in her life that it would devastate her. They agreed that they could never live with themselves if they did that to her. In 1969 he wrote to Isabelle Evans about the affair: 'Yes, about my marriage I "made up my mind" (one cannot be certain of such things) about 26 years ago, when I almost allowed it to break asunder. It was a terrible time, but worth it, for the relationship in consequence became closer. We are now so close we are more like one person than two. In a sense this is bad; it stifles creativity.'

So, 'the beloved, delinquent brother' – Sybille Bedford's interpretation of Jimmy's relationship with Tania – returned to a fold which he had little wish to leave in the first place. Joan says now that she wanted to be with Jimmy forever and ever: 'I think I realized that that was never to be, so I just put up with whatever time he was willing to give me.' It is possible, too, to discern in Tania's letter and from her earlier remark – 'it's all right by me' – that her confidence in Jimmy's devotion to her had not been misplaced, though it had taken a severe blow.

For Joan, Jimmy was the love of her life, a soul mate – 'he was magic'. She became suicidal after the ending of the affair. On the rebound, a year or so later, she married her first husband, the sculptor Sidney Simon, with whom she had five children. A composer, librettist, novelist, poet, and teacher, now in her eighty-first year, Joan lives with her second husband, the designer David G. Crowell. She and Jimmy were to remain in sporadic contact until three years before his death. His last letter to her is addressed, in July 1990, to 'Dear Granny Joan'.

Jimmy could never remember whether it was Mia and James Agee or Alice Morris, the editor of *Harper's Bazaar*, who introduced him to Walker Evans (1903–75), the renowned photographer. *Let Us Now Praise Famous Men* (1941), Evans's classic collaboration with Agee, had recently been published, and Jimmy had started work in the offices of *Time*. Jimmy's memoir is as much a picture of part of his own life at that time as it is a portrait of Evans:

> … for those of us who knew Evans only during the latter half of his life [Walker was a year older than Jimmy], I for one find it difficult to dissociate his name from that of James Agee. Jim, as he was generally known, died in 1953 of a heart attack in a New

York taxi at the shockingly early age of forty-five. Not that the two men were in any way alike. On the contrary. It's as though the short, dark, diffident, deliberate, fastidious, slow-moving, slow-speaking Walker of those days is all the time in danger of being eclipsed by his larger-than-lifesize friend …

[Jimmy first met James Agee at a dinner party on Riverside Drive, Manhattan in the company of the English poet George Barker, and the American writer and critic Lionel Trilling. Jimmy recalled that Agee 'looked poor and dirty and modest and nice'.]

Let Walker himself have the first word as he remembers the Jim of just over forty years ago: 'He didn't look much like a poet, an intellectual, an artist, or a Christian, each of which he was … His clothes were deliberately cheap, not only because he was poor but because he wanted to be able to forget them. He would work a suit into fitting him perfectly by the simple method of not taking it off much. In due time the cloth would mold itself to his frame … He got more delight out of factory-seconds sneakers and a sleazy cap than a straight dandy does from waxed calf Peal shoes and a brushed Lock & Co. bowler. Physically Agee was quite powerful, in the deceptive way of uninsistent large men. In movement he was rather graceless. His hands were large, long, bony, light, and uncared for. His gestures were one of the memorable things about him. He seemed to model, fight, and stroke his phrases as he talked. The talk, in the end, was his great distinguishing feature … Many a man or woman has fallen exhausted to sleep at four in the morning bang in the middle of a remarkable Agee performance, and later learned that the man had continued it somewhere else until six …'

I have quoted this passage not only for the sketch of Agee by Evans, but also to suggest that however great a photographer Walker may have been, his talent as a writer lagged not far behind …

… [It was] while Europe burned and in the all-but-audible blaze of collapsing cities, [that] we all met – Tania and I, Walker and Jim and their wives – and became friends. In fact, we ourselves had recently moved into an apartment in an old house just off Third Avenue … Although that day is more than twenty-three years ago; although during the past two decades Walker has often come to visit us here in England, I still cannot think of him without seeing Jim.

For this there is an additional reason beyond that of urban friendship and the book on which the two men had collaborated. One morning not long after its publication I was sitting working in my room on East 52nd Street (no doubt wondering as usual how the month's rent was to be paid) when the telephone rang. The voice was that of an English friend ... He was writing the weekly Books column for *Time* magazine, and he will need no introduction to readers of these pages, for he is the author of *Cards of Identity* [1955] ...

'Just thought I should tell you,' Nigel [Dennis] was saying. 'I know you are not very flush. The Art column here is free. They are wondering if I know anyone ... ? You wouldn't consider it, I suppose?'

The first lesson I learned in America was never to say No. And when I heard the sum the magazine was prepared to pay, I swallowed twice and said Sure!

'Splendid!' exclaimed that exuberant English voice. 'Just one little word of warning. Didn't you once tell me you'd wanted to be a painter?' Yes, I probably did. 'Then you've lived in Paris, haven't you?' That's true. 'Well, for Heaven's sake forget it. Please remember: you've never met an artist in your life!'

... a few days later ... I started off in an office, just vacated, I remember, by John Hersey, and next to that of my friend Nigel Dennis. Almost at once, however, I was moved to another room, an office overlooking the Hudson River and next door but one to that of Jim, *Time*'s 'famed' film critic.

I was destined to spend a whole year on that corridor. 'Group journalism', I believe it is called. It may sound cosy enough. I did not find it so. What kept me going was the pay. And the people. As well as Agee, Dennis, Evans (who arrived after me), anyone would count it a privilege to have known Hamilton Basso, Saul Bellow, Louis Kronenberger (who sat beside me twice a week to write the Theatre column), and Winthrop Sargeant, who married Walker's first wife ... What got many writers down were the hours, the uncertainty, the insecurity, and – as a result – the Benzedrine, nicotine, and alcohol.

Jimmy was fired by his boss, T. S. Matthews, who remained a friend. He did it so politely that Jimmy didn't realise he'd received 'the chop'. The penny dropped only when he returned to his office to find somebody else's name on the door. He maintained that his dismissal was due to an interview with Djuna Barnes, the only interview, he claimed, she ever granted to a journalist.

The story appeared, castrated to the hilt, in the weekly, which some of the 'poor hacks' who worked there called '*Slime*'.

When Djuna Barnes showed her first oil painting, 'Portrait of Alice' [Jimmy wrote in the issue for 18 January 1943], at Peggy Guggenheim's Manhattan gallery last week, many critics were surprised to find the woman who wrote *Nightwood* (1936) could paint with similar distinction. In *Nightwood* no less magisterial and exacting a critic than T. S. Eliot found 'the great achievement of a style, the beauty of phrasing, the brilliance of wit and characterization, and a quality of horror and doom very nearly related to that of Elizabethan tragedy'.

Now the output of original and talented Djuna Barnes consists of a total of six paintings and six peculiar books. The 'Portrait of Alice' is a full-length study of a woman in a burgundy robe standing against a background of gold. It suggests the quality as well as the style of the great Italian primitives. Asked last week how she came to paint Alice (1934), Djuna Barnes said: 'I asked myself one day, why not paint a painting? ... I painted most of it on my hands & knees, because I couldn't afford an easel.'

Thin, pale, 50-year-old Djuna Barnes was born in Cornwall-on-the-Hudson. Her father was a jack of all talents who played five musical instruments, so disliked his father that he changed his name Buddington to Barnes. Djuna was named after Prince Djalma in *The Wandering Jew,* but her young brother's mispronunciation changed everything. She prefers to call herself The Barnes.

The Barnes studied art at Pratt Institute in Brooklyn, later at Manhattan's Art Students' League. She started to earn her living on the Brooklyn *Eagle* as an illustrator and reporter. For the *New York Press* she covered 'Gyp the Blood'. For the *World* she did 'stunt' stories, including being hugged by a New York gorilla, being forcibly fed in order to tell what it felt like. For *McCall's* Magazine she went to Europe, interviewed the American-born Duchess of Marlborough in her fabulous Blenheim Palace. Said the Duchess: 'This may be a palace, but there isn't one decent bathroom in the whole bloody place.'

In 1928 her novel *Ryder,* written in many different styles, parodied Fielding, the Bible, Chaucer. That same year The Barnes published privately and anonymously her self-illustrated *Ladies Almanack* ... Says The Barnes: 'By tramping the Paris streets I sold about 500 copies to book-stores and friends. Ten copies shipped to the U.S. were banned. The remainder are in France, in the hands of the Nazis.' ...

In a dark, one-room apartment in Greenwich Village last week Djuna Barnes said she was 'writing one more book, painting one more picture', felt she was 'going slightly mad'.

Although he could ill afford to be jobless, Jimmy left the *Time* building whistling with joy.

Jimmy's memoir of Evans continues:

'In those days', said Walker many years later, 'there was a certain satanic naiveté in the very top editorial direction of Time Incorporated, perceptible only from below: gifted, intelligent employees were expected to work hard and long hours under crushing pressure at many tasks no man with a mind could put his heart into.'

I have little doubt that this 'pressure' helped to curtail the lives of some men who had the misfortune to be of such value to that 'editorial direction' that, from a sense of loyalty or dire need, they dared not or refused to count the cost to their brains, livers and hearts. I have a vision when passing Jim's office (doors were kept open except on rare occasions as when a cover story was being written!), of Jim sitting in that bolt-upright posture, head nevertheless bent in intense concentration, pencil – always pencil – careering back and forth across the page in that tiny, totally legible hand. And then one morning of seeing Walker crouched in equal concentration beside his friend in such a position that even a stranger's eye would recognize it at once as that of the pupil. Pupil? Agee teaching Evans? What? A language known as *Time*se.

The morning hours over, some of us, seldom fewer than four, more often six or eight, breaking open one more pack of Camels, would swiftly fall the fifty floors to the teeming street, and hasten round the block to the Ristorante Del Pezzo. In my memory, however many of us turned up, we invariably sat at one large round table, which Nigel and I called our *Stammtisch*, in this most excellent of Italian restaurants. And just as invariably, at the same neighbouring table for two, sat the fascinating figure of Sergei Rachmaninoff!

In this civilized atmosphere, its comfort and décor so *fin de siècle* Europe, so remote from that lofty, over-heated, clinical cage of our labours, who could help but rest and revel? Confronted by the *Scaloppini al Marsala*, the delicious *Carciofi alla Veneziana* cooked to perfection and served with southern grace, who could blame these overworked men for sitting on, evidently oblivious of the hour, of their empty coffee cups, the vacant tables, deaf even to the call of that corridor?

… He [Evans] was a passionate Anglophile. He loved this country's literature, its eccentric public customs, its titles, honours and colourful ceremonies. Himself an eccentric, a diffident dandy, favouring the most expensive black or dark grey suits and neckties (usually of wool and narrow), he was fascinated by London's West End tailors, hosiers, hat and shoe shops, subjects on which he would occasionally reveal his knowledge. How many Europeans or Americans can talk, or have even heard, of 'waxed calf Peal shoes and a brushed Lock & Co bowler'? In clothes as well as in cameras he was wildly extravagant. I have often thought that his initial interest in me derived from one particular Savile Row suit (which he so coveted that I promised to leave it to him in my Will).

In nature, in man himself (except in the young and in pretty girls), Walker took little interest. What did interest him was what man had made of nature, how he lived, what he had invented, built, and left behind him. What Walker called civilization. Like most photographers I imagine, he was immensely inquisitive, continually on the snoop. He didn't walk, he prowled, and pretty slowly at that. His eye was for what is there for all to see, but few notice.

Jimmy's appointment as Art Critic of *Time* may have been surprising, as initially it surely was for him, but after some months in the job he wrote this letter to Alfred H. Barr, Jr, Director of the Museum of Modern Art, in which he justifies his position:

A propos our conversation yesterday a remark you dropped about my colleague Winthrop Sargeant has made me wonder if perhaps you do not exaggerate the rather worn out maxim about *Time* writers being employed as such only on condition they [know] nothing of what they are asked to write about ...

As for myself, I take pleasure in confessing that I do not look upon myself as an Art Critic, have never written about art. But may I, in self-defense and in defense of my criticism of the maxim referred to above, say this: that I was brought up between horses, a father who was, if ever there was one, an *artiste manqué*, and a Viennese grandmother, one of the last great Victorians who died last year aged 90, and who was a close friend of all the Pre-Raphaelites & 19th century English poets. Millais and Browning were her best friends. From the pictures in her London house, including the portrait of her by Millais, and the magnificent collection of paintings in the house of her sister, Mrs Bischoff-sheim, I learned a great deal about bad painting and good. From my earliest childhood I was fascinated by painting. When my grandmother exhibited a picture of mine done in Africa in 1925 (without telling me) I was so horrified by the idea of publicity that I never painted again, except for a few months of private lessons under the German painter Nussbaum in Frankfurt, where I spent most of my spare hours in the Staedel Museum, my weekends in the Museums of Darmstadt, Cologne, my holidays in those of Basle, Munich, Madrid, and later, while continuing my hateful career as a banker in Berlin, in the Kaiser Friedrich. I came to writing only through my intense dislike of the banking profession, my fear of ever being good enough as a painter. The eight years I spent in Paris before coming here, I lived almost exclusively with painters, very little with writers. This I have realized only lately, looking back.

I realize perfectly well, in spite of all this, that I 'know' very little about painting. I know only that all my life it has fascinated me, that I believe I have a 'feeling' for it, and that I have seen more pictures than I have read books ...

It had been thirteen years since he had worked in an office, and the prospect of having to sit with dozens of others – he didn't get a room of his own for several weeks – made him literally tremble. His first days there were nerve-wracking and brought on a bout of insomnia. 'The New Boy is not told how or where or when to do anything,' he told Joan Lewisohn, 'but [is] simply left to his own resources: to review a magnificent new book by Epstein, and to tell a story – in my case in 22 minutes – on Nazi art robberies in Holland. The atmosphere of the office is not like any other office I have known. It has made me draw the conclusion that when American men are nice they are nicer, individually and en groupe, than any other people I have ever met.'

He worked late into the night and early morning at the office, but never on Mondays or Tuesdays, and at one time wrote six stories – at *Time* everything anyone wrote was called 'a story' – in three days, one of which was about Jean Helion's escape from the Nazis, 'an incredible affair, ruined by editing – but which will be nevertheless worth reading, as not even *Time* can spoil facts'. He had furious disagreements with 'the powers that be involving ethics, smut, & friends'. 'I believe, simply by being a little quicker & more slippery than anyone else, that I won ... But they can always outwit me at the last moment by phoning to Chicago (where the rag is printed), & inserting smut it took me two days to delete.' His tenure was soon to end: 'I very nearly stepped out of the *Time* office for good last week over the filth they made of my piece on Chagall. I despise the blasted rag, and am not sure I can stick the kind of muck they expect me to pour out. If it wasn't for this, I'd quite like the job, and the money more ...' He was earning $440 a month.

It was during his stint at *Time* that Jimmy came into contact with Whittaker Chambers, a connection which was to cause Jimmy and Tania great angst and may have been one of the factors in their decision finally to leave America for England in 1956.

Chambers, who had spied for the Soviet Union in the 1930s, became an impassioned anti-Communist after he left the Party. He said he was the Soviet's courier between 1934 and 1938. In 1948 he claimed that Alger Hiss had given him classified government documents. Hiss denied that he'd ever been a Communist or a spy; he was convicted of perjury in 1949 and jailed in 1950, serving nearly four years. Many believed him to be innocent and today the case is still fiercely debated in the US.

'The fat priest', Jimmy's name for Chambers, whom he never trusted, knew that Tania had had two Communist brothers in Germany and thus became interested in the Sterns. Lewis Mumford, a friend and benefactor whose cottage in Amenia the Sterns would rent in 1947, was a passionate supporter of Alger Hiss, while James Agee took the side of Chambers, as did Alwyn Lee, and so Jimmy and Tania were inevitably divided in their allegiances.

Two pro-Hiss psychiatrists – Karl Binger was one – came to call on the Sterns looking for real 'dirt' on Chambers, which they didn't have. But was pressure put on Jimmy to testify against Chambers at Hiss's sensational trial, as Jimmy's friend Malcolm Cowley did? It is not clear. The Sterns were very unpolitical, yet found themselves under scrutiny by the FBI, to whom it was alleged Agee suggested that Jimmy be interviewed about Chambers, thus, according to Tania, souring for a time a close friendship. However, from the evidence of an undated draft letter to Agee, this version of events assumes a greyness:

> I'm so glad you wrote ... You are quite mistaken, Jim, in assuming that I feel you have 'betrayed' me 'on several counts' ... my silence to your rejoinder [on the telephone, a means of communication with which Jimmy was always uneasy] about the importance to you of our relationship was the result, Jim, of a sudden strong emotion which I could not find, fast enough, the words to express. These words you have given me in the last paragraph of your letter, they are warmly reciprocated, Jim.

It is difficult to believe that this letter was never sent, and that a rapprochement between the two friends and colleagues wasn't swiftly arranged.

Were the FBI interested in Tania's connections and her youthful flirtation with Marxism, or were there stories which Jimmy had told 'in his cups', partial 'inventions', which made the FBI think that he knew things, perhaps about others? It is impossible to know for certain; the Sterns repressed all memories of those months of stress. And understandably, for Jimmy, close to paranoia, took to the bottle in earnest. Tania feared a breakdown, which he narrowly avoided. She had given up her regular work and was travelling with Jean Arthur, on tour in *Peter Pan*, in order to give the actress physical therapy, while simultaneously, with Jimmy, translating Erich Maria Remarque's novel *Spark of Life* (1952). Jimmy, profoundly upset by the Chambers/Hiss affair, joined them. Since the producers of the touring company would have banned him from accompanying their star, when breakfast was served in his and Tania's hotel room, he would disappear into the bathroom to avoid being seen.

Later, in an undated letter, Chambers hinted darkly at information never divulged: 'Dear James ... I must congratulate you on what you have done, on what you have gone through. It isn't easy. Still, it isn't gun-fire, and afterwards there's the proud feeling of being a survivor among survivors – if that's worth anything. I must get well some day if only to tell you some parts of the battle that only I know …'

Over thirty years later, in 1976, Jimmy was reluctant to confide, anyway in a letter, his memories of the case to Nora Sayre. He wrote to her:

> … Did I know Wh. Chambers??? He 'hired' me. He was Our Boss. Us being Jim Agee, Walker Evans, Nigel Dennis, Louis Kronenberger (with whom I shared an office), Hamilton Basso, Winthrop Sargeant, et al – How did Wh. Chambers strike me? Short answer: All of a heap. Long answer: Far too long for a letter. Let me recommend an article by Sidney Hook in last month's (January) *Encounter*. Wh. Chambers a 'friend' of Jim Agee? I think in *Witness* [Chambers's book] he claims Jim as the best writer *Time* ever had. Yes, they were very close friends. Our other boss (editor) in that year (1943, I think) was Wilder Hobson, and the Managing Editor Tom Matthews.

'You have only begun to do the great work as a novelist that it lies within you to do: there is no one writing in either America or England today that you need fear comparison with.' Despite this praise – and faith – expressed by Lewis Mumford, the sociologist, literary critic, and author of *The City in History* (1961), Jimmy's creative drive began to waver during the early and mid-'40s. Although he continued to write and submit stories to American magazines, to Cyril Connolly's *Horizon* and to John Lehmann's *New Writing* in England, his best fictional work had been achieved. As Auden was to write in April 1942:

> If I read your stories right, they have been your catharsis of your childhood, and that particular task is almost or quite over; so you feel stuck because the amount of resolution that writing can do is very limited and in your case the residue of *ressentiment* is still too great for you to look at your later experiences with the necessary combination of freedom and interest, while at the same time your artistic conscience is too acute to allow you to do what so many writers (eg Housman) do, endless variations on the same theme. Maybe you will have to wait till your father dies (it won't be long now I suppose), when you will be able to forgive him and forget him, and relive him. I hope that you won't have to: it's my guess that you are the kind of writer who must write directly about their

own experience, so that your next stories will be about Ethel Mannin and Brian [Howard] and Tania ...

In March 1968 Auden was still exhorting Jimmy:

I have just been sent Calder-Marshall's selection from your Short Stories [*The Stories of James Stern*, 1968] ... You don't need me to tell you how first-class they are. What concerns me is what you should do now. Your 'drying up' since you returned to the Old Country has worried me as I am sure it has worried many others. I am convinced that what you should do now is write a straight-forward and truthful autobiography. For a poet like myself an autobiography is redundant since anything of importance that happens to one is immediately incorporated, however obscurely, in a poem. With a novelist or short story-writer like yourself this is not so.

Some people, like myself, have an uninteresting family back-ground and, from a reader's point of view, an uninteresting life (except as a 'queer' which is nobody's business.)

In your case both are of the utmost interest. I implore you, therefore, to write what I know will be a document of the greatest historical and, because of your talent, the greatest literary value.

(One of many explanations, but apparently the most considered one, of Jimmy's inability to write can be found in his letter of 23 November 1964 to the South African poet and novelist William Plomer on p. 216.) At the very end of her life, Tania Stern told Nora Sayre that she may have damaged Jimmy as a writer, that in 'trying to give the love he didn't have as a child' she diminished his creative powers by lessening the necessary pain. Jimmy's judgement that he and Tania were so close that their relationship stifled creativity is also of telling significance. On another occasion Tania worried that she had curtailed his 'powers of invention' by always insisting on the truth, correcting the stories which he told about their life together. This emphasis on 'the truth' may have been a throwback to her youth in Berlin with her two brothers who became Communists. To her, Marxism had been appealing initially; but while she liked the idea of giving herself to a great cause, she violently recoiled from the dictum 'the end justifies the means'. She couldn't abide the bending of the truth, the telling of lies in the name of the cause. An understanding of the concept of 'fictional truth' seems to have eluded her.

Apart from his already well-developed prowess as a letter writer, Jimmy now began to hone his critical powers in an increasing number of book reviews for the *New York Times,* the *New Republic,* the *Nation, Partisan Review,* and other journals. That he was asked to review books by such authors as H. E. Bates, Elizabeth Bowen, Simone de Beauvoir, Pamela Hansford Johnson, Paul Bowles, Salvador Dali, Georg Grosz, Mary Lavin, Le Corbusier, Alan Paton, Tom Hopkinson, Sean O'Casey, Frank O'Connor and Cyril Connolly is an indication of his standing as a reviewer in the judgement of literary editors, and he was to develop in the decade which followed into a critic of influence and repute. He also reviewed a number of books which were to become landmarks: *Lucky Jim, The Sheltering Sky, Room at the Top, Enemies of Promise, Lord of the Flies, Thin Ice,* and *The Catcher in the Rye.*

Patrick White, the Australian Nobel Prize winner, was 'put on the map' in 1955, especially in the USA, by Jimmy's front page review of *The Tree of Man* in the *New York Times.* It is an excellent example of his reviewing style.

> Almost all novels are transients; very few remain on, permanent residents of the mind. Of those that do, some cease to be books and become part of the reader's past, of an experience felt so deeply it is sometimes difficult to believe that the illusion has not been lived. From these rare works of literature characters emerge better known than our most intimate friends, for every human being has a secret life, one unknown to all but himself and which he takes with him to the grave. To reveal in a novel this life (which is that of the soul) in such a way that by the time the last page is reached all questions have been answered, while all the glory and mystery of the world remains, is not only the prime function of the novelist but the artist's greatest ambition – and surely his rarest achievement. Were I asked if I had read a book called *The Tree of Man,* I might hesitate. But if someone in my presence were to start speaking of Stan and Amy Parker, I would immediately wonder how he had come to be in a certain region of New South Wales, Australia, when I was there, how he knew this obscure and simple couple about whom I feel I know all there is to know ...
>
> Some no doubt will complain that this is a 'sad' book. It is. In it is all the sorrow and senselessness of living, the profound loneliness of mortal man, his cowardice, his cruelty, as well as dignity,

his indomitable courage, and the comedy, the fun his imagination is able to create ...

The Tree of Man, it seems to me, is a timeless work of art from which no essential element of life has been omitted. A magnifying glass has been laid over a microscopic world in the center of which loom, larger and larger, man and woman, married, bound by love, and from whom radiate the beauty and the tragedy of humanity.

From this apex he continued to write reviews in American journals and newspapers regularly until the early '60s, and it is a matter of speculation why, with a body of critical work behind him, he was not taken up by London literary editors when he returned to England in 1956. He wasn't, and it is perhaps one of the reasons for the frustration which showed itself in later life.

Whilst the Sterns' early years in their adopted New York were marked by financial anxiety ('We lived hand-to-mouth,' he wrote to Nora Sayre), by their search for a permanent home, and by Jimmy's continuing insecurity about his role as a writer, they were nevertheless outstandingly handsome and popular, a 'golden' couple in the Scott Fitzgerald sense, who had the reputation for giving spectacular parties. They had a genius for friendship and, as the screenwriter and playwright Donald Ogden Stewart has said of Sara and Gerald Murphy, those expatriate American luminaries of the '20s on whom Fitzgerald based his protagonists of *Tender is the Night* (1934), 'they had the gift of making life enchantingly pleasurable for those who were fortunate to be their friend.'

'Our life has been completely dissolute almost since I can remember,' Jimmy wrote to Joan Lewisohn. 'We never get to bed before about 2 & seldom stop talking until 4.' They were good times, indeed: a continual, lively interaction between soul-mates, writers, painters, and older men of letters like Malcolm Cowley and Van Wyck Brooks, both of whom became Jimmy's regular correspondents, Tania's successful professional life and, not least, the freedom of a country materially untouched by the war in Europe.

With still vivid memories of Limerick point-to-points and race meetings at Punchestown, Hurst Park, Goodwood and Sandown, Jimmy kept alive his youthful excitement by visiting the track at Jamaica, a grey suburb half an hour from the city. He also became keen on skating which in mid-winter he would perform on a frozen-over tennis court among the skyscrapers. A particularly bad fall resulted in delayed concussion; while buying vegetables in a shop on Madison Avenue, he passed out. His condition was diagnosed by a young Russian physician whom Tania had known twenty years earlier in Berlin. As Jimmy began to recover, the doctor introduced him to his old mother, a peasant-like woman with a wrinkled face and bony hands which, so her son alleged, had extraordinary healing powers – something Jimmy came to question as she forced the knuckles of her hands, which looked and felt like walnuts, into the sockets of his eyes, giving him the most appalling headache. For years he suffered from dizzy spells and bad hangovers – his skating legacy.

The Sterns became fast friends, too, with Alexander (Sandy) Calder, the creator of the mobile (a delicate suspension; the balancing and twisting of metal shapes), and his wife, who was a niece of Henry James. The Calders were neighbours of Arthur Miller in Roxbury, Connecticut, and of the irascible, reclusive Djuna Barnes, who described her *Nightwood* as '[The soliloquy of] a soul talking to itself in the heart of the night'.

During 1942 Jimmy saw a lot of Barnes. '*Nightwood* is a very peculiar book,' he wrote to Joan Lewisohn, 'and she's certainly a very peculiar person. I'm prejudiced agin the book (though I see wonderful flashes in it) by knowing all the characters. I think she should have stuck to painting. But she was very ambitious. Oddly enough, *au fond*, she's a stupid woman – but I should have to explain what I mean by stupid. She's a wonderful friend ... She lies in bed (sometimes for 10 days without moving) and phones me at any hour of the day or night.'

In *Being Geniuses Together* (1938) Robert McAlmon describes her as a 'haughty lady, quick on the uptake, and with a wise-cracking tongue ... Djuna is far too good-looking and fundamentally likeable for anything but fond admiration, if not a great deal more, even when she is rather overdoing the *grande dame* manner and talking soul and ideals. In conversation she is often great with her comedy, but in writing she appears to believe she must inject into her work metaphysics, mysticism, and her own strange version of a "literary" quality.'

A good impression of Barnes is also provided by David Gascoyne in his *Collected Journals 1936–42* (1991), in the entry for December 1938:

Spent an hour talking to ... Djuna Barnes ... glummer than ever, ironically derogatory about everything, imparted an atmosphere of defeat and gloom to the household, I felt. It was twilight and misty and bitterly cold outside. She sat huddled in a corner of the sofa, unable to keep warm, although the heating of the chalet seemed quite adequate ... She seemed detached from everybody. Did I know Henry Miller, she asked me, and what was he like? Wasn't he a shit? Look at his picture, she said indignantly, he surely must be a Jew? – His name is really Mueller, I told her, and he rather tends to think he is a modern Goethe. He always talks as though he hates the Jews. – All the more reason to suppose he is one, she said. In spite of all this, she seemed ready to admit there was 'something' in *Tropic of Cancer*. 'Three hundred pages of bickering, bitching and buggering: but yes, it has a sort of strength.'

Arthur Miller, who dedicated his play *A View from the Bridge* 'To James Stern for his encouragement', has a story of him in an Irish bar on 42nd Street and 2nd Avenue, frequented by *Daily News* journalists. Jimmy's friend, the barman – Jimmy, throughout his life and all over the world, developed friendships with barmen – told him the bar had to shut down because 'the Jews' had bought the building. 'I'm a Jew,' said Jimmy. To which the barman replied: 'How did that happen?'

'Why I am always made *happy* seeing your short name on the back of an envelope I do not know,' Miller wrote to Jimmy in January 1971. 'Your news is always dreary and bleak and yet I find myself ready to smile at the least crumb of a joke or a good remark.' In a letter to John Byrne in 1974, Jimmy wrote: 'Arthur Miller? Yes, a hilarious friendship. We make each other howl with laughter. He is one of the funniest men I know.'

In various letters over the years, Arthur Miller expressed his fondness for Jimmy: '... I miss you. It's a damned shame life has kept us apart. We had much to talk about, I think.' (2 July 1980). '... God, it's good to hear from you. I've thought of you more than you'd believe, and I can't exactly say why either. Just good to know you're in the world.' (8 December 1964) '... I've never been able to forget your stories; among the ignorant I tell them as my own.' And this long letter of 17 August 1958 reveals the mental, emotional and physical background to the play he was working on at the time:

... I am gladly settling for this beautiful land in Roxbury. We've been remodeling the old Ray Leavenworth house which is across the valley and within view of the Calders. I have a fine little studio apart from the house with a fireplace and an electric heater and windows all around. Bought a door and made a fine long desk, and our Basset hound, Hugo, lies faithfully at my feet.

But I madly miss my wife who is in Hollywood since early July making a movie, a mad farce of the Twenties, called 'Some Like it Hot', with which she is thoroughly dissatisfied but will be wonderful in ...

I'm at work on a play – which begins sometime in 1952, has been through nearly four reams of paper, and suddenly, by dint, I suppose, of my old Jewish conviction that God will put his hand on my shoulder if only I'll stand still – I have hit the rock from which water is finally flowing. It is, as usual, out of my poor life but a hell of a funny tragedy, if I may say so. I am trying to set down the American disaster in the midst of the hilarity which accompanies, for in the laughter is the hope. I believe that finally, and quite without plan, I have come to recognize my optimism. Looking back, for instance, at my eleven-day trial in a Federal Court, it is clear that the lawyer and I were always laughing when we weren't under court duress not to. It was bitter laughter often, but laughter nevertheless.

... I've just got word that John Huston has agreed to direct an original movie I wrote last summer. I did it really as a gift to Marilyn when she lost the baby. It's called 'The Misfits' ...

On the page, Jimmy underlined in red the words '... in the laughter is the hope'.

In New York during the '40s was Jimmy's oldest friend and schoolroom companion, Harold Acton. In *More Memoirs of an Aesthete* (1970) he wrote:

Others I met in New York and saw more of in the following years were old friends from Eton, Oxford and Paris: James Stern, Wystan Auden and Pavel Tchelitchew. New York was their temporary anchorage. Auden had become acclimatized ... James Stern was more *dépaysé* [disorientated], and he made me realize that I might become a fish out of water if I stayed on. He had written some of the best English short stories of his generation but he was too fastidious for a sensation-seeking public and perhaps too bitter. His experience had been varied, for he had travelled in Africa and Hawaii, he had visited unemployed coal-miners in

Wales and Derbyshire, and the ruins of Germany just after the war – his book *The Hidden Damage* is a masterpiece of tragic irony and compassion. He had been brought up by fox-hunting parents in Ireland but he had broken away from that horsy world whose limitations he understood thoroughly. Edwardian parents expected their children to conform, and it cannot have been easy for him to leap over the hedges and ditches of the Irish country-side into the field of letters. His handsome features were signed with the strain of his divided allegiance. Like Somerset Maugham he could make you see persons and places in primitive isolation, but he penetrated the loneliness and frustration of individuals more deeply than Maugham, without that slick artifice which makes you exclaim 'How clever!' and forget them. The reverse of facile, he had to wrestle with his material. He and his wife Tania seemed more isolated in New York than other Europeans.

During 1943 and '44 the Sterns spent many months on Fire Island, a forty-mile strip of sand on the ocean side of Long Island, where they had rented a shack in Cherry Grove. It could be reached by ferry from Sayville, the whole journey from New York taking two and a half hours. Cherry Grove consisted of about thirty houses, mostly on stilts, inhabited by wealthy European homosexuals. Without trees, without a road or a street, it looked like an outpost in Alaska.

Two years later they were to be the owners, with W. H. Auden, of another shack, which they called Bective Poplars – Bective after Jimmy's childhood home and Poplars after a house owned by a relative of Auden's.

Jimmy edited and translated a new edition of *Grimm's Fairy Tales* (1944), which was lauded by W. H. Auden in the *New York Times*. He also translated speeches, articles, books and plays by Stefan Zweig, Bertolt Brecht and Hermann Kesten. In July 1944 Auden told Jimmy that he had 'long cherished a secret wish to collaborate with you on a play about marriage, the *only* subject' – a wish never realised. But that autumn the Sterns and Auden began a translation of Brecht's *The Caucasian Chalk Circle*. It was completed, as Humphrey Carpenter has written, 'with Auden providing what were in effect entirely fresh song-lyrics which recreated the originals in his own terms. But he took no part in the prose translation, and Brecht complained that there was "too much Stern and too little Auden". The proposed production never took place, though the Stern-Auden text, somewhat revised, was eventually published, and became the standard English version of the play.'

The following March the genesis of Jimmy's momentous return to Germany came about. Auden, by then an American citizen and already recruited into the US Army, arrived at the Sterns' New York flat from Philadelphia to announce that a 'certain man' was trying to recruit civilians to go overseas. They were to wear uniforms and to travel under War Department orders, but just what was to be their function was unclear – and remained so until Jimmy and Auden eventually landed in Germany after V-E Day. Jimmy, in fact, was to become a member of the US Strategic Bombing Survey, whose task was to interview citizens of the American Zone and to discover the effects of the Allied saturation bombing of their cities and towns and what the people felt towards their victors. Obviously, they were chosen because they both spoke German.

Although they both signed a contract with Harcourt, Brace in New York to collaborate on a book describing their experiences, the project never materialised. Instead, two years later, in the summer of 1947, the same publisher brought out *The Hidden Damage,* Jimmy's own account of the spiritual damage suffered by the people of Western Europe during six years of war. From the experience of four summer months in a country with which he had ties of blood, but which also had left him with so many conflicting emotions, he created a portrait of Germany such as could be painted only by a practised storyteller. Driving a pony-and-trap in the English countryside, he recalls the Edwardian era in his native Ireland; landing in Paris, he begins to relive his half-forgotten life; in Frankfurt he is reminded of people he used to know twenty years ago. The remnants of one such family he finds by searching in an old address book; another by recognising an old man on a balcony. He listens to a father's story of his son who was beheaded by the Gestapo, and to a strange tale of suicide told in the silence of an American cemetery.

A many-faceted, not wholly successful book, *The Hidden Damage* is in parts a travelogue, a memoir, a personal pilgrimage, even a 'sentimental journey', which was how Stephen Spender described it in his Introduction to the English edition (1990). '... in this book', Spender wrote, 'it is the writer's interior search for a hidden self striving to understand the most terrible events of our century which deepens sentiment with diamond-like determination.' In its journalistic grasp of

detail and its sympathetic and acute observation of the social conditions prevailing, many parts of the book recall Jimmy's earlier exercise
in reportage, 'A Stranger among Miners'.

On 15 May 1945 he wrote to Tania: 'I'm in a dream, half nightmare,
half I don't know what … the most exciting and saddest day of my life
… The silence, the silence is what envelops Paris & terrifies one and
tells one everything.'

Two weeks earlier Tania had written revealingly and positively to
Jimmy:

> What a strange letter this No.4 of yours was – what a strange idea
> to start out on your 'recherche du temps perdu' in the middle of
> your hurried stay in London [on his way through England to
> Germany, Jimmy made a sentimental journey to Wimbledon
> where Ethel Mannin had lived]. The strangest thing about it for
> me was my own reaction to it – because much to my surprise I felt
> the same old jealousy for Ethel surge up in me! Probably it isn't
> even wise to admit this anyway. Now on second reading the sensa-
> tion has entirely gone. But how deep these feelings go and sit! And
> on analysing it I realised that never for one moment have I had the
> same reaction about Joan (although in some ways there would
> have been more reason!). But even the idea of your standing in this
> place of 'crime and punishment' and reliving the past made me
> feel lost – curious, considering that I am a comparatively rational
> human being (or am I flattering myself?). Actually, and looking at
> it objectively, I find the scene quite moving and beautiful and
> worthwhile writing a story about one day.
>
> … Strangely enough, I've never in all these 10 years felt quite
> so married to you, or perhaps better quite so much your wife as I
> do now and as a result I feel very happy.

Before leaving London for France Jimmy discovered that on his
father's death he and his brother Peter were each to inherit $80,000
(£20,000) 'which sum would bring us an annual income (at 4%) of
around £800 a year ($3,200). That, it seems to me, if not magnificent,
would be very pleasant indeed! … my darling, we may have a little
house & some peace & a garden yet!'

On 10 June he wrote again to Tania from Germany, complaining
that Auden was 'selfish and domineering': 'Wystan has turned as anti-F
as he is anti-R. I sometimes find him very stupid. His reactions are so
quick, so impulsive & he's always so convinced by his quickly acquired

prejudices, which he tries to make others accept as facts – and very often succeeds.'

On 19 June, with reference to his love affair with Joan Lewisohn, he wrote to his wife again: 'I had got over her completely, but I guess the experience, terrible as I know it was for you, poor darling, was good for me – and perhaps even necessary, up to a point.'

Tania, who was dividing her time between their Manhattan apartment and Fire Island that summer, replied:

> My ego doesn't seem to need any longer the affirmation which goes with teaching and helping other people ... Apparently this old ego has been mysteriously saturated or at least is completely satisfied with being needed by you (which I hope I am!) and perfectly willing to retire into private life and inconspicuousness. The only thing I seem to be day-dreaming about (as one always seems to do about something) is a quiet life anywhere in the world with you, with time to read, perhaps to translate, to cook – in one word to *live*.

That July Tania stayed near Woodstock in Vermont with an entirely German-speaking household, while also hobnobbing with Dorothy Thompson, a friend of Jean Stafford, and the novelist Sinclair Lewis – a 'very degenerate, loudmouthed and badly brought up young man'. In another letter she wagged a reproving finger at her husband: 'The only thing I can't refrain from warning you about are my two bogies: sleep and drink – by which I mean I would like you to have as much as possible of the one and the rest you know!'

Malcolm Cowley (1898–1989)[7] had postulated some interesting ideas in a letter to Jimmy of 6 May 1945 from Gaylordsville, Connecticut:

> It's no use for one guy to try to pass on an idea to another guy – but there's a novel I wish somebody would write, and you could do it better than anybody else. It's the novel about the French and/or German literary exiles in New York since the war, their cliques, their literary and political quarrels, their love affairs, their passport difficulties, their doubts (in case of the Germans) about what country they belong to and what language they're going to

7 Cowley, a critic and literary historian, was literary editor of *The New Republic* from 1929 to 1944. His book, *Exile's Return* (1934), described the lives and work of the illustrious group of American writers who congregated in Paris after the First World War.

use – the ones who fling their arms around American business and make their thousands (like Willy Schlamm), the ones who starve as tutors or whatnot (usually the best of them), the Surrealists and their millionaire friends – not all the picture, for nobody could do that, but some one story picked out of it. None of the French or the Germans could write it himself, because they're either superficial or brutalized by their experiences or too full of self-pity, but you know them and still are completely outside them. Most people can't write good fiction about what is happening now, but the task isn't impossible – Scott Fitzgerald turned the trick more than once, but especially in *The Great Gatsby*.

And another, much smaller thing I wish you'd write, just as a duty. When you get to London, if you have any free time at all, I wish you'd dash off something for some English paper about what's happening to the literary world in the U.S., for apparently the connections between the two countries have been pretty well broken. Tell 'em at least Swarthmore isn't a boys' prep school, as somebody described it in *Horizon*. Tell 'em about the publishing boom, occurring at a time when almost nobody is writing good books; it's a dead point for letters. Tell 'em about Jeannie Connolly in the dining room in the inn at Amenia, in shorts and bra – and the beautiful countryside with lots of kitchen machinery and bathrooms but no such thing as a servant, so that people have a hard time meeting. This is still a lonely and non-gregarious country... Actually what has happened here is that the inter-war generation has dominated things for a long time, and now there's a sort of interregnum, while people look around for something new and don't find it – when they rake up a new literary hero, like Katherine Anne Porter, it's one of our old friends who simply didn't write much in the 1920s, though she batted around with the rest of us. There's a process of stock-taking and literary excavation going on, a great deal of scholarship being applied to the American literary past on the new theory that it composed a separate literature – maybe you don't hear so much about that, but it's a biggish movement, and even if it is in the hands of college professors, mostly, they are more intelligent than American professors used to be...

And finally, I wish you'd write me one letter from England or Germany. I ought to have talked to you about this on Saturday, but it slipped my mind. I have to write a long piece on American literature abroad since 1900, and I haven't got the data. Could you ask a couple of people for me – in England (and in France and Germany if you get the chance) – what American books they continued to read, what American authors they valued, and why – and scribble off a page or two to me? I'd be very grateful...

It wasn't until Jimmy had returned to America (on V-J Day, 15 August 1945) that he wrote at length from Fire Island a month later in reply to Cowley:

You may not remember that you wrote me a very good letter on May 6. This letter has haunted me ever since. I have it in front of me. I often had it in front of me in Germany, but I can only trust you will believe me when I tell you that I was never able to sit down & write a letter from that country – a letter, that is, that required thought, such as an answer to yours did.

Actually, to answer your letter properly is next to impossible. We would have to talk – for hours or rather you would have to ask questions & I would do my best to answer them. (I have been put through this kind of thing ever since I left Germany, naturally – & I am rather tired, & very depressed & very depressing: but it does depend a great deal to whom one talks, & it would be a pleasure to talk to you. So let us arrange a meeting next month in New York, unless of course you feel that by now, or then, you have nothing more to ask!)

Let me tell you now, anyway, the (to me) very depressing news that I am not allowed to publish a word of any knowledge I gained of Europe while working for the United States Strategic Bombing Survey. So that's that. You probably want to know what I did in Germany. We were only in Bavaria & Hessen. The cities & towns I can tell you most about are Frankfurt (where the Germans call the undamaged I.G. Farben – AMG H.Q. – the 'Phariseen Ghetto'!), Munich, Nürnberg, Heidelberg, Darmstadt (93% destroyed a year ago this week; the one raid lasted 28 minutes and killed 21,000 people), Erlangen (unbombed) & Kempten (almost unbombed). I spent the entire day, every day, interviewing Germans – the 'Man in the Street' – picked in the good old American way: by 'random sample'! Each interview lasted from 1½ to 3 hours, & each had to be fully written up before the day was over. I interviewed 90 men & women between the ages of 16 and 80. When the day was over I usually went in search of liquor – any kind of liquor – usually in the rain. Then I took photographs, & wandered about in the ruins. Then, on our own, we held long, long interviews with what is left of the intelligentsia (they took some finding), professors, doctors, a *very* occasional writer, a psychiatrist, a whore, a cheese-maker (who recited to me by heart the most famous poem in Germany today. I refuse to tell you what it is, because that is a story in itself!) & an odd publisher (Piper Verlag, Georg Callwey, both in Munich) still existing, but almost unfindable, in one room in the midst of the unbelievable chaos of the once beautiful city. All that is left of Munich are the towers of the Frauenkirche (which will probably collapse after the first frost) and the monstrosities that Hitler built – Der Haus der Deutschen Kunst & the Führerbau – which are untouched. In Nürnberg only the towers of the Lovenzkirche & the medieval towers survived... Auden found one good young novelist & poet, near Munich. Aged 30 he had fought 3 years in Russia & written an unpublished novel about it. Auden felt sure it was good, but couldn't get out the MS. Ernst Wiekert, who gained great respect in 1934 and 1938 for two brilliant anti-Nazi speeches, continued to write novels which I believe are not at all good but which sold all through the war & in tens of thousands. He wrote, for us, a third anti-Nazi speech (not yet delivered while we were there, simply because there was no audience to whom he could deliver it) which I found rather embarrassing; but one doesn't know – the average German is in such a terrible state of confusion, hopeless-ness, helplessness, that it is very possible what would embarrass us would give them the lift from utter dejection they so badly need.

The average German/ Bavarian asks only two questions; & in this order:

1) When are we going to get more to eat?

2) When are the Russians coming?

By now there will be a third question:

3) How are we going to get through this winter without freez-ing to death?

Can you answer any of these? I couldn't. Quite intelligent Germans – well, let us say Germans who want to know of the world outside their own country – read every *word* (Germans, of course, always read every word!) of America's super-bestsellers. I spent two hours in the library of a doctor in Kempten. He was a man of 50 who had himself written a dozen of what the Germans call '*Unterhaltungfs-novelle*', the greatest expert at which he considered, no doubt quite rightly, Vicki Baum. He had also written essays, short stories, even a movie-script. He was a modest man & never showed me even one of his efforts. But what he did show, with great pride, was his collection of books by American writers. It included every super bestseller you have ever heard of, as well as a number of the products of what the Germans call (without the trace of a smile) the '*Hartgenossene Schule*'! – all in translation, of course. Steinbeck (*Grapes of Wrath* [1939]) is in the shelves of all those who read modern translations, Erskine Caldwell, Hemingway (*For Whom the Bell Tolls* [1940], ditto) *et al.* Towards the end of our talk he disappeared & came back beaming, holding in both hands a volume so huge, so reverently wrapped in what looked like a velvet covering, that I presumed, for a moment, he was about to quote from the Bible. Instead he sat down & said: '*Mein gute Freund*, it was not until I had read *this* book' (here he stroked it as though it were his own new-born baby) 'that I realised I knew nothing about America. Ah, if only you Americans would write one or two more books like this one. I am now reading it for the second time & at last I am beginning to know what your country is like.' The book (as you may have already guessed) was *Gone mite ze Vind* [1936]. And he was an admirer of Rilke, expressed a great admiration for both Manns.

Even *highly* intelligent Germans, however, know next to nothing of American literature. They have not *heard* of Hermann Melville. (The Irish? Ah, that's different—weren't Yeats & Shaw played in Munich theatres thoughout the war? – A nice touch: The last opera (August '44) to be performed in Nürnberg was the *Götterdämmerung* & the last play *Much Ado about Nothing*).

Dear Malcolm: I have now scribbled you half a dozen sides of paper at random and have not answered one question in your letter. American literature abroad since 1900? Perhaps I have half-answered this re Germany. Re France I couldn't have (I was in Paris for one day, by far the saddest day of my life). Re England I *should have*, but my stay there was so hectic I just didn't. But I still can. Is there time?

In spite of his statement that he was not allowed to publish 'a word

of any knowledge I gained in Europe', on Fire Island he applied himself
to the writing of *The Hidden Damage*.

On 20 December Jimmy cabled Malcolm Lowry, having read *Under
the Volcano*, which was to be published the following February:
'*Hombre* am lying under the volcano consumed with excitement jealousy gratitude and indescribable praise. Hasta la vista. Saludo amigo.'
To which Lowry replied the next day: 'It was lovely of you to wire me
so generously your appreciation of *The Volcano*, which wire I received
with delight this morning and I can't say how much it meant to me.'

From Djuna Barnes, on 24 June 1946:

How wretched of you not to drop me a line! Here I am sweltering
in June with much mental concern. For one, Laurence Vail has
been cut off 'with a month's notice like a chamber maid' (which is
31 days more than I was once given); secondly, I understand that
Peggy [Guggenheim] is suffering from a disease known as lucemia
(if that is the way one spells it) which I'm now told is fatal within
2 or 3 years – this because T. S. Eliot's brother has the same thing
– apparently a sort of galloping anaemia. I hope it's not true in any
of the two cases. A greater concern is T. S. E. himself. He looks so
worn & tired & thin & troubled, naturally, about his brother. I
am wondering if any one on earth is doing anything for him, his
comfort & his health – knowing the world, I feel not. I was so
happy to see him ...

... At the moment am feeling ghastly having been out last night
with Laurence & his wife. I called him before I heard of his bad
news, not quite able to let him sail after his efforts to make up.

I'm still of the same opinion of his weak character, but I'm sorry
for his own destruction – we all make one kind or another, & even
a noble one is as painful as one can bear ...

... Mad creatures continue to write me or call – being known is
very overestimated. The whole blasted world is falling apart.

Jimmy replied from Fire Island the next day:

I pray you are an alarmist, at least to some extent. I was so horrified by your letter that – knowing Laurence was leaving tomorrow
– I called him from the pub an hour ago. I got 'his wife'. She
seemed remarkably calm. The money business is apparently not a
very new story. During the 24-hours I was in town last week, I saw
them both – and neither mentioned it, although the story was not

new then. In fact, Laurence talked at length about six-figure sums of money he was going to inherit from his mother. There, I guess, is the rub. Though why Miss G. [Peggy Guggenheim] should have chosen just this moment to act I really don't know. Anyway, Laurence's wife's reaction was expressed in these words: 'Well, you know, I can understand her point of view; after all, I've done it myself!' Rather nice, I thought, considering ...!

As for Miss G's disease, she said: 'I wouldn't take that too seriously. In my opinion, there's a good deal of chi-chi about that!'

You are certainly justified in accusing me of not having 'dropped a line'. It's no good my telling you how often I've been on the point of doing so, especially since I had dinner with T. S. Eliot on the evening of the day you invited us. (That was why we came into town; Auden had invited us.) It was an experience. Surely no more charming, more modest man ever lived. You are indeed fortunate to have such a man for a friend and admirer. I cannot remember ever having been so impressed by a first meeting – all the more wonderful because I had expected a great deal. And the marvel! The greatest expectations would have been satisfied.

I had no idea, of course, about his brother. Tania, by the way, says this disease is NOT fatal, that there has lately been discovered, she is almost sure, a cure. But I won't try to write of it until I know more.

You say you are wondering if anyone on earth is doing for T. S. E. I really don't think you have to worry about what the English call his 'creature comforts'!

He is staying, to begin with, at Frank Morley's, to which the Ritz is a Gaelic cabin in comparison. As T. E. said: 'The living-room is so vast you can't see the ceiling; everyone avoids it like the plague.' God knows, that sounds dismal enough, but – well, comfortable. Secondly, he is, after all, not in a strange country. I should imagine, though he complained as little of this as of anything else, that his greatest trouble would be in refusing the offers of those who would sell the shells of their souls (presuming they had lost long ago what once may have been in them) to have him sit for five minutes on their only chair.

From Djuna Barnes on 18 July 1946:

I should, but don't know better than write when I am worried.

op:
...tive

...ove:
...nnie Stern

Right:
Harry Stern

above:
Jimmy and Reggie

left:
Reggie, Leila
and Jimmy

Jimmy at Eton

Below:
Jimmy 'guiding'
British tourists,
Victoria Falls,
Rhodesia, 1926

Right:
Brian Howard,
Frankfurt am Main,
1927

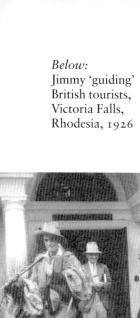

Reggie Stern

Peter Stern

Sir John Squire
and Jimmy
watching the Lord
Mayor's Show from
the *Mercury* office,
1931

Tania and Jimmy
on their
wedding day,
9 November 1935

Above:
Joan Crowell

Below
Tania and Jimmy,
Manhattan,
November 1942

Right:
Jimmy,
Manhattan,
1940s

W. H. Auden
and Jimmy,
Bad Nauheim,
Germany, 1945

Tania and
W. H. Auden,
1945

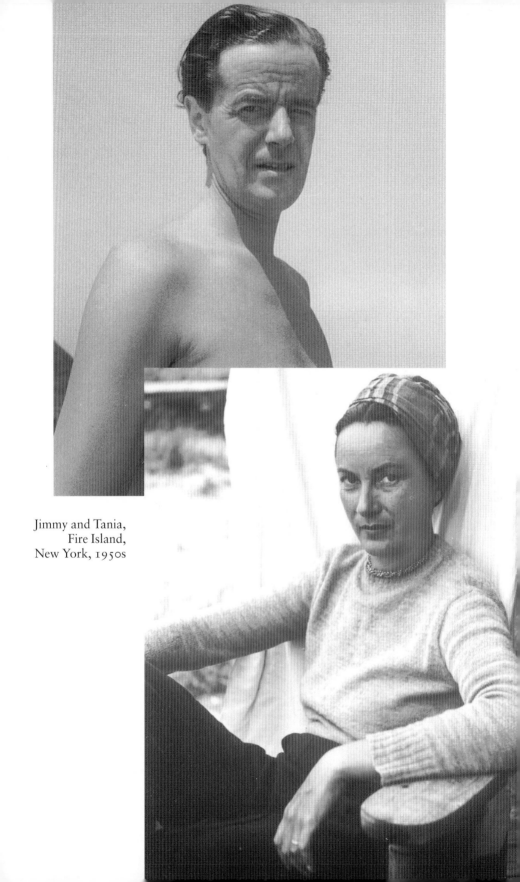

Jimmy and Tania,
Fire Island,
New York, 1950s

I am glad you like T. S. E. I think everyone does, thank goodness, it proves that there is something in human nature that can recognize an honourable man.

And thank you my dear for asking me to come & see you & Tania ... also were I not quite mad I'd come, but as I've said before, no one has ever been happy to have me Period.

Did I tell you that I've a 'sort' of job with Holt, reading manuscripts – entirely due to the kindness of Mr [Allen] Tate, to whom, I am ashamed to say, I've been rather grim, merely because he is so dashed American – calling me by my first name in 2 minutes, & asking himself & wife to my room to see my painting, how he knew anything about it is beyond me – I am too nervous for such immediacy.

If you really want to know how it is with me – extremely nervous, due to fear, a new job – something I've not had for a million years, the arrival at the same time of Mr Eliot, my respect for him & my terror of Time – we have not seen each other for some years – the knock at my door by Emily Coleman & the long emptiness of Summer days, when you sense, tho you never see anyone anyway, tho the city is empty & you are alone with your vitamins & your vertigo & your personal history.

I've been writing slowly crouched in ambush. And you? And the book? *And* are you getting a bit of health there in spite of everything?

As for Laurence [Vail], darn him, if, as you say, he is inheriting something in 6 figures – that's a frightful fist of money, I can't believe it. That poor lump of a wife he had got for himself – it's such a blasted compromise, but then he always has walked out on difficulty – if perchance there be no God, it would seem to pay, he has about everything in sight, including a black bitch dog.

5
'The Hidden Damage'
1946–1950

The winter of 1946–7 was a terrible one; the snow fell ceaselessly from Christmas until late March. While Tania remained in New York City to work, Jimmy lived alone in Lewis Mumford's house in Connecticut. With not a friend within thirty miles, he talked to no one but a much-loved cat. The temperature dropped to 25 degrees below zero and milk froze in the bottle. Tania, the breadwinner trapped in the city, was afraid that he would be lonely and would start to drink, so she asked their artist friend from Germany, Vita Petersen, to go up and stay with him, which she did, taking her six-year-old daughter Andrea. In the early mornings the child watched Jimmy shaving and both would be amused by the streaks he would make with his cut-throat razor down the white mask of his soapy face. When it snowed, Andrea and Jimmy threw snowballs at each other. At weekends Tania would come to stay, and at Christmas the two German expatriates decorated the Christmas tree and became nostalgic for the ceremonies and traditions of their mother country, feeling like conspirators in a secret rite. Jimmy found the two women ridiculous and would take no part in their festivities.

On 6 January 1947 Jimmy wrote to Malcolm Lowry:

In a hot confusion of guilt, my dear Malcolm, a confusion of guilt! And before I tread another step, the top of the morning to you and, a trifle belatedly, the tiptop of the year. By all the stars and portents, it should be propitious for the Novelist: does it not close with a seven on its rump, its four digits add up to vingt-et-un, its as yet pubic-hairless little body beautifully divisible by the magic number three!

To fla – fall, I mean – flatly into platitudes, my honored & talented friend, thank you for your card, your seasonable greetings, your warmth of expression (which you still wear like my Papa, the Major, his military moustache), for remembering so unfailingly one of my early *contes*, and finally for encountering, in some typically Malcolmian manner, one of my latest (according to this city's *Times*) 'delightful Irish lullabies' – God rot the reviewer's wretched little soul!

Since my telegram of cheers hardly a night has passed, need I tell you that I have not dined out, and wined out and thought myself into alcoholic slumbers on the *Volcano*. ('Oh tell us, tell us, Jimmy Stern, what's he *like*? – 'Oh you moronic miseries you, you and you, by their works shall Great Men be known! Read and get thee hence! A flea's phart could be heard further than your loudest scream!')

O friend, am I to write you a book about your epic? Have patience, and have my love, you have done a mighty deed. Praise and damnation will ring in your ears, and you will live. By the highest standards you deserve to be judged, but that will not be your lot, for there are not more than two or three in 140 million competent. And of these I, alas, am not one. I am the tired salmon, a worn and scraggy fish, making fishy-goggle eyes at the moby-blubber blunderer, the Whale. The skinny salmon swoons and makes his little leaps, the Whale squirts, rolls, belches, moans and groans and finally, with one horrendous subterranean phart, moves a mountain, an inch.

From Jimmy to Djuna Barnes on 26 February 1947:

You probably don't know how perfect you were yesterday, how I admired your poise & patience, & in what fear & trembling I was before our arrival. The presence of the beer was miraculous, for without something things get pretty bad. I'd had him [Malcolm Lowry] six hours (on one beer myself!) wandering all over New York. To get him past a pub you had to think up a certain thing to say, to change that thing every time you know another pub is coming, then say it quick. And he has to be kept on the move. It was his fourth day & night of drinking, & the stories he told you I had heard maybe a dozen times, never a word altered. Since noon yesterday he had had a Scotch, Bourbon, beer, red wine, Bourbon, Scotch, beer, a bottle with you, 'my' sherry, & later at Auden's a tumblerful of brandy & then a minute or two with a gallon of claret out of the spout. On the way 'home' he insisted on buying two gallons of burgundy to take up to his hotel room, & on the way another Scotch because he remembered that it was after six & that that is when I have a drink. Just as I'd got the drink to my mouth, he said in great trepidation: 'Oh, I say, old fellow, should you! I mean, don't let me lead you astray!'

Sometimes he makes me laugh more than anyone in the world. Other times – and you never know when they are coming – he puts the fear of God into me. He's stronger than an ox. Two nights before, it took me two hours & a great deal of my precious sedative to calm him down & prevent him breaking up his room, while his wretched wife sat trembling in the next room.

Well, all this just to thank you and explain my gratitude. I have a most unusual affection for that guy.

From Jimmy to Malcolm and Margerie Lowry on 25 March 1947:

This morn the snow came falling, Jamesy Joycey, and I thought of you, and there was your welcome nosey-nosey. Hurroops and hurrah that all's well.

… Brentano's window is bursting with the third edition of the *Volcano*. A fake *Kunstgewerb* piece of 'Mexican' cloth hangs down from the ceiling: *Kunstgewerb* (Hart and Craft, old boy) watah colours of Kakakopapetl hang on the walls, whence a Niagara of Lowry foams down to the glass, where, so that a hooded nun could read (I stood next her, but she said nowt to her fellow magpie), a Volcano lay on its face, bottom up, with a dozen extracts of reviewage, as I say, readable, eggstatick. 'He's ma friend!' said I to the nun, but Nun, she gimme a cold convent look.

From Jimmy to Djuna Barnes on 18 April 1947:

… I can quite imagine that you won't know what to say about *The Hidden Damage*, which is why I don't like giving it to friends to read. Reading it of their own accord is quite another matter. It was a chore, a pot-boiler in the sense that I did have to get it off my chest & I did have a good 'advance'. If I'd had $100 a month for the next 5 years (or rather, for my lifetime!) I think I could have written a good book on that subject, even a minor work of art. As it is, it's a self-indulgent hotch-potch in which there is too much about the not very interesting past of the author. But the *personal* technique was my only hope. I'm not a journalist.

PS. Please remember us to T. S. E.

PPS. *Please* look after yourself: I think you had better get a damned telephone.

From Jimmy to Djuna Barnes on 23 April 1947: '... Sorry you don't like the book at all, but I had a good laugh when I got over the initial shock. So in keeping, dear. There's no one like you – thank God!'

After nearly a decade in America, the Sterns became restless for Europe. In the spring of 1947 they rented their apartment in New York for the summer to Christopher Isherwood and his friend Bill Caskey. The two men learnt from Auden that they were being charged in excess of what the Sterns themselves were paying for it. Perhaps Jimmy calculated that the long-established and surely affluent scriptwriter and novelist from Hollywood could well afford it.

So they returned to Europe many times, until in the late '50s they spent a trial period of two years in various rented accommodation before making the final break with the United States.

From Gerda Mosse's house in Hampstead, on 15 May 1947, Jimmy wrote to Malcolm Cowley:

Have you heard that publication of *The Hidden Damage* has been postponed *again* – until June 5? And that the price has been jacked up from $3.50 to $4? Aren't these two facts enough to kill the book? H.B. [Harcourt Brace, Jimmy's publisher] sent me a copy by air-mail ($7.20 postage!). I was agreeably surprised by the paper, but the photograph on the jacket has made everyone here swoon. They are convinced it's a bad joke on my part.

...London this week has been a dream. The sun came out, & the lilacs, chestnuts, tulips, laburnum, bluebells leapt into glorious bloom. The soft voices, the quiet, & the *friendliness* of friends & the man in the street are overwhelming. We eat too much, all at the expense of other people. I'm just going to have lunch with Peter Watson (proprietor of *Horizon*), Frank Taylor (now at Random, as you probably know) & John Davenport, from whom I expect to hear all about Conrad Aiken. I will make every effort to see him. Had dinner with Tom Hopkinson, who was charming.

Going to a party for Thomas Mann on Monday. Shaw was invited. His reply: 'Sorry, too old to go so far. GBS.'

From Malcolm Cowley, Gaylordsville, Connecticut on 26 May:

Yes, I heard about the delay in publication of *The Hidden Damage*. That meant I didn't have to submit my review to the *Times* until last Thursday, May 22. I wrote about 1600 words and Hutchens said he thought he could front-page it – I do hope so, for I like the book and want it to get a break ... But you'll see what I wrote, in time, and I hope you like it; the publishers will, anyway.

If I'd been editing the book ... I'd have wanted you to omit the first and last chapters (although both are good) and put in more and more Germans. And, to continue the criticism, there are two stories where I'd have wanted you to make the point clearer – the one about the doctor's wife who cut her throat (why?) and about the two GIs who landed in the cemetery (why did the ?lover? shoot the husband?). I think you sometimes make your stories too brief at the very climax of them; but they're wonderful stories – and that's what you wrote on Germany, a collection of stories about people.

The following day, from his parents' house in Henstridge, Dorset, Jimmy wrote to Djuna Barnes, who had lived in London and Paris and was acquainted with some of the Sterns' friends there:

... We were entertained twice by Tom Hopkinson [editor of *Picture Post*] in his enchanting Queen Anne house in Chelsea – the first time with whisky *before* dinner & Champagne *at*! I like them both, though they are of a type a little strange to me. They belong to the middle & coming class. A little too bourgeois for the likes of this old rake. He *dresses* so well & is so hellish polite; & she, while charming, is somehow very hostessy. I felt a little out of place & rather as though I were among my Elders & Betters. None of this is *quite* fair; I would not say it to anyone but you – partly because I know you'll know what I mean & won't repeat it. Second time was a real Party – what they call 'Cold Buffet Supper' with guests divided at tables in different rooms & a weak punch to drink, mostly globs of pineapple. I sat between Tom & a terribly *polite* English lady, wife of an actor called, I think, Raymond Miles – or something like that. And opposite Feliks Topolski's wife, an Irish hussy whom I met here in '45. After dinner I spent an hour with Antonia White, who talked far too much (for me) about Emily C. [Coleman].[8] I gathered (after I'd

8 Emily Holmes Coleman, an American novelist and poet, was Antonia White's best friend, and a friend, too, of Djuna Barnes and Peggy Guggenheim. She was converted to Catholicism by Jacques Maritain and, while in England between 1953 and '58, developed religious mania.

put my atheistic foot into it too many times) that she is a 'staunch' Catholic. I quite liked her, but again I couldn't quite see you & her together. And again she was all dressed up in long skirts & looking very matronly. Altogether it was too grand, without being in the least grand, for me. Middle class is the only way I can describe it. And their accents were all slightly off. Sounds horribly snobbish of me, don't it! Can't help it. I can't say I felt at home, though I'm very grateful to the Hopkinsons & feel rather embarrassed that they made such an effort.

England looks much too beautiful for anyone coming from & returning to America. This country at every glance is Ruisdael & Constable & Turner at their best. The world is velvet green & the trees of an indescribable loveliness. You just stare & itch to be able to paint. I sit surrounded by flowers – lilac, clematis, tulips, roses – listening to the cuckoo & the dreadful row of distant peacocks. It is all timeless & terrible – that one has to turn one's back on anything so sublime. But that is something which you probably cannot understand.

The two weeks in London were the most hectic I ever spent – partly because we slept miles away in Hampstead & never had anywhere to close an eye in by day. I never realised I had so many friends. The largest number at one time I met at Thomas Mann's party, given by Secker & Warburg at the Savoy. I had forgotten that I ever knew such an adorable old umbrella as Rose Macaulay & would have sniggered if anyone had told me she was alive & that she still wore a man's cap dated 1904. Lady Colefax looks like a painted coffin on crutches. Tom Driberg has several hairs in the middle of his cranium. Tom Mann, aged 72, looked as young as most.

I saw that you were among those at tea with Eliot. Do write to me about it.

Djuna Barnes replied on 1 June 1947:

What a delightful letter & glad to hear at last. Eaten up with fury to hear others had word & I had not one!

I was afraid you would be disappointed with Tom Hopkinson. I said as much as you probably recall. He's nice & correct &, I found, dull – I can't stand Tony [Antonia] – I warned you! We call her Queen Victoria of Surbiton or however you call that suburb – your description of the 'party' sounds even more stuffy than those

I attended, tho no one there ever put on a show like that for me. I do adore polite British people until I get with a group of them like those you mention. You are exactly right, they *are* middle class & bourgeois & well informed & beastly dull...

...Tony *would* rave on about Emily – they are at it 'buttering' each other up – only I do not trust, & you know what I think of Emily of this Season's Vintage – She has seen Peggy [Guggenheim] but told her she did not 'dare' to come to see me – now what's *that* about!

T. S. E. seems older – I am afraid for him – his hands shake & he is too thin. Everyone on earth at The Frick, & his spell worked again. E. E. Cummings acted ruffled & silly – drawing caricatures – in audience dancing up Park Avenue. To the Clapps [for] tea as if tight – which he was not – all because he can't stand the spot-light turning. Eliot was tall & [indecipherable word] & polite, balancing a tea cup & a small slice of cake—mine, while A. Roberts & Georgia O'Keefe stood, one reading & the other remarking (why are people nervous?) 'I think I am the *only* person in the room who *can't* read.'

Two days before the above letter, Jimmy had written to Malcolm Cowley from Ernst Freud's house in Walberswick:

It's a strange sensation, four days after you wrote me your charming letter in Gaylordsville, to be answering it in a thatched cottage in an English village on the North Sea. From where I sit, surrounded by hawthorn, iris & lilac, I can see the miles of rusty 'scaffolding' & barbed wire put up waist-deep in the waves in 1940 to keep out the approaching barbarians. At that time the bombing of Rotterdam shook the timbers of this ancient cottage. This I would not have believed, had not Ernst Freud (architect son of Sigmund & father of Lucian, the boy who painted the picture of the 'Rose' in 207 [East 57th Street]) been here at the time. The beach, still ruined by the aftermath of war, is strewn with pieces of planes, both British & Nazi. The contrast between this coast & the inland parts of Somerset (where my people live) is remarkable: in the latter place the only sign of war I saw during many miles of travel was a single man on a road. On the left cheek of his arse was painted a large white P and on the right a large W. 'Poor devil,' said my father. He would not have said that 25 years ago.

…Yes, you are right, of course: I went to Germany subconsciously to find 'Good Germans'. You are also probably right about the first & last chapters. I particularly dislike the first; yet there are things in it which I don't see how could be left unsaid – 'the guilt of the unbombed, uninvaded,' my brother, Paris etc. I somehow had to identify myself, you see. Who am I, after all?

I was interested by what you said of the two stories without solutions, the mystery stories, as I call them. The cemetery story is my favourite in the whole book. That is exactly how it happened, how I heard it. I have five different solutions to that story, & if I were a novelist I could imagine writing five different novels about it. The *New Yorker* wanted, almost implored me to tie up some of the knots. I couldn't. Or wouldn't. For me it would have spoiled everything. As it stands, it is *life* and probably no one knows, or ever will know the truth, for probably no one is alive to tell it. What I like to think is that the two boys had a subconscious homosexual relationship, & that when the Negro said: '… they were always together. That's how it gets some guys…', he half knew, had half solved the mystery. Those words are the only clue I allowed myself to offer the reader.

As for the doctor's wife having her throat cut, or cutting her own throat, I again don't know. Maybe the doctor does. What I believe is that she went once a week (20 years ago) to Frankfurt to her lover (that much, I hoped, was clear), and that one day, years later, that lover threw her over for another woman, & that she, rather than seek him out & maybe murdering him, paid him back by committing suicide with *his* razor in *his* apartment in his absence! To me that sounded like her & quite like life. But again I don't know, & all through the book I was trying my utmost to tell only what I saw, heard, & knew. That's the trouble with 'non-fiction'.

When on 5 June 1947 *The Hidden Damage* was published in New York, having been turned down in London by Secker & Warburg and John Lehmann, who had started his own publishing house, one of the most gratifying reviews to Jimmy was that by his mentor Malcolm Cowley, on the front page of *The New York Times Review of Books*:

One of the world's best short story writers turns his brilliant powers on a section of gutted Europe … His moving account of the people he knew, his search for them, is far more interesting and illuminating than any amount of statistics; though the statistics are here too, and in a highly sinister and concentrated form. In brief, there is much in *The Hidden Damage* of value to the historian of the future. But it is also an absorbing piece of work, almost as witty and nostalgic, as it is horrible and punishing.

The critic and biographer of Henry James, Leon Edel, wrote in *Partisan Review* that

Stern looked with that extraordinary optic eye of his ... into the abyss with a compassion and understanding that do not minimize the brutal record ... The point is that Stern uses all his senses, instead of just pencil and paper ... It is his greatest success that nowhere is it necessary for him to sum up, to tell you explicitly what the damage is. You see it constantly with him and through his eyes ... You put down the book feeling that you have seen the whole picture ... *The Hidden Damage* lives because it fuses the past with the present and because every page is *felt*.

In *The Commonweal* his friend from Fleet Street days, Anne Fremantle, author of *The Protestant Mystics* (1965), thought that 'the whole, long, complete book is a miracle of understanding ... an overpoweringly impressive book ... What Mr Hersey did for the single bombing of Hiroshima, Mr Stern has succeeded in doing for the whole aftermath of the German war and for the allied occupation – nor could even Tolstoy have done better.'

The very favourable press reactions to *The Hidden Damage* may be marvelled at now, for no 'midlist' book, in publishing jargon, could expect such recognition today.

In June Jimmy received a letter in unstinting praise of his book from his soon-to-be landlord, Lewis Mumford. It was dated 28 May.

It is a long time since we met, and I little suspected, when we finally did meet a few days ago, that you would hold me, with your glittering eye, with miraculously swift descriptions or presentations, with the lilt of a remembered phrase, with your grim insight and your humble self-knowledge, with your unerring eye for the significant little detail and your painter's sense of the overall design – when finally we did meet. Obviously, I have been reading *The Hidden Damage*, and just as obviously I regard it, not merely as a significant piece of reporting but as one of the very best books of imaginative interpretation that has been done in our time. Only a born novelist could have recreated scene upon scene in the fashion you have done and only one who had come to terms with himself could have dealt, in a spirit of such penetrating pity, with the good and the bad that he found in post-war Germany. Even in those few places where I found myself giving a slightly different emphasis or interpretation to the facts that you presented, I respected your own treatment. If this book is read as it should be, hundreds and thousands of readers should come to it; and I know no better preparation for the political decisions that we must make than to have the picture you have painted freshly before us. To those who know Germany it is a useful refresher and corrective of stale reactions; and to those who don't know Germany it is, in addition to being as fascinating as a novel, an essential guide book. I have respected and admired your African short stories; but I doubt if I realized how steadily you have been growing since writing them ...

By chance, Jimmy had written to Mumford just before receiving the latter's letter above. He wrote on 19 June from his old childhood home, Bective, to which, it is supposed, he had been invited by either the Lavins or the house's owner, Charles Sumner Bird. The native had returned.

I have before me a clipping of Harcourt's 'ad' in the *New York Times*, with your statement regarding *The Hidden Damage*. I read it & re-read it, barely able to credit my eyes. I still cannot believe that it is I who can have evoked such words from a man of letters such as you. How can I thank you, what am I to say? How near I came last summer to tearing up the MS. of that book, borrowing the money to return the publisher's advance, I will not tell you! I can only say that this wretched hand that wrote it is powerless to express my gratitude for your generosity.

And the next day another letter to Mumford from Bective:

I had just posted you my wretched thimbleful of gratitude when in came your letter. I never dreamed to get a letter like that from anyone. It makes me feel very humble & proud & thankful to know you, & it almost gives me the urge to go up the road to the 'prisonlike church' which still smells of dust & where the butterflies & flies are still dying on the never-opened windows, & say: 'I'm sorry, forgive, I didn't really mean it; but O Protestantism, do, for God's sake & mine, cheer up!'

I'm so, so glad you mentioned my having 'come to terms' with myself! That's a most penetrating poke, & that, of course, is what the book's about. You're the first to have pointed it out, & I'm so delighted.

Jimmy had sent a copy of *The Hidden Damage* to every member of his family. Uncle Bertie Stern (Sir Albert, KBE, CMG etc), who had so demolished Jimmy on his return from Africa decades before, rang the bell in his South Street, Mayfair house and told his butler to 'take this thing and have it burned in the oven'!

More benign was the reaction from his old *London Mercury* editor, Sir John Squire: 'I was delighted with your book … [it] is absolutely first-class: my intellect respects it, and my heart is warmed by it. Above all, it is human and not party-political.' And Malcolm Lowry wrote from Dollarton, British Columbia, on 16 June:

Just a note to wish you and your book godspeed. I enjoyed *The Hidden Damage* enormously – we both did – and I wrote to Harcourt of Harcourt and Brace of Brace to tell him so. Here's to its great success, from us both!

(The only thing one regretted were the brilliant short stories buried therein, that would have had your unique form and those endings that taste like a good pipe after a pewter tankard of strong Falstaff and a hunk of Cheshire at the Ring O'Bells; but that was what had to be, once you had set out.

But perhaps you only buried them sitting up like the Indians and you will pull them to their feet, and blow new breath into them at some later date when you feel like it.)

Jimmy replied from Bective on 19 June 1947:

Malcolm, you unique, unbelievable old dear! D'you know what you've gone & done? D'you know that before me, in this room from which my infernal loveable [!] old Pop banished me every evening from 1910 to 1922 (because, as he said, 'This room's mine, not yours, see?') there lies a *New York Times* clipping on which your name appears as having the audacity, the decency, the generosity, the thundering thingamebob to say that your old wreck of a pal of 15 years sitting is 'one of the world's best short story writers'! There, before me & under the rheum-sodden eyes of the old bay mare at my elbow (not the wife, old man, but a real mare on four legs, grazing at the moss on what used to be the most perfect tennis court in the County Meath) there stand the words in the *boldest* of black print on a page of Yankee making & less than a week old – an infant-in-arms of a page a-sucking at his bottle (of Guinness) & squinting at me with the wryest of Third Avenue smiles. 'Take a deep breath & pull at your belt', it bids me, 'and offer up a word of gratitude to the Almighty that Malc's in Vancouver & yourself in your native land!' The idea being, I presume you will understand, that were we together, by the end of the week there'd be no Power's or Jameson in Ireland, & only bones & what remains of our tuskies left to ourselves. My hat, sir, my stick & gloves, sir – my gratitude, & my eternal affection, my Guinness, to you & Margie.

On succeeding days, 20 and 21 June, again from Bective, he wrote to Malcolm Cowley and Djuna Barnes. To Malcolm Cowley:

I have your review and needless to say I was mighty pleased and grateful: for the place it got in the paper, the length of it and for what you said. I particularly liked the third paragraph, and the first should give the publishers some quotes. Talking of quotes, I've just got Harcourt's first 'ad' in the *Times*. I've had to read it several times to believe my eyes! Well, a little embarrassing though it is, it's mighty nice to have some friends. Mighty good of Mumford. At least I know that did not come from a nostalgic past, from memories of memorable days & nights in our cups in distant lands! As for Lowry, he never was one for moderation, even in print. It would be a queer thing indeed if I were able to pay a few debts with this book. But I suppose I'd better not think in those terms at this date. So glad you quoted the bit about the woman in the Nürnberg ruins.

Having read the book, you will probably recognise this house's name. The sensation of sitting in this room ... is stranger & more complicated than many experiences of 1945. It's strange to gaze out of the enormous windows, at an old mare grazing on the moss where in 1912 I first learned to play tennis on a perfect court. And it's strange to meet a very old man sitting on the side of the road, and to be greeted with outflung arms: 'Ah, Masther James, 'tis here you is at last. Welcome home!' And to realise that he'd heard of my coming and had been sitting there from dawn to dusk for three days. This particular man was with my father in the Boer War. 'I've still ten years in front of me', he said, 'to be gazin' at the folly of mankind.' I hope he has. He still sleeps sitting up in a chair, dressed, 'to be ready should anyone want a doctor in the night'. He has no teeth and lives on bread and Guinness.

To Djuna Barnes:

Dearest Djuna: Thanks for your good letter and please forgive the time I've taken to answer. You must also forgive me making this short, for I'm suddenly inundated with rather important mail about the Dreary Damage – foreign rights, agents' frantic questions, ('Where are you, for God's sake?') etc etc. Well, thank God I'm here and not in New York. You, darling, seem (I might have known it) the world's only good critic, for from what I've seen of reviews of that infernal book, not to mention alarming quotes from 'private' sources displayed in the publishers' 'ads', all but yourself appear to have found interest in the wretched thing. The adjectives they use, the things they say! Oh bless the star that brought me back to my native land, and bless you for being different from everyone else – ha, and bless them from being different from you. Imagine a world of Djunas! Or even two (Djunas, not worlds!).

    ... It's 25 years since I spent a night here. Everyone is 80 and I'm still 'Masther James' ...

A month earlier Katherine Anne Porter had written to Jimmy from California: 'Dear Jimmy: And dearer by two at least since I read your book. I have rather deep feelings and beliefs about Germany, and what the real trouble is there, and I read almost everything that comes out, and *The Hidden Damage* is so much the best of all there is no comparison... I had rather given up hope that anyone capable of hearing and seeing and writing it down would ever get to that place. Stephen Spender made a brave try ...' To which Jimmy replied on 13 June from yet another address: Delgany, Co. Wicklow:

    ... I am quite overwhelmed by what you say, and *you* will know how grateful. I do hope the wretched book deserves such generous treatment from such a practised master craftsman. I have no idea what to think of it myself. There were not many pages where I felt like myself, very few where I didn't feel Bogies looking over my shoulder, laughing & sneering. An 'I' book is a terrible thing; I hope never again. I forced it out, feeling it was now or never. A whole winter went by with only a couple of stories (the short cemetery piece, and the Pregnant Girl) written. Then, on June 1st, in desperation, with just the summer left for my deadline, I sat down in the shack on Fire Island and wrote the whole thing.

...Ireland depresses me beyond words. A defensive mockery seems about all that's left. Or perhaps it's me. I'd find it hard to live in a country where people simply cannot be *bothered* to blow their noses, not even with a bare finger. I do believe that in the end, to retain your sanity if not to save your soul, you'd be forced to drink, in camera, with priests. The front page of the *Irish Times* shows Mrs Peron shaking the hand of a bowing Franco, and underneath de Valera opening an exhibition of architecture (!) with the Earl of Rosse (at Eton with me!). De Valera even attends *cricket* matches with Lord Dunsany, and a horsy woman in the Dolphin bar denounced the invasion not of the English but of the Jews. I suppose all this is more obvious from afar than it is from here. It's pretty ugly under one's nose, where everyone else thinks it's funny. Lately a sadistic abortionist set up shop in Merrion Square. Only the fact that he tore down the 18th century door and supplanted it with one of chromium got him caught, after 5 years' practice. Not a word in any paper of this story which was told me by an MP in the Dail!

... In the last house we stayed in – that of Joseph Hone, George Moore's and Yeats's biographer – there was no coal, no electricity, no hot water. They had no car, no horse, pony or donkey, no whiskey, 10 cigarettes a day for the whole family and the price of meat higher, eggs as high, as in New York. Also no flour, so what I have looked forward to more than anything, Irish home-made bread, was unobtainable and now but a memory of the Good Old Days during the war.

On 26 July he received another characteristic letter from Djuna Barnes:

... Many things have happened since I last wrote, but have no memory of those I've mentioned and those not. However, had lunch with Peggy just before she left 'forever', and I've never seen so many beautifully packed cases in my life as stood in her chambers. Emily C (why are the waters of the Arno so distant?) along, without my invitation. Peggy looked very vague and black haired, seemed (and said) she was ill. That white blood cell eating the red or vice versa I am sorry to say. Emily looked faded (cat!) and fixed.

She sang snatches of secular music and a pass or two at liturgic as she tripped along Fifty Seventh street remarking, in answer to my report that Eliot seemed very tired and troubled (he has now about a thousand degrees conferred by U.S. Universities, the darling), 'He *wouldn't* were he a Catholic. He'd be gay' – so I take it that all you have to do to enrol in Emily's paradise is to touch up your technique on the viola-de-gamba or what.

On 17 September Malcolm Lowry replied to Jimmy's June letter from Bective:

It was swell to hear from you, twice, from the auld sod and Paris both: you gave no address, and I hesitated to write care of American Express in the Rue Scribe (a good playwright by the way) and now I regret not having done just that. But we gathered you would be back by the 11th, and so I and we arise from contemplation of your gloomy and handsome mug upon the jacket on *The Hidden Damage* – quite indeed the gloomiest I have ever beheld albeit with that part used to be called: character, not to say soul, writ large upon it – to welcome you back.

For ourselves we are riding rather high. I have gone into a kind of Indian wrestler's training to commit a new opus: Margie's book coming out (did you get the copy she had Scribner's send you?) and we have done some short stories in collaboration, both doing good work: at least we are making the effort. One has even gone some distance toward — in your own words – 'purging oneself of one's filthy little fears'. At least we have put a new roof on the house and rise before dawn. It is superb here in the autumn – the only inhabitants, and the tide coming up so high you can dive out of the window into the sea ...

Meantime also we seem to have a spot of cash, for once, thanks to the good Albert [Erskine, Lowry's editor at Reynal & Hitchcock, and sometime husband of Katherine Anne Porter], and subsequent sundry pieces of awesome luck, in fact quite a lot of cash, so this place being really a bit too tough in the winter I had thought to betake Margie and self where it's doubtless even tougher, in short to the place lately vacated by yourself, namely Paris. To which end I wonder if you could give the family any information (we propose to go by freighter, and if possible later shift for a while to Morocco, even look at Italy, before returning here) of this nature: what can you live on in Paris? How far does the franc go or does that matter? Can you live on $200 or does it cost $500? Hotel? Do you have to write for reservations? Is Sylvia Beach still there? Do they demand that you have any set sum of money? General advice. Places to eat, drink, starve; friends alive or dead – or messages to be delivered for yourself, and so forth. Can you get an extension in France on the three-month tourist visa procured here? Are tourists in general frowned upon? What not to do: Chesterfieldian council. We both have the status of landed Canadian immigrants so we do not come under the English ruling that forbids travel; Margie still has American citizenship. Since ironically I don't think I shall be able to go to England, that is, I could, but it might take too long to get out again, how does the ruling against travel affect Englishmen from travelling for business etc? In short anything you can think of, or have the time for. The *Volcano* is coming out fairly soon in France, also Norway, Sweden, Germany, Switzerland and Denmark, so I have a sort of raison d'être for being in Europe: but perhaps it would be a bad idea to mention it.

All our very best love to Tanya – as to Albert, Jim Agee, [Alfred] Kazin, Dawn Powell – not to say Djuna Barnes and the wind-blown Auden – drink a health at the Lafayette – I hope you had a good trip and the very heartiest congratulations on the swell *Hidden Damage* and I hope it is bringing in the pennies likewise – where and under what title do I look for the next? (Do not either, reproach me for liking 'The Force' so much – perhaps if you will examine it again you will see how universal it is. The monotony – the dream – the town that was so much less than its glow – the disillusion, the savage almost creative act of intercourse; a sort of mating with the fissure between the dream and reality. That is a wonderful scene also at the dance, and it remains one of the finest short stories I know, though you have done better, and of course can.)

The mails brought further news and gossip from friends. The following spate of letters illustrates the preoccupations of Jimmy and his close friends.

From Lewis Mumford's cottage in Amenia, Jimmy wrote on 31 October 1947 to Katherine Anne Porter:

... I thought a lot of you while in Paris. I even went as far as the fate of your old house in the Notre Dame des Champs. Zadkine has his name on a studio door there, and a young American told me that an elderly couple now live in that lovely corner behind the faded blue door. It has not been painted since. Have I evoked sad memories? Please forgive. Paris was sad and gay and more beautiful than ever, all at the same time. Had we gone to sleep there in 1937 and woken up in 1947, you could go around for a very long time noticing only these differences; total lack of edible bread, almost total lack of 'vrai café', no cheese, very few taxis (an awful bore when you arrive at a station with baggage, or need to catch a train) and prices for most necessities 10 to 12 times higher. The smallest tip you can give a porter is 50frs – that's an odd sensation for the first few days. A decent room and bath is 500 frs on the Rive Gauche.

I went in search of Sylvia Beach and found her, ran into her in the street – a little vaguer, a little stooped, definitely older, as quiet & christian as ever. She lives at 12, rue de l'Odéon, if you would like to send her a line. I often thought of calling on your translator, but found that Ann Desclos (now known as Dominique Aury, writer) is still where she used to be when she began to translate *The Heartless Land* before the war. As with so many people, I found her by pure chance – yes, by looking through that 'little red address book' and taking a chance. She had translated 'The Man Who Was Loved', which is to appear in the next number of *L'Arche*, edited, I believe, by Gide and Camus. I would have known none of this if it hadn't been for that address book...

... But I cannot care; I am so happy – viz. my address. Can you imagine anything more wonderful! I have a house with a womb – or just a womb. The womb has one room of four walls, each packed from floor to ceiling with books. I have room for guests – oh, I do wish you could be one – (I hope there'll be darned few!) – I have an oil-burner (what magic!), a brand new gas-stove (which I'd have taken for a juke-box had I not known better), two open log fire places, no neighbors, an ancient automobile, 3½ miles from the nearest shop, 100 miles from New York, and fields and cows and hills to stare at. I cannot remember feeling happier. The very day after we arrived back from London – bang! – I ran into Lewis Mumford (hadn't seen him for years, but he wrote me a letter about 'The H.D.' which darned near made me weep): I'd a face as long as from here to you, all because of the prospect of another winter in NY and the knowledge that I CANNOT write a book there. I told him what was wrong, and he loaned me this place for the winter. I've never felt so much like kissing a man with a moustache – I mean, it's the only time I ever have! – My foul Irish superstitious nature, of course, is already raising its hideous head. I keep touching wood and spitting when I see a magpie and wishing the moment I see a black cat cross the road. And T has, or will so manage her work that she can come out long weekends. Oh, it's so wonderful – and to think that three weeks ago we were in London. Life is really worth living if only for its uncertainty. I've been saying that ever since I was a child.

Lewis Mumford, although only nine years older, was a man whom Jimmy respected whilst finding him too much 'the schoolmaster', authoritarian and lacking in humour. Mumford wrote to John Byrne, in August 1974, saying how much he 'admired James Stern's work and have the warmest personal feelings towards him, for some emanation of his personality still haunts this house, where he spent a winter many years ago. (By some miracle of memory & tact, he had replaced on the bench beside my chair the very book I had carelessly left there, months before!)'

Mumford wrote from Hanover, New Hampshire, on 13 November 1947:

> ... At the moment, all my appetites are burgeoning: I act as if I were a young man again, and as if I didn't know that doom hangs over us all. Since nothing that I say or do affects my contemporaries as much as the distant rustle of a skirt would, though I shout from the house tops, it's probably a saving grace, or at least a saving sanity, that my own juices for the moment are flowing so freely and gaily... Even my reading has become wide-ranging again, and very carefree: Chekhov's letters, which are quite wonderful, and Meredith's letters, which are often pretty terrible; and for the first time in my life, I'd almost swear, I have read *The Blithedale Romance* [by Nathaniel Hawthorne, 1852], a novel I never guessed, when I read it as a young man, would hold me as completely enthralled as it did the other day. There is a sort of fine needleworker's delicacy in Hawthorne's prose that my taste at this late date finds very graceful: what George Moore called in one of his Ebury St. Conversations, an almost Greek absence of emphasis ...

To which Jimmy replied from Leedsville, New York, on 21 November:

... How warm and near it made me feel to hear that you are reading Chekhov's letters! Aren't they magnificent! What humanity, what a human-being! If anyone ever taught me anything about writing, it was he ... Alas, I have never read *The Blithedale Romance*. I was brought up in the belief that the Open Air Life is the Only One and that books are things you put in the Guest Room. So I'm ill-read and I'll never catch up now; but what better time & place to try than here & now? I'm in the midst of the strangest assortment: [Johan Peter] Eckermann's *Conversations with Goethe* [1852], [Leonardo] da Vinci's *Notebooks* [1938], and, for breakfast, Gertrude Stein's *Three Lives* [1909]. 'Melanctha' I guess is the best thing she ever did, but the book, for me, doesn't hold up, for all of it is Stein. Why would a German-American family, a German girl from Germany and a half-a-dozen Negroes from the South ALL speak exactly alike? The answer the old girl would have given, I suppose is: A Rose is ALWAYS a Rose!

From Lewis Mumford in Hanover, New Hampshire, on 20 November, a letter which had obviously crossed with Jimmy's:

... I must add one more word, as an older writer to a younger one. All your pains and difficulties, dear Jimmy, are normal to a writer's pregnancy; only trivial books can be written without undergoing them, and I am not sure but that even they exact their toll! For me, the hardest parts of the book are those days when one is not quite sure whether or not it has been conceived: when one is full of discomforts but has no reassuring external evidence of growth: that part and the final days of finishing a manuscript, when one needs one's utmost energy and has spent everything, are the worst. But pain, anguish, and despair, yes, and nausea, are the price of any kind of creation; and in the end one can ask nothing better in life than to get them in *tolerable amounts* ... with an occasional moment of relief or ecstasy to wipe the slate clean.

So I can honestly wish you more power: but not less pain!

Jimmy replied on 2 December:

... last night I picked up yr *Values for Survival* [perhaps *Programme for Survival*, 1946] and read your 'Letters to Germans'. I have read lots of Letters to and from Germans, but I certainly have never read any 'to' letters to compare with these. They are really magnificent, if you will pardon my little salute and handshake. I believe the internationally ignorant of all countries could get more idea of the German character out of these few pages than out of most books published since 1918. It has always been an enormous satisfaction to me that you – the emphasis is on the you – liked the H.D. [*The Hidden Damage*]. But since reading these letters, and learning therefrom your knowledge of the people I was trying to write about, that satisfaction has greatly increased. So has my humility vis-à-vis yourself. I would like to see these letters printed alone, in a kind of pamphlet form, translated into all languages and dropped from the sky over the globe like snow. The letter to Alfons F., with its masterly analysis of the Brothers Mann (and Heavens, how briefly done), is superb. The language into which these letters should first of all be [put] is, of course, German – for Germans in Germany, in their millions, to read.

Lewis Mumford replied from Hanover on 30 January 1948:

Shake hands! I have been going through the same devilish period of frustration that you have encountered, only mine has lasted for the better part of a year. Knowing that it might easily come to you, I had forborne asking about your work. Part of it is normal to all writing. I don't think I have ever written a book without, at some point, wanting to drop it forever or to chuck the manuscript in the fire. As an old hand, older at all events than you, I'd warn you against such counsels of despair: they are the insidious inventions of the devil. He has a way of making one pleased and jubilant about utter tripe; and he often persuades one to treat in the most scurvy fashion the very best outpourings of the spirit. So if you have written at all, cling to what you have written till a better moment comes. One of the things that has made me respect Ignatius Loyola was his counsel never to go through with a decision made in a moment of desolation; but to wait for health, confidence, and clear vision before carrying it out.

Jimmy answered from Amenia on 7 February:

That letter of yours is the most sympathetic & understanding it has ever been my fortune to receive. Coming when it did – at a moment of chronic neurotic lowness – my hands & heart went out to you in deepest gratitude. They still do, & will, for I shall certainly not forget. Though Loyola would no doubt have looked askance at my letter to you, written in 'a moment of desolation', I cannot bring myself to regret it.

But to hear that you, too, have been going through such devilish frustration makes me sad, and, at first, sorry that I should have chosen such a time to express my lamentations. Let us pray that the first bud of spring & the melting of these white mountains will put creative life in us.

I *have* written a little; I even started off quite well. Then things went very badly for Tania in town, & I began to worry, impotently, for her at this distance. That seemed to start the rot. But I don't know. I don't like to blame circumstances, least of all the snow. Deep down I believe that what I am trying to do is too trivial for our appalling time. To be able to write today, it seems to me one needs colossal strength, or rather to feel that what one is trying to say is of great importance.

And this I simply cannot feel. But there is no need to tell you all this. You know it.

An infrequent correspondent, Christopher Isherwood, wrote on 29 October 1948 when he had heard on the Californian grapevine that Alan Paton, the South African author of *Cry, the Beloved Country* (1948) had asked Jimmy to write a film script of the book: 'I'm not surprised Paton wants you to write the movie version of his novel ... I do wish you were here! Would you come if I could get you a job in the Studios?! But I suppose you'd loathe it.' Isherwood was right. To imagine Jimmy in Hollywood is to conceive of the Pope converting to Judaism.

The following year the venerable American Academy of Letters awarded the $1,000 prize for short stories to Jimmy. The other recipients of grants were James Agee, Alfred Kazin and Joseph Campbell. Sixteen years later Lewis Mumford was to become a controversial president of the Academy.

Jimmy was half-way through a long life; this moment could be deemed its crowning point.

The Sterns continued to see Carson McCullers (1917–67) whom they had first met in the early '40s. During the Second World War she was at the height of her powers as a novelist and short story writer. The following are extracts from three touching, lonesome and affectionate but undated letters written from her home, Columbus, Georgia, and from the Yaddo writers' colony in Saratoga, around 1949:

I have written a good many letters to you in my mind. I know I should apologise. It was very wrong of me to have behaved as I did. I should have left the party and gone off somewhere. I knew it well enough. But there was a real reason why I did not want to go home that night. And I just kept staying on, watching you walk around, Tania, and drinking and being in a room with lights and people. I knew perfectly well that I should have gone away. Forgive me ... Jimmy darling, please be well. It makes me very unhappy to think of you being ailing in any way. Do just exactly what Tania says. I love you both very much ...

Are you really coming at Easter? Remember you promised. I look forward to your visit so keenly. Have planned all sorts of little festivals. I will cover the walls of your room with wild-flowers and hunt up a fresh present for you every day. Tania, you are so very beautiful, and so good. And Jimmy, I am fond of you greatly as you know. So please try and come ...

I am getting a divorce [she and her husband Reeves were twice divorced] ... Our marriage has been one long struggle – which both of us were unable to change. I love him deeply – but in a curious way I have always felt as though he were my young and rather mad brother. Both of us have hurt each other. I feel very much alone, and rather lost. But I will be able to work. That I must, otherwise my life would have no point at all. I have finished my Ballad [*The Ballad of the Sad Café*, 1951]. It is a cruel sort of faery tale ... Don't forget me. You know that I think a whole lot of both of you, and being your friend is cherished by me ... Tania, you are the person I dream most about at night – almost every week I dream about you.

On one of their visits to England, Jimmy wrote from the Freuds' house in Walberswick, Suffolk on 23 July 1950 to another of his mentors, Van Wyck Brooks[9]:

> We often think & talk of you these alarming, beastly days & wonder how you are. A week of as near as one can get to peace – in this silent countryside where Crabbe, Edward Fitzgerald & Constable are not yet forgotten & the local living genius is known as great Britten – is coming to an end, & tomorrow we return to hectic London… Even here, as a matter of fact, our translation of a book on Asclepius (for Bollingen, God bless 'em) has been interrupted by several welcome visits, among them one from A. S. Neill [founder of the controversial Summerhill School in Suffolk now run by his daughter Zoë] & family & Anna Freud & Dorothy Burlinghame, out of whose mouth it seemed peculiar but pleasant to hear the short 'ä' emerge. Poor Neill, Gladys, is terribly depressed: he's just been refused his visa to the U.S. (where he has been twice since the war) on the grounds that once, many years ago, he favoured the government of 'another country'! Can you imagine! (For the moment, however, let this be entre nous.) We were once more fascinated to see how all his ideas about child education work like magic with his own. He is 69 and little Zoë 3½.
>
> Last Saturday we spent the night at Cambridge … in the afternoon went to the wedding of C. P. Snow and Pamela Hansford Johnson (both novelists) in Christ's Chapel, the most splendishous affair I've seen in years. I made the error of congratulating the Best Man, who looked about 50, instead of the Groom who is bald, fat & looks about 65. Champagne, however, was flowing & my mistake flowed down happily with it. Two highspots of our London life were a meeting with Henry 'Green', whom I'd not seen since schooldays & who kept me in fits of laughter about his recent visit to N.Y., & an evening at the Stephen Spenders (he is due for 3 weeks at Harvard on August 10) where William Plomer

9 A cultural historian and conservative critic, Van Wyck Brooks approached a writer's work through his life, personality and character. He was an authority on Melville, Whitman, Emerson, Washington Irving and Henry James, and 'his love of letters as an art and his integrity as a lonely scholar' distinguished him, wrote Malcolm Cowley. Edmund Wilson was less generous, calling Brooks 'the darling of the women's clubs'. Brooks also published in 1970 his correspondence with another of Jimmy's benefactors, Lewis Mumford.

(one of my heroes) regaled us on his favourite subject, English eccentrics, living & dead. After we had competed on the exploits of Horace Cole (Virginia Woolf & the 'Dreadnought Hoax' etc), he got going on his great love – British Generals with huge moustaches who in 'reality' or 'private life' are roaring sissies. My favourite was a Brigadier (retired) who spent the war under the cliffs of Dover with a dipsomaniac & a dog, all of whom (including Nellie, the collie) managed to write a novel each during the blitz! It was an unforgettable evening...

I feel that if I stayed long enough – a few months, perhaps – in this village I'd start writing stories again. It is full of characters of which stories are made – quite impossible people like our 75 year old neighbour Holman Tupper, son of Martin Tupper, godson of Holman Hunt, whose house is full of pictures by Rossetti & Hunt, of buffalo heads & tiger skins, the relics of 25 years in India ('very warm out thah') & who lives with an unbelievable lady called Mrs Taylor whom he picked out of a bombed house during the war & who whispered in my ear as though she were about to produce a pornographic postcard: 'You look hungry, I'm going to get you a *bicky*!' Poor old Tupper now has to leave the house (in which he has spent the last 30 years) for a box-like horror because the frightful Mrs Taylor (she has a puce face & immense false fangs) wants to live in 'something modern and manageable – why, we haven't even a W.C. hee-ah, just a bucket which Holman's getting too old to carry!' Pure Paradise! How you'd love it! Perhaps, Stalin permitting, I'll take your advice & stay a couple of years. All these people, of course, are grist for the mill of Angus Wilson (have you read *The Wrong Set* [1949]?) whom we met recently & took an instant dislike to. But Walberswickians are not all Tuppers. Over the hedge on the one side of us lives Sir Charles Tennyson (with a *very* grumpy wife) and behind us, in a shack overlooking the tidal River Blyth, A. E. Coppard.

Seven months later Van Wyck Brooks wrote from Bridgewater, Connecticut, on 22 February 1951:

You would have heard from me long ere this if I hadn't been toiling over my attempted demolition of T. S. Eliot. Gladys was improving it up to the last minute when we took the MS to town yesterday morning. Since T. S. E. can now consider himself demolished, I can turn to other matters, being out of a job, a twenty years' job... You were good to send me Joyce Cary's book, and I do most heartily thank you for it. Though I've only been able to read a few pages, I gather it is all chuckles & good cheer, so I shall probably like it – unless it drives me back to the paranoid Kafka. And on that subject I don't disagree with you. What you say in your letter is exactly what I meant; but our talk that evening left in my mind a sort of bruise, for I felt I had *seemed* to be attacking something you cared for ...

Van Wyck Brooks from the Shelburne Hotel, Dublin, on 12 May 1951:

Can't you jump on to the rudder & come over that way, or perch in the rigging? ...we had a fine day at Bective. We lunched with the Walshes [Mary Lavin and her husband] (who are darlings, both, and came in yesterday & spent a good part of the day with us here). Then we walked up the avenue – through squads of daffodils. It was like the story of Turgenev (*Torrents of Spring?*) that opens 'In the springtime in a beechen grove'. The beech-trees were all in first leaf, with the sun shining through, and when we reached the house there was your old friend Kevin raking the gravel (as you probably saw him raking 35 years ago). He was delighted to have news of you & said 'Oh, Master Jimmy, *he was a wild little boy.* They had to send him away to a farm' ...

6
'The Man Who Was Loved'
1951–1957

Jimmy was not in America when his third selection of a dozen stories, *The Man Who Was Loved,* was published in April 1951. In fact, during the decade 1950–60, Jimmy and Tania lived in five rented locations, all in south-west England – Dorchester, Sherborne, Marnhull, Sturminster Newton and Shaftesbury – before settling in 1960 in the hamlet of Hatch, near Tisbury in Wiltshire. Each was an hour or so's distance from Monmouth House, the Stern parents' home near Templecombe.

In retrospect, they were not sorry to leave their third floor New York apartment, which they had lived in for fifteen years and which is now no longer in existence, when they finally left the States in 1956 never to return. 'I never really liked 207; it was ruined for me always by that blasted crackpot upstairs who bawled her head off all night & stuck loving & insulting notes under my door all day.' But in a characteristic letter to Maeve Slavin in 1978 Jimmy described in nostalgic detail some of the colourful aspects of the neighbourhood: 'We were still paying $52 a month when we left! The Moped shop ... was the home of our landlord; our land-lady was a most formidable dame who as a girl used to milk the cows at the westernmost end of that street and who, in our time, upholstered for the Dook of Windsor, Mrs Simpson (that was!), & Sirry (?) Maugham, who once got her foot stuck in her upholsterer's dark & gloomy Loo. Mr & Mrs Meers (for that was their name) slept in one bed with a large & rather obscene French bulldog between them. No, I am *not* romancing: I saw this with my own eyes. I might add that all three snored in unison ...'

The Man Who Was Loved appeared over a year later in London. In retrospect, it seems a dereliction that Secker & Warburg did not reprint Christopher Isherwood's encomium which was proudly displayed on the jacket of the book's American edition: 'There are characters in it who are big enough to dominate a major novel. Stern writes equally well about Ireland, Africa and America; about landowners, peasants, city people, Negroes, children, horses and snakes. He always knows profoundly and feels warmly whatever he describes. What more can you ask of any writer?'

The stories had originally been published in *The London Mercury, New Writing, News Chronicle, The English Review, Esquire* and *Harper's Bazaar*, while five had been included in *Something Wrong* (1938), a book which had been long out of print.

The collection begins with the title story (Carter, a major of the Black Watch who while in Australia has learned the art of killing snakes, in Rhodesia becomes the fatal victim of his prowess) and ends with 'The Woman Who Was Loved' (in the privileged home of the Turners, Ethel B. Higgins, 'the governess who married', is replaced by Miss Whitmore who causes a revolution in the schoolroom, and pays for it with her dismissal). 'I guess that story contains about all I want to say – an all-is-not-gold-that-glitters story,' Jimmy was to tell Isabelle Evans in 1969.

In four of the stories, his subjects are the effects of adult behaviour on children. In 'Our Father', a mother's lover assumes the role of father to her children, a welcome and happy function which is terminated by the startling reappearance of the children's father. One of two brothers, on a summer holiday with their hunting-shooting-fishing aunt, in 'Under the Beech Tree' ('Riding, nine to twelve – shooting, three to six! I presume you know what to shoot... And what not to shoot!') witnesses a fight to the death of a vixen and a swan. 'Something Wrong' and 'The Broken Leg' are two of Jimmy's most well known and admired stories. In the first, a sensitive and impressionable boy is looked after by attractive, loveable Bessie who, because of his fear of the dark, shares his bedroom. One night he awakes to find a man crouching over 'his Bessie' as if assaulting her ... The second is a study in courage, cowardice and retribution: Mrs Archer, an expert and obsessive rider to hounds, suffers an accident which prevents her ever hunting again. Instead, she pursues her passion for horses and hunting vicariously through her two sons, with a fatal result. The presence and dialogue of Jimmy's parents are evident in every line of this terrifying story.

'Travellers' Tears', set in the Hawaiian islands, and attempting to reproduce the colloquial speech of the islanders and the visiting Americans, criticised by Katherine Anne Porter, is Jimmy's only homosexual story and the only one he ever wrote in which 'no part of himself played a role'. It goes nowhere as a narrative, but it captures the exotic atmosphere, sticky heat and sense of rootlessness which he found there as a young man.

'Solitaire' draws upon Jimmy's knowledge of Manhattan and the brittle life of the city-goer and his hectic existence. A medic reluctantly agrees to lunch with a girl-friend of long ago, who still holds a torch for him. The story colourfully evokes the city as much as it does one girl's loneliness. They meet, she gets drunk and embarrasses him with total recall of the incidents in their affair. Sad and poignant, it displays Jimmy's acute ear for speech, hesitations, and hidden meanings. 'The Face behind the Bar', too, is set in New York and is a result of Jimmy's experiences as a boy in Ireland when the IRA actively threatened his family. A German map of Ireland becomes a matter of contention between an Irish barman and the first person protagonist who visits a Third Avenue tavern.

'Ever since I can remember I have had a passion for pictures,' begins 'The Idolater of Degas', the story of an amateur artist whose pursuit as a 'copyist' appears to be justified.

'Two Men' is about male bonding in the African *veldt,* and ends with a frenzied massacre of wild birds.

The collection underlines the fact that Jimmy was a master of reportage and descriptive writing. He drew exhaustively on his own very varied experiences and because he was a writer of unusual honesty and rigour, his best stories have a powerful impact, although his dialogue inevitably seems dated now. (A discussion of some of the stories between Kay Boyle and Jimmy in 1957 may be found on p. 164.) A near contemporary, Jean Rhys, who was fourteen years older than Jimmy and a novelist of high standing, who also suffered a childhood of loneliness and rejection, said this of her writing: 'I can't make things up, I can't invent. I have no imagination. I can't invent character. I don't think I know what character is. I just write about what happened. Not that my books are entirely my life – but almost.'

To Jimmy's great delight, V. S. Pritchett, the writer of stories he most revered, reviewed the collection in the *New York Times*:

> His descriptions of the crucial action: the killing of a snake, the rise of a jumping horse, the physical crisis of illness at night, the astonishment of a child at seeing his nurse in the arms of her lover, have a burning, exact stillness which is tremendous … The hunting story, 'The Broken Leg', is a superb picture of the grueling human standards traditional in English upper-class life and, I think, one of the best stories of its kind to be done since Lawrence.

In any collection of English stories in the last twenty years it would have a high place.

Two English critics, both friends of Jimmy's, picked 'The Broken Leg' as his finest achievement: '... one of the most penetrating of all stories of adolescence ... There are penalties for producing a masterpiece, and this story is clearly doomed to appear in every competently compiled anthology from now on,' wrote John Davenport in the *Observer*, and in *The Listener* Arthur Calder-Marshall, with a sting in the tail, wrote: [In 'The Broken Leg'] 'all Stern's themes, of courage and cowardice, love and misery, life and death, are fused at white heat. In its forty pages, the author says with absolute assurance all that he is fumbling to say in the rest of the book.'

During the '50s, Jimmy and Tania were busy translating: Erich Maria Remarque's *Spark of Life* (1952) was the direct result of the author's persecution by the Nazis; thereafter the *Selected Prose of Hugo von Hofmannsthal* edited by Hermann Broch (translated with Mary Hottinger and not Tania) appeared in 1952, *Letters to Milena* by Franz Kafka in 1953, the anonymous *A Woman in Berlin* in 1954, *Casanova's Memoirs* (with Robert Pick) in 1955, and Leo Lania's *The Foreign Minister* in 1956.

Milena Jesenska, a writer herself and translator of Kafka's early work into Czech, handed hundreds of Kafka's letters to Willy Haas (founder and editor in chief of *Die Literarische Welt* before 1933) at the time of the German occupation of Czechoslovakia. Haas edited the letters and had them hidden in Prague, from where he rescued them on his return in 1945. In the *New York Times*, the Sterns' friend Harvey Breit wrote of *Letters to Milena*: 'It is an extraordinary document – touching, horrifying, brilliant, sickly, heart-breaking and infinitely convoluted. The challenge of translation from Kafka's subjective and idiomatic German into clear, conversational English is a heroic one, and it is met with unbelievable grace by Tania and James Stern.'

That December (1951), Van Wyck Brooks wrote from Bridgewater, Connecticut, describing a visit to him and his wife by Alyse Gregory.[10] '...My book will follow – *The Confident Years* [1952]. You don't have to read *all* of the 611 pages; but I will take it ill of you if you don't read

---

10 Essayist and novelist, Llewelyn Powys's widow, who preceded Marianne Moore as editor of *The Dial*.

what I have to say about that old poisoner T. S. Eliot, your pal... Alyse Gregory spent a day with us here, looking this time, not so much like Juliet's nurse as like Shakespeare in person...'

Ten days later Jimmy replied from Sherborne, Dorset:

Dear Van Wyck, cher Maître

... Forget if I told you that we made haste to visit Sylvia Townsend Warner & Valentine Acland, & found them, in the wildest, gloomiest of Tom Hardy weather, in a house so surrounded by swirling water that, sitting over tea, I should not have been at all surprised to have looked out of the window & found ourselves sailing merrily towards you across the Atlantic. Valentine Acland, of course, I had imagined to be a distinguished-looking member of our sex, with a pipe and possibly a beard. Imagine our surprise then, when the door opened & in marched, arms laden with 'tea things', a large, handsome lady – albeit with reddish hair about the length of mine but needless to say, properly, perfectly groomed. Recovering quickly from this shock we promptly received another in the form of the unmistakable sounds of an infant howling near at hand. On this occasion the door opened – or rather was opened – to introduce the most beautiful (& certainly the noisiest) Siamese cat I have ever seen. After that we settled down to a very pleasant hour. These ladies have over the years been intimately acquainted with all eleven (?) members of the Powys family. Upstairs Miss A. works in the loveliest of small rooms surrounded on all sides with precious books, many of which – including an early 16th century bible which had been in the same Dorset family since its 'birth' – the ladies had rescued (at the risk of their lives) from the 'Paper Salvage Drives' during the War. Another volume we were shown was a perfect copy of a Father to Son memoir with a frontispiece by Blake dated before he had published his first poem...

In March 1952 Jimmy heard from Constantine FitzGibbon[11] who

---

11 Born in America, the four-times-married FitzGibbon was a direct descendant of the first Earl of Clare, and a grand-nephew of Norman Douglas. During the last months of the Second World War, he served on General Omar Bradley's staff throughout the preparations for the invasion of France and Germany. A gifted linguist, he was a versatile writer of fiction, publishing fourteen novels, the best known of which is *When the Kissing Had to Stop* (1960). His account of the Stauffenberg conspiracy to kill Hitler, *The Shirt of Nessus*, was published in 1955 and his biography of Dylan Thomas in 1965.

lived near Sawbridgeworth, Hertfordshire. '... I go to Dublin immediately after Easter ... you were good enough to say once upon a time that you'd tell me the names of some pleasant people to look up over there ...

'... Did you hear a man say on the wireless that you're writing "the Great American novel"?'

On 1 April 1952, the day the Sterns moved from Sherborne to Bottle Knapp, Long Bredy, Dorchester, 'a dark, damp, gloomy hole, with a studio attached, the kind that reminds me of Montparnasse after some awful night before,' Jimmy replied to FitzGibbon:

> ... I know almost no one in the South except hunting & racing relations who wouldn't interest you. How about Elizabeth Bowen, who's there all the time now, I hear. Bowen's Court, Kildorrery (Tel: 4), Cork. Joseph Hone, Ballyornery Ho, Enniskerry. In Meath, at Bective, Robinstown, Navan – my old home – there's Mary Lavin. She's lonely & would love to see you. But that goes for anyone in Eire. O'Connor (Frank) I don't know, but I'd certainly look him up if I were over there – 57 Strand Road, Sandymount, Dublin. And Hester Plunkett-Connell (Desmond [Ryan]'s late hostess) at Shillelagh, Wicklow. Oh, you shouldn't miss the country's one philosopher, Arland Ussher, 14 Strand Road, Merrion Gates, Sandymount. And Lennox Robinson – I know only his phone number. Dublin 83125.
>
> Yes, that chap on the wireless was a nice bit of irony. Equally ironic is that someone on John Lehmann's programme is to read a mutilated chapter (on account of some remarks I made about the Royal Family) of an unfinished novel of mine (needless to say, I've never finished one!) on the 7th & 13. This is *not* a suggestion that you should listen.

In the spring of 1952, Jimmy had the first of many letters from William Plomer[12] (1903–73), whose autobiographical book, *Double Lives* (1950), he had read two years earlier. 'Since that day [when they had first met] I have felt for him the fraternal affection seldom found, I think, outside a family united by blood. As though there were between

---

12 Jimmy had first met Plomer in 1947 at Thomas Mann's seventy-second birthday celebration. A South African-born poet and novelist, he succeeded Edward Garnett as principal reader to the publishers Jonathan Cape. With Laurens van der Post and Roy Campbell he started the magazine *Voorslag* ('Whiplash'), which attacked racism in South Africa. His works include the novel *Turbott Wolfe* (1926).

us a secret bond. A bond there was. And I call it secret because, as in a family, I – and I like to think he, too – took it for granted. The bond was Africa. We had both been to English public schools. And we had lived, in the white man's lonely isolation, before the days of cars and telephones and radio, on the African veldt.'

In the autumn of 1973, in the *London Magazine,* Jimmy wrote this appreciation of Plomer:

> With his clipped moustache, dark hair brushed straight back, the thick-lensed horn-rimmed spectacles, the considerate, enquiring, courteous manner, he struck me as a cross between a doctor and an army chaplain with a sense, a surprising sense, of humour ... I don't think I have known any writer inspire affection so quickly. It was not simply charm. When William was with you he gave you, like a good doctor, all of himself. And so, unlike most good talkers, he could listen. Indeed he was such a good listener (how rare a gift!) that he seemed to know what one was thinking, before one spoke. Which can be disconcerting.

From London on 4 May 1952, Plomer wrote:

> I have been very much enjoying *The Man Who Was Loved* & I must tell you so & say how much I admire your range – of subjects, experience, & treatment – your great skill – & your attitude to the human, and so often inhuman, race.
>
> I hope this book of selected stories will bring you the sort of success you would wish for – perhaps renewed appreciation from old admirers, plenty of new admirers, & I hope good sales. I see that my old friend Christopher [Isherwood] says on the dust-jacket that you are the most unjustly neglected writer of short stories alive today. If you are neglected, then that is not only unjust but stupid of the negligent, & I must say I think on this book alone your status must be recognised as one of the best of living short-story writers – & by no means only about Africa. If you are horrific at times – well, so is life most of the time – & the ability to be stirred by human suffering is evidently dwindling on all sides. However much it dwindles, I shall return to warm myself at your flame, which may be 'gem-like' but is, thank goodness, neither hard – nor soft ... .

On 29 May 1952 Jimmy wrote to Van Wyck Brooks from Dorchester: '...Djuna Barnes, having polished her one-room parquet in

Patchin Place in preparation for a visit from your pal Mr [T. S.] Eliot, slipped on the polish & fractured her shoulder ... After an hour's crawling, she managed to get to the phone & called Cummings across the way. e.e.c. had to climb the drainpipe & get in through the window, then phone for an ambulance to take her to the French Hospital, where she now lies. I'm sure there's a moral to this tale, one certainly involving TSE...'

Four days later he wrote another letter to Brooks from Highdown, Goring-by-Sea, Sussex:

> ... I write from the home of Uncle Fred [Sir Frederic Stern, who created a celebrated chalk garden, from which Enid Bagnold took the title for her play], the gardener, of whom I believe I've told you a number of stories. At the risk of boring you – oh, the daily risks one runs! – I will tell you one more. It appears that the present Queen Mother is quite a gardener & that it was recently Uncle F's duty, as Hon. Secretary of some distinguished Horticultural Society, to invite Her Majesty to attend some exclusive function. Several days later, *at 7 in the morning*, there was a loud knock at the bedroom door of his London club. A voice informed him that he was urgently needed on the telephone downstairs – 'Your butler, Sir, in the country'. In the worst of tempers, convinced that Highdown was already reduced to ashes, Uncle F., in pyjamas & dressing gown, descended the stairs. 'A registered letter for you, Sir,' said the voice of Barnes (whom I remember as being here in 1911). 'Brought by special messenger on a motor-bicycle, Sir, at 6.30 this morning.' – 'Letter!' howled Uncle F., 'where from?' – 'From Buckingham Palace, Sir – written in hand, Sir, & stamped back and front with the stamp of Buckingham Palace.' (He could have added that the envelope was also stamped with G. R. & the writer's ER. in a corner) ...

On 7 August 1952, he was again writing to Brooks and his wife:

> ... A few days ago I saw my parents who, as usual, wished to be remembered to you both. My father had taken a new lease of life. He insists he is a Manic Depressive – to which I can only say 'Oh'. In any case, at the moment he is planning a party in October to celebrate the 98th Anniversary of the Battle of Balaclava. When I asked why the 98th, he said because he wasn't sure he'd be around on the 100th. Considering he has often hinted that he expects to

outlive his elder son, I thought this most modest. And when I asked why Balaclava, he said because his regiment had been in the Charge & he is now one of the oldest members of that regiment. Well, manic he may be, but you can't say he sounds depressed. Oh, I should have mentioned that he came here one day & that from the lane to this house there is an incline so steep up a stony little path that for generations it has been the Talk of the Village.

Before he set out I warned him by phone to put on his tennis shoes (sneakers to you) so as to be able to get up & down – to which he replied that never in his life had he gone to lunch with anyone in tennis shoes & he wasn't going to begin now. What was more, if *I* could get up & down why couldn't he? (I managed to refrain from remarking that his reputation for falling down on the flat had not been earned for nothing.) Well, coming up the precip-itous incline all went very well & he was full of pooh-poohs about its famous slipperiness. Going down, however, was another mat-ter. I had suggested (unknown to him) that T should lead the way & I bring up the rear, so that in the event of his slipping he could lean on her shoulders & I could steady him from behind by hang-ing on to his coat. And this, in fact, was just how he made his descent – though I had not foreseen that we should both be attacked by a fit of the giggles when, in a voice breathless with embarrassment, he kept exclaiming: 'This (slip) – no really (slither) – this is really *too* (slip) – damn it (slither) silly-for-words!' This path has never been mentioned since.

Jimmy, having moved from Dorchester to Sherborne on 23 October 1952, wrote to Constantine FitzGibbon:

I started *Cousin Emily* [1952] in the train coming down here about 10 days ago & got bogged down when they started (& went on) fucking after swimming in cold water. Forgive me, but this is one of my bêtes noires; I can think of nothing less conducive to a 'hot encounter' than a cold douche. Maybe it's just envy on my part!

Then I picked it up again yesterday pm & read it through at a sitting & with very great pleasure as well as admiration. A damn good description of a proper bitch. How I admire all the things that I would be quite incapable of doing & which you bring off with such consummate ease – the linking up of the years, the moving forward & backward through time, not to mention space.

One episode, that of calling up her husband after all those years on account of the stolen pendant, I couldn't quite swallow whole – though, needless to say, I see the point you were trying to make. The disintegration of the one-book writer I found superb. And I liked as much as anything, I think, the chapter on old Maureen. This is really first-class & deeply moving.

On 21 January 1953 Jimmy wrote to the Brookses:

We have much to thank you for: a long letter & those beautiful things – those socks (*just* my line) & that tie! I sported them both last week at a luncheon for 35 writers in London arranged by Henry Green in honour of John Lehmann who was recently kicked out of his own publishing house – by the printer, an act that has shocked literary London. Toastmaster was Van Wyck's old friend (TSE[liot]), next to whom I was very nearly made to sit. At the last moment, however, I persuaded one of the two ladies present, Rosamond Lehmann (the other was Rose Macaulay) to move into the ominously empty chair. Afterwards I thrust out my legs and pulled up my trousers (all right, *pants*) under the eyes of the author of *Passage to India* [1924], who beamed appropriately. Though the following day's papers reported that nothing to compare with this occasion had been seen in London since the 18th century, I am sorry to say that I found it extraordinarily dull.

A few weeks later Jimmy wrote again:

I wrote you a letter yesterday, in a bleak, unthinking hour an empty letter, and just wish to say that in the evening I read – oh, with such pleasure & hearty agreement – your chapter entitled 'Beyond Adolescence'. So many things I was glad about, above all, I think, that you included Hemingway among the adolescents. Never could I forgive him for that childish bombast – 'knocking Turgenev out of the ring'. That a serious writer should ever talk of knocking another out of anywhere! I was interested at the same time that you should consider *The Old Man and the Sea* [1952] a 'great' story. Not long ago I was having a drink with Louis MacNeice. The subject cropped up & I expressed astonishment that among all the reviews I had read in this country of this story I had heard but one dissenting voice. Even the intellectuals, I said, including such as Cyril Connolly, had referred to it either as 'great', or as a 'masterpiece'. I said I thought it was 'a damned good yarn'. 'And is not that', came the answer, 'exceedingly high praise?' (I added, I think, that it was a story I would have been delighted to give – did I have one – to an adolescent son.) I don't think L. attempted to suggest that there was more in it than that – the good yarn, excellently told. Perhaps he added how wonderful it was that the suspense was kept up for so long. The conversation passed on quickly to Kipling, & here I insisted that I could remember no story by Kipling that was not either highly symbolic or highly satirical. (I have just re-read 'The Maltese Cat' with disappointment, but 'The Brushwood Boy' with frank amazement.) What I have against Hemingway as a writer, apart from anything else, is that in all his works I have not yet discovered a line of humour. Enough, one could go on for pages. But I did want to express my agreement & pleasure.

(Just now a letter from my mother, who says Papa had something wrong with his 'Gaul bladder'; unlike her to get historical.)

Yesterday was a Red Letter day: Theodore Powys. Fascinating. He & his wife ('Vilutt') & adopted daughter Susie, 20, live in what was once the school of the village of Mappowder, which is near absolutely Nowhere. As you know he has almost always been a 'hermit'. I often wondered how hermits – he in particular – write fiction. I'm now convinced she – a Dorset peasant girl of 66, they have been married 48 years – tells him the stories (*echt* village gossip) and he, rolling them round his allegorical tongue & spitting them out & allowing them to curdle in his Biblical bowl, writes them down. Or did. He has not written anything for 16 years. 'I am out of business.' 'Writing makes my head ache.' From pictures I always thought he looked like a prehistoric grandmother; he doesn't at all. He looks like a sage with a ruddy complexion, huge white eyebrows, the hooked nose, a mane of white hair, & black eyes which stare at you. All through tea he rolled cigarettes of black tobacco & passed them round for each person to lick (the paper) before handing them the cigarette. But his hands shook a bit & he wasn't very good at it. After ½ an hour a row of 'bad' ones lay by his plate. Then he 'undid' them all & replaced the tobacco in a little tin. He's very conscious of his age (he's only 77) & maintains it's by far the best time of life – 'for then, you know, one enjoys *everything*; every day is a year. No ambitions, no fears, no regrets. Once ceases to be; one just isn't anything.' In the evenings V., the Dorset peasant, reads Jane

Austen (tonight they are to finish *Emma*) aloud to him & Susie. (Susie was adopted after the second son died – was eaten by a lion, I believe, in Kenya, about 20 years ago.) At breakfast they discuss what they have read the night before. V. was promptly told to produce *Emma* for me to read a passage aloud. Which I did, whereupon TFP exclaimed: 'Mr. S., he has a voice, a voice of his own, not someone else's – that's a rare thing.' Wasn't that nice?

That July of 1953 Jimmy was made a Fellow of the Royal Society of Literature. At the General Anniversary Meeting, which was held on the 15th, the Chairman, the Earl of Birkenhead, in the presence of the society's President, R. A. Butler, welcomed twenty-seven new Fellows, among whom were Noël Coward, Daphne Du Maurier, and Jimmy's contemporary at Eton, Henry Green.

In December, Jimmy confided to his journal his agonised preoccupation with the inability to write, to create. Although in years to come he alluded to the problem in letters to his more intimate friends, this is the last wail of self-reproach before a series of translations occupied him and he began in the final decades of his life to produce the fragmented attempts at an autobiography which he modestly dubbed his 'knitting', some of which Alan Ross published in his *London Magazine* and much of which is contained in this book.

> T believes that at worst a diary should be kept – à la K. [Franz Kafka], & that the horror should be poured out, that this would be something. Better than complete stagnation, than staring hopelessly into the void. As with everything, it's lack of faith. What good? There have been too many disappointments. How is it possible that the person who from time to time (not often, but sometimes, & for what reason?) has been able to clinch, to *see* the story, the drama, the end, the *inevitability* of the end, & at the miraculous moment rise like a fish to the surface, at that miraculous moment of conscious creation – (it's the moment in which the bell rings aloud in the ear: 'You've got it! Nothing else matters! No one in the world but you can do this! No one in the world but you *knows* this!') – live again, lose fear, find faith: how is it *possible* that for this person such moments (& it is the moments that make, that *are* the stories) have gone, vanished, seemingly forever? Is it because he has gradually driven himself into a hole,

always away (after the first years of experience) away from experience, & thus lost the link with life? Is this why the spark has
gone out, why the imagination simply ceases to function? And is it
because I don't *want* to believe it a sign that it is true?

Lay awake all night, nearly all night, feverishly trying to *pump*
the imagination into action, into catching a glimpse of a person or
a place (not even a situation, but the person or place that might
possibly produce the situation) that would set off the spark. In
vain ...

Sixteen years later he was to write to Isabelle Evans that 'the frustration from which I suffer is so old a story that it should not be mentioned
... I expect (and have done for years) that I am "a burnt out case".'

After a considerable time, Jimmy heard from Katherine Anne Porter
in Liège, Belgium, on 11 January 1955:

... The way I landed here is very simple; simple for me, that is. A
year ago last July Allen Tate and I were driving from a writers'
conference in Connecticut, that is, he was driving and gave me a
lift towards New York, and he was sailing very soon on a
Fulbright Grant to Rome, and I said, 'I wish I could get my eager
hot little hand into one of these numerous grab-bags. I haven't
lived on public money since the Guggenheim fellowship. It would
be nice to have something that would take me to Paris.' 'Get a
Fulbright,' said Allen, 'just ask for it, they'll send you to Paris'... I
have not seen or heard of Allen since, he disappears out of my life
for years at a time, but the consequences of my taking his advice
are still marching on, on the double.

I got the Fulbright grant all right, but they explained that
simply everybody wanted to go to Paris or Rome, and their supply
of grants was used up for those two places. BUT –Liège would be
delighted to have me.

... There is nothing wrong with the city – but the sun just
doesn't exist so far as I have been able to learn, it is the most stub-
bornly dreary, wet, cold, dank, smoky, grimy, *morne*, triste, did I
say dark? climate I ever was trapped into, worse than Berlin this
time of year if I remember truly. The Gothic north is simply not
for me, I am not a northerner in *any* man's country, and I have
been using up too much of my energies fighting cold, physically,
and then fighting the melancholy that fighting cold always gives
me.

Jimmy answered her from yet another address, in Sturminster Newton, Dorset, on 24 January 1955: '...I write book reviews for the "*London Mag*" and for Mr Spender's *Encounter* & hardly an hour of any day goes by that I don't weep internal tears for all the stories I've begun and never finished, & for all the stories I've not begun. I am, or feel beyond asking What Is Wrong, yet no power that I have will smother that question to death.'

It was on a transatlantic liner returning for the last time to New York from London in November 1955 that Jimmy wrote the first of many letters which have survived to John Davenport[13] (1908–66).

> Glory be to God ... I assumed there would be some Germans (I dislike them so much I can barely refrain from bestowing on the breed all the four-letter words the British have invented) but I was not prepared for a quivering, obsequious, arrogant, cigar-stinking *horde*! At the end of November? How come? Seems more than half the stye grunted over en masse in the summer, are now farting back again – to Chicago, Milwaukee & other such Schwein stadte. 'Me, I haf a husbond in Chicago, a tochter in Hamburg – she sings in Konzerten, very goot!' And the youngish glassy-eyed dining-room steward: 'Why so many people on this ship? Because it is ze cholliest ship on tze ocean. In St. Pauli Taverne Blasmusik till tree in ze mornink! So is why we always full, all uzzer ships empty!'
>
> And the uninterested, asinine agents in Jermyn Street swore that I should have what for me is the most necessary of all

13 In her book, *On the Wing: A Young American Abroad* (2001), Nora Sayre describes Davenport: '... literary critic, aesthete, editor, and former heavyweight boxer ... It was said that T. S. Eliot had pronounced his poetry most promising when he was a student at Cambridge in the late 1920s. It was repeated – with some awe – that he had been expelled from the Savage Club for putting a small bishop on the mantelpiece: nettled by some discord in their theologies, Davenport had lifted the little prelate into the air and deposited him above the fireplace, declaring, "You talk like a bloody clock and that's where you belong." ... Others recalled that Davenport hurled tureens of tomato soup over the snowy shirtfronts of club-men whose perceptions of Marcel Proust displeased him.'
    John Davenport was one of the most highly regarded non-academic critics of his generation. In the '50s and '60s he was the lead reviewer of fiction for the *Observer* and also wrote for the *Spectator* and the *New Statesman*. For a time, he was the literary editor of *Vogue*, theatre critic of *Queen* magazine, and a frequent broadcaster for the BBC. In 1940 he and Dylan Thomas collaborated on a detective story, *The Death of the King's Canary*, which was published in England in 1976 and in America in 1978.

necessities on a voyage of more than 24 hours: a Table for Two. Here no such table exists. It does not make for cholliness. Well, nor do I, as unsere Nachbaren have already discovered. From one of them, however, I did hear a remark that struck me as making most un-German sense: 'I tell you, mein Herr, zis ship – it is crook-ed.'

The strong anti-German feelings in this letter compare strangely with the sensitivity of *The Hidden Damage*. It is possible that, like many Englishmen after the Second World War and especially given his Jewish blood, he harboured an ambivalent attitude to Germans – tourists in particular – or that a residue of his unhappy days in the Frankfurt and Berlin banks still remained.

Jimmy also wrote to Constantine FitzGibbon from New York:

... Now for the '20th' [Constantine FitzGibbon's *The Shirt of Nessus*]. I find it very hard to describe, to find the words for my admiration of it. I always knew you are a first rate man for fiction, but I did not know you are a *historian* of the first rank. The construction, the way you managed to sort out & piece together this vastly complicated story to make it so clear, not to repeat yourself except when necessary, & never to drop a cliché – it's quite fabulous. This book is not superb journalism, it's literature. And how often is a work of non-fiction that?

I have so much to say about the 20th – I mean about the whole ghastly story – that I guess I'd better not begin now. I suppose it could be boiled down to this: that the Resisters in Germany during the War were given the cold shoulder by the Allies not so much from distrust as from fear that such a step (to court them) might lead to a separate peace between Germany & the West. Or rather (I am expressing myself abominably) the Allies could not afford so much as a gesture, for fear of offending & alienating Russia.

Your book told me many things I did not know. Needless to say, I have not read all the books you list – Ian Colvin's study of Canaris [entitled (in England) *Chief of Intelligence*]. I had never realised that it was almost entirely (or so it seems) owing to Canaris & his friendship for Franco that Hitler did not drive through to Gibraltar. I had always assumed that he had been warned against doing so on account of the impossibility of guarding the Spanish & Portuguese coasts. However, it is probably not as simple as all that.

Stauffenberg certainly emerges as one of the few great heroes of the century. To me, psychologically, Canaris remains the most fascinating figure. I still cannot figure him out – his early life, his pre-war activities & his behaviour during the war: he does not emerge all of a piece, as one man. Maybe he wasn't! He was a Fouché, yet he cannot have had Fouché's detachment. But now I am wandering ...

He received a reply from FitzGibbon under a week later, 11 January 1956:

... I'm glad you liked the book, and delighted by the flattering things you say about my talents as a historian. As old Norman D. [Douglas] used to say, 'You can't lay it on too thick, my dear.' I wonder how many people will agree with you? Not many over here, I'm afraid. People over here are anti-German the way the French used to be anti-Semitic, even intelligent people, like Arland [Ussher] or [John] Davenport. Most depressing. And for the same reasons, too, envy, fear and xenophobia. Contemplation of the political emotions of the human race is really the most horribly discouraging business. I have largely given it up and am writing a series of works almost entirely about sex ...

John Davenport replied to Jimmy's anti-German invective on 12 January 1956:

Delighted to get your letter from the boat. ... Somebody tells me you're with the Calders ... Christopher [Isherwood] arrived and is staying with John Lehmann .... Brian [Howard] came over looking very ill indeed and has gone back to France to spend 6 months in his bed. He may have to go back to Switzerland. He was sweet and pathetic. He has not been both of these together before. Malc [Malcolm Lowry] is still in hospital and will stay there until the end of Feb. They've just been putting him through a hideously exhausting and nauseating 'Aversion' treatment. Expensive, too, for the ratepayer: the analyst is dazed by the amount of whisky that goes down daily. They seem to think it will work for a time sufficiently long to enable him to get down to the book. Margerie needless to say has been vexing to a degree .... The new ed. of Old Calabria [by Norman Douglas, 1915] has had some rave reviews, which is nice for me. No acknowledgement, by the way, from [Edmund] Wilson; perhaps he never got it, or perhaps he's digging up another culture, white, in Iceland? Joan [Churchill] dressing-gowned, amiable, gin-fogged; her husband getting on with his book & in fine form. Nigel [Dennis]'s *Cards of Identity* is coming on as a play in the spring, in a highbrow repertory season at the Court Theatre, together with plays by Angus Wilson and Bert Brecht. So you'd better be home by April 1st. Cyril [Connolly] is so upset by Barbara [Skelton]'s (final) elopement with [George] Weidenfeld that the appearance of his novel in *Encounter*'s been indefinitely postponed. A pity – I was longing to read it & he's written 40,000 words: 2/3rds of it, in fact.

Jimmy from New York to John Davenport on 21 January 1956:

... The *Observer* arrived this morn, & I opened it hoping to see my Dav. But it was Stevie Smith saying So Long. Giving way to John Wain, I see. Never liked that one since reading his last novel. What I did find with pleasure was that article by Philip Oakes, whoever he may be. I think I'll quote it in my [Kingsley] Amis piece. This Wain, this Amis – they seem so bad-tempered. They don't like anything or anyone, seems to me. Guess I said that before.

Only news since last letter is the party we had last night for Alec [Waugh]. He is a sweet man, I must say. I got into a violent rage before it began & was in an Amisian temper all the way through. Alec said he had never seen so many 'pretty girls in one room' – which suggests he enjoyed himself. Who were they? Well, the new Mrs Harvey Breit (who someone seriously insisted used to be Mrs Charles Addams, which I refuse to believe); Augusta Billings, a grand-niece of Poe, ex-*Vogue* model & great friend of Jamie Hamilton [English publisher]; Ruth Ford, sister of Charles Henri & great pal of [William] Faulkner; Vita Petersen, a beauty from Hamburg; Nan Taylor, wife of Frank (whom you know, I think); Emmie Kronenberger, wife of Louis. And a few others. Men. Wystan, Ben Huebsch [a partner in the Viking Press, later to be Patrick White's editor], as young as ever. And – back to the other sex – someone whom you may also know: Elizabeth Eliot, author of a novel called *Alice* which I glanced through in the library yesterday afternoon. A very strange-looking number. What age? Seems to pop back & forth between here and London even more erratically than we do. Alec brought her. Seems she is also Lady E. Kinnaird. Who may he be? [George Kinnaird was a literary adviser to the publishing firm of John Murray.] She appears to be an old friend of Ernestine Evans, who was also here. So was Rosie Constable, also as bouncy as ever, talked of you. Walker Evans was another. Has an exhibition of photographs at the Modern Museum – old ones. Mr Auden brought Mr [Chester] Kallman, who has grown in all the wrong places since I saw him last.

From John Davenport on 19 June 1956:

... I had several letters from N.Y. saying thanks for the little bit on Ted Weeks I wrote for the *N. S. & N.* His horrid little book [*The Open Heart*, 1956] smells of artificial tweed. So you saw the new Professor [W. H. Auden]. I missed him in Ischia by a matter of hours, without regret by him; or by me, come to that. I thought the *N. S . & N.* went rather far in devoting a number to him. I told John Raymond that W. H. A. was not the forgotten but the *remembered* man. But there, I know we feel differently on that subject.

Enjoyed de-bagging Mr Brinnin [John Malcolm] in the current number of the *XXth Century* ... Mary McCarthy says I was far too kind to him. I suppose she's not exactly renowned for charity herself. All the same, she made Rome for me. Odd that we should click so firmly. She turned out to be a J. D. fan, which helped at the kick-off. After that it was roses, roses and an occasional negroni all the way. Joyce Cary *is* a saint, just as David Cecil is a bore. Glad you heard from Malc [Lowry]. He's in better shape than he has been for years. Jim Thurber writes from Bermuda that his new set of fables has begun to appear in N. Yer. Haven't seen yet, have you? Very many thanks for *The Aunt's Story* [by Patrick White, 1948], which shall be carefully guarded.

While in England during the summer of 1956, the Sterns drove on 11 June from their roadside cottage in Sturminster Newton, conveniently next to a pub, and across the River Stour from the house where Thomas Hardy wrote *The Return of the Native* (1878), to Oxford for W. H. Auden's inauguration as Professor of Poetry. Lord David Cecil gave a party in New College attended by, among others, Neville Coghill, Enid Starkie and Isaiah Berlin. They ended up after midnight at the home of Dan Davin, son-in-law of Joyce Cary, a writer Jimmy much admired.

A month later they were in London to meet Walker Evans and Jean Stafford.[14] They also enjoyed a party in Sonia Orwell's Percy Street flat, attended by Clive Bell, John Lehmann, V. S. Pritchett, Stephen Spender, Ruth Ford, Zachary Scott, John Russell, Lucian Freud, Cyril Connolly, Nigel Dennis, Dwight Macdonald and Nora Sayre. They walked to the Etoile for dinner with Nigel Dennis, where they saw Patrick Leigh Fermor dining with Cyril Connolly. Such a collection of literary luminaries is an oft-repeated feature of Jimmy's journal entries over the following decades!

One evening in October, Lawrence Durrell and Diane Ladas, the English ex-wife of Durrell's friend Alexis Ladas, who owned a cottage nearby at Donhead St Andrew, turned up at the door of the Sterns' Sturminster home. Although they had many mutual friends, this was the first time they had met Durrell. 'He was charming,' Jimmy remarked, 'very short, fair, with tiny hands and feet. Very English ...' The four spent over two hours discussing friends or acquaintances, most if not all of whom were writers living in France: James Joyce, Robert McAlmon, Laurence Vail, Eugene Jolas, Samuel Beckett and, at great length, Henry Miller.

The deaths of friends – Peter Watson, the wealthy backer of Cyril Connolly's *Horizon*, Allan Ross Macdougall and Bertolt Brecht – cast a shadow over another celebration: the first night on the 26 June at the Royal Court Theatre of *Cards of Identity*, a play by Jimmy's colleague at *Time*, Nigel Dennis. That evening he was introduced by Walker Evans to Nora Sayre,[15] the only child of Jimmy's friend Joel Sayre, whom he described as being 'one of the best writers the *New Yorker* ever had'. Their friendship, which lasted for thirty-seven years, was conducted in part through a lively and voluminous exchange of letters between Wiltshire and New York. She also became a frequent visitor to Hatch, the manor house where the Sterns lived until their deaths.

On 8 August 1956 Jimmy wrote to Djuna Barnes:

... 10 days or so ago we went to a party in London given by Sonia Orwell (O's widow). Who do you think was there? Ruth Ford &

14 The humorous, hard-drinking American novelist (*The Mountain Lion*, 1947) and Pulitzer Prize winning short story writer, who married the poet Robert Lowell and was an integral part of Philip Rahv's *Partisan Review* in the '40s.
15 Then a fledgling writer, Nora Sayre became a cultural historian and critic, and was from 1965 to 1970 the New York correspondent of the *New Statesman* and film critic for the *New York Times*. She was the author of four books, including *Previous Convictions: A Journey through the 1950s* (1995). She died in 2001.

Zachary Scott. I could hardly believe my eyes. Apparently he is doing a movie here, or working in one. There were several other Americans, including Jean Stafford and Dwight Macdonald, the latter with a roving job on *Encounter*.

Plans? As unsettled as ever. Would like to stay on, & Papa – to him it really means something, I can actually help in his old age, but there are the usual difficulties. Passport etc. Talking of passports, Arthur Miller & his new wife were supposed to come through here last weekend on their way to see Sean O'Casey in Devon, but A. phoned at the last moment & said Miss [Marilyn] Monroe had been called upon to 'work', would come, however, soon. He's a good sort, with a very special sense of humour which, alas, he forgets he possesses when he writes a play.

Domestic discord marred the first two months of 1957: 'T in bed all day with throat-cold & a hateful temper,' Jimmy wrote in his journal. 'Mine none too good, after her laying-down-the-law & bullying of last night.' And: 'T can't stand my "silence" any longer & let go over late breakfast. She feels done in, ill – don't blame her! Not on speaking terms all day after last night – & I don't even remember what it was I said.' On many occasions during the next thirty years, Jimmy was to use his retreats into silence as weapons in their marital battles, just as he had used the same armament against his father as a boy: 'I felt at an early age that to surrender an inch would be to risk losing my independence, my personality …' Tania, more than ready to verbalise her concerns, became increasingly frustrated by this tactic.

More deaths that spring and summer contributed to the gloom: Wyndham Lewis, Jack Yeats, Joyce Cary, Roy Campbell, Auden's father, Dr G. A. Auden, Joan Churchill (née Black), Malcolm Lowry, and John Davenport's wife, Marjorie, who threw herself from the 8th floor of the Strand Palace Hotel in London.

Although the event is unrecorded in his journal, Jimmy returned to Ireland twenty-five years after his family had left Bective, at the invitation of Mary Lavin, the little girl he'd glimpsed at the door as they'd driven away. The now famous author welcomed him and Tania and gave them tea in the Stern children's old schoolroom. He'd never felt so much at home. 'Glory be, what was I after saying! I was home!'

In late May, Jimmy recorded some thoughts on J. D. Salinger: 'He is close to Kafka, & knows it. But does he know why? Because whatever either of them writes about, he is writing about *love*. Why? Because each of them has been deprived of it in youth. This may be subjective reasoning, but it is true. Both are the really lonely ones. S. quotes K.: "The happiness of being with people". Think of the "being with".'

And an anecdote about his beloved O. W.: 'Walter de la Mare said that Henry Newbolt once found Wilde in a drawing-room surrounded by a crowd of female admirers. They were asking him which he thought were the best passages in Shakespeare's plays, & O. W. quoted them at length. Newbolt didn't recognize them; on looking them up afterwards he found that Wilde had invented them all on the spot.'

Another row over breakfast flared up on 1 September: 'The bloody feminine threat as usual. The usual recriminations because I do not respond – in other words I retire ... from mortal weariness, into silence. Drown my misery & weariness in correcting Kafka proofs. Thank God for Kafka & his sense of humour.' Later, in the May issue of the *London Magazine*, John Lehmann published Jimmy's and Tania's translation of Franz Kafka's story 'The Refusal'. In the same number, Lehmann included 'Letter from a Reviewer', in which Jimmy paraded his Hemingway antipathies.

Meanwhile earlier that year the wider world had encroached, presumably to Jimmy's relief, in the form of a letter from Kay Boyle in Connecticut on 2 February asking for his professional advice:

... Well – what I am really writing to you about is to ask for your help, for I have got myself into a job for next summer that is really terrifying. I have agreed to give thirty lectures at the University of Delaware in a six weeks period, one lecture a day, which means seventy-five minutes a day, all on THE SHORT STORY. It is utter insanity, of course, but I just could not turn the money down, as well as the prospect of being alone for six weeks so that I may, by some miracle, get closer to finishing my book. If only it were a story workshop I would not be so terrified, for there is always something to go on with that, and a lot of group discussion involved, but this is just getting up and tracing the history of the short story, dealing with various short story writers, and going totally mad, as far as I can see. The students will be teachers, and they all undoubtedly know far more about the short story than I do. And it is a credit course, so I have to give them an examination, and give them grades! It is too appalling.

I am going to borrow your *Man Who Was Loved* from Herman [Rappaport, a book collector whom Jimmy called 'The Magician from Brooklyn'], of course, and discuss you with the Irish group. (You see how I am falling into the academic patter already?) But I wondered if you could suggest to me an anthology, or collection, of Irish short stories with some sort of introduction which would contribute to the history of the Irish short story, at least? I am trying to do the same thing with the Welsh. Do you know of any Welsh collections? … I know enough to feel that Dylan Thomas was good because he was very deeply of his people, as Joyce was, and the words they used were the words that their own people used to speak with. (Frank O'Connor to the contrary). (Incidentally, I feel an increasing antagonism to O'Connor and hope I can forget he is a short story writer for the entire summer. Every time I walk into the room and see his arrogant, self-enamoured face on the cover of his collection, I turn it around, face down with a bang. I can't bear the man).

To which Jimmy replied immediately:

Lord *how* I agree about O'Connor. I simply cannot *bear* the divil. When I think of all the nice things I've said about him in print over the years …

… As far as the Welsh story writers are concerned, the best I can do is put you on to a most excellent young man, [Idris Parry] a professor of German at the University of North Wales & with whom I am in constant communication. Just drop him a line & mention my name.

… My native land is another matter. (By the way, if you mention my name as that of an Irish writer, be prepared for loud raspberries from the American brand who, as you know, are far more Irish than the boys still in the bog.) I am neither an authority nor a literary historian, and I feel bad that I cannot suggest exactly what you need straight off the cuff. My suggestion, banal as it may seem, is to ask Devin Adair (that is his name, isn't it, the American publisher of Irish-ry?), who produces tomes like A THOUSAND YEARS OF IRISH POETRY & PROSE. He himself of course doesn't know a book from a bottle (unless it be filled with John Jameson), but someone in the firm must. Sean O'Faolain, of course, is the man who'd know, but I'm sure he's not in the States right now.

I have one suggestion (nothing to do with what you have asked) which I feel would put up your stock (if that is possible or ever needed) among the more up-&-coming Delawarians (if any) and that's my opinion that since Joyce died there's only one man writing today in the essence & spirit of the ancient tradition of Irish Letters: Sam Beckett. If you could possibly get hold of that first book of his (stories), I really believe that within a few days your services for this kind of racket would be demanded in every State in the Union. There's the awful possibility, of course, that you don't like Beckett's work. That of course would be a terrible thing entirely, so it would.

John Davenport, who in many letters used to address Jimmy as 'Jymes', presumably a Cockneyism, wrote on 5 April 1957:

I thought Lolita would get you. I've sent a detailed description of you to the Chief Constable of Dorset. He's rather down on that sort of thing, so be careful.

A Film! Carson [McCullers] ... How would Cyril C. do for H. H. [Humbert Humbert]?

Yes: what is so amazing is the fusion of emotions – as you say, 'wildly funny, so serious, so shatteringly moving'. And so marvellously written. Of course, it's amazingly Russian = *Russian-American* of a very special kind.

Malcolm Lowry's last letter to Jimmy before his death on 27 June 1957:

We looked for you all day through the storm but didn't even see a flash of lightning (though just now, a week later, I heard a great roar of thunder).

The poppies blew over in the bloody brood, however, and we still live in hopes you may be coming, as when a certain magician was thinking, the churchbells started, elsewhere, ringing, though I'm not quite sure who the magician was. I hope you didn't have any trouble with your car on that stormy day, on which I also received an extraordinary letter from Germany about the *Volcano* couched in terms rather more suitable to the young Hofmannsthal than to the Cydraddict of Ripe. I would be extremely glad of your translation. Don't be put off by the rumour of Cydrax either, as my other friends seem to be. There's plenty else in the house. I don't even drink Cydrax myself for that matter, not to any excess, that is: in fact remembering that [Robert] Burton (not on Trent) somewhere said that borage was an aid to melancholy, and finding the garden full of borage, I have taken somewhat to borage: borage, I discover, on the contrary, *hugely induces melancholy*, so I can suppose that Burton (not on Trent) meant that he found it an aid in writing *The Anatomy of Melancholy*. Well, life is full of little touches like that. Do let us see or hear from you soon. The phone number is Ripe 282.

Everything you say can be heard next door by our landlady's sister, who just lent me *The Psychic Life of Jesus*, so don't say anything too metaphysical. For the rest I am doing a bit of fairly good work that is boring me to death but we do have – largely thanks to Margerie – a marvellous garden, in which everything is to be found in flower, except henbane, which is to be found in the churchyard. Let us hear.

Jimmy and Tania drove to Sussex on 3 July for Malcolm Lowry's funeral and burial in the parish church in Ripe. Among the small group of mourners were Lowry's widow, John Davenport and the novelist's eldest brother, Stuart Osborne Lowry, whom nobody knew and who held Margerie Lowry's hand throughout. Jimmy thought he was a hired mourner.

Kay Boyle continued her reports of her students' analyses of his stories on 11 August 1957:

... Thank you for your letter, which arrived in good time to make use of to refute my analysis of 'The Broken Leg'. This will be scattered and incoherent, but I must tell you that a member of the English Department at the University called Sproul (who rides to hounds in Delaware) was so excited about your work that he took your address to write to you ... Several students in my class (of over thirty) told me that your stories had been the ones they had enjoyed the most of all that we had read (and torn to shreds). There was bitter controversy over the closing line. Did you or did you not intend the arms that gathered Max in to be the mother's arms? Students practically killed each other in class. Several maintained that the whole meaning of the story was that Elliot was dead, and now the mother finally understood, and gathered her one remaining son to her heart. Others cried out that Elliot was not dead, despite the yellow waxen color of his flesh, and that other arms caught Max as he fell. If ever you want to decide the issue, let me know by a word or two for I have promised two students I would try to let them know ...

Well, if you think for a moment that I attributed gifts of prophecy to you which you do not possess, you should have seen what a young man did with 'Our Father'. I gave it to him to analyze (each student had a story or two to do, and two weeks or more in which to prepare analysis) and he took for granted that it was written after the Second World War instead of the First and read such symbols into it as you would have been amazed to see. In the final scene, when the toy boat sinks, the boat represented Hitler's Reich, and the wall which it hit was the second front. The rescue of the boat by the one-armed man was indication that the veterans (German) of World War II would be the ones who would salvage what hope was left and build a new world on German soil ...

... Dear Jimmy, had you been there this summer you would have realized how much your work means to people ... you would have sat down and done a short story, started a book, confirming all that they believed and said. You were one of the very finest short stories [sic] they had ever read, and they wanted more and more ...

... Love to you both, and remember how we need your work and how the halls of Delaware rang in your name.

Jimmy replied by return of post:

... Good Old Sproul! No, I've not heard from him yet.

What a maddening profession writing is! To be so, and so often, misunderstood! Surely if I had meant Max to fall into his *mother's* 'out-stretched arms' I would have said so. That woman would never have stretched out her arms to that son. But someone in the crowd, seeing he was about to faint, instinctively stretched out their arms – his or her arms, rather. However, that so many people have misread this sentence does show, I guess, that it is badly written. As I have said before, I hold no brief for the writing of this story. It is, or should be, the beginning of a novel, but I am simply not a novelist, I haven't the breath, the stamina, the patience, for steeplechases. Seven furlongs is my limit, and I prefer five. There I go, talking as though I still wrote stories…! When I was really writing, by which I mean at the time when almost nothing else was in my head, all I could think was: Oh God, please let me live until I have finished this. So you see why the few things I accomplished were brief!! I was always convinced I was going to die when I was 37. I very nearly did – but there, not quite!

… Of course Elliot did not die. Nor was he 'brave', for he had not known fear. I honestly do not believe that authors who write from the heart, who write because they must, because they feel they'd burst if they didn't – I honestly do not believe that such people know, certainly not at the time, what is the deeper meaning of what they are doing. This sounds awfully sententious. By 'authors who write from the heart' I mean at those *times* when a writer is writing from the heart, which cannot, in the case of writers who have a long writing life, be always. Which is one reason, I think why the first work of most writers is so often the best. Very few can keep up, can sustain the power, the enthusiasm, the naiveté, the innocence. D. H. Lawrence was an exception, I think. Most of those who managed, I believe, had TB and died young. And the best writers keep saying the same thing over and over again. Everything I have written, so far as I know, has been about EL O Vee EE, or the lack of it. It's really all I'm interested in. That is what 'The Broken Leg' is about.

It is also what 'Our Father' is about. This story I wrote in an hour on the backs of envelopes while sitting on a rock overlooking the Mediterranean in Majorca in 1932 or 3. Suddenly, while walking alone over the hills, I remembered a photograph I had taken of my mother and a friend sitting outside a tent on the lawn of our home in Ireland. The year was 1915. My father was 'at the war' in France, and I 'knew' even while I took the photograph at the age of 10, that man was my mother's lover. Suddenly I saw the story. To disguise it I placed it in Germany, a country with which the story has as much to do as I have with the Moon.

Dear Kay, I should of course be highly honoured by the dedication of your new book of the stories in paper-back, and I already look forward to reading the one I don't know: 'Decision'. And thank you, thank you for writing so generously of the things I used to do. Writing for me has been for years something akin to what your tooth was to you when you wrote me this letter. I have learned to live with impotence, to coddle it and even at times to laugh at it (it has such a ridiculous face), but I find it hard to accomplish with dignity. However, I do not utterly despair. A week or two ago I rose at 5 a.m., dashed downstairs & with my face streaming with tears poured out 3,000 words in an hour. I knew then that springs do exist in the Sahara.

A spat with the crabbed Djuna Barnes erupted in December 1957. Jimmy complained to her on the 21st:

> I wrote you a letter yesterday which may easily arrive at the same time as this. In it I referred to a 'bloody' remark you had made in a letter earlier this year. On waking this morning I thought maybe it was bloody of me to talk of a 'bloody' remark made by you months ago, and that since Christmas has to do with the Christian spirit I should have omitted to mention altogether my reason for not having written for so long. To my surprise I found the remark; I also found that age has almost mellowed the words, which I still think nevertheless most un-Christian & just the kind of thing to stop a chap writing altogether. Added to this, there was no doubt my own guilt for not having written. And the rest of the letter, I note with relief, was downright affable ...
>
> I ran into Peggy [Guggenheim] in goggles in a *Time* magazine ... I now wear bifocals, with the result that my head goes up and down like a chicken pecking... We drove to Bournemouth (30 mi.) last month to see Ruth and Zach Scott in the première of Faulkner's *Requiem for a Nun*. She was marvellous, 2 hours without a break, but the play was... turgid I think is the word. Great Success at the Royal Court, I'm told. In March I had lunch with Sam Beckett. I was all set to tell you about that, when you went and spoilt it, y'ould barnes, you. Now that's enough. Unlike you, I can't write in bed, I just ache all the way from crown to coxis (?) [coccyx].

To which The Barnes exploded on 28 December 1957: 'As I have not the *faintest* notion to what you refer in your two angry and rude letters, perhaps you will have the courtesy to enlighten me, as I can not defend myself in darkness.'

From Jimmy in answer to the above on 31 December 1957:

How can you say that I wrote you '*two* angry and rude letters'?

What I took offence at in your letter of June 9 was: 'You wrote last, but you said you hoped you were going to write a longer letter very shortly, *I knew better*.'

I thought this unfair, and the first of my two 'Christmas' letters was stupid enough to say so. In the second, mailed a few hours later, I intended to say that I was sorry for being petty. But evidently you thought my letter 'angry and rude'. *Surely* not? It was meant to be just the opposite. So is this.

7
Hatch Manor
1958–1962

The bleak first months of 1958 brought forth this reflection from Jimmy: 'The darkest, saddest year of our lives. We began to lose, one after another, close friends. Some contemporaries, some younger. All in England ...' It also appears to be a time when Jimmy and Tania's marriage was under a further degree of strain. For again in January he recorded:

A late night argument in which T. maintained that she had made a tremendous effort to behave normally ... & that my New Year's Eve behaviour, not wishing to sit up until midnight together (she was almost too drunk to cook at 8.30, & I certainly was less sober than usual), has sent her down into the depths of depression ever since. Back of it all is the old, beastly animal: Race. Or 'Blood'? It's what D. [his father] meant, of course. But look what he did – or rather what M. [his mother] did! Could that possibly be what he really meant? That he 'regretted' it, & so would I? I think the only way Anglo-Saxon men can live with women, in the way women *want*, is to have an endless succession of rows ...

This is the only mention of his Jewishness in relation to his marriage and that of his parents.

It has been suggested that the Sterns' rows fuelled their marriage, as is the case in many households, and it is difficult for one who knew them well not to be astonished when reading Jimmy's accounts of their bitter disagreements. One couple, subjected to a meal at Hatch Manor during which the Sterns rowed furiously and continuously, had retired in confusion, then returned to collect a favourite umbrella. They found Jimmy and Tania sitting close together in marital tranquillity on a garden seat, deep in conversation. If their public battles, which were numerous and witnessed by many over the years, were a form of theatre which subconsciously they needed and enjoyed, they were an embarrassment to many of their friends.

In London they ran into a host of these at a party of John Lehmann's. The 'great and the good' of their world were there: Christopher Isherwood and Don Bachardy, Moura Budberg, William Plomer, Graham Greene, Jocelyn Brooke, Keith Vaughan, Rosamond Lehmann, Stephen Spender, Tom Hopkinson with his wife and daughter, Alan Pryce-Jones and his son David, Robert Medley and Rupert Doone.

1958 was a tragic year for John Lehmann: his niece, Sally Kavanagh, the daughter of his sister Rosamond, died suddenly of poliomyelitis. Also, he had been forced to relinquish the editorship of the London Magazine which, since the collapse of his publishing house, had been his 'life'. Besides which, he contemplated the necessity of selling his elegant South Kensington house in Egerton Crescent, where he was a frequent and accomplished host.

Lehmann had known Jimmy since the '30s, had published him in Penguin New Writing and the London Magazine, but had never become a close friend, which was a disappointment to him. (His letter on p. 269 reveals his affection for Jimmy.) Indeed, in 1939 they had an altercation over an article on refugees in which Lehmann's characteristically overbearing manner elicited this outburst from Jimmy:

> I was so completely taken aback by your behaviour last night that I am afraid I acted like a schoolboy confronted by his Headmaster, of which the situation reminded me in every detail but one – which is that a third person was present. (T tells me she remained as mute as I did, because she was 'flabbergasted'.) Had she not been there I suppose, if only because I am in my thirties [Lehmann was three years younger] and not in my teens, I should have walked out of the room; or, had I had a drink and not felt so 'low', 'boxed your ears'.
>
> In future, should we ever do any 'business' together – which God forbid! – I shall see that it is conducted between ourselves, and in private.
>
> The manner in which you set about getting me to finish this article was, as I have suggested, the way in which my masters at school, and my parents at home, tried to get me to do things. It never worked, with me. And it never will.

'Business' was subsequently done, but their relationship appeared never to have recovered from this early fracas. Lehmann's schoolmasterly, authoritarian manner offended many; to Jimmy it was like a red rag to a bull. Forgiven maybe, but never forgotten.

Meanwhile Jimmy and John Davenport continued their exchange of literary gossip. From Davenport in Duxford, Cambridgeshire on 26 March 1958:

> Yes, there's quite a lot to be said for John Wain as a critic – that cheerful sharing of ignorance. (V. the assumption that Djuna [Barnes] had only written one previous book, that no one had heard of Henry [Miller] until Orwell's essay, *etc, etc.*) He's lucky, I think, to have been born into his particular age. As to his *own* age, he and Amis are 34 if they're a day and have 3 wives and at least 5 children between them. 34 is young, but not all *that* young. They'll be puppies all their lives, which will be long ones and studded with 'awards'.

From Davenport a month later:

> … Did Larry [Durrell] *really* say that he was 'by now an important figure' in Paris? A bit steep. Even as a joke.
>
> The countryside here is bright with lambs and daffodils & young birds of every description, but I'd like to be sitting on a terrace with a pretty girl – or two – and my favourite refresher: a bottle of dry white wine in a jug & a good measure of brandy and a squeeze of lemon. The sea not an absolute necessity, but not far away; & real *undiluted* sun.

From Davenport on 12 May 1958:

> … What is so awful about being fifty is that I am quite unable to feel differently from what I felt when I was sixteen. I spent most of 1924 in Touraine & I can still taste the Vouvray, the Chinon, the Bourgueil & the kisses of the girl from Baltimore who made the captain of cricket seem so sadly spotty when I got back halfway through the summer half.

On 21 May, at the age of eighty-five, Harry Stern died, a fact unremarked upon either in Jimmy's letters or in his journal. Harry's first-born had spent his whole life thus far 'too busy hating his father', in Isherwood's words. The fact that Jimmy's considerable literary achievements had gone forever unacknowledged by both his parents had surely

created a void never to be bridged, while Auden's hope that after his
father's death Jimmy could forgive, forget and relive him and thus be
creatively renewed would prove forlorn.

In January 1959, Jimmy was averaging eight personal letters a day.
Despite his avowed writing 'block', he was daily driven to write many
hundreds of words. Thus the truth of his alleged remark to the customs
officer in New York on his first visit is confirmed. In the late '70s he
wrote to Maeve Slavin: 'I am going through an (even for me) awful
period of being unable to "work", so I pounce upon the opportunity to
talk on paper ...' and 'I never had much desire or ability to work
(write). *Now* I will invent *any* excuse (best of all: writing to you) *not* to
put pencil to paper.' To Isabelle Evans in April 1963 he struck a note of
self-comfort: 'The art of letter writing, as Macaulay knew, is just as
much an art as the writing of fiction or essays or of painting.'

At the end of February 1959, he and Tania took off for a month to
France and Italy. On his return he noted that 2 April was the last day of
his status as an American citizen, which he had been for the past fourteen years.

Although some seven years later he told Isabelle Evans that if he
should survive his mother's death he and Tania planned to sail to the
West Indies via New York, the reason why the Sterns never returned to
America, even for a short visit, after their final departure from New
York in 1956, has remained obscure. The mystery deepens when it is
remembered how many friends and regular correspondents they had
living there, whose annual 'invasions', of which they fondly complained, were one result of their continued absence. On a practical
level, their aversion to aeroplanes was a factor, although passenger
liners still plied the Atlantic route. Jimmy's revocation of his US citizenship, it has been suggested, induced a crisis of loyalty: why would they
welcome his return if he'd turned his back on them? A theoretical
display of rectitude, which is not wholly convincing. Again, it may be
imagined that Tania was fearful that with the inevitably lavish reception from their wide and devoted circle, Jimmy might eventually
succumb to an alcoholic end à la Dylan Thomas. The answer is probably more simple: 'There's no doubt it [New York] *is* an exciting place
to visit,' he wrote to Pauline Wynn in December 1980, '— *if* one has a
few friends & a good deal of cash. But no, I should never want to *live*
there again. If I could go by sea when I *liked*, & return by sea when I

liked, I'd go like a shot, simply to see friends, of whom we have more than elsewhere in the world. Not, of course, just in New York: but in most of New England. There's the rub; how could we see them all, & not give offence by seeing only some?' That last sentence is the key. 'V. diffy.'

In London, the Sterns dined with Hamish (Jamie) Hamilton and his wife in Hamilton Terrace, Maida Vale. Truman Capote, Raymond Mortimer, Steven Runciman, Cyril Connolly, Ernestine Carter, and Vivien Leigh were the other guests. The Sterns have been called literary snobs and lionisers, yet when asked for an account of their exploits on returning from many of their visits to London, their priorities were invariably the plays they had seen and the art galleries they had visited, not the famous they had met.

A sentiment expressed in a letter that autumn from John Cowper Powys amused them: 'The only other human forehead I've wanted to kiss after I *did* kiss Augustus John's was Tania's ... I was so delighted my dear Tania to see your *forehead* again for save only my Phyllis's forehead I've never seen a lady's forehead of such obvious intellectual acumen and power and wisdom as yours ... I've got a mania for seeing inside ladies' foreheads.'

While staying with the Freuds in Walberswick in Suffolk, Jimmy overheard a conversation of Tania's with another guest – '... the sort of thing that shouldn't happen, much less be overheard, & made me feel v. sad and low. Such bitterness. "He doesn't know me; one day I'll just get up & walk out".' It was a threat to be repeated.

In November, they moved from Bees Cottage in Marnhull, the village in the Blackmoor Vale which is the original of Thomas Hardy's 'Marlott', the home of Tess in *Tess of the D'Urbervilles*, to Hays, a large house divided into flats, in Sedgehill, near Shaftesbury. From there, Jimmy wrote to Constantine FitzGibbon on 12 February:

This latest [*When the Kissing Had to Stop*, 1962] is by far the most superior work of fiction by you that I have read. I am aston-ished & filled with admiration at its scope, at your powers of invention, at its construction, the ease with which you move in a few pages all over the globe without any sign of strain, and above all at your characterization.

What I kept noticing in myself were the varied moods it provoked. I found that within half an hour's reading I had been thrilled, fascinated, horrified, deeply moved, and that I had also laughed out loud at least twice. Could any reader reasonably ask for more than that from a novel? And at least three times I found myself thinking: This is a very courageous book, a very serious book.

And here a minor criticism: as a distinguished novel I think it deserves a more dignified, more distinguished title. Browning or no Browning!

FitzGibbon replied by return:

I am, of course, delighted by your very positive reaction to my novel, and extremely grateful for all the agreeable and flattering things you say in your letter. Your criticism over all, I think, tenable. (Although I like the title – a matter surely of taste. The comparison with 18th Century Venice, riches, corruption, decay and surrender, seems to me just right. But my very sensitive N.Y. agent agreed with you, saying it was novelettish. I hope you're both wrong.)

Apart from another violent row in late February ('I letting loose apparently pent-up bitterness, no doubt saying things I shouldn't ...' Adding, ominously: 'Now our moment has come. I always knew it would ... Don't let us make it more dramatic than it is ...'), Jimmy and Tania were actively looking for a house to buy, in spite of their differences. On 30 March they viewed their future home for the first time: 'Terribly "steep" house, on four floors with frighteningly steep staircases' was their first impression. On 5 May their offer of £5,000 was accepted for a small sixteenth-century manor house in Hatch, a Wiltshire hamlet whose adult population was twenty. But they didn't move in until 23 November.

In fact, except for the treacherous stairs, which curled in a slippery spiral from top to bottom of the three-storeyed house and became a hazard in their old age, but which Tania later declared were good for the heart, Hatch Manor suited the Sterns, who were to live there for the rest of their lives.

After moving in, they quickly stamped their own personalities on the house. The drawing-room, with its low ceiling and open fireplace, and books lining one complete wall, exuded an air of comfort and cosiness. Across the hallway, in Jimmy's oak-panelled study, a huge 'partner's' desk stood importantly among more books. An anonymous door in the corner concealed a bountiful drinks cupboard; leaded windows looked out onto the lawn below.

By the end of their lives, Jimmy and Tania had accumulated an impressive array of pictures: there were oils, drawings in pen and ink, charcoal and chalk, and prints and lithographs, many by prominent artists. They included works by Max Beerbohm, Jacques Emile Blanche, Edward Burra, Alexander Calder, Dora Carrington, Jean Louis Forain, Lucian Freud, Arshile Gorky, Augustus John, Henry Lamb, Pablo Picasso, Pierre Auguste Renoir, Henri de Toulouse-Lautrec, Keith Vaughan, and John Butler Yeats. These had either been left to Jimmy in the wills of relations deceased or bought by him in galleries and salerooms over the years.

In the kitchen, down one flight of the dangerous staircase (where hung a particularly striking pen-and-ink portrait of W. H. Auden by Don Bachardy), an Aga stove, a plain pine table and an ancient, noisy fridge dominated what was very much Tania's domain. Here special guests would be 'syphoned off' to talk to Tania, while Jimmy appropriated their partners, wives, husbands, friends or children in a curious selection process which was intriguing and sometimes hurtful or mildly insulting. Jimmy feared that Tania, in her enthusiasm at having people to talk to, would otherwise monopolise the conversation.

More anger erupted that June. 'Swear I'll not be "abused" in this way ever again ... A ghastly row begins at 11am. & lasts till 3pm ... Finally she lay on the bed & had hysterics ... I have never [felt] so unguilty in my life!'

From Jimmy to Constantine FitzGibbon on 8 June 1960:

... [Richard] Aldington is not sane. He has the biggest chip I have encountered on a human shoulder. I once spent a fortnight under the same roof with him in Colorado – of all places (also present, down the road in Sorority Hall, sat that remarkable campaigner, Katharine Anne Porter. Falling foul of the filthy food in the Men's Dorm, I was looked after by Witter Bynner, the most humane example of she-men). I look upon R. A. as an extreme example of the class- and minor public school-conscious Englishmen, one in whom the ambition this 'consciousness' mostly breeds (among the talented) has never been realised. Hence the bitterness, the introspection, the bitch-hunting – in his case, for fairly obvious reasons (though one might be wrong to assume illegitimacy & suppressed homosexuality) – against English homosexuals. T. E. [Lawrence] was his perfect target: not only was he (presumably) homosexual, he did not go to Eton or Harrer, he was an intellectual and a soldier, a military hero & author of *Seven Pillars*. This was just too much for the man who, to this day, cannot forget that he served for 2 years of the Great War as a private. See *Encounter*! It is also possible that he cannot forget his origins – whatever they may be. It would be interesting to learn about his ancestry & childhood. I believe he was educated at Dover Coll & London U ...

... To return: Whatever his faults & weaknesses, one cannot deny that TE was, above all for the young & romantic, a highly romantic figure – just as I still think Cecil Rhodes was – but for whom Africa today ... well, *quien sabe*?

From Jimmy to John Davenport on 4 July 1961:

... I expect I have news or gossip of sorts, but I cannot think what it is right now. In fact, I cannot think – for I am engrossed, absorbed, overwhelmed, in the Patrick White Country. Viking sent me proofs of the new huge work [*Riders in the Chariot*, 1961]. Looks like 750 pp. Since I never skip a word of White I have been sitting with these proofs for a day & a half and have still a third of the book to read. My God, how puny in comparison every other living author I can think of! – An exaggeration? I wonder.

... Hemingway? His early work, the stories, were a revelation – the prose, what could be done in an opening sentence. And the war book (*A Farewell to Arms* [1935]). And the bull-fighting book (though I have heard real *aficionados* deny it) was good, may live. But the others – no, I cannot abide sentimentality, & the worst, for me, is the 'tough' (soft as a Bratwurst) American variety. This may sound pompous; I can't help it. I even once said it in print, but the best bits had to be cut. I just don't like 'Hemingways'. Also, there's no humility. It's all 'Hem, here I come...!' And the ghastly attitude towards *women*. Oh dear.

In mid-August, the Sterns were involved in a fatal accident. 'We were involved in a car smash in which a woman was killed & a child very seriously injured,' Jimmy wrote to William Plomer on 22 October. '... the very fact that one was there at all, at that moment, is enough [for the police to 'proceed' with the case]. If one hadn't been, it wouldn't have happened.' Eight days after the accident the boy died. In October a court, which Jimmy attended, found that he had done so accidentally. From many this tragedy was kept secret, even from Jimmy's brother Peter.

That month the Sterns were fighting again. Jimmy felt 'miserable, depth of depression & unhappiness'. Sybille Bedford and Eda Lord left after a short visit. He was 'genuinely sorry to see them go. Wish lack of vitality & deep unhappiness would allow me to ask them to stay. Feel ashamed – & so low ... Neither of us can communicate – feel miles away & not *so* guilty ... Crisis reaches climax in bathroom, where I break down ...'

In February 1961 they were in London on one of their many flying visits to see two of their old friends from New York, Harvey Breit and his wife, who were staying at the Connaught Hotel. Breit was an assistant editor of the *New York Times* and was a friend of Ernest Hemingway and William Faulkner. They had drinks at the Connaught with Ian Parsons of Chatto & Windus, Truman Capote and Cyril and Deirdre Connolly, with whom they had dinner afterwards. Jimmy noted that a friend of James Agee, Sam Spiegel, was in the restaurant, as was Lucian Freud, though, one assumes, not at the same table.

This evening was followed by an even more exalted occasion, a meeting at the Royal Society of Literature at which W. Somerset Maugham, John Masefield, E. M. Forster, G. M. Trevelyan and Winston Churchill were made Companions of Literature. Churchill's scroll was received by his daughter, Mary Soames.

They returned to the Connaught to have dinner with Arthur Miller who remembers Jimmy entering the hotel's lobby in his father's immense overcoat and a wide-brimmed hat. 'Jimmy treated hotel servants like the upper-class gent he was. They loved it!' he said.

In September and October they were in London again for two exhibitions: Max Ernst, Jimmy's friend from the '30s, at the Tate (Jimmy lunched at Scott's with John Davenport and Henry Miller) and Don Bachardy's drawings at the Redfern, where they met Christopher Isherwood, Joe Ackerley, E. M. Forster and Hester Chapman. Henry Moore, a neighbour of the FitzGibbons, and his wife visited them at Hatch in mid-October.

'My dear old Irish Harper,' Jimmy addressed Van Wyck Brooks on 20 October 1961,

To your Shadow of the Mountain from the green slopes of Hatch (only 7 miles from that Grosvenor! [the hotel in Shaftesbury]) I write to tell you that 'il est arrivé', as the special editions of the *Paris Soir* greeted the arrival of Monsieur Lindbergh 35 years ago!

But what a pleasure this volume [*From the Shadow of the Mountain*, 1961] is! I don't know why, perhaps because so many pages strike so many bells, but here, far more than hitherto, I can see you in that corner of that booklined room, can hear your voice – reading the proofs – like several rambling brooks (ha ha!) hour after hour. And what you do with your astonishing memory, your files, your reading, your letters! It strikes me as curious & oddly significant that each time I open the book it is to hear that you have 'long believed that the best writers are now the writers of natural history…' Oh, *how* I agree – about the 'permanent things', the 'immutable themes'. One of the most violent storms I ever remember raged and tattered at this old house last night (it is now 8am on Oct 23) & while I went up & down the stairs mopping up the windowsills with my pail & sponge, I kept thinking of you & Gladys in that sensible spacious house where, so far as I know, the rain did not penetrate & you mixed your evening drink in the cosy warmth of that drawing room in front of my favourite circular table; I thought of your hospitality, your taking me in as a guest, when I was broke or alone, or both; & later, on going at last to bed in the howling gale I put down your *Mountain* & picked up & re-read Jack's [John Hall Wheelock's] *The Gardener*, then picked *you* up again to read your tribute to those grand poems & that grand man, & I went to sleep thinking what an honour it is for 'the wild little boy' from Bective to have you both as friends.

From Jimmy to John Davenport on 31 October 1961:

… First, I couldn't help being disappointed that Angus [Wilson] had got hold of *Riders* [*Riders in the Chariot*]. Was it ripped out of your admiring hands? Did you actually do a review which was thought too uncritical? Though I had to agree with some of the things Angus said, I thought his objections were pretty trifling. And I couldn't help sniffing a little bile, if not outright envy, behind his words.

Davenport replied the next day:

Yes: the *Observer* was afraid I'd go overboard about White, as I probably should have, and Angus asked for it particularly – so there we were. (You will – I hope – be pleased to read that V. S. Pritchett wrote to me yesterday to say that he was sorry I hadn't been able to write about his short stories: 'Nobody has so wide a grasp as you or so fine an eye.' Ahem!)

.... Why does White have to stay in that antipodean inferno? Is it sheer masochism? After all, other parts of the world have as good a climate and are infinitely more congenial. *No* good Australian writer or artist stays in the bloody place; & he must have enough 'material' to last him a life-time.

Augustus [John] has gone. Only three weeks ago I had a letter from him written in a pretty tremulous hand. I must quote the beginning: 'My dear friend, whenever I come up to town I ring you up – or get somebody to do so as I am now struck down with deafness & am under treatment. I would so much like to renew our so genial acquaintance but have no luck. You are probably the most evasive figure living... if indeed you are still alive; though most certainly, what is better, marked down for a niche in Paradise in due course.' So I felt rather weepy when I heard the news on the radio last night.

.... Nadine Gordimer is a darling. When we were first going to meet some years ago in a bar I described myself as a gigantic dwarf, and she said (on the telephone) 'How nice! I'm a dwarf, too.'

From Jimmy to Davenport on 3 November 1961:

... Now it is [James] Thurber...Golly, what a week! Still, dear old Augustus was 83. And what a life! My most vivid memory of him is running into him in a bistrot somewhere in the middle of France during the worst days – or day, perhaps – of the Munich crisis. He struck me as like a lion at bay, both furious and fearful.

...I quite agree with what VSP said in his letter to you. I have been a great admirer of Pritchett's stories, and I think reviewed the 'collected' volume. The awful thing is: I read recently in the *New Yorker* a couple of his stories which I assume are in the present volume, & I must say – although much of the old Pritchett vitality and vivid dialogue were there – I was very disappointed with the stories *as stories*. Something essential – depth, I think – was missing. One could not help feeling, at the end: So what? I feel I should read this book & write to him (he has treated me very handsomely at least once), but can't help feeling apprehensive ...

... Re White (from whom another letter this morning): I think there is little doubt that he *is* masochistic (the streak of the female is strong). But I think I understand his attitude. I believe that among the things he would say in self-defence would be: It is just *because* 'No good Australian writer or artist stays in the bloody place...' At some time, immediately after the war, I imagine, he had to make his Big Decision: to return or not to return. And I think he has said somewhere that he knew that if he stayed (in Europe) it would have been to become a dilettante in London. And instead, chose to become a writer in the country he knows and loves, among people he despises and hates. Oh yes, I find it quite comprehensible. A certain masochism no doubt, but courage too. And I cannot imagine him leaving now; he has made his decision, and in doing so, his Name. To leave would be letting himself down, and the essential part of himself behind.

From Davenport on 6 November 1961:

I wonder if you know what pleasure your letters give me. They're solid without being heavy.

You make White's position vis à vis Australia perfectly clear. The love-hate is obviously necessary to him, and my God, what doesn't it produce!

From Jimmy to Davenport a day later:

Well, that *was* a nice thing to hear: oddly enough, it is the second time in a week (as well as years!) that someone has commented on my hastily scribbled letters. (The other was dear old Van Wyck B[Brooks].) Let me honestly and quickly reciprocate the compliment.

Oh, I do agree: there is no one like VSP. God, the number of words that man produces over the years! And such *good* words – nearly always. I can think of no better model. I would rather read his criticism than Bunny [Edmund] Wilson's. More 'human'.

Off and on throughout 1962, Jimmy was at work on the autobiography everyone had been waiting for and which so many friends had urged him to write. The work was interrupted by recurring family problems: his sister Rose's nervous illness, and his widowed mother's domestic arrangements. (He records in his journal a characteristic verbal near-miss from the latter about one of her innumerable cooks who came and went in rapid succession: 'Of course I don't think she's very well. If you ask me, I think she's having the time of her life.')

From William Plomer in Rustington, Sussex on 9 January 1962:

… At Aldeburgh I saw nice Heywood Hill, & both the Gathorne-Hardy boys – Eddie & Bob. The latter is editing the memoirs of Ottoline Morrell, he told me, in two vols. I expect he will have to leave out a lot because of people being alive – & alive to libel and scandal, I seem to remember Virginia Woolf telling me that Otto-line's memoirs weren't much good because she couldn't write …

From Jimmy to Plomer three days later:

… As I was saying to your nice friend Joe Ackerley (at the party to which you did not come), for a writer to have a 'place' of his own is nowadays, without servants or help of any kind, absolutely hopeless. He couldn't have agreed more, as they say, and he told me you agreed too. Good old Wm. But since I don't aspire any longer to be [a] writer (let alone a *Writer*) – shish, Wm – I should not complain.

… Oh, those wastepaper mongers! So you know Schwartz[16] as well! He lives alarmingly near you. I say alarmingly because he is constantly threatening to come here, and he is really one of my *bêtest* of *noires*. How that nice Irish woman (do you know her name? Take a deep breath: Sharp-Bolster!) can go on living with…a case of 'chacun à…' if ever there was one. Last time I saw him was at Sotheby's; he had grown one of those goatees, so I was quite innocently able to ignore his rude stares across the room. But of course he nabbed me, and began telling me who Dame Edith Sitwell is and how Pavlic Tch. [Tchelitchew] was her 'good friend' and 'Look here, that's what he made of the Dame in middle-age. And look at this, that's what Sir Max Beerbohm thought of Kipling. Max didn't like Rudyard, you know …'

… No, I too should not have thought that Lady O. could 'write'. But I shall always remember her handwriting: the image of herself – an elderly Edwardian heron (or should it be heron*in*?), don't you think? (Or heroness? Her Royal Heroness, Lady O.?) I remember going to occasional parties in that house and feeling intolerably uncomfortable & shy. I managed to take

16 'Dr J. Schwartz who buys MSS & waste paper for American universities' – W. P.

occasional refuge with him, I suppose because I thought he didn't look like a Writer and didn't seem very much at home in his own home …

From Jimmy to John Davenport on 14 January 1962:

It strikes me as very odd that we have not discussed the work of Jimmy Baldwin before now. I call him by his first name, for I have known him for some 10 or 11 years. I met him first in St. Germain-des-Près in, I think, the spring of 1952. He was the Black Chief of a little tribe of fairly poverty-stricken white Americans who hung out at the cheaper bistros of that quarter. I remember that from the first moment we started talking of the Eternal Problem, of Africa & America, & that after half an hour I realised that I was sitting with a Negro who talked more profoundly about colour than anyone I had ever met or read. From then on I sat back & listened & have here all his published books bar the second novel, *Giovanni's Room* [1956], which has been swiped. Ever since his first book of essays, *Notes of a Native Son* [1955], I have been convinced that he is the only living American who has ever dared to show white Americans the colour of their own shit (his favourite four-letter word). The moral courage (let alone his talent for reasoned polemics) of this boy has always struck me as one of the wonders of the world. When I first met him he was seeing a great deal of Richard Wright, loved him, admired him, but was magnificent in explaining why Wright's work was doing almost as much harm as good. Wright had fury & power, but not the brain, the reasoning, the delving you have read in the long *New Yorker* piece ['Letter from a Region of My Mind', later published as *The Fire Next Time*, 1963] your phone call jerked me, belatedly, into reading. It is probably the most daring thing Jimmy has yet done, yet some of the shorter things among the two volumes of essays, simply by their brevity, are nearer to knock-out blows even than this sweeping, devastating survey. (Incidentally, it must be one of the longest things the *New Yorker* has ever printed?)

From Jimmy to Davenport again on 8 February 1962:

… Believe it or not, I am still writing…though I shouldn't say so. One of my appalling weaknesses is if and when I *do* write I feel compelled to go and spill the beans. Fatal. So far, however, I have not told a soul (bar Tania) but you. So don't let on, please. The moment I hear someone ask 'How's the Book coming', I shall shoot – both the questioner & myself.

I am so nervous about the bloody thing that I dare not return & begin to type out a legible version. I write in longhand in pencil in a cahier (the only way I have ever been able to write anything); I write on the right hand side of the cahier, but by the time I have reached the bottom of that page the opposite page is a criss-cross mass of deletions & insertions. The result *looks* as though several Balzacs had been over it in their boots, and the right-hand page is illegible. But I dare not go back, I dare not type; it would take me a week, at the end of which I should never be able to continue. Forgive me for using you as a kind of vast towel to mop up my [word missing], stifle my inward screams.

And again to Plomer on 3 April 1962:

… There is so much to talk about that I hesitate to begin. I will *try* to be brief. There's some good news, & some bad, but the latter has improved. The good news is a dead secret, which I am divulging to you (& no one else at present) because (1) I believe you to be one of the very few people I know capable of keeping a secret; and (2) because I feel I must at last tell someone, preferably a writer, a contemporary, & above all a friend. I have already told a number of people that on February 3 I suddenly began to *write*. By the end of the month I had down on paper, typed, 25,000 words. What I have not divulged to a soul is what I am writing *about*. Well, my dear Wm, it really is not all that interesting: I hush it up simply because of the fear that if I talk of it I shall dry up on the spot. I am writing an autobiography – straight: full names, no punches pulled etc. It cannot of course be published – for years, if ever, or rather possibly not in my lifetime, although that does rather depend on how long I am allowed to fiddle about with a pencil and paper. However, I am not worrying about publication; the words flowed, day after day, so I let them; I lived all through February in a kind of dream, the kind of dream I experienced last in the summer of 1946, when *The Hidden Damage* somehow wrote itself.

Then, early in March, my sister fell seriously ill ('nervous breakdown') & we both had to leave here & look after my mother. We slept at her house & I commuted back and forth 40 mi. morning and evening by car. It was a bit of a nightmare, both physically and psychologically... By this time, however, *I* feel ill ... I am definitely recovering & have managed to crawl to page 115 of the opus. The *élan* of course has evaporated, but simply by sitting with my cahier & pencil I find that I can take it up & drop it more or less like knitting ...

... Isherwood's 'novel' [*Down There on a Visit*, 1962]? It left a nasty taste in my mouth. I know or knew most of the characters & *don't* find them v. interesting. But than C. I. I suppose there is no one more *readable* alive.

'The good news is a dead secret': it can fairly be said that Jimmy was uncommonly secretive. 'We're coming up to London, but don't tell a soul ... we'll be incognito' is an exclamation his friends heard many times. The fear or anticipation that the capital's telephone system would be jammed with the hot news that the Sterns were coming to town is a risible notion. But, of course, his ego could never be accorded that strength. No, the fear of being found out, checked up on, called to account – perhaps a throwback to childhood when he suffered those ignominious inspections under his father's derisive, military gaze – may have accounted for a desire for anonymity, a wish not to be beholden, not to be seduced by drink or blandishment from a preconceived course, not to disappoint by exclusion – when time is so precious – one or many of his friends. In short, to be in control.

In the case of his 'confession' to Plomer, his fear of failure should the fact be widely known that he was writing – at last! – an autobiography, would have been paramount. But to share this miraculous renaissance with a trusted confidant on whose encouragement he could count, would have been exquisite, too. The springs of creativity being as remotely located as El Dorado, his phrase, 'If I talk of it I shall dry up on the spot', would ring a bell with every writer since the beginning of time.

From William Plomer on 6 April 1962:

Let us speak of your *good* news first. It is very good, & I will keep the secret. I am most anxious that you should go on and complete what you have begun. When almost everybody writes too much & too often, you write too little & too seldom. You are perfectly equipped to write an idiosyncratic & brilliantly lucid & unforeseen kind of autobiography, & I shall be furious if it isn't printed in my lifetime.

… I haven't read Chrisherwood's novel. I don't feel any curiosity or appetite for it. I think I should find it distasteful and boring, and that 'nasty taste' has evidently been left in other mouths besides yours …

Jimmy replied three days later:

… Somewhere in his letters Freud says that a truthful autobiography is an impossibility: there can be no such thing. And I know I should not be attempting it & I already feel that it is not even 'interesting'; but … I started it with that 'no uncertain feeling' that *by God this is what I should be doing*; the words began to flow, so I let them …

… I came across in my old tin trunk (which I acquired for Africa in 1925!) the other day the script of a radio version of a D. H. Lawrence story Wystan & I did together for CBS in New York exactly 21 years ago. The music, I see, is by Benjy B. [Benjamin Britten]. I re-read it & thought it so lively, funny, sad, & so *very* Wystan that I sent it to the BBC. They seem to be quite excited, despite its age, shop-soiled condition etc. It's called *The Rocking Horse Winner*, I think, about a child who takes to backing horses through his parents' chauffeur …

… Guy Chapman. Isn't he the Chap(man) who wrote a 'Life' of Wm. Beckford, our neighbour? I am in violent disagreement with all Beckfordians: I long ago came to the conclusion that he must have been one of the beastliest men who ever lived …

Five days later from Plomer:

… So you have been invaded by Schwartz – and Miss Blunt Pillow, whom I have not seen. There is something I can't help liking about Schwartz, but he makes me just as nervous as he does you. I feel he might suddenly want to buy one's socks & insist on one taking them off & signing them, with an inscription 'To J. Schwartz, with whom one is pleased to be on such a friendly footing, with somewhat restrained good wishes …'

Yes, it is Guy Chapman who wrote about Beckford [*Beckford*, 1937]. He is a splendid, genial, irascible, highly intelligent little man, & the husband of Storm Jameson (whom I don't know, & who has just taken a running kick at Chrisherwood in the *Lit. Supp.*).

… I meant to say, I have no doubt you are right about Beckford.

It is unusual for you to express such strong feelings about an author – if that is what one thinks of him as being.

From Jimmy to Plomer on 13 June 1962:

… No, I am not reviewing the Wilde Letters. I suppose, perhaps, I should be. I say this because I know someone who is reviewing them, and who has no business to be doing so, someone who did not know that Bosie wrote poetry. Needless to say, I can't wait to see *your* review …

Re-reading these letters sent me back to Bosie's autobiography, which I don't think I had looked at since soon after its publication in 1929. I had quite forgotten, for instance, that he and I went to the same prep. school. He in 1884, I in 1914! But good heavens, what an appalling book! It is hard for me to believe that this was the man with whom (also in 1929) I once spent an hilarious hour in Fleet Street, the handsome (nothing like the photograph, the frontispiece of the autobiography), tweedy, aristocratic-looking gentleman who told so many (and such marvellous) stories about OW that I of course cannot remember one of them. Dreadful thought.

I think the most awful moment in the book is when he finally leaves prison, goes straight to the Sphinx [Ada Leverson], manages for an hour or so to be his Old Self, then asks for pen and paper, writes a note, asks for a messenger, then sits and waits for the answer – which is in the negative. What, I wonder, would have been the result if the answer had been Yes?

There was a man here last night who insisted that had it not been for the scandal, OW would have been but a 'footnote in English literature'. These letters are a pretty fat footnote. But I suppose the 'man here' would have answered that these letters would not have seen the light of day.

From Plomer on 15 June 1962:

… I am quite horrified that somebody so ignorant about Bosie should be allowed to review the Wilde letters. And for several reasons I think the other *somebody* wrong in suggesting that Wilde, apart from the scandal, would have been 'only a footnote'. What about the comedies? the aesthetic revolt against plush-and-mahogany Victorianism? his gifts as a talker & wit? his place in his period? I think all those of *some* importance.

So you were at Bosie's prep. school, and I was at a prep. school kept by the son of the man who kept Norman Douglas's prep. school – 'a hog in human form', wrote Douglas somewhere. My meeting with Bosie was not hilarious, like yours. It was in Hove, & he was old and poor & I think hungry, but I didn't feel sorry for him.

... That awful moment when the R.C.s wouldn't let Wilde go into retreat is perhaps linked with his crack about not liking Christians because they weren't Catholics & not liking Catholics because they weren't Christians. At the one moment in his life when he needed sanctuary, tolerance, forgiveness, &c., he gets a dusty answer ...

'Noble William!' Jimmy wrote to Plomer two weeks later,

Your OW review is grand. One can feel the affection behind every sentence, as well as the hatred of philistinism shared by your subject. And what a *lot* you managed to get into 11½ columns. I still have not written to the King of the Footnote. I must do so at once and address him thus, since I don't know him well enough to call him Rupert [Hart-Davis]. And oh, how glad I was to see OW's description of Queensberry quoted. (Odd thing: I don't think I have ever consciously seen the word 'aberrancy' in print before. But I am very much aware of my poor vocabulary.) And I did not know that disease – oh, how appalling it must be! – is known as 'middle-ear'. I have always wanted to know more about the relationship between OW and his wife. What a heartbreakingly sad picture that is of her! The more I think of these Letters the greater grows my admiration for OW's moral courage (viz. 'his playfulness to the very end'). It seems to me particularly impressive in one who just could not resist 'turning to the bottom of the next page'. (Incidentally, is this an apocryphal crack, do you think? Also incidentally, is Bosie's case against Arthur Ransome the same Ransome who wrote all those books for children & who once lived in the farm a minute's walk from here & where, in 1917, just before leaving for France to be killed, Edward Thomas stayed with him?). I believe this Ransome is still alive, at 85 or so. Today, Bosie would be 92 ...

In the summer of 1962, Jimmy became friendly with Sonia Brownell, who had married George Orwell, virtually on his deathbed. Although subsequently she had been married briefly to Michael Pitt-Rivers, she had reverted to the name Orwell, a cachet not easily resisted. A confidante and colleague of Cyril Connolly, with whom she had worked on *Horizon*, she was also a great Francophile and generous hostess in her South Kensington home to the leading literary figures of the day. 'Sonia, with popping blue eyes and a complexion that grew rosier with every additional glass of wine ... liberally sprinkled her conversation with Gallic phrases – *"et comment"*, she would trill.' – Jocelyn Rickards (*The Oldie*, October 2000).

From Sonia Orwell, Percy Street, London on 18 August 1962:

Kindest Jimmy,

In a way I'm sorry I wept all over you, but in a way it was so marvellous that *you* were there to weep over! What I really want to say is that I couldn't have had a lunch more necessary to me, that it was lovely seeing *you*: that altogether this has been one hell of a summer for us all, and that the Sterns have been one of the rare illuminations in mine! OH FOR FRANCE! I was just thinking *how* odd it was we had all come to like that huge country and see it as a province of our own in many ways. Anyhow thank God it exists. I can't wait to hear those cross, intelligent voices again and be told 'c'est jamais trop tard pour bien faire' when one wants lunch at 3.30!

... Yesterday evening I spent with Henry Miller in transit and am already quite exhausted! However, it was very nice when you were mentioned and he said 'Now, he was always one of the most generous people anyone ever knew!' He was talking so much I couldn't make out whether this was because you had known each other personally, through Max Ernst, or he was just repeating hearsay. Anyhow that's what he said. And he meant with ideas as well as with kindness as well as with the little money you had.

'Chère Chumme,' Jimmy wrote to Sonia Orwell on 3 September 1962:

... These few lines will have to be written in snatches, for Wm. Plomer, that dearest of men, is sitting in the next room, waiting to be driven to Salisbury, whence he takes a train to Portsmouth, & thence to Angmering-on-Sea, and his bungalow home.

Which reminds me that John O'Lehmann was here last

weekend, on a very brief visit. I am more than ever convinced that he should have been in the City, where he would have become a real tycoon & possibly a Governor of the Bank of England. Wm. P., on the other hand, should be Prime Minister of the U.K.

... An oddment of today: About the City of Salisbury I always say that it has only 2 advantages – 1) Beach's Bookshop, and 2) I never see anyone I know. In 30 minutes today I saw (& managed not to be seen by) a character known to me in Paris of the 1930s as Benvenuto (Sherard?), who used to hang on to (rather than out at) the Flore, was a chum of Desmond Ryan & a pupil of Blanche Jouve. (So what? Nothing, *rien*). And a strange-looking gent of a very uncertain age who had half-white, half-bleached-looking hair & on his face dents rather than spots. 'Look!' I said to Wm, 'Look at that!' 'That', said Wm, as though taking it for granted that the stranger would be on that spot at that moment, 'is a very good poet, from South Africa' (most of my conversations with Wm. tend to circle in & around South Africa); 'he is unfortunately stone deaf. Could he hear, I would have suggested that you halt your motor & I would have made the introductions. He is co-editor of a magazine that might have the name of X or Y – or possibly even Z. I alas am not what I believe is known as UP in these things. His name? Ah. Now – Wright? David Wright, would it be? *You* would know.' No, said, I, and to myself: Sonia would. – Well, that was today's wild excitement.

On 16 October in London the Sterns gathered at the Savoy in distinguished company – Stuart Hampshire, Geoffrey Gorer, Alec Waugh, Jimmy's publisher Fred Warburg and his wife – for the annual W. H. Smith Award, presented this year to J. R. Ackerley's *We Think the World of You* (1960), which Jimmy thought was 'an astonishing tour de force. V. brave. To write such a book must not the author have known the depths of degradation & despair? How can it *not* be accused of "obscenity"?'

During that autumn of 1962 there began a correspondence between Jimmy and a young actress and aspiring writer which would span three decades and amount to over four hundred letters and postcards from himself alone.

He first met Pauline Wynn, the second wife of Humphrey Spender, painter, photographer and pioneer of the Mass Observation Movement in the '30s, five years earlier at Kitty West's house near Blandford

Forum. Pauline's first love was acting but the uncertainties of that noto-
riously insecure profession led her eventually to the writing of stories
and to the adaptation of the work of others and of her own for radio.
With dark hair, a strong-featured face and a versatile, expressive and
well-modulated voice, she was regularly employed as a reader or in
acting parts by such as Douglas Cleverdon, the discoverer and first
producer of Dylan Thomas's play, *Under Milk Wood*, and the BBC's
Reggie Smith, husband of the novelist Olivia Manning. Pauline, with
the actor Douglas Leach, also took part in 'An Evening with Thomas
Hardy', a series of dramatised lectures and poetry readings, which
Desmond Hawkins, the novelist, critic and founder of the BBC's
Natural History Unit took on tour in the UK and to America, Japan,
Malaysia and India.

It was her search for material to adapt for radio plays which first
drew her to Jimmy's stories and in time she would be successful with
his 'The Woman Who Was Loved' and *Sons of England*. Their letters
were wide-ranging and covered every subject under the sun from the
price of apples to cures for depression, from the iniquity of neighbours
to the tedium of lawn-mowing. Yet paramount were the subjects of
writing and the literary life.

Of a tenacious, fiery and passionate nature, Pauline was to react at
first with knee-jerk sensitivity to any criticism, real or imaginary, which
she received from her new mentor. ('Why on earth did you get angry,'
Jimmy wrote in January 1966. '... Be peaceful & unprovocative &
uncomplaining for as long as you possibly can.') And it is a feature of
their correspondence that Jimmy's tact, indeed tenderness, mixed with
straightforward and constructive help, is invariably apparent throughout their thirty-year relationship. 'I am an idiot of infinite patience – as
you know,' he told her. He addressed Pauline with the mystifying
epithet 'Squif' and signed himself 'Croc' or 'Croque' (meaning, with
characteristic self-disparagement, 'old crock', a sickly or worthless
person).

From 1964 to 1985 their epistolary affair is charted chronologically
in the following selected passages from Jimmy's letters to his often
importunate and demanding young pen friend who 'longed and
yearned' for his immediate replies to her own:

You ask me what I would have done about ending that play. I
don't know. My powers of invention no longer seem to exist. But
I do think you would or rather should have thought up an entirely

new situation or idea. Perhaps the Dr could have given the girl something more concrete on which to work out her salvation. Or allowed the older man to visit her or write her a letter. Or could she not have literally confronted the girl in the next cell?

If you wish me to criticize your work in general I would say their one flaw is a lapse into sentimentality; also that you are inclined too much to dot your i's and cross your t's. You say too much. The intrinsic *art* of all story-telling, no matter what form it takes, is that of implication. When one has finished reading a story one should be left wondering how on earth it was done ... I feel very strongly about this subject – I suppose because I feel in my bones that I know, instinctively, intuitively (& I function only in this way, which makes me, I insist, the opposite of an intellectual), what I am 'talking about'. [25.7.64]

In several passages there are suggestions that their relationship was not confined to letter-writing: 'I was immensely relieved to hear that your state of "desolation" after our meeting lasted only until the end of that day. My reaction to seeing you go lasted much longer.' (25.7.64)

I am so relieved that you took my 'criticism' so – so well, so charmingly. I am afraid of being mis-read, misinterpreted, of the tone of my voice being misunderstood ...

Please never think that 'it is cheek to ask' me to vet mss; I am such an old hand at it I could do it in my sleep, almost; and, since I find it easy I rather enjoy it, provided I am not under pressure. The only difficulty is to word one's remarks without appearing offensive or 'superior'. I am continually amazed how few people can 'take' criticism of any kind. [2.11.64]

You are a sweet creature and I am glad I know you ... Please take care of yourself, Squif, & try not to get 'het up' (*that's* the phrase) if I don't write as often as you think I should. [1.12.64]

I cannot forgive myself for allowing you to leave the way you did. I know it is all my fault, of my inability to show my feelings in the manner most women want. The more emotional, the more frustrated, the greater the yearning, the more passive I become.

As for you, I imagine that this particular meeting was worse than any other simply on account of the weeks of waiting & the agony you had gone through when for ten days on end no word came.

Another thing that you perhaps do not take into account is the difference, at each meeting, in what is going on in the back of your mind and mine. I can never be completely unaware of the ticking minutes, of the knowledge of where I am and where I ought to be, and how I am going to explain my afternoons. On reaching Durrants [Hotel], for instance, where I was supposed to have been 'lying down' since 4pm, T. herself was the one who was lying down, & rather understandably furious that I had been 'on my feet' – or foot – since 6.30 that morning, in fact for 12 hours. – I am not trying to 'excuse' myself, but to explain & analyse why it was that you left that taxi as you did. Please try to understand, and to forgive. [20.12.64]

In the first of two letters that December, Jimmy's capitals may be decoded with some ease by the prurient: 'In pants? I'd much rather L Y A O *without* them. In fact, I would find it v. difficult otherwise. So lie down & I'll take them off. Save you the trouble. I'd like that. How about you?' The second ends: 'I would like very much to K U A O & be K A O. Look after yourself and "take it easy".'

Dearest badly-treated Squifling [begins his letter of 7 March 1965], oh dear oh dear, there we go again. And this time it does look as though it's the Old Croch's fault. From what you say he must be a very nasty old croch indeed. Fancy him making generalizations to the detriment of the opposite sex, of which his girl-chum is such a delicious example – except, of course, when she's X. And it's so easy to make her X; she takes a little irony so personally, so much to heart. A croc hardly dares put pen to paper sometimes. He's now made a vow never to write after midnight – though some days that's about all the time he has.

Dear Squif, you know I cannot 'decently' phone, ever, from here – unless I am on my own, which is as rare as sunshine in England. [undated]

I am more than ever terrified of disappointing you ... If I tell you that it is possible for us to meet only for a short time I am disappointing you; but if I didn't tell you, you would have every right to say that I *should* have told you. See, Squif? I wonder if you *really* can see the dilemma I am constantly in vis-à-vis your sweet self? [1965]

My darling Squif, I thought you looked quite miserable as you got out of that taxi ... You harp only on my not being able to 'look at you'. If I have not explained already, it is because, after such an absence, I feel I could explode, or burst into tears. And that is the woman's prerogative. I also know from long experience of 'absences' that nothing one can say or do or how one looks can possibly rise to the expectation of either oneself or the Other Person ... What it all amounts to is that you and I, both of us, are emotional brutes who have been starved of affection at the most crucial years of our lives. [17.7.66]

Do I think of you sometimes? Considering that I have been writing to you pretty regularly for 3 years, this seems an odd question. [17.7.66]

Re the possibility of reviewing books ... if you have never reviewed a book, yet consider the idea at all, you must have a little practice before beginning in earnest. So I am having you sent a book (for Christmas, it won't be any surprise), with the suggestion that you review it in 500 words & send it to me, on condition of course that you do not resent anything I may have to say. [12.12.66]

The following month, Jimmy's lengthy, considered and tactful critique of her review produced profound disappointment, according to Humphrey Spender.

Squiflet cara! Your two nice letters, not a word of complaint. Very nice. Almost makes me feel I am not so awful after all. One of the nicest, most generous things about you is that one only has to give you one slight pat on the shoulder, and you begin to glow. [26.7.67]

No, I did not answer your next to last letter because I am incapable of doing what is expected of me; I am *most* incapable of being 'demonstrative on paper'. Surely you should know that by now? 'How can I tell that you are fond of me if you don't say so from time to time?' Heavens above! That's a schoolgirl. What a silly you are. To whom but you do I write letter after letter after letter? But they are no good, for in them I don't tell you that you are nice & have lovely eyes! Oh, do please let us be a little more adult ... I'm *ever so fond* of you, Croque. [2.9.67]

You need take only one of my comments seriously, and that (as you know) is the rewriting of the final paragraph. Personally, I don't think it would matter if you made it obscure or cryptic. The point is to force the reader to raise an eyebrow, to *think*. The great thing *not* to do is to treat him (the reader) as an idiot, even if you have no doubts at all that that is just what he is. My advice would be: put that story away until you get a brainwave, which will come when you least expect it, even if you have to wait 6 months. [28.4.69]

The trouble is I am not in a position to judge the market ... People don't read any more, as we are constantly being told ... in a world that feeds almost entirely on Sensation, your stories are probably too quiet, too subtle. Which does not mean that the time, *their* time, won't come. One trouble with you is: you want quick results. When I wrote it was because I had to, I felt I had something to say, had to say it. Whether it was published was a comparatively minor consideration. And what, if anything, I received for my efforts was even less important. I looked upon writing almost as a luxury. I still do. To this day I am astonished when a cheque arrives for anything I have done. [18.6.69]

I am naturally pleased & grateful that 'The Woman Who Was Loved' is at last (and owing to your suggestion, it would seem) to be *read* over the air ... But of course I should have preferred you more than anyone else to have read it, & if it could not have been you, then I should have liked to have read it myself. [25.6.70]

Your visit certainly perked me up; if only it would last! It also had the effect of persuading T. at last to confess how little if any encouragement or interest I get from her. This has always been a great sadness to me, and something I have never told anyone before ... [25.11.82]

On 12 December 1990 Pauline, who called herself 'Head Groupie of the JS Fan Club', showed her appreciation:

For some time I have been wanting to tell you how very lucky I am to have met such a responsive pen-pal as yourself.

Before I met you I'd always been searching for a willing letter-writer. Someone who would be prepared to answer my letters, and wouldn't mind if I kept on writing; but no one ever quite lived up to my expectations. Then miraculously, I met you; and you seemed not to mind how often I wrote, and always responded so splendidly ... What I really wanted was a dialogue on paper; which, dear Croque, is exactly what you have given me. And that is why I still love writing to you; and receiving your letters in return. You are a marvel.

A few months after beginning his extensive correspondence with Pauline, Jimmy met Isabelle Evans, the young Swiss wife of his friend, Walker, and another very close relationship ensued in many hundreds of letters until the end of his life. Thus he was intimately involved with two young women simultaneously over a long period. It must have brought him great satisfaction and a bulwark against the lasting deprivation of his skills as a writer.

Isabelle, a beautiful woman of thirty from Berne, working in fashion design, met Jimmy in the Redfern Gallery in Cork Street on 21 February 1963.

My heart was jumping when I entered [she wrote to her husband]. Nobody was there and I looked at the paintings ... Finally a most handsome man with gray hair, lovely tweeds and a wonderful face came in ... this most attractive man nodded, smiled and shook hands with me. We sat down and Jimmy asked *all* about you, your work, your health, your car, our apartment, your habits, your flasks, your tweeds and more. We had a wonderful time. I *am* in love with him ever since I saw him and more so since he kissed me good-bye in Waterloo Station ... Finally Tania returned from shopping ... She is nice, very German, and I had the feeling that she bored Jimmy just a tiny bit ... For tea we went to Brown's Hotel ... Jimmy kept filling my plate with sandwiches and every so often he'd wink at me kiddingly, all while Tania was talking, talking, just like Vita [Petersen].

8
Writer's Block
1962–1965

To resolve the conflict between Jimmy's pathetic sister and his ageing mother needed extreme tact and endless attention on the part of the Sterns. Visits to France and Italy relieved this burden and their sorrow at the death of friends. While Jimmy exchanged literary gossip and opinions on books and writers with four of his most faithful corre-spondents, he was also plagued, yet again, with 'writer's block', a state with which William Plomer was particularly sympathetic, without suffering from the same condition himself.

'Dearest Friends,' Sonia Orwell wrote to the Sterns on 28 November 1962: '... Mary McCarthy has been visiting to buy furniture ... [She] was in splendid form and always fills me with resolution, rather like a school mistress one has a crush on, with her remarks such as: "No, Sonia, even though the drinks were poured out we didn't have to drink them. After all we do have free will." I revert instantaneously to the convent and stay off the bottle for a week!

'Tea with Ivy Compton-Burnett on Saturday ...'

From Jimmy to John Davenport on 23/24 January 1963:

What would we, what would I do without you! The only living soul who has an unbiased, unbitter eye for the GOODS, who knows at a glance, can tell at one squint of however jaundiced an eye the gold, the silver, even the copper, from the lead, the mediocre, the meretricious! God bless your heart, above all your objectivity, generosity, & ENTHUSIASM – and all this in the dread, demon-cold of Duxford. Would that old Malc. [Lowry] were above the sod to celebrate. For he would, be Jasus. He'd kick us all in the balls first, but in the end he'd say Yes, Yes, Yes ... and finish every bottle in all our houses, bless his soul.

It's a funny thing: only last night there arrived indirectly from New York a copy of Jim Agee's *Letters to Father Flye* [1964]. I don't know what you think about Jim, but anyway he was very

much like you, and I loved him, and he died of drink and tobacco
and of talking until 5 a.m. for 25 years, and he was the only person I have known outside yourself to whom I could not only say:
'Look, Jim, read this ...' and who would react the way you do.

I have been reading these letters all day and feel an awful sense
of sadness, irreparable loss. Not that he died last week, he died in
1955 I think, but there he was on the page, in the middle of the
night always, tight, and saying so, & knowing he could not last
much longer, and asking Father Flye, a heavenly Saint of a Man if
ever there was one, what Fr. thought he might do to be saved. And
a moment later: 'To bleeding hell with being saved, Father, I have
something to say. Say! have *you read* ...?'

All of which is meant to say, as you may have guessed, God
Bless You.

From Katherine Anne Porter in Rome on 25 February 1963:

... I don't believe what Maugham says [that he replied personally
to every letter he received, a fact conveyed to KAP in a letter from
Jimmy], and I think he has crowned his life of falseness by
disclaiming his daughter. I see that a group of hotheads – or would
you call them die-hards – including my old friend, Dame Edith
Sitwell, have banded together to write a memoir, or something of
the sort in defence of Maugham's unfortunate wife who had such
a pretty name [Syrie], I can't remember it now. It is a rather futile
attempt to defend the dead and harass the living, because I am
sure the shameless old crock doesn't give a damn what anybody
thinks of him.

From Jimmy to Katherine Anne Porter on 26 March 1963:

... All my life I have known that one – *I* rather – should never
'make plans' ... [The Sterns and KAP had arranged to meet in
Paris]. My nature is to act on the spur of the moment; but 28 years
of marriage to a wonderful woman – whose dislike of 'moving' has
been beaten in my experience only by my dear friend Hermann
Broch (who actually burst into tears when informed that he was
to be liberated from a concentration camp) – have caused me to
try to compromise with my instinct. The result is of course fatal:
'on ne change pas, malgré tout – mieux, malgré la femme!'

From Jimmy to William Plomer on 8 April 1963:

... Ernestine [Evans]![17] I have been inundated for weeks. Her very velleity makes me positively vellicate (how's that?) Yet in her dottyness she had sent me a book (from Virginia) I very much wanted to read. (I later discovered it came from the widow of Sherwood Anderson!) In one of her hundreds of paragraphs I lit upon the name of someone I had heard of: Arthur Ransome. I wrote and said so, which of course was asking for trouble. But she did say that his wife had been Trotski's secretary. I like to think of the link between Hatch and Trotski.

... No, indeed, Hervey is by [no] means a stale bun to me; indeed, the good man is hardly a bun at all. I had been thinking of acquiring his Memoirs. And now will. Paperbacks are less of a temptation to me: I am a book snob. As a child I used to steal books off the open boutiques on the Dublin quays. Later I 'traded' in books, buying and selling through the mail. Then I began to 'collect'. But I always hated to buy a book, even by a favourite author, which I did not like the look or feel of. I abandoned collecting long ago, but the snobbery remains. I believe Mr C. Connolly suffers from the same affliction ...

... Since I last mentioned my 'autobiographical writing', I have added a couple of chapters, and started on a third, about my 'prep', and there I got stuck. What *can* one say about this institution that has not been said before? And yet it, the experience, cannot be omitted. I think I began floundering after re-reading what Harold Acton wrote about the same place (we were there together) in *his* Memoirs. He does it so well, that old extrovert; with such glee and gusto ...

... I have just read for review 'part of an autobiography' by Mr John Wain, a gentleman about whom I know little & that little I did not like. Having read the book, I still have no desire to meet him, nor do I know what to say about his book. He wrote it when he was 36½. He never went to a boarding school, and feels that if he had he would not have survived. He maintains that the schools that he did go to made him understand perfectly the totalitarian state: they were synonymous. A cut above the working class, he lived in terror of them, because in the Staffordshire pottery town where he was brought up he was surrounded by them. His life was 'saved' by going to Oxford, where he was mentally seduced by

17 Ernestine Evans, who was married to Kenneth Durant, head of the newsagency TASS in America, was a freelance editor and book reviewer for the *New York Herald Tribune*.

that crackpot Meyerstein, Wain's portrait of whom is by far the best thing in the book. (I had read it before, in *Encounter*. Perhaps you did, too?) I have since been told by a neighbour, who was told by Desmond MacCarthy, that when Meyerstein himself was 'up', he faked the Newdigate Prize. Mr W. does not mention this. If true, it would explain a lot about Mr M.

From May to July of that very hot summer the Sterns were forced to stay in London; Tania underwent a cervical cancer operation followed by a hysterectomy at a private hospital in Chelsea. Jimmy, who was anxious, caring and attentive to her needs, stayed with Kitty West in Regent's Park Terrace. Tania recuperated in the house of their painter friend Billy Henderson, near Barnstaple, north Devon.

Straddling the fall of John Profumo in June were the deaths of two people particularly important to Jimmy, Van Wyck Brooks and John Cowper Powys. The latter was a novelist and poet, who during a lecture tour of the US before the First World War had been lionised by Kay Boyle's mother, Katherine, and is best known for his *Wolf Solent* (1929) and *A Glastonbury Romance* (1932). He was one of a Dorset dynasty of writers, his brothers being Llewelyn Powys and T. F. (Theodore Francis) Powys.

In September another old friend, Louis MacNeice, also died. This loss affected Jimmy badly: 'In bed burst into tears from a feeling of utter emptiness, expressed as "loneliness". Unable to sleep & not wanting to keep T. awake, go to attic.'

From Katherine Anne Porter, Villa Adrienne, 19 Avenue du Général Leclerc, Paris on 23 July 1963:

... Yes, this was Avenue d'Orléans in the days before, and it should have been left with that lovely name. Who was this faceless Général Leclerc? ...

... Do you suppose Lowry ever lived here? To think I never knew you and he were friends. I had a strange kind of introduction to his work: far back, in 1946, I think—I was in California – the publisher sent me the page-proofs of his book, *Under the Volcano*, and I remember it as one of the most painful, really appalling books I have ever read; a lost soul really in hell just beginning to realize it, who yet did not know why he was there. It was strange how long it was, after his death and all, that certain writers began to discover him: he had a tremendous gift.

... N.B. This is important: Where was your piece about Lowry

published? I must see it. I am working on a little recollection of
Sylvia Beach; of course Mercure de France was getting out a
special number for her, and asked me to contribute my article
which I had already begun of my own accord. Of course I didn't
make it! But they dug up a letter of mine to Sylvia and are printing
that instead ...

From Jimmy to Katherine Anne Porter on 28 July 1963:

... You ask where my Lowry Memoir was published. Alas, my
dear, it wasn't. This, briefly is the history of its not getting into
print. I sent it to *Encounter*. Spender said he liked it, but could I
see my way to cut the alcoholic content by half and substitute
several pages on what I thought of Lowry's work. In reply I
shouted a loud No! Some time later he said he would accept the
piece, after all, as it stood. Six months later he wrote to say that
the typescript had been lost, could I send him a copy. I sent him a
copy. Where upon he wrote back that he was sorry that 'they' (he
and his co-editor, Melvin Lasky) could not accept it after all. And
he enclosed a cheque for £20, which I promptly cashed. – I then
sent the typescript to the *London Magazine*, one of whose editors,
a young Australian, sent me an extremely impertinent letter of
rejection. [This was Charles Osborne, poet, critic, biographer and
musicologist, who as Assistant Literary Director at the Arts Council in 1966 was to announce to Jimmy that he had won a £1,000
prize 'for the short story']. Another copy of the Memoir has been
in the hands of Brandt & Brandt for well over a year. I know only
that it was turned down, not surprisingly, by the *New Yorker*, as
being 'too literary'! I wonder if you know that the one person
responsible for the publication of *Under the Volcano* was that
handsome ex-husband of yours, Erskine. You probably do know.
I never saw a human being work so hard for a book.
    ... Leclerc, was he not the man, or at least one of the men,
responsible for the Liberation of Paris?
    I am most interested to hear that you are working on a Memoir
of Sylvia Beach. I still would not know what to say about her; I
guess I never knew her well enough. She was always so
surrounded by authors, and I have always fought shy of meeting
authors, believe it or not!

Jimmy and Tania darlings ... [Katherine Anne Porter wrote from

Paris on 9 August 1963]. I read your account of your first meeting
with Malcolm Lowry, and it is delightful ... YET, I have this to say:
the history of your first encounter is just certainly touching and
very absorbing. But, many things have happened since; I have read
somewhere that he died of a terrible, stupid-sounding accident,
was smothered to death in some way – was he near you? Did you
know about this? You do know that after all these years – after all
poor Albert's terrible efforts, and God, *didn't* he work? Lowry is
going to be – if he isn't already, the next fashionable literary furore
... I don't like fashion any better than you do. And I am not
suggesting that you join the parade. Bandwagon-hopping is not
your style any more than it is mine. But it happens that you had a
friendship with him when you were both young and unknown
and life and literature were one and the same thing – as they
always are, but we didn't know it then, we just took it for granted
– and you must have a good deal to say about him, his temperament and his work, and the thing that gives a weight to all of it is
this untimely tragic death, and the mystery of his being so unable
to live ... So, let's try to get this piece published, but I beg of you to
summon your memories and your feelings and your good critical
faculties and make a study of him before the little Me-Too boys
get to picking his bones ...

'Dear Generous Friend,' Jimmy addressed Katherine Anne Porter on
12 August 1963:

... I *could* hazard a pretty shrewd guess as to why Malcolm found
living impossible, but of course it would involve dissecting the poor
devil, poking into his 'private' life, and I am not prepared to do
that. His widow, for one thing, is alive, and she does not like me (to
put it mildly), and I feel the same about her. Another thing: a young
American, who knew Malc. intimately during the last years of his
life and for whom Malc. still remains a Hero, has done more or less
what you suggest I do – a little job of some 100,000 words. He even
lived for more than a year in Mexico to get the local colour of the
VOLCANO first-hand! Of course there are many stories about Malc.
which this young man does not know. One of the most hilarious is
about him and the French translator of the *Volcano*, a French spin-
ster who, until she met Malc. in Paris, had (so legend has it) never
drunk a glass of wine. Within 24 hours of their meeting both of
them were in jug – in both senses of that word.

Malc. died in May of 1957 (eight close friends of mine died that year, all under 50) in a tiny village in Sussex. At the grave were five mourners, of whom I was one. I believe the precise circumstances are known only to the widow. It was a grisly end, involving (needless to say) alcohol and sleeping pills.

His work – and in my opinion only the *Volcano* is worthy of serious consideration – is little known here, and this despite the reprinting of that book quite recently. Were he still alive he would of course be even less known. He has a coterie of fans in the U.S., but the odd thing is (and I believe this goes for Lawrence Durrell, too, does it not?) that it is the French who consider Lowry a second Melville. (That is poorly expressed, but you will know what I mean.) I suspect that this admiration may have something to do with the French admiration for Joyce, by whom Malc. always adamantly refused to admit he was influenced. Which is of course nonsense.

... *Later*. ... It is typical of your modesty that you have not drawn attention to a *Paris Review* which lies in front of me containing a 65-page piece by Malc. (which I have not had time to read), and a fascinating KAP interview. Anyone watching me reading it would have probably thought I had some peculiar disease, for I just went on nodding my head in agreement, occasionally quite violently, from beginning to end. And when I came to what you said of 1920s and Scott Fitzgerald, I let out a hoot of assent. Oddly enough, on the very same day I was sent a copy of *Esquire* devoted entirely to American writers (did you see it? Did you see that double page spread, in colour, of ageing faces?) and there, almost word for word, is Faulkner echoing what you say about what it was like to be brought up in the South: 'In those days you belonged together, you lived together, because you were a family' ... etc. It was somehow tremendously gratifying.

August 13. A most peculiar thing has occurred: the mail has brought suddenly out of the blue, marked URGENT, proofs of the Lowry Memoir from *Encounter*. What can the explanation be? It is almost as though *you* had a hand in it! Of course it does not mean that they intend to *print*; they are *so* dotty. Still ... You remember what I said about coincidences in matters, no matter how remote, connected with Lowry? Dead or alive, they seem to continue ...

'Malcolm Lowry: A First Impression' appeared in the September issue of *Encounter*.

From Katherine Anne Porter on 16 August 1963:

... It is very clear to me why you do not undertake a memoir of Lowry ... I have the same thing with Hart Crane. There is no point in writing anything unless I write what I know – there is already too much lying and inventing of romances and just plain ignorance at work on that history. I do have a certain undeniable first hand knowledge and experience of the horror of that unhappy doomed life, and I have refused steadily to write about it ever since his suicide. Yet I may, sometime. It depends on how I feel later about it ...

1957 was your year of loss. Mine was 1955. My only brother, my favorite cousin, my friend and publisher of twenty-five years, a friend and photographer for the same years, and two other dear and bitterly missed friends just left the world—all within less than six months. There is only space where they were: no one comes to take their places. Every one his place and no other.

The mystery to me is, why one human being can bear his life to its natural end, and yet his fate may be no less terrible and incurable than that of his friend who will despair and make an end to himself. We blame bad marriages and so on, but no one needs to go on with a bad marriage. There is in *Under the Volcano* expressed a most horrible hatred of women, but many men hate women even worse than he did, and many women hate men, and yet they manage to live rather cheerfully, all things considered. No, it *cannot* be what actually happens to any one, it is a matter of resistance, of a fibre that can take any strain, that accounts for survival. I used to think I would die of my troubles, and more than once meditated suicide. But every time I was seriously threatened, I resisted instinctively, even against my will as it sometimes seemed; but I know now that only accident or the natural wearing away of vitality will put me down ... So my mind is all made up, and I intend to make the best of what is left of this quite gruesome (in spots) world.

From Jimmy to Katherine Anne Porter on 20 August 1963:

... Yes, Lowry hated women – because he feared them. Can you hate without fear? Why he feared them *you* probably do not need to be told. Every drink he took was a sip at self-destruction. I guess he and Crane had much in common. Apart from their common means of self-destruction. But he did not have the fibre you talk of. His instinct was to self-dramatise. And the manner of his death would have made him shudder, and rage. For of course if he had to die prematurely, violently, then it should have been at sea. Like Crane.

From William Plomer on 20 August 1963:

... The allusion to Janet Frame rings a rather warped bell with me. She was first recommended to me by a very remarkable pen-friend with whom I have corresponded for many years – Frank Sargeson, a writer in New Zealand, at least one of whose books has been published here. He sent me her first book. I thought it gifted but too New Zealandy and non-popular to stand much chance here, and Sargeson said, I think, that she was in, or had been in, or was in and out of one or more asylums. But two or three of her books *have* been published here by somebody else & have received some very favourable reviews, though I can't believe that they have been much bought. There is a distinctive oddity and intensity about her view of life & use of language, and such a talent is so uncommon in those 'new' countries that it may perhaps seem more important there than to us talent-weary Europeans. From all of which you gather that I am not myself madly responsive to Miss Frame[18] though this may be my fault, not hers ...

From Jimmy to Plomer on 23 August 1963:

... EE [Ernestine Evans]. Latest news – or 'Final Buff' as the evening newsboys used to yell in the streets of Dublin. We asked her to come here tomorrow for the night or two nights. She accepted the invitation but said she could not come on train we suggested, she would come on a later one. Since on the last occasion I was with her in New York she opened her mouth on Fifth Avenue and her 'lowers' fell into the gutter (where they were 'mislaid' for several minutes among leaves, cigarette-butts, & the usual city offal), we thought it would be 'nice' (for her) if we drove to Salisbury & bought some special 'dainties' (American-style) in case her lowers, or even her uppers, were still (or again) a bit loose.

18 'Perhaps I may allow myself to say that I am not quite "in the picture" with Miss Frame.' – W. P.

... Yes, P. White *is* alarming. I suppose all self-absorbed people are. Poor sweet Manoly [Lascaris], *what* a time he must have, what a masochist he must be. Apparently P. W. wanted to buy an 18-room house on the top of a remote mountain on a remote Greek island, & when M. finally put his 'foot down' (which I imagine to be something like a kitten putting forth a paw on a Turkish carpet), P. W. wouldn't speak to him for a week.

From Plomer on 2 September 1963:

Your p.c. asks whether my lunch was less exhausting than your dinner. *Well*, can exhaustion on such a scale be measured? I had arranged to call for her [Ernestine Evans] at her hotel & take her round the corner to lunch at Prunier's, where I had booked a table. When she appeared she said she was afraid something had happened – it was she who was taking me out to lunch with a Mr & Mrs Ewer at Rules, but we should begin our lunch & they would arrive at 1.30. I hate Rules, I didn't want to meet any Ewers, but with what is called a good grace I told the porter to cancel my booking at Prunier's, then drove E.E. to Rules. The monologue which had begun as soon as we met was now largely inaudible as well as unintelligible, because we sat near an open window & a constant roar of traffic, but most of it seemed to be fragmentary reminiscences.

The service was bad, the food indifferent. I was hungry & wanted to get on with lunch & get away in reasonable time. Our old friend wouldn't get on with her food, perhaps hoping that the Ewers would soon pour upstairs. At 1.35 she became a little restive & asked me to go downstairs & see if they were there. I had left instructions that they were to be shown up, but to satisfy her I went down at 1.45, & of course there had been no sign of or from them.

A slight anxiety about this seemed at times to show itself in the monologue, but perhaps she still hoped for Ewers. At least, she had coffee three times, at intervals of about half an hour. Having missed a train I particularly wanted to catch, I apologetically began to show signs of wanting to go at about 3.15 (impatient waiters doing a sort of ballet in the background for some time past). We then had to go and find a taxi, which took some time, & decide where she wanted to go in it.

I don't think I have ever felt so tired – all my diminished vitality seemed to have evaporated. The strain of listening and of not hearing, the strain of waiting for Ewers who were evidently not coming, the strain of not being able to get on with one's food & get *away*, the strain of trying not to appear impatient, were almost too much …

And *yet*, you know – there is something so admirable about E. E., about the rightness of her instincts, even about her widely, too widely, dispersed interests, & her varied acquaintance. She has, surely, a generous & somehow un-self-seeking nature, & so often minds about what is wrong, in the treatment of children, in political matters, in attitudes to life; and minds intensely about what is good in literature.

'And how were Jimmy & Tania last night?" I said. (Almost the only words I got in.)

'Jimmy seemed nervy,' she said, 'but he has something that Chekhov had – whenever he writes a story, whatever he writes, I *believe* it, I know it's true.'

From John Davenport, Cambridge on 29 September 1963:

… The widow [Margerie Lowry] wrote to me. Yes. With a rather phony p.s. asking after 'my wonderful boys'. Harvey Breit met Malcolm once in N. Y., drunk, at a party. He has no right whatever to have a hand in such a book [Harvey Breit, with Margerie Bonner Lowry, edited *Selected Letters of Malcolm Lowry*, 1965], the thought of which makes me shudder. He's an artful necrophilist; a great tagger-oner: Hemingway, Dylan T. I found him quite an agreeable little bumsucker, but …

Yes: I *am* very well physically, but then I usually am; but this is the absolute nadir of my life. I can scarcely go lower. Naturally I don't moan in public, but I'm in the most desperate economic plight. It is all too depressing to talk about.

From Jimmy to Plomer on 2 November 1963:

… I have just finished reading Lady O's [Ottoline Morrell's] *Memoirs* [1974]. I find my opinions fighting like cats – with gloves on. I cannot help admiring her moral courage, especially after the outbreak of and during the War. Much of this admiration, however, must go to Ph. M. [Philip Morrell] as well as to her. (One cannot help wondering: but for him, what?) That said, I found myself constantly irritated, sometimes embarrassed. I am allergic to Yearners, no matter which sex. Also to Beauty, Soul, Spirit, & Ecstasy. As usual, I was far more interested in the Child than in the endless list of Names with which the Woman was so determined to surround herself. Still – and this does surprise me – think of the men who stuck to her and sought her out, above all Bertie Russell, that intellectual aristocrat (still running away at 90). Those talks and walks. I wonder what *he* would say …?

I don't think I learned much from the book, and I laughed only twice, once when (I assume) I wasn't meant to. On page 213 Roger Fry accuses her of 'spreading abroad' the news that he is in love with O. 'I was so utterly dumbfounded … this thought had never entered my head.' 17 lines later: 'Since that day I have never had intercourse with Roger.' Now anyone who can write that … ! And Bob G-H [Robert Gathorne-Hardy] didn't even drop a footnote. My second laugh came on page 237: 'There is Mummy eliminating' …

From Plomer on 8 November 1963:

… I am much interested in your 'reactions', as they say, to Ottoline … Yes, she was an old Yearner, but I think all that gush about Beauty, &c., was part of the whole rebellion against Philistinism & conventionality of the relations & the background that oppressed her when young. After all she was young in the Nineties, when the rebellion of the imaginative did take the form of aestheticism & yearning. But she did what she wanted to do, she stuck to her guns – and pretty big guns, or big shots, some of them were. The streak of absurdity in her was often obtrusive, but her zest for life, her courage, her independence & all sorts of other qualities greatly I think outweighed it (if one can outweigh a streak). She was good to me when I was young, & encouraging, & introduced me to persons I might not otherwise have met – e.g. Yeats.

Once in her house somebody said of somebody else, 'Of course he's mad.' O. turned to me and said in her extraordinary strange deep doting voice, 'I adore mad people, don't you?' This seemed to me a silly & affected remark, & I replied brusquely, 'Well, I don't, you know, I prefer sane ones. They're so much rarer.' I think now this was rather rude & priggish of me; but you see, don't you, how that sort of remark, made in a gushing fond unconsidered way, could annoy one when one was looking to one's elders for good sense?

In early 1964 the Sterns suffered eleven weeks of illness in the comfort of Magouche (Agnes) Phillips's[19] house in Chapel Street, Belgravia.

Magouche had first met the Sterns during the war, when she was in her early twenties, in the Connecticut house of the sculptor Alexander Calder. She was a friend of Jimmy's ex-boss, Tom Matthews, the editor of *Time*, and when Jimmy had become bedridden with an obscure malady, she and Matthews took down to Hatch an antique commode as a present. One morning, during the local doctor's examination of Jimmy, they heard loud laughter from behind closed doors. After the doctor had left, Jimmy confessed to the diagnosis – 'the clap'. Later, in London, this was denied by a specialist; instead, Reiter's Syndrome – a combination of urethritis, arthritis and conjunctivitis – was the verdict.

In April, back at Hatch, Jimmy complained to his journal: 'Depressed. Long for sun & calm windless day. Don't know what to settle to. Dare not pick up "knitting". Don't feel like reading, & don't know what to read. Can't keep awake. So slumber – till 4.30.' But six weeks later they were off to Ischia via Paris and Rome; sunny days had returned. They met the French actor Charles Boyer and Terence Rattigan at William Walton's house. Jimmy and Rattigan discussed the hypnotic effect televised cricket had on them. A letter to Pauline Wynn records that he told Rattigan that 'part of myself felt rather ashamed: that it must derive from a part of life that had not been lived; a hangover of adolescence. But he thought this idea quite dotty, and cited a whole row of literary people who were unashamedly devoted to the game. None of these names surprised me until he suddenly came up with one, an Irishman whom he, Rattigan, had been instrumental in getting elected a Member of the MCC: Sam Beckett! I can't wait to ask Sam if Godot ever played for his county? And which county was that?'

'Poor, dear Chum,' Sonia Orwell wrote from Paris on 4 February 1964:

19 American by birth, Magouche was the wife of the Armenian painter Arshile Gorky (1904–48). After he died, she married the painter and printmaker Jack Phillips and came to live in Europe with her four daughters. Her third marriage was to the writer and translator Xan Fielding.

I spend some afternoons in the Ritz Bar with Edmund Wilson who never wants to go back to America again and gave me his book on the Income Tax with the dedication: 'To Sonia, with much pessimism, from Edmund'. He reminds me now somehow of Wystan, ie marvellous until he passes straight out early in the evening! I just feel sorry for his poor wife who can't then leave and go on jaunts to queer bars. Maria Jolas has set off for America in the wake of Nathalie Sarraute in a certain spirit of trepidation, but smugly pleased at the signs of collapse in all her contemporaries who she claims are younger than she!

... [Marguerite Duras] is dedicating her next novel to me – which raises the name problem: apparently after a long discussion with a mutual friend she decided simply to put 'Pour Sonia' because all my strings of other names had lost their reality in some way. I feel I [have] achieved the status of a super-tart, known only by her first name!

From William Plomer on 16 March 1964:

... You have certainly provided me with a most lively entertainment in the memoirs of Lady Glenavy [*Today We Will Only Gossip*, 1964]. I think she is rather honest & doesn't put on side or humbug, & she gives one a curiously factual panorama of her life & times ... The photographs are madly funny or sad ...

... I got a clearer idea of Gertler than before, & the account of Koteliansky is fuller than any I have seen in print. Leonard Woolf has often told me of him & how like an Old Testament Prophet he was – but he does sound a bit tiresome in some ways, & perhaps a bit warped by his would-be self-sufficient way of life. And that wrecking of the preparations for somebody else's party by him & Gertler doesn't seem very Isaiah-like. I should have thought he might have hesitated before running amok & biting, not the hand that had fed Gertler exactly, but the food that was going to feed somebody else – to say nothing of the drink. And *how* could anybody take to James Stephens & his writings, I wonder?

I like all the many touches of 'period' detail in the book, & was quite unable to skip. Some of K. Mansfield's asperities – e.g. about D. H. Lawrence – have a good sharp tang of vinegar – and not necessarily of vinegar misapplied ...

From Jimmy to Sonia Orwell on 11 April 1964:

Chère Choom: ... The past 3 weeks were interrupted by a hectic & near-disastrous 24 hours in London. I think I told you I had an 'interest' in a volume of Memoirs by 81-year old Beatrice Lady Glenavy (neé Elvery: Mr Elvery used to make our 'macs' when we lived in Ireland!). Well, I was prevailed upon to broadcast a review for the 'World of Books' programme, & meet the author later for a drink. The broadcast was a near-disaster because I heartily disagreed with the manner in which the young man at the BBC insisted I should read. By the time I reached Her Ladyship (a glorious Irish woman, as I had anticipated) in the house of her novelist son Michael Campbell (whom you may know; he is charming, I thought), I was in such a state of nervous tension that I drank what would have been a considerable quantity of gin at any time. But I had not drunk gin for 5 months. Needless to say, I did not get drunk there & then, but later, after a bottle of Chablis, I sure did. Next day – no, I will leave the rest to your imagination & experience! Incidentally, I had the publishers [Constable] of this book send a copy to Cyril [Connolly], Raymond [Mortimer], and [V. S.] Pritchett. I even wrote to them all personally, emphasising that I was having it sent to them *not* for review but for their amusement. Not one of them acknowledged the book or the letter. Don't you think that's rather rude? Or do they receive *so* many books in like manner? Perhaps.

... Wystan is in Stockholm; can't remember why. He says Ishyvoo's [Christopher Isherwood's] new long story is the best thing he has ever done; am glad to hear it; hope I shall agree.

... *Sunday*: My latest Pet Hate is Brigid Brophy. Such intellectual arrogance: artificial, pretentious, conceited, & seems to think she can outfirbank Firbank & that no one will notice, that the American male's castration complex is somethin' noo.

From Sonia Orwell in Paris on 25 May 1964:

... I rather enjoyed my weekend in London, although I've never felt so tired. It was all very giggly, very childish and rather tipsy as might be expected. Wystan explaining religion to that super-rationalist Richard Wollheim was a 'gem' and Geoffrey Gorer defending me against Wystan by stoutly declaring he was 'anti-Kraut' and 'pro-frog' was a moving spectacle! Wystan absolutely defeating Edmund Wilson by saying: 'Well, Edmund, I pray for you every Sunday' was superb, because poor Edmund suddenly looked so pleased! ... I also had lunch – *very* drunken – with Lucian [Freud] and Francis [Bacon] and Francis's most extraordinary new 'friend', which I adored (I mean what I can remember of it) but was *horrified* to learn that Lucian had won £5,000 gambling that week which inevitably means he will lose another £10,000 next week. Ah well!

From William Plomer on 18 August 1964:

... Thank you for your kind condolence about Ian Fleming [who had recently died]. He was a much more interesting person than one might imagine from hearsay. He had vitality, versatility, curiosity, & various kinds of skill. I had a real affection for him & admired his originality & ability ... But I don't see why you should read any of the James Bond books, world-famous as they are. I see them as brilliant fairy-stories which have answered some craving in the modern world for 'wishful' conflicts between a dragon-slaying hero & forces, roughly, of death & destruction.

In February the Sterns had visited James Joyce's daughter, Lucia, who was confined in a sanatorium near Northampton. 'I am not at all well these days,' she wrote to Jimmy at the suggestion that the Sterns visit her. 'I don't like the people in this place they are very strict and unkind. It will not be very interesting for you as I am very run down and nervous.' While they were there, Lucia remarked: 'Do you think I could be sent to London to be buried with my Aunt Kathleen when I will be dead? I think one should make plans for the future, don't you think so?' Later, on the same morbid subject, she remarked pathetically: 'They are putting up a monument to my father in Zurich; my brother wants me to be buried there, but I think it is a bit too far to go, what do you think?'

That autumn the Sterns were off again to Paris to see old friends: Maria Jolas, wife of Eugene Jolas[20] and intimate friend of James and Nora

20 The Jolases were Americans, he from New Jersey and she from Kentucky. Maria, warm and unfailingly hospitable, had lived in Berlin and Paris, studying for an operatic career before marrying her husband. She sang in German and French, in New Orleans patois and American Negro songs. Eugene, who formed a close personal and intellectual bond with James Joyce, was also a talent in his own right: a poet and critic, he was a political journalist whose activities in post-war Germany led to the establishment of a free democratic press there.

Joyce, Sonia Orwell, who was living there permanently, and Sybille Bedford and Eda Lord.

In late October the Sterns dined with Tanya and Anthony Hobson in their elegant Georgian house near Salisbury. Hobson, seventeen years younger than Jimmy, followed his father, a distinguished expert on book bindings, into Sotheby's, of which he was a director from 1949 to 1971, heading the book department. He is an 'historian of the book' with many publications, lectureships and honours to his name.

Deirdre and Cyril Connolly were staying and at dinner a lively discussion about a poem of W. H. Auden's turned into a mock court of law. With phrases emanating from Connolly and his host such as 'Irrelevant, tendentious and liable to prejudice the witness' and 'Objection! Mr Perry Mason is trying to lead the witness', the charade led to Cyril covering his head with a red table napkin. Lifting a corner over one eye, he pronounced: 'Objection overruled!' Later, Jimmy produced a copy of Auden's poem about a lavatory typed by himself, a gift which Connolly, the great collector, after the Sterns' departure, pronounced as meagre – 'not even typed by Auden!'

From Sonia Orwell on 24 October 1964:

... The scene has been enlivened by Mary [McCarthy] who is doing a TV script on Paris for the BBC in which a curious amount of her dislike of this place is emerging! She gave a dinner party to be televised – to which I was not invited on account of my well-known pro-feelings – in which she exceeded herself by announcing that French women were frigid. This brought down rage upon her head from all the guests including her husband and she was naive enough to be so surprised that she turned on him and asked: 'Have you ever been to bed with a French woman?' I assume that the BBC will cut that bit out but I told her she mustn't be amazed if a new set of rumours starts! Anyhow we are all – except Mary – now doing serious 'field-work' into this lamentable frigidity of *les dames du 6e arrondissement* and I have been assured that you can't even buy a lettuce in *le marché de Buci* without its having serious obscene overtones!

From William Plomer on 27 October 1964:

I duly went to the W. H. Smith thing & should much have liked to see you both there ...

... [R. A.] Butler made a suitable little speech, & I had some nice talk with Toynbee – one of the judges – & a little with E. [Elizabeth] Bowen, one of them too. Butler, who always looks as if his face had been stung by a party of queen bees (if they have stings), on this occasion had a tightly packed overnight-bag under each eye, poor man, the stresses and strains of political wrong turnings, if not blind alleys, having been rather too much for him.

From Jimmy to Sonia Orwell on 26 October 1964:

... Now for our Titbit No. l: We have seen that book-eater Cyril [Connolly] on two successive days. Night before last at the Hobsons & yesterday. D. [Deirdre], Sarah [Craven, CC's stepdaughter] & Cressida came here. The adults drank nothing (it was 11 a.m.), but the girls fairly let in to the Coke-on-the-Rocks. C. shuffled into the house trailing behind him on his shoes several large lumps of dogshit (I hope you are not just about to eat a delicious meal in the Av. de Beaumarchais!). For several minutes I took no notice of remarks from both of them about there being some 'mud on the carpet' until all of a sudden the room began to stink like – well, that I think I will leave to your imagination. By this time, of course, the books had been seen, a lump had been well trodden into the carpet, and I was being informed that my *White Peacock* (1911) may be a first edition but certainly not a first issue. 'The difference between £100 and £5, you know.' I knew only too well. Then his eye lighted on the *Oxford Broom*, Vol 1. No. 1. 1923. 'You have no need of this, I imagine.' Me: 'Well, yes, I have.' C. 'Oh, it's not that *I* want it. But I know someone who does. Hobson will give you a fiver for it any time you like ... ' To get him away from the books, out of that by now extremely smelly room, I suggested that since he was here he might as well sign one or two Connollys. He was delighted, rose to the occasion like a leaping trout. 'Sign anything you like.' I had produced my 'first' of *Enemies of Promise* [1938] & was opening *The Rock Pool* [1936] when I saw to my horror that 'my' copy belonged to, and was signed by, ... Annie Rogers Davis, C's ex-sister-in-law!! It was too late, of course. No going back now. He pounced. 'Oh, she must have that back. He (Davis) collects *everything* I write.' ...

I was glad, really. At least he did not go away empty-handed – though I did feel like frisking him as he got into that scarlet car. All this, my dear, is for *your* delectation; I would prefer that my report did not get back to the Dean of Letters verbatim!

[Jimmy frequently quoted eight-year-old Cressida Connolly's remark: 'Daddy likes other people's books'!]

The night before was a very pleasant evening [at the Hobsons' house] – though 52 miles in the dark is too far for me, and, what's more, D. had retired to bed with a streaming cold. At dinner C. and A. did an act out of the Law Courts (re books that might or might not be at Hatch Manor!), but it was lost on me because it was a skit on some TV serial which I always turn off the moment it comes on. – What an enoRmous room that is: I felt we all ought to be wearing medals and jewels and preparing to swing our legs to the lilt of the Blue Danube.

… I loved your letter. In my experience, somewhat limited, of French ladies I would utter a loud YES: they are definitely frigid. I must admit that as far as I remember I had to do with the intellectual type only. *Very* hard going. I remember two in particular whose only desire was that I should meet – and have a *good long talk to* – André Gide! That, alas, was not my idea of sex.

The Sterns were to meet the Hobsons again, on the last day of October, at dinner with Judge Billy Hughes and his wife Jenny. Jimmy entertained Anthony with a long story about his days at private school with Harold Acton, who 'looked very foreign in a grey checked suit, with a face of brilliant white and raven hair'. He described Acton standing on a desk giving a sermon – 'very camp'. Jimmy had never forgotten that Acton pressed into his hand a copy of Oscar Wilde's book of essays, *Intentions* [1891] with 'Read this, my dear.' For Jimmy, a boy brought up in a supremely philistine home, the book was a revelation.

From Sonia Orwell, Paris on 3 November 1964:

Many thanks for that lovely letter. The only bad thing about it was it made me feel life was far livelier round Tisbury than in the *septième arrondissement*! Golly, you certainly got Cyril *en plein* and of course I will never breathe a word, but it did make me laugh! It had everything about him in it, particularly his immense clumsiness. No one else brings dogshit into a house. I remember once at *Horizon* bursting into a rage and shouting at him: 'Can't you do anything to help instead of just sitting around?' Well he was startled and sheepishly tried to put the stamps on the post. At the end of five minutes I gave in, as the French say, to the evidence. The stamps were everywhere but on the letters – on his forehead, on the walls, on the floor but nowhere near their proper destination. Since then I have never tried for anything but the hope that his contact with the physical world will be minimised. As for wanting to frisk him: well, you should have.

In all honesty I felt compelled to pass on your tit-bit about French women to Mary as she had been so teased about her pronouncements. She gave one of those whoops which really terrify me – a mixture of some Red Indian blood with the original girl guide! My friends are certainly a strong mixture! I sometimes feel like a thimble in a pudding full of Louis d'ors!

From William Plomer on 21 November 1964:

... It took Sybil C. [Cholmondeley] & me a good half hour to drive to Heytesbury – a larger house than I had supposed, and oh, it's all rather sad. Room after great grey room, all dank & chill & unheated, & full of stray, unused furniture and vast allegorical pictures painted by S. S.'s [Siegfried Sassoon's] mother (a pupil of Watts), and some good pictures, and mementoes of the dead & of the past. The house is on flat ground, not well kept, with two fine cedars to the south & east, and a well-kept wooded hill at the back. And there is S. S. himself, looking and I think feeling older than he should, and doing nothing, and easily tired, and shabbily dressed, and very very restless and nervy and never still for a moment, and to some extent looked after by some sort of Belgian maid in bedroom slippers.

... S.S. talked without a pause, not once I think asking any question, & following his own flow of memory & opinion, particularly when showing one his things.

... S.S. [is] essentially I believe a kind & modest man, but perhaps turned oddish by age & solitariness. He feels that his later poems were & are ignored, and that he is remembered only for his earlier ones. Said little about his prose writings, except that the strain of producing them gave him ulcers, & that if they are good it's because he has always been an amateur, not a professional, writer, with a slow, ruminant mind.

... I didn't find him for a second boring, & in a quick, glancing way he said two or three very kind things about me to me. And at one moment I teased him a little, and I think the playfulness kindled his own a bit. But he looked so sad when we went away. But one never knows – perhaps he was relieved to get rid of us.

From Jimmy to Plomer on 23 November 1964:

What a good description: I can see it all – the dark, empty house, one of my nightmares (childhood, the ruins of Ireland). And him. '… and doing nothing, & easily tired, & shabbily dressed … ' I almost got the giggles, it sounds so familiar, so fitting, so very close to home! But the 'Belgian maid in bedroom slippers'. That – surely that is most peculiar, incongruous? I should have thought at least an ancient male retainer, or even a not so ancient ex-batman.

  … My dear Wm, I am always so touched when you show concern for my – my what? – my *mental* (as well as physical) welfare. And invariably I repay this concern with a few embarrassed & none too truthful clichés. Of *course* it's no good or not true to mumble something about 'getting back to writing again *one day*'. What evidence is there that I will? None. The fact is (I do think) that my writing, or rather failure, lack of desire, to write is all tangled up with my *marriage*. I wrote at all (so I think) to get away from my boa-constricting family, to evade the Army & the Bank. This, still to my amazement, I accomplished, with some 40 stories, in a very few years: 1931–5. Then, in the latter years, I did the only thing I can remember ever wanting to do 100% since my earliest childhood; I found someone I was convinced I could live with. Thereafter (I do think) any tiny ambition I may have had, any little creative talent or desire, began to fade. I felt I had had my say, achieved what I had set out to do: gained my 'freedom', shot my bolt. I had always thought that at 37 I should die. I almost did. But didn't. And here I still am, having overstayed my welcome (*sic*) by some 23 years. – I don't think I have ever told anyone this before, partly because no one has ever been sufficiently interested (and I suppose it is presumptuous of me to think *you* might be), & partly because I feel it may be a kind of negative reflection, an accusation, even a form of betrayal of one's (my) Better 'Alf! In any case, my dear Wm, you will surely agree that if I felt I had something really worth saying, worth writing *about*, no one would prevent me from sitting down tomorrow morning & every following morning & banging away till every cow had come home & my fingers all blood from banging.

  There now, that is what you get for coming & staying a night here & generously showing concern for my welfare …

Jimmy had written to Joan Lewisohn twenty years earlier: 'Originally, I wrote for two reasons. The latter I realized only lately – 1) to escape from a terrifying future, & 2) as a substitute for Love. I believe, as a matter of fact, that even the best artists do this. The result is that my work has been done in unhappiness – i.e. loneliness, misery.' Three further remarks on the subject of Jimmy's writing and his inability to do so are revealing: 'When I wrote it was because I had something to say, had to say it,' he wrote to Pauline Wynn in June 1969. Tania also once remarked to Nora Sayre that she thought he was initially driven to write by his sense of injustice – to black people and to children, and that he stopped writing when the conviction dwindled. And in a letter of advice to Isabelle Evans, who had begun to write fiction, on 30 March 1987: 'The desire, no, the *passion*, to write must come from another passion: *Love* or *Fury*! I had, at the age of 23–4, not known any kind of love, but I was v. soon to be visited by anger – in my own person.'

From Plomer on 29 November 1964:

... I am immensely impressed & touched by your account of the reasons for your writing & not continuing to write stories. You see yourself as clearly as you see others, & this is a very rare gift. Your oeuvre, or corpus, of short stories is unique and durable. One can feel their freshness whenever one returns to them ...

Your explanation why you don't go on writing is so clear and wise and dignified that I feel I must never again nag at you with impertinent questions about whether, or if, or when. But I don't see why I shouldn't secretly harbour a hope that there may be moments when you will feel driven to write, if not a story, some passages of reminiscence, for example ...

In January 1965 the marriage break-up of Constantine FitzGibbon and his third wife Marion was much on the Sterns'minds. They went to see FitzGibbon and found Kay Boyle, Laurence Vail and Walker Evans there too. While their own marriage seemed in jeopardy once more: 'Sleepless night of near despair. Contemplate flight. Anywhere. As a result, begin to translate K. [Kafka's Letters] ... that awful cul-de-sac deadness: words of no avail, nor gestures, however loving & deeply felt. Weeping jag alone at breakfast ... Poor T paralysed in kitchen. Try & analyse my behaviour.'

From Jimmy to Sonia Orwell on 16 January 1965:

... Walker & Isabelle were here last weekend. But I will tell of this later, probably tomorrow. I *must* stop, feed the pigeons, get the car, & drive through the grim, sopping landscape.

To recap: the Walker weekend is too long a story for a letter. As a guest he had always been a nuisance, needs so much looking after, demands too much, & is so unbelievably slow. He was more of a nuisance than ever, and infinitely slower, but by the time he left I found myself as fond of him as ever. For two days before he arrived, The White House in Washington phoned for him twice each day. There was also a cable: URGENT. He himself had phoned me from Paris, asking me to get him a room in London. I did. I then wrote two letters & the cable to the hotel. But he never went there, never received the letters or the cable. He stayed with Tom Matthews. By the time they arrived at Tisbury he was in such a state about the White House urgency that I thought he has going to have a nervous breakdown. I foresaw him sitting by the hour at the phone here, calling Washington DC – at, needless to say, my expense! As I opened the front door the phone went. I muttered a prayer. It was granted. 'Mr Goldman at the White House calling Mr Evans.' (I had of course asked already what his connections were with Mr G. of the White House; they both answered that it could only be bad news: the very serious illness or more likely suicide of a woman friend – whom I happen to know.)

Well, what Mr G. wanted was Walker's approval of a job he had been offered as one of four 'overseers' of photography in the U.S. Government; should he accept, the document saying so had to be signed by President Johnson the next day. – Well, you can probably imagine the relief from tension, from any likelihood of further calls from the White House. How did the White House get my address & phone number? That still remains a mystery.

… Most of the rest of the weekend Walker spent drinking vodka, beginning with two 'snorters' before breakfast. He polished off just over a bottle per day. He showed no signs of tipsiness: he simply repeated himself more than usual, and his movements became slower – and slower – and slower. Until by the time he left he was hardly moving at all. I will say this for him: he bears not the slightest resemblance to anyone else I know. And that is sumpin'.

From John Davenport, Worthing, Sussex on 27 February 1965:

I can't tell you how your letter cheered me. I feel so far out on the lit. limb. Appreciation from you, who *know*, is invaluable.

... There is much that is 'difficult' about him [Brian Howard]. I was saying to Roger [Senhouse, senior editor at Secker & Warburg] that being with him was all too often like skating on thin ice over a sea of sulphur. All those paradoxical snobberies ... Of course he had panache when young, but spoiled it all by malicious jealousy and sheer spleen. So lazy: after all those years in France and Italy he could still only speak high Windsor. M. J. [Marie Jacqueline Lancaster, author of a biography of Brian Howard] seems to regard him as a sort of Oscar Wilde; but Wilde was benign as well as brilliant. Brian had all too much of Bosie about him! Forgive this bluntness. Unfair.

The hours at Rye were delightful. Roger was at his best, which as far as I'm concerned is *the* best. We zig-zagged dizzily about in space and time from Catullus to Ullswater. Millions of books and bottles. Endless laughter. Wished you were there; which you were, of course, in a way – somewhere between Rome & Carlisle. Unfortunately I had to stay with old John B[anting], and I found it rather depressing. He had a dreary pear-shaped Sam, who said that when he was house-boy in a Catholic seminary the oblates all wanted to suck him off when he brought them their morning tea. I was sceptical, saying that surely it was unlikely before Prime and breakfast; after supper and Compline, perhaps. J. B. was rather cross with me. But, seriously ... John will swallow anything, tall stories and semen included.

Well, dear old boy, I must go and totter about with the other cripples. This place is killing me, but terribly slowly. We must eat an oyster or two together before The End.

It was at this time that Tania decided that she had had enough of translation and that gardening was a more satisfying and rewarding occupation. So, with the immediate prospect of Kafka's *Letters to Felice*, a massive task, a new collaborator had to be found. This was Elisabeth (Lila) Duckworth. Originally from Vienna, but married to an Englishman, she was introduced to Jimmy and Tania, with whom she became great friends, by her compatriot Dorli Percival, a relation of the von Hofmannsthals. One of Lila's two daughters was at Cranborne Chase School in Wardour, a mile or so away from Hatch.

Lila and Jimmy hit it off from the first moment. On her frequent visits, she seldom saw Jimmy and Tania together – 'Come to my room, we'll talk,' he used to say. It was a confidential approach experienced by many; abandoned to Tania's voluble embrace, the visitors Jimmy wished to monopolise would be lost to him.

The American publishers, Schocken, with whom Jimmy had signed a contract back in the '40s, published the Felice letters in 1973 and Secker & Warburg a year later. The delay was caused partly by a clause which did not allow publication until Felice's death. She died in 1960.

Jimmy's and Lila's method of translation was the same as that he had used with Tania: Lila would write a first draft and then Jimmy would anglicise and polish the prose. In the copious correspondence which inevitably ensued, Jimmy would address Lila affectionately as 'Dearest Marvel', 'Meine liebe Marvel' or 'My dear Favourite Sister'. It was to be a successful professional liaison of more than two years' duration, after which they repeatedly met in London.

Jimmy replied to John Davenport on 1 March 1965:

What a generous letter, dear boy. *You* have no reason to feel 'so far out on the lit. limb'. Some of us are long ago beyond the point of no return.

About BH [Brian Howard] I do not consider you are unfair at all. I am equally censorious (as I should have thought Roger S. would have told you) & for the same reasons. I am angry to think that this 'M. J.' is one of those (Sybille [Bedford] is another) who dare to mention BH in the same breath with OW. In the hundreds of pages of the latter's letters there is hardly a malicious word; even after the tragedy only sorrow at the vile behaviour of others. You are absolutely right: there was far too much of Bosie in B. H. I feel anyway that I have a far better 'right' to speak – God forbid that I ever should! – than any of those ladies, who knew him only during the later years & then only that side of him which he revealed to the opposite sex – the *flattering* side.

Where B was marvellous was – alone, with no audience – in the country, by the sea. I have never known a more wonderful companion. Cities were his undoing. (As indeed, they are mine.) The only person I know who *influenced* him was Eddie G-H [Gathorne-Hardy] – alas, it was not a very helpful influence. E was far more *daring* than B, behind whom there always loomed the critical but alas ever-indulgent eye of Mom. I suppose the two most important factors in B's life were his *name* and that he was an *American*.

From Davenport on 4 March 1965:

Yes: Roger had mentioned your attitude toward BH – an attitude I share and sympathise with ... of course Eddie's influence on B was disastrous. Eddie's influence on Eddie has been pretty disastrous, too. Your adjective 'daring' is absolutely just, though. He had – one always writes of him in the past tense – a sort of gallant insolence. Poor old B adopted more of the insolence than the gallantry. But how good he was without a goggling audience! He used to like me to play for him – Fauré, Debussy, that sort of thing. He was beautifully *innocent* at such times. Of course you knew him better than anybody – longer and more intimately. Damn it, he was in love with you for years!

... Long letter from Roger, tidying-up, so to speak, our Rye conversations, beginning 'Dearest literary individual'. People so clever are rarely as kind. He behaved with amazing understanding during the days following Marjorie's [JD's wife] death. Made me deliciously (not horribly) drunk every night, without *too much* sympathy. He is a 'gentleman'. How many of them are there, one wonders? It's a dirty word. I suppose we're all gentlemen in a seedy sort of way. Not being just that old-fashioned thing was Brian's doom.

Lunched with Graham Greene on Tuesday, just back from Vienna, off to Paris, on to Saigon – 'for a pipe or two'. I arrived at 12.15. When I got out into Piccadilly it was seven o'clock! He is wonderful value. Amazingly *objective* about his work.

From Jimmy to Davenport on 8 March 1965:

Just a *petit mot* to say that (snow permitting; we have been imprisoned since Tuesday) we are off tomorrow to Berlin and Paris for 10 days. Wystan (I think I told you) has been asking & asking us to come for months. I did not think I could persuade T. to go (she has a block about Berlin, which is understandable). Can't say I am longing to go myself, but I know it is now or never, & I would like to see what it *looks* like, sniff the atmosphere of that hideous city. It is 37 years since I was there, as a bank clerk. I have never been so lonely & miserable in my life. It was the year my elder sister (aged 18) died (of 'sleeping sickness'); it was also the winter BH got caught in Paris by Cocteau & Co. & failed to turn up – though he did eventually, to catch 'crabs' with which he insisted on having 'races' on the kitchen table, even on the ship coming back to England. At the time I did not think this was funny; but in retrospect I find myself giggling at the memory.

What a day you must have had with G. Greene. I have never even met him, only caught occasional glimpses of him – haggard-looking & raincoated – dashing out of Albany.

From Jimmy to William Plomer on 22 May 1965:

Turbott Wolfe [1926] arrived an hour ago; since when I have read the Introduction. Perhaps 'read' is incorrect; I was hypnotised by it. The telephone was ignored; even the chatter of T. and our 'help' and the clatter of crockery beneath me failed to arouse my customary bellow of resentment.

I now feel exhausted, as though I had been trying to swim as far as I swam 40 years ago (apropos that number of years, it is 40 years ago today that I set sail for the Cape). My head reels with a storm of thoughts. Uppermost among them is that you are clearly an even Greater Man than I had thought; and then: 'How *very* extraordinary it must be, to be you!' That you are alive! That you are but a year older than myself, and in spirit years younger! This 'Introduction' is the kind of thing that is, occasionally, written ten, twenty, fifty years after the death of a rare and original artist. What must you feel? That there are (were?) two William Plomers? That you have been born again? What *can* your reservations be when you look at that *marvellous* photograph? How sturdy and strong you look, and how confident & *un*-neurotic – a born Leader of Men. Poor [Roy] Campbell (poor my eye!) he looks like a middleaged wreck washed up from Tristram da Cunha; and L. van der P. [Laurens van der Post] little different from the way he looks today. And that just visible girth of yours round your waist!
...
Of what L. v. der P. *says* I will not write now. There's too much to say, & it would bore you, & there would be too many questions. But how good it is, what a lot he has packed into it, & nothing irrelevant, & so much less Jung than I had anticipated ... What Wise Men you two are, and how *good* of Fate to have spared you both. And selfishly-thinking, how strange and rather awful to know now that in order to escape from my own solitude of 40 years ago all I

would have had to do was walk away from that Rhodesian farm and keep on walking, south & south east, until I reached the south coast of Natal. And even stranger thought: this was precisely what I dreamed of doing, every day for a year, for I had a girl-friend there, to whom I wrote long letters every week.

And now, dear Wm, my blessings & my thanks as I embark on your first great work.

From Jimmy to Kay Boyle on 9 July 1965:

I have been a great admirer of [Robert] Lowell ever since the publication of *Lord Weary's Castle* [1946]. God, what that man must have been through since then! I am less familiar with his more recent activities & though I knew he had been here I missed the BBC interview. He seems to feel much as we do about Freud the man. But I often wonder, what a mess this world has made of his work. It has always seemed to me that of all men Freud was too far ahead of his time, that he arrived, pioneered too soon, that the latter half of this century is not yet prepared to digest what he was only *beginning* to discover. Or, to put it another way: although he lived to be an old man he should have been allowed to live half as long again. There has been no one, it occurs to me, capable of carrying on where he left off. And I feel that he himself was deeply pessimistic.

... Within a few hours of our arrival in Dublin we found ourselves by pure chance in the midst of the Irish Academy's celebration of Yeats' centenary; and as a result met again in one somewhat hectic hour all the Irish men & women we know connected with literature, including that remarkably active & vocal octogenarian Padraic Colum. The Irishman I have by far the most admiration for is Sean O'Faolain. Have you read the first vol. of his autobiography *Vive Moi!* [1964]? Please do, when you have time.

From Jimmy to John Davenport on 6 September 1965:

... It's true that for the past two months Reiter has been at me again; for much of August the right wrist was in a splint & I could not sign my name. It's really appalling how little a guy can do bereft of his right hand. Worst perhaps is the continual state of apprehension in which one lives: where is it going to break out next? The knees, neck, ankles? Is this the price of post-middleage, of 40-odd years of various excesses – including, & probably above all, indolence?

... I was more or less all right for several months, until mid-June, when we took off for th' Ould Sod for a couple of weeks: Dublin, Donegal, Derry – where I had not been for 50 years. And where I met a number of cousins for the first time. In Dublin, by pure chance, I saw in one hour everyone I know in Ireland who has written a book. The only exceptions I can think of were Frank O'Connor & Liam O'Flaherty, both in Dublin but not attending the Academy's celebration of the Yeats centenary. The only reason we were there was because we got caught, a few minutes before the party, in the lobby of the Shelburne, by Sean O'Faolain. If one has to be caught by anyone for anything, let it be him. We saw him again later, *chez lui*. *What* a grand man he is. Do you remember the hint in *Vive Moi!* of the collapse of his life-long friendship with O'Connor? It's true. And a great sadness to him; but perhaps a greater bitterness. They are very different people.

Between 21 September and 16 October the Sterns visited their favourite city, Paris, and then moved south to an equally treasured part of France, to the Pont du Gard between Nîmes and Avignon. Jimmy referred to the bridge as 'his spiritual home'.

As his letter of 19 October to John Davenport relates, Lawrence and Claude Durrell visited them for lunch in their hotel.

In a desultory way the Sterns – Tania was keener than Jimmy – were looking for a house to buy, having fantasised about a French retreat in the sun, a dream which they shared with Daphne and Xan Fielding who were living in the area.

From William Plomer on 15 October 1965:

... Looking back over the last few months, I feel I have been active, but it would be boring to catalogue my activities for you. I rather wish you had heard, on the 3rd Programme, a 'conversation' in which a fairly young S. African writer, Dan Jacobson, who lives in this country, was put on to draw me out apropos of *Turbott Wolfe* ... They called it 'A Long Shadow on the Veld'. I also wish you had seen – perhaps you did see – a poem by me in the *TLS* called 'The Taste of the Fruit', an elegy on two young S. African writers who killed themselves in July – one, white, an Afrikaans poet, female, drowned herself at Cape Town; the other, black, male, extremely talented, threw himself out of a window in the US. Three different anthologists have already wanted to use this poem, & it brought me some striking responses – one from Nadine [Gordimer], for instance, & a really extraordinary letter from the head of one of those American 'foundations', calling it one of the great elegies in the English language ...

... This letter is perhaps egocentric, like an article by Angus Wilson I have just read, in which the words 'I', 'my', 'mine', and 'myself' occur 94 times.

From Jimmy to John Davenport on 19 October 1965:

... Larry [Durrell]? Yes, they both came over to lunch one beautiful noon, in the dappled sun dropping through the branches of the plane trees, at a table overlooking the Gardon and facing the Pont. He brought me his *Lear in Corfu*, published there with a Preface by himself, and the copy of *Fact* about the trial in the US, which I see advertised obscenely all over some Sunday paper. She, Claude, has gone through all kinds of illnesses, accidents, & operations, & looks ten years younger than when I last saw her. Dapper, smart, marvellously made-up, very much the well-to-do, French bourgeoise. Larry with a real settled look, relaxed, *arrivé*, warm, unpompous, charming. Only when a 17-year-old French girl, daughter of my doctor, arrived & recited some poems by Jacques Prévert & Anna de Noailles, did a really fiendish, diabolical look leap into those blue eyes. Over several bottles of local Lirac we seemed to talk about everything under the sun except literature.

9 November was a special day: for their thirtieth wedding celebration Jimmy laid on a small, secret dinner party at L'Etoile in Charlotte Street, Fitzrovia. Tania, sartorially unprepared, believing the dinner to be *à deux*, was astonished to see approaching their table several friends in evening finery – Eda Lord and Sybille Bedford, Elaine and William Robson-Scott and William Plomer. Perhaps not intentionally unkind, it was a treat which he had arranged for her on a previous occasion: 'Last time the secret was so well kept that Tania burst into tears as one friend after another, fifteen in all, came marching into the restaurant ... ,' he had told Isabelle Evans in October. Tears of joy? Probably not.

From Davenport on 19 November 1965:

Thank you so much, dear old boy, for your heartening letter. Cheered me no end. Even the thought of Truman C's [Capote's] new apartment, of which I feel not the slightest envy. Think of the *people* in it!

... Very glad you didn't think the Malcolm [Lowry] thing too terribly bad. The trouble was I was overburdened with instructions: told that no *Life* reader had heard of M. L. or of *Under the Volcano*; that he was a 'cult' for an 'obscure clique'; that I shouldn't attempt an analysis of the book; that I must try to explain *who the author was*; that I was not to be 'highbrow' etc. etc. Anyway the editor (who seems to be as asinine as his TV-doped readers) hasn't complained so far, touch wood.

... To drag oneself arbitrarily into a book review is very bad, but if one's presence is part of the texture, so to speak, it can help. Darling old Desmond [MacCarthy] was *the* master of the personal touch. Always relevant, always illuminating. A most under-rated writer; except by writers – a dying race, one sometimes feels. Am perpetually enraged by condescendingly derogatory remarks about D. MacC. from people with names like Kermode. Very glad indeed they all treat *me* with contempt, like P. H. Newby. I misread your W. H. A. quote as: 'Being one of those perverts who generally look like an unmade bed' etc. Thought it was carrying the personal touch just a leetle far. But later realised you'd written 'persons', not the other thing, & felt relieved all round. God, what a boring, what an *unbelievably* boring, book that is about Max [Beerbohm]! David C [Cecil] *is* a bore, of course, and always has been and will be. A hymnologist. If he hadn't been a Cecil I suppose he'd have been a dim schoolmaster-parson. Odd to think that he's Desmond's son-in-law! They tell me he's a good husband and father – nobody could accuse him of being licentious or unkind – so I say no more, not being notable for virtue myself. Isn't it extraordinary how even so perceptive a one as W. H. A. will persist in finding 'suppressed queers' whenever they are puzzled by someone who obviously isn't. I lunched with Robin Maugham, Terence Rattigan & Cuthbert Worsley recently, and they decided that *everybody* (except, rather oddly, me) was a sup. qu. It just isn't true. One might as truly say that all homosexuals were suppressed mulierasts (Alfred Douglas's word).

... Thanks again for your letter. I love you dearly. Perhaps I am a suppressed queer after all. What fun!

Eight months later John Davenport was dead.

9
The Prize
1965–1971

While Jimmy was mired in his own slough of non-creativity, behind the scenes his admirers were at work to bring him the recognition he deserved. Their endeavours were to revive both his spirits and his literary reputation.

'A James Joyce evening' at the American Center organised by Maria Jolas took the Sterns to Paris in early February 1966. Nathalie Sarraute, Alain Robbe-Grillet and Michel Butor were three of the New Wave writers who attended. Before leaving they had spoken to Arthur Miller who was in a Brighton hospital suffering from hepatitis. He insisted on their meeting his wife, the photographer Ingeborg Morath, when they were in Paris. They dined with her and her frighteningly precocious three-year-old daughter Rebecca.

But back at home, there were recurring problems over Jimmy's mother's nurses and domestics, which occupied much of their time.

> Yesterday was particularly bad [he wrote to Pauline Wynn two months later], I had to get rid of the one good highly-trained nurse; she was driving my mother literally up the wall … She had also so antagonized all the other females in the house that one had collapsed & another phoned & said she was leaving. On bidding the woman farewell she pressed into T's hand a little packet wrapped in tissue-paper. On reaching home we discovered in it a diamond wristwatch, a diamond & ruby brooch, & an emerald ring, which the nurse had ripped off my mother's body – another story I had taken *avec du sel*. (Actually the act is professional hospital rules, but it was how it had been performed that mattered.)

In early October the Sterns were driven down by their now near neighbour, Billy Henderson, to his house in Georgeham, north Devon. They were even to have a holiday from each other, for Jimmy slept alone in a house on the beach, to be as near as possible to the sea. He described the scene to Isabelle Evans: 'As at Bandol, I can spit into the sea from where I sit ... But what a sea! The fury of it has turned it into what looks like curdled cream. When the tide is in, it comes up the wall, when it's out you have to walk several hundred yards to reach it.'

It was not until later in the month that he received a morale-boosting letter from Charles Osborne, the 'impertinent' young Australian of the *London Magazine*, now at the Arts Council: recommended by V. S. Pritchett, he had won a £1,000 prize, the first the Council had awarded for the Short Story.

At the ceremony, Jennie Lee, then Minister for the Arts, gave the prize to a poker-faced but emotional Jimmy in the presence of Cecil Day Lewis, chairman of the Arts Council Literature Panel, Edgell Rickword, who was there to receive an award for his poetry, Rayner Heppenstall, who was honoured for his fiction, and Angus Wilson. A week later his publisher, Fred Warburg, was pressing him for 'a chunk of autobiography'.

Early in the new year Jimmy retained an agent, following the publicity he had received from the prize. Elaine Greene was an American, and had been married to Sir Hugh Carleton Greene, Governor of the BBC and brother of Graham. Jimmy's work was in demand: Tom Maschler of Jonathan Cape was very keen to publish Jimmy's stories, but Warburg wouldn't release him and immediately laid plans to publish a new selection, to be chosen by Arthur Calder-Marshall. It was proposed that a dialogue between Arthur Miller and Angus Wilson should preface the book. Miller wrote that he would do anything he could to further the public recognition of Jimmy's stories. But this idea never came to fruition. Jimmy's last book, *The Stories of James Stern*, which thereafter he nicknamed 'my stale buns', was published the following year.

In February Warburg read Jimmy's memoirs, or as much as he had written, and, while offering an advance of £750, wasn't insisting on a deadline for delivery. Earlier, Jimmy had re-read the material he had started four years ago and wept: '... oh, the lack of organization, the repetition.' And he was feeling gloomy, too, for another reason: the wife of Alan Thomas, a dealer in rare books, vanished from their home in Chelsea and nothing was heard of her for two weeks. Then her coat and handbag (with a considerable amount of money still in it) were found at the foot of the cliffs near Swanage. Jimmy had known Thomas for more than forty years and had found his wife a woman of sound mind and common sense. The Thomases lived for years in Bournemouth and whenever Lawrence Durrell was in England he always stayed with them. It was a tragedy which haunted Jimmy, whose mental state during these years was particularly vulnerable.

The Sterns, on 1 October, drove to Fordingbridge for the unveiling of Ivor Roberts-Jones's memorial statue of Augustus John, described by John's biographer Michael Holroyd as 'standing like some chocolate pugilist', but which Jimmy thought 'had a certain wild dignity'. Lady Melchett and Lord Mountbatten and various other dignitaries 'howled through a gale into a microphone which kept breaking down'.

By the end of the following March, proofs of the stories had arrived: 'Awful experience. How can anyone believe a word of it? But what wasted material, how could anyone believe in "The Man [Who Was Loved]"? Even "The Cloud" is more credible! ... Begin to read *The Heartless Land* – am so horrified I am almost physically sick.'

From his new home in Hassocks, Sussex, William Plomer wrote on 29 May 1967:

> ... It's a worry about John L. [Lehmann]. He really minds about writing & writers, he has done a great deal for them, he is a loyal friend, he is not in the least ill-natured, one can't (at least I can't) help being rather fond of him in some ways, but some lack of imagination, of sensitiveness, of seeing things from other people's points of view, some heaviness of touch, puts people off him and off his writings, & prevents them from seeing or allowing for his solid good qualities.
>
> Years & years ago Rosamond [Lehmann] used to sigh over him & say 'I *know*' in a resigned sort of way, half sad, half amused.

From Jimmy to Plomer on 9 June 1967:

> ... Of John L. you write in such loyal terms of defence that I wondered if I had said something you thought I shouldn't have about that imposing figure? Surely not. I agree with all you say. His greatest trouble, it seems to me, is his inability to express any emotional feelings, above all in his writing, at least in his prose. About his poetry (by which I feel he sets great store), I wouldn't know. Rosamond by now is more 'sad' than 'amused' about her brother, I think ...

... Alas, there is little that's funny in the world of the moment. When will there be an end to the deaths, and mostly premature deaths, of writers – and writer friends? I am afraid you will have been terribly upset by that of Joe Ackerley. I knew him hardly at all, but I know that you and he were very close ... And then, today, Pamela Frankau and Dorothy Parker ...

From Jimmy to Plomer on 4 September 1967:

... Alas, alas, dear sweet Alyse [Gregory, who died on 28 August] – and you thought of me. Then Sassoon. And at once I thought of you. I do have a kind of mild, selfish regret: he lived so near. I would like to have just *seen* him once. As I am sure I have told you: the only occasion on which I agreed with my father – or vice versa – was when he expressed admiration for the *Foxhunting Man* [1928]. Or was it that book's successor? Anyway, I can hear him: 'Yers. The war. The winters. The trenches. The rain. Riding back. At the head of yer men. Yers. It was just like that.' I could have kissed him. (Of course I couldn't.) But there came an inner glow: he was human. He could read. And recognise. Yers. Poor man, who should never have been a soldier, never have had children. *What*!

Seamus Heaney. Now there's a man. 'A perfect dear'? Now isn't that grand! I am going to surprise you:
'Prevention of cruelty' talk cuts ice in town
Where they consider death unnatural,
But on well-run farms pests have to be kept down.
My copy of *Death of a Naturalist* [1966] looks like a barbed-wire fence. Why? Well, his poems are smells – stinks familiar to this uneducated, farmyard nose: Of blackberries:
It wasn't fair
That all the lovely canfuls smelt of rot.
Each year I hoped they'd keep, knew they would not.
Bless the boy. How Belfast can produce broth or butter, God knows. I suppose just *because* it is so awful. – I long to hear more about him, his face.

From Plomer on 24 November 1967:

... Of course Chips C.[Channon, whose diaries had just been published] is awful – vulgar, shallow, conceited, and probably far more 'poisonous' in the bits left out than in the bits left in. When I said 'comedy' I meant in the sense of 'life regarded as a spectacle' (C.O.Dic.). The self-revelation, and the picture of a certain corner of society at a certain place and time, seem to me to have a horrid fascination – especially as one lived through the time he is writing about and to some extent was informed at the time about what went on. I don't mean that I laughed – though I was amused (if it was in C. Channon that I read it) by the story of Mrs Greville saying to Queen Mary: 'I always say that that little Lady Cunard isn't as bad as she is painted.'

ALL I was trying to convey was that reading such stuff, such tinselly stuff, after *250,000 words* of the letters of a giant bore (female) of the early 19th century was like – no, I won't say it again. And surely from a novelist's point of view (I don't mean mine, I mean generally) that kind of gossip is fascinating, and from a social historian's, too? But what would Henry James have thought? Proust? Balzac? Perhaps the vulgarity would have been too much for them; but the 'poison' would surely have engaged their curiosity.

From Jimmy to Plomer on 29 November 1967:

... I feel sure that Lady C. not being as bad as she's painted was uttered by, of and to another, before any of the ladies were born. One of the repetitions by Chips (which I had not heard) and liked was the occasion (during the climax of the Abdication crisis, I think) when Churchill ran smack into Baldwin in one of two H. of C. *pissoirs*. 'Well,' muttered Baldwin, buttoning up, 'it's nice to know that there's at least one platform on which we can still both stand.' And walked away.

Latest on the subject [of the Channon Diaries] came over the air last night from (of all people) Tom Driberg. Perhaps you heard: 'Of course he was the most ghastly snob, of course he hated Americans, of course he was a rabid anti-Semite, greatly admired Ribbentrop, *but* ... (what seemed like 5 minutes later, in the anti-climax of the year) ... I knew him, he did have charm.' So, I am sure, did Ribbentrop. And Goering.

1967 ended with some depressed entries in Jimmy's journal, and no wonder, for in October he had suffered a heart attack brought on, he maintained, by frustration and the distractions of the household: Tania talking on the telephone, the cleaning lady vacuuming the floors, cars in the lane outside his study. Noises at any pitch – music included – had become purgatorial. The sound of silence; that was what he craved. 'Silence is now the most expensive commodity on earth,' his contemporary Graham Greene said to Shirley Hazzard, who recorded his remark in her memoir, *Greene on Capri* (2000).

Although there had been a positive renewal of interest in his work, his 'stale buns' were indeed stories he had written many years ago, about which he felt less than proud. His feelings about the so-called autobiography, too, were tentative. But the Arts Council had now invited him to judge a prize for the best book of short stories; it could be deduced that life, on the whole, was not too bad. Yet, after seven years at Hatch Manor, the black moods persisted.

'... I am convinced ... ', wrote Auden from New York on 13 March 1968, 'that your greatest work lies ahead of you ... and what it will basically be is an act of *thanksgiving* for your marriage ... '

The irony is that only a month earlier he had written in his journal that on leaving the car one day,

> T. lets her bag fall on my left arm so that I am incapable of using the gears. On such occasions there is no chance of being 'polite' & in any case the very gesture is an outrage (perhaps impossible for her to recognize); in any case she bursts out with such abuse that my breath is taken away. I have for so long felt that there's so little left in the world worth living for that this is the last straw, I'd rather die, seems extraordinary that a couple who between them have lived 126 years on this earth should still feel capable of creating such scenes.

That he deemed Tania's unwitting and obviously involuntary gesture an outrage is an indication of his mental state and of the strain the marriage was under. It is no wonder that Tania once remarked to the writer Anthony Sampson, their neighbour across the valley in Wardour, that 'it is a full-time job keeping this marriage together'.

Yet his letters, as ever, maintained a balanced, humorous insight. In them he emerged more generous, outgoing and *simpatico* than he did face to face. In person, he came more and more in old age to resemble his father. Before the wry smile, the humorous, quizzical twinkle in his eyes – and often a wink – his face in repose or when disagreeably surprised was forbidding. On the telephone his hatred of the instrument was penetratingly conveyed. Communication by post was, as ever, the safest mode.

On 26 February 1968 Secker & Warburg published *The Stories of James Stern*. Of the nineteen pieces included, sixteen stories had appeared in his three previous collections, and the remainder were non-fiction: 'A Stranger among Miners', 'A Peaceful Place' and 'Home'; the last two sections were extracted from *The Hidden Damage*. His 1931 account of a visit to the coalfields of Wales and Derbyshire, told in the first person and in the present tense, is his first published attempt at journalism, complete with dialogue, whose faithfully recorded cadences now appear outdated. It reveals, however, the political awakening of the twenty-six-year-old writer, whose background and upbringing were so dramatically different from those of his subjects.

His immediately post-war visit to war-ravaged Germany is the background to a description of two encounters, one with a Negro corporal whose account of a double suicide is succinct and poignant:

> These two were buddies, see. Ever since they left home, about three years back, they were always together. That's the way it gets some guys ... One of 'em was married and had just heard he'd got enough points to go home. He was all set to leave for one of them French ports end of this week – today it would have been. Then he gets a letter from his wife. A short letter. 'Just to congratulate you,' she says, 'on bein' the proud father of a beautiful baby boy ...'

The other encounter is with a young pregnant woman, all her belongings stolen, who is cycling, walking and hitchhiking from Rome to Frankfurt. Against orders, Jimmy gives her a lift.

The first of the sixteen stories, 'The Cloud', which was also his first to be published in *The London Mercury*, is set in the Transvaal. Its protagonist, a Dutchman, vents all his anger and unhappiness on his innocent and defenceless native workers. For his companion (Jimmy) the pure, relentless azure blue of the sky becomes a symbol of pain and suffering. But 'the cloud', a portent of salvation, does not bring rain and relief, only fire – and murder.

'The Force', much admired by Malcolm Lowry, is a story of frustration, miscegenation and sexual desire. George Newman, thirty, a bachelor sent alone to administer justice and keep the peace on what is known in the British South African Police as a 'one-man station', is desperate for relief when on leave after nine months' isolation. During a Saturday dance in the local town on the first evening, he impresses a policeman's wife with his prowess on the floor. His sexual need thus aroused, his fulfilment is sought with the black girl who brings him his night-cap: '... a torrent whose power was irresistible surged up in him, possessed his stricken limbs as his arms went about her, and the rocks called colour were conquered as the man and the woman fell slowly together where they stood, on the floor.'

'The Beginning and the End' is about Sam, aged ten, who falls in love with Lena: '... in the middle of a laurel bush ... our love was consummated in innumerable kisses ...' At home Sam and Lena are banned from his mother's bedroom; he's told she has whooping cough, a euphemism for pregnancy, and in the cloakroom, also out of bounds, mysteriously, they find an empty cot. Back at boarding school, his letters to Lena become more and more of a burden as school life takes over. Soon, he returns for the holidays and is shown his 'new' brother. But the devastating news that Lena is dead leaves him almost unmoved. The story ends: 'The next day but one, at the party after my brother's christening, I fell in love with a girl called Mary – Mary Jameson I think was her full name ... '

'I bain't a-goin' with 'ee over theyurr – t' see them gurrls,' says Joe Gurney in 'On the Sabbath', to his three brothers. But uppermost in his mind was the desire to 'treat 'em rough, the kiss-and-cuddle wantin' 'ussies ... I'd like to ... ' Joe sublimates his desire by bird-watching and cliff-climbing. Out on the cliffs, with the gulls and the curlews weaving maddeningly above him, he finds himself trapped. 'In one blind flash he knew that if he fell he would hurtle to certain death on the rocks, and he knew even if he were able to spring from his position on the face he could not hope to fall in the sea ... At last, in a hollow, failing voice he called the names of the girls he had refused to go and see with his brothers only that afternoon. He raised his head and called them into the night ... And his brothers' words came back to him mocking him. "Ah, then bez 'ee afeard o' gurrls, Joe? Bez 'ee afeard ...?" And he screamed till the pain shook him. "I bain't afeard of 'ee – I love 'ee, I love 'ee ... I love 'ee, Mother, I love 'ee ..."' The story is a *tour de force*; the empathy with Joe's loneliness and frustration is marvellously conveyed.

In 'Mister and Miss' a gentleman apprentice farmer is involved with a local millionaire's daughter to whom he makes love but whom he despises, while secretly desiring the daughter of the head groom. At a dance attended by both gentry and villagers his dilemma is resolved in a dramatic denouement. Class consciousness and the sexual frustration of the educated English male is again a subject which Jimmy handles with knowledge, restraint and fine judgement.

On 18 March he received a heartening accolade from Patrick White in Sydney, to whom he had sent a copy of *The Stories*:

> What a remarkably modest person you are to keep yourself so dark. Of course we knew you had written stories, but I didn't imagine they would be anything like these ... I can think of no other writers in the Twentieth Century whose stories are so satisfying and at the same time so subtle as yours ... The stories in your volume which give me most are 'The Man Who Was Loved', 'A Stranger among Miners', 'Under the Beech Tree', and 'Something Wrong'. Some of the English stories I find horrifying. I don't think anybody else has brought out that particular horror of English family life. I can re-experience the temperature of the bedrooms. Ugh! You made me cry three times – in 'The Man Who Was Loved', 'Next Door to Death', and 'Home' – whether this is a good thing or not, I don't know, but I like to think it is, and so I record it ... I think 'The Broken Leg' one of the most horrible things I have ever read ... It is a great relief to find that somebody one knows and likes is a master in his art.

To have retained over many years White's respect and friendship was a remarkable feat considering the famous volatility of his disposition. David Marr, White's biographer, once wrote to Jimmy: 'No one else, I think, had your authority to grill Patrick about his work ... [yours] are the letters that most put him on his mettle ... ' Marr has also declared that were it not for Jimmy's support, in his opinion White would not have been awarded the Nobel Prize.

A review of *The Stories* by William Plomer appeared in the *London Magazine* of April 1968:

> Comment on the Arts Council awards to authors has been mixed, but the award to James Stern last year seems exemplary. It shows recognition of merit in a writer of short stories long known to discriminating contemporaries but not recognized widely enough ... all Stern's stories are disturbingly vivid – vivid because exactly in focus, and disturbing as all reminders that 'ordinary' life is a cat's cradle of tensions ... All Stern's stories deal with moments of crisis; all are dramatic.
>
> They are set in various parts of the world. The stories of

Rhodesia, written a good while ago, indicate, like all the others, Stern's own unilateral declaration of independence. They show his independence of accepted ideas, his seemingly inborn inability to take racial or class or sex taboos for granted, and his unerring ability to detect foot-and-mouth disease in sacred cows.

... The stories speak for themselves as the work of a man who had to fight to free himself from early trammels, and who, in adapting himself to differing environments and ways of life, has seen men, women and children with senses capable of delight, looking for happiness, for emotional anchors and emotional fulfilment, and sometimes having to fight for them ...

In acknowledgement of these perceptive words of praise, Jimmy wrote to Plomer on 31 March 1968:

Your opinion of the *Cakes* ['stale buns'] and your letter arrived on the same platter. In the latter you write that you 'feel uneasily that I may be irritated or even enraged by what you have said and/or left unsaid'. You cannot of course feel anything of the sort ... That you should have considered saying anything at all makes me feel pride, humility & gratitude all at once. What you actually wrote made me do what I am quite sure I have never done before when reading a review of my efforts: burst out laughing twice in two minutes. Briefly, my 'unerring ability to detect foot-and-mouth disease in sacred cows' had the effect of 'propelling me headlong over hedges & ditches' (well, chairs & sofas) into the next room where the LW [Little Woman: Tania] was sitting over the fire. Her subsequent shriek was even more piercing than mine ... I have omitted to mention the *tone* of your review – its quietness & discretion & (I trust) lack of exaggeration in your judgement. I do so hope, my dear Wm, that you did not find it so terribly difficult as I know I would have – in reverse, I mean. ... You may not believe it, but I don't mind much what people I don't know say or write about my Buns, it's being *ignored* that irritates me. I know of course that this is a shoddy and madly expensive reprint & that I should be delighted with so much as a nod of recognition, as indeed I am; but there have been no nods from my native land, not even from the *Irish Times*, whose charming editor Terence de Vere White took the trouble to write & tell me that he would see that the book got 'properly treated' – and no nod from the *New Statesman, Spectator, Guardian, Daily Telegraph* – but goodness me, as if it mattered!

Ignored he wasn't by two of the 'heavy' Sundays. Montague Haltrecht in the *Sunday Times* wrote: 'James Stern shapes his narrative masterfully. He projects his characters vividly, and exposes them, through a completely assured and deliberate highlighting of incidents, with a dramatic clarity. It is difficult not to be thrilled by characters who are splendidly vigorous even at the point of pitiful defeat.'

Paul Bailey's review in the *Observer* was more critical:

[Stern] is so obviously serious, intelligent and humane that it must seem little short of miserly to complain that his stories, for all their virtues, have a heavy-handed, premeditated air about them. Studiously conceived, they lack spontaneity and immediacy – it's as if they were written long after the initial inspiration had cooled off.

Yet in all of them there are marvellous passages, descriptions of landscapes and animals that are sometimes worthy of Lawrence … Even so, only one of these stories completely satisfies – the macabre and poignant 'Something Wrong'. It is so good, so rivetingly true, that one wishes Mr Stern would write with more passion more often.

In the early '90s, Sean Wyse Jackson, a director of John Sandoe's Chelsea bookshop, who had published the English edition of Jimmy's *The Hidden Damage,* commissioned the novelist William Boyd to write an introduction to a projected selection of stories, alas never published. The following is part of his text:

Stern possesses a talent that is idiosyncratic and multifarious. He is not to be pinned down by setting or style, or tone of voice, or by literary fashion. Some of these stories reflect the modes and manners of their time of composition (over half a century ago) and others seem as strange or as sophisticated as to have been written today. And reading through them one senses that this variety is not willed or striven for but rather has arisen from the unique demands of the individual story. It exemplifies, I believe, a kind of unreflecting confidence in the writing: when a Hemingwayesque taciturnity is best suited to the tale then that is the mode employed, but if at any moment a surge of emotion is apposite then the tone will change accordingly. Romanticism of a distinctly purplish hue is not shunned and neither is ellipticism or ambiguity. The lush imaginings of 'The Pauper's Grave' are a far cry from the worldly cynicism of 'The Force'. The unclassifiable mood of 'Travellers' Tears' (High camp? Surreal farce? Ortonesque fantasy?) is hugely removed from the Kiplingesque, Conradian verities of 'The Man Who Was Loved'. Each story, it seems, is written with an integrity of purpose in the manner that will best produce its destined effect and the result of this candour is a distinctive freshness and honesty in the narrative that is both potent and beguiling.

While celebrating James Stern's exuberant variety this collection also illustrates one significant unifying trait: seven of the stories are told from the point of view of a child or young boy. There is evidently something about a child's vision of the world – at once clear and occluded – that Stern relishes. He is not alone: the innocent's gaze on the adult's world is one many writers have exploited from Voltaire to John Updike. Its attraction is not hard to divine: a child's interpretation of what it witnesses will be simultaneously unblemished and incomplete, pure and yet flawed. It is the reader who supplies the adult subtext, who sees what is implicit behind the bafflement and incomprehension. And it is a device particularly well suited to short fiction. At greater length it becomes wearisome and over-obvious, but for the short story (whose working maxims should always be 'show not tell', 'suggest not delineate', 'distil not expand') such a trope plays to the form's strengths. Stern handles it with a natural confidence, particularly in 'The Ebbing Tide' and 'Something Wrong'. In addition both of these stories, as do many of the others, draw on the author's own Edwardian Anglo-Irish childhood for atmosphere and detail: a lost world of governesses and scullery maids, riding to hounds, gentry and peasants, large houses and narrow horizons. Three others are set in Africa, Rhodesia to be precise, where Stern farmed as a young man. In each case these familiar, remembered worlds colour the fictions with an exactness of detail and ambiance that is impressive, and bestow on the writing a conviction and relaxed authority that is enviable. From Bim, the over-excited Sealyham on an Irish beach in 'The Ebbing Tide', to the solitary hell of a one-man station in the African bush in 'The Force', the authenticity is exact and irreproachable.

… What I haven't touched upon is the large area of questioning opened up by your allusions, in your previous letter, to Patrick White [Plomer wrote on 2 July 1968]. You know him, I don't, & you wouldn't speak of a 'cruel, sadistic' side to his nature without reason, but Sidney Nolan kept assuring me that White is a 'compassionate' man. I think it is because I feel that he, like Mary Hare in *Riders in the Chariot* [1961], has a 'love for all living matter' that I made that remark about my own disinclination or inability to evolve as a novelist. I feel sure I am more cruel than he is, because I tend to reject, despise, dislike insolence, vulgarity, self-importance, to say nothing of (other people's!) lies and violence instead of patiently unravelling or tolerating or being *interested* by them ...

From Jimmy to Plomer on 9 July 1968:

... And yesterday an invasion, headed by one Harrison Birtwhistle (how did anyone come to be called that?) – I have a hunch you may at least know 'who' he is? The opera *Punch & Judy*, performed recently at Aldeburgh, perhaps you even saw it – and hated it?

HB (let us call him) came to me yesterday professionally, under the impression that I am *un Homme de Lettres*. I guessed before he opened his mouth what he wanted: a librettist. And I don't have to tell you that a vision of yourself promptly reared itself (if I may be so vulgar) out of the lawn upon which we were sitting.

Now what would you say to a young man (though he reminds me rather too much of a sober Dylan Thomas – I prefer my Thomases tight – I do like him very much) who is seriously in need of a librettist? He is very much aware of one thing: He knows exactly what he wants to do, has it all in his head, which makes him think that this might scare the Word Man (librettist) away. As you can imagine, I am not the 'very man' for him to consult on such a subject. So I told him I would dare to 'drop you a line'. I also have dropped Wystan a line, partly because years ago I introduced W to HB at a concert near here, & W. was greatly taken by HB's music. It so happens that I was in the middle of writing to W: did you hear that he fractured his right shoulder – drove his car into a telegraph pole while trying to save some eggs from falling off the seat? ...

... In moments of relaxation I have been reading Harold N.'s [Nicolson's] Diaries, Vol. II [1967]. The most unputdownable book I have read for many a day. Every question everyone is asking about de Gaulle vs. the 'Anglo-Saxons' is answered here. *What* a marvellous writer HN was. He is one of the few writers I wish I had known; I don't think I would have been scared of him—though I remember feeling rather scared on the one occasion I met him. At a party of Richard's [Rumbold], I think. He (HN) was the only person in evening clothes. He looked so terrifically dapper, and grand, and he stared me straight in the eye (why not eye*s*?) – most disconcerting, I found ...

From Plomer on 18 July 1968:

... I do thank you for suggesting me as a librettist, but I don't feel that I could really help him. (Between ourselves, after working with Ben [Benjamin Britten] with such mutual understanding, I don't feel I could expect to find that with any other composer.)

... Of course you're right about P. White, and it's perfectly easy to be both cruel & compassionate. I do hope I didn't convey some fatuous opinion of *Riders in the Chariot* inadvertently to you. I really can't think of any living novelist with such force & variety, or of any contemporary novel more disturbing and, in places, more touching. It is even *funny* at times (the brothel scene). On the whole it fills me with alarm about the human race: I am seven-eighths full of that without his adding to it.

Desmond MacCarthy, once asked what he thought of some novel, said quietly, 'It's a very good book, but powerful.' That 'but' is wonderful. (It was Harold Nicolson who told me this story.) ...

... Oh, I do so agree with you about that tiresome Schweitzer. He's on my list of non-favourites, which gives quite a high place to that infinitely tiresome T. E. Lawrence ...

From Jimmy to Plomer on 26 July 1968:

... Yes, to me Patrick White is a giant. I think you are the only writer friend (at any rate in England) who shares my opinion. By which I mean whole-hearted admiration. Some people grunt affirmatively, but grudgingly. Others talk of his prose as being 'turgid'. I maintain that I could recognise his 'signature' at once, in a short paragraph, a sentence even. I believe this is supposed to be a sign of 'greatness' – whatever that is. John Lehmann said: 'Well, Jimmy, I'm afraid you will never convince me!' I have no doubt he was right. Of one thing I am sorry: that PW ever wrote a book called *Voss* [1957]. It won a £1000 prize, and put thousands of people off the author for years, possibly for good. Have you read *The Aunt's Story* [1958]? Once launched upon PW I am afraid I can only too easily become a White bore ...

From Plomer on 3 August 1968:

... I like much what you say about Patrick White. So far as I know (which may not be very far, because I read little fiction, & less than that with pleasure) he is the most imaginative of living novelists. I agree with you that he is a 'giant'. One doesn't like, does one, comparisons & categories, but him I think as important as, let us say, Thomas Mann or D. H. Lawrence.

I see what you mean about *Voss*, but don't share your regret that it exists. (Dare I confess that I was one of the committee which awarded it that £1000 prize?) I do hope you're not altogether right in saying that *Voss* put a lot of people in the off-White fold.

Yes, I have indeed read *The Aunt's Story* & have often recommended it to 'people'. I think it a more 'difficult' book than *Voss*, but it wasn't difficult to me, it was an extraordinary feat of imagination, & a work of intense newness. One goes on being haunted by White's persons & by what happens to them. It is the largeness of his views, his feelings, and his imagination which make him appear a giant among all the European & American fictionists who remind one of dung-beetles.

From Jimmy to Plomer on 7 August 1968:

I am sure I should not have said & certainly would not want to say that I regret the existence of *Voss*. I am equally sure that had I been in your position on that committee I would have done likewise. Only a most extraordinary man could have written *Voss*, and whatever its faults I have no doubt they would be virtues in comparison with almost any other work of fiction of that (or any other one) year ...

... Between that paragraph and this I have been talking to the Author on the telephone. Since he did not tell me where he was going to stay in London, I had written to him care of his publisher (to be forwarded). He now tells me that he is not on speaking terms with his publisher & that they refuse to forward his mail ...

'... as important as ... Thomas Mann or D. H. Lawrence'. That certainly is a mouthful, as our 'cousins' say. And I certainly will not argue with it ...

From Jimmy to Kay Boyle on 20 September 1968:

There are two references (pp. 204 & 352) [in Robert McAlmon's autobiography *Being Geniuses Together*, 1938] to Hemingway having physically attacked Bob [Robert McAlmon], one by Bill Bird, the other by [Hilaire] Hiler. I wonder if the two occasions could have been one & the same? For some months of the winter 1933/4 Jimmy Charters had a bar in what had been a grocer's shop right next door to the apartment house at the top of which I lived, in what was then the rue René Pauline, a very short street running from the Blvd Montparnasse into the Notre Dame des Champs. One night when I came in, Bob was sitting (alone, I think) at the bar with a strip of plaster along his upper lip. He said that Hemingway had used a knuckleduster on him. That very day, or possibly the evening before, I think. And I believe I am right in saying that it was at this time that *Esquire* had come out with a terribly funny and very malicious cartoon (in a series of coloured drawings filling a page) of Hemingway in many attitudes in Africa, the central drawing depicting him rifle in hand, foot on a dead lion's head, & dressed (as I remember) in nothing but a tiger-skin—and perhaps a sporran. I am almost certain the cartoon was by Wyndham Lewis, and I have a hunch that some other journal at just that time ran an attack on Hemingway called 'The Dumb Ox', a title which became famous & which I am sure you remember. Could Lewis have written that, too? It's appalling how one's memory fades.

In late October W. H. Auden came to stay and Jimmy complained irritably to his journal that 'WHA simply never leaves the house ... Over dinner probes how I came to write. Could not get over what he found the hilarity of my belief that if only I had a room of my own [which he had, but the noise ...], incognito, pen & paper, "something wd come" ... To go near WHA, alas, is for him to dive into the Commonplace Book ms, pick a "plum", & bring it to me to read in his presence – & this after I have told [him] I want to read it in peace, *alone*.'

From Jimmy to Sybille Bedford on 11 December 1968:

Kay Boyle,
Connecticut, 1960

Malcolm Lowry,
Mexico, 1946

John Davenport

Katherine
Anne Porter

Walker Evans

Alexander Calder

William Plomer

Cyril Connolly
and Barbara Skelton

H. Auden, 1972

Nadine Gordimer,
1980

Pauline Wynn

Isabelle Walker

The elegant
Mr and Mrs Stern

Tania and Jimmy,
Tisbury, 1980s

... Of your novels I like *A Compass Error* [1968] best. I cannot tell you how much I admire your courage in dealing with Flavia as you did. It is the kind of thing I have been turning over & over in my mind for years (because there are so many occasions when, and so many reasons why, the first person won't work), but when it comes to the point I cannot face it. You overdo it, I think. It's as though you felt: Well, here goes: If I can summon that much courage, I may as well go the whole hog. I found that early monologue far too long. And I wonder very much (you being you) why you did not cut, or break it up? I meant to ask you at Wilton's that night, but did not dare because I had not finished the book. One is bound to conclude that you had some definite reason. – What I like next is the ruthlessness. That, too, must have required courage. Especially *with* the ruthless, where it 'works' beautifully, or rather hideously! I had almost forgotten, my God, how frightful women can be! It's a fine feather in your cap that you do not spare them. – I was particularly glad to have read this novel after so recent a visit to the South. There it all was again, the marvellous dryness, and the smell of it, on the page, in the dank grey wetness of London.

From Sybille Bedford in Del Mar, California on 31 December 1968:

... Very touched about your writing to me about my knitting. It is a thing I most like to talk about, but seldom do. Curious what you say about courage. It must have come into it, I suppose, but then I don't see myself as a courageous person, on the contrary; I live beset by all kinds of fears, and it is getting worse. Other kinds of fears. In writing, I seldom think of readers, known or unknown; seldom but sometimes, then try to keep them out of it. The ruthlessness is another matter. That had to be stuck to. I don't like writing about odious people, bad behaviour, violence. Never did.

From Jimmy to Sybille Bedford on 21 February 1969:

... Boulder. I wonder what you will think of it. I found it very beautiful ... do try to get someone to take you by car to New City. I long to know what it is like now. You know, of course, that this is where Oscar Wilde drank the miners under the table, where Sarah Bernhardt *et al* performed at the opera ... The very air of New City struck me as wildly romantic ...

On 27 April he wrote a rare but affectionate letter to his benefactor and contemporary, Alan Pryce-Jones, who lived in America:

Every so often I have a great longing to see you & to talk, or rather (& as usual) listen. One night a few weeks ago your ears should have gone up in flames. It was after dinner chez Alan & Jennifer Ross, & among the guests was John Betjy [Betjeman]. Suddenly he & I began to reminisce about 229 Strand [offices of *The London Mercury*], & everyone else was silent. Never have I heard laughter as loud as John's, & it's a very long time since I have laughed so much & so long. The anecdotes were mostly about you, of course.

While on a visit to London in April, Tania produced with an apology – 'I've done an awful thing' – a drawing which she had bought for £30. Again Jimmy overreacted: 'I blew up – and feel ill for the rest of the day ... can't eat lunch, so retire to lie down.' It is difficult to condone or excuse such unkindness, yet it is another example of the ill-suppressed rage which inhabited Jimmy during these years. At this time he was also beset with money worries: he discovered that through the agency of what he described as a criminally inefficient solicitor, if he died tomorrow his entire fortune would disappear in death duties, leaving Tania all but penniless. He made instant plans to rectify this dire situation.

On the morning of 22 July Jimmy's mother, Connie, died, after 'failing' for a long time. The great ever-present shadow which had shrouded his whole life was no more. 'Love – or the lack of it. It's really all I'm interested in,' Jimmy had written. Now, the embodiment of that lack, the object of his life-long resentment, had ceased to exist. The release was palpable at Hatch Manor, and six weeks later the Sterns escaped to Paris, Toulon and Bandol, where they caught up with old friends: Eda Lord, Nora Sayre, visiting from the US, and the Swedish actress Mai Zetterling and her husband, the writer David Hughes, who were living near Uzès.

During this period Jimmy had achieved what he had often bitterly complained of being denied – a quiet room of his own. For three or four months he rented an old stable which had been converted into an apartment by Sir Anthony Rumbold, then H. M. Ambassador to Austria, in the extensive environs of Hatch House, the home of the Rumbold family, only three miles or so from Hatch village. Jimmy called this retreat Mon Repos. (Subsequently named Cherryfield Cottage, it was where his young friends, Humphrey and Solveig Stone – dubbed by Jimmy 'The Pebbles' – lived for nine years). There he forbade himself to write a letter or read a book, two of his 'besetting sins', he claimed.

On 11 November 1969, Jimmy wrote to Nora Sayre:

> I did not realize that Daphne F. [Fielding] is in so many Memoirs. I think I have told you that I have known her for horribly near 50 years … I don't think Daphne had even met Nancy Cunard. But your question[21] is a good one. I think the answer is the extreme *intensity* she put into everything she did. She was a huge exaggeration. (And I did not know her well. And I did not want to: she was just too intense.) She was very elegant. She was devoted to Underdogs and Causes (often already lost, in itself an attraction to her). She was always writing, and I think always badly, but not as badly as Daphne. I should like to have heard Norman Douglas's answer to your question. That she was an intimate friend of his, does say quite a lot for her. She was liked, I think, for her irreverence, her unshockableness, and I fear, among some people, for the appalling things she said and wrote about her mother!

Four days before the year's end, Jimmy went to London for a rehearsal of a short play of his which Pauline Wynn had adapted for radio, *Sons of England*, which was scheduled to be broadcast early on 9 January. 'I have not enjoyed a day so much for years,' he wrote to Isabelle Evans. 'It is a very strange sensation to hear one's own words spoken perfectly by highly professional actors, even if it is nearly 40 years since one wrote those words. One actor, aged 72, is very famous: Carleton Hobbs. Another played for six months in the first production of *Godot*. A sweet man. But my favourite was a boy [Charles Pinner] of 13, a ravishing child playing his first part, and a very difficult one, too. The whole thing was also unutterably sad as well, for it reminded me too acutely, too painfully, that if ever a man had "missed his proper vocation", it's me.' The play's cast included Judith Fellows, Hugh Burden, John Ruddock and Pauline Wynn. It was produced by R. D. (Reggie) Smith.

The play is about the limitations of traditional attitudes, the misunderstanding between the generations and the *plus ça change* … aspect

---

21 Jimmy didn't keep Nora Sayre's letter, but 'the question' was obviously: why was Nancy Cunard so interesting to others? Or, how or why did she capture others' imaginations?

of life. An upper-middle-class drawing-room satire, much of whose dialogue now creaks like an old oak in a high wind, it nevertheless contains passages which make a sharp point with which present-day animal rights activists would agree. An eight-year-old boy asks his father to describe his, the boy's, grandfather: 'He was very wicked, extremely immoral. His greatest joy in life was to go out and kill. Four days a week in the winter he'd put on a red coat, get on a horse, and together with a crowd of other people also on horses they'd gallop across the country after a pack of dogs chasing one wretched fox … What happened next? Oh yes, on Fridays Grandpop went killing birds. During the summer he spent a lot of time rearing pheasants and partridges. Then in the Autumn he'd "organise" a shoot …'

In February 1970 the hoary subject of a house in the south of France was again discussed – with some acrimony: 'The usual nightmarish bitterness over the future: cannot continue to live here. So to build? Or emigrate once more? This argument or conversation cannot be conducted in normal voices.' Jimmy was against it.

Another reason for discord was of a more personal kind. In the seven years since Jimmy had met Isabelle Evans a hitherto platonic and epistolary friendship had gradually grown into an affair which promised to become full-blown and physical. The crisis came during a visit to Paris, after which Jimmy wrote this letter to Isabelle on 8 April:

> After Paris T. seriously thought our marriage was threatened … I have never known for certain if you realise that – I myself did not know that W. [Walker] had 'given you permission to have affairs'. I understand that he even 'censored' both your friends and your reading of books! If what you say in this letter is true (and I have no reason to doubt it) then we must put our relationship onto an entirely 'different footing'. Briefly, crudely, we must look upon each other, or at least I upon you as a niece.

A week later he wrote again, drawing a line under the affair:

> Apropos our relationship & the good sense you talk in this last letter & above all about it being 'up to me' I agree. And have decided that we simply must, both of us, 'be our ages'. I have even less 'business' to 'court' someone 30 years younger than myself (however 'free' she may be) than you have to sleep with a man that much older than yourself & who is not 'free'. So we had better make a pact, a Gentleman's Agreement. If we do this in

total agreement & in the proper spirit, it should make us feel more free, especially you who have (unlike me) *your life to live*. And you cannot live it with me. You simply must free yourself from your obsession (too strong a word, no doubt) with men so much older than yourself ... I suddenly feel much closer to you, probably because I feel I am at last being brutally honest.

In 1973 Isabelle divorced Walker Evans and later married James (Jim) Storey, a Boston lawyer.

In April 1970 Jimmy had to give up his 'bureau'. It is not apparent that he had achieved much in the way of writing there, for in September Fred Warburg was asking again about the autobiography. 'What a moment to receive that enquiry!' Jimmy noted.

Another of those liquor-induced accidents to which he was so prone occurred in July. He had joined Le Petit Club Français off St James's Street and, at 11pm after a particularly good dinner, hearing Bal Musette music and people dancing in the street outside, decided to dance alone, tripped over the kerb and fell flat on his back, missing his coccyx by a whisker. Four months later an accident of a different kind left him with a very bruised right hand and with a bill of £100 for repairs to his car. In a narrow street in Shaftesbury, at night, in the rain, he had driven into a wall.

From Jimmy to Nora Sayre on 17 October 1970:

... We left Bandol from Toulon (if you see what I mean) to Avignon, where we disembarked, cabbed to the Pont du Gard, and an hour later were dining there with Daphne and Xan Fielding. We were asked to leave the dining room some time around midnight, and 12 hours later Xan was back again, to fetch us to lunch chez Fielding, where we had not been for five years, when the house was beginning to be built. This was difficult to believe, for round it grew large trees, and up its walls crept Virginia creeper as far as the roof and over. Inside sat the chap I irreverently called Old Tunc [Lawrence Durrell], looking plump and very clean, almost with a white bib and a brilliantine look about the hairs (as T calls hair!).

Our hostess, in red velvet, looked even taller than ever. She is arriving any minute in London, where she has a book (mostly about herself, I believe) coming out. And she is appearing on TV 'as' Rosa Lewis. I suggested that *I* should appear as Rosa, and she as my Lord Ribblesdale – which did raise a laugh. I found the house rather like this [Hatch Manor], in the sense that both are grossly over-furnished. Here one is inclined to fall over bookcases and small tables, there one collides and knocks over objects, bibelots, photographs in frames, & ornament after ornament all made of china. Among it all sat Mai [Zetterling](so thin – well, so much less plump that I fear the word skinny escaped from my embrace), stood David [Hughes], and a young fuzzy-haired Englishman whom I had not seen before, of whom indeed I was ashamed to admit I had never heard: John Bulmer, photographer. He was so charming, had such a passion, such a genuine passion for our Dark Brothers, such a wide, if naturally rather superficial, knowledge of Africa that I talked to him almost exclusively that day, as well as the next – which, part of which, was spent chez Hughes. This day was so long and so strange that I simply have not time or the energy to describe it properly here. It started in a hired car driven by a blonde Bonnie (of the movie), who sulked when T appeared, and refused to speak when asked (by T) to drive at less than 80 mph. She carried everything but a gun at her hip. We drove all over Provence in search of a ruin harbouring Kay Boyle's eldest child (I have known her almost all her life) & her 20-year-old son ... The astonishing thing is that though we had no address we did in that glorious desert of stone and scrub and occasional hovel, find them and that was all. Later Bonnie drove us madly & in deadly silence over hills and into valleys & over more hills to Belvezet & chez Hughes, where Mai and David, half a dozen Swedes, John Bulmer, a toothless darling of a peasant woman, and a young man with long hair & a beautiful face lay asleep under an umbrella ... all these people were finishing their lunch in the sun, and were about to start, one at a time, leaping up and down on a very small basin of grapes ... Some hours later we were driven back to the Pont du Gard by a Swede (girl) who lived in Aigues Mortes & seemed to spend her time & energy in the preservation of fighting bulls much as the English try to preserve trout in the local river.

In October Jimmy and Tania went on an extended visit to Ireland, principally for the Irish Academy awards, where Jimmy, in the presence of Mary Lavin, Arland Ussher, Aidan Higgins, a prize winner, Monk Gibbon and Constantine and Marjorie FitzGibbon, got very drunk; but also to visit Bective, where Jimmy enjoyed a nostalgic tour of the house, impressing his guide and hostess by his memory of the two steps down into his father's dressing room. They visited Dunsany Castle nearby and had dinner with his Lordship.

A brief stay in Paris to see Samuel Beckett ended the year.

In a depressed state at the beginning of 1971, Jimmy nevertheless felt the beginnings of a new story, 'The Man Who Knew the Time', but it never got beyond the initial stirrings.

During February, having been commissioned by the *Irish Press* in Dublin to write an essay on the stories of Sean O'Faolain, he had to admit failure. His rule never to review the work of a friend and the necessary use of superlatives – inducing boredom – which naturally ensued from his deep admiration for O'Faolain both contributed to his inability to produce the piece. From writing so little he had lost his nerve. Defeats of this kind had a devastating effect on him. He felt suicidal.

'Try to suffocate depression partly by reflecting on J. [Julian] Fane's melancholia & obsession with death,' his diary relates. Jimmy had been introduced to Fane, an unmarried brother of the Earl of Westmorland, in March by Stephen and Natasha Spender. Besides admiring *Morning* (1956), his highly regarded first novel about the privileged childhood of a small boy surrounded by nannies and servants, which must have struck a familiar chord, Jimmy had also read Fane's *Memoir in the Middle of the Journey* [1971], and was keen to cement what he saw as an affinity with the young man, many decades his junior. Fane's partial portrait of Jimmy at sixty-one is illuminating:

> He compared his writer's block with my description of the diffi-culties I had been having with my writing. He lived in a manorial house, and was a respected literary figure. He was really the man who had everything, but was disappointed and discontented.
>
> Our occasional meetings in London were unsatisfactory – at least I could not engage Jimmy's attention for long, and feared I was letting him down and boring him. Once he brought Tania to dinner with me and spent most of the time snarling at her. His letters to me in his beautiful handwriting were less enthusiastic and more demanding – had I received his last one, why had I not answered it? Moreover the question of when I should stay with him was repeated naggingly.
>
> ... At last I paid a visit to Tisbury ... I think I only spent one night ... It was not much of a success ... Jimmy was cross with

Tania all evening and cursed her, and was closeted in his study the following morning. Just before lunch he emerged and took me to see a drawing of his greatest and late friend Brian Howard, whose excesses and homosexuality had become a byword. After lunch he seemed relieved to bid me goodbye.

But I continued to receive letters of an increasingly carping nature. I did not and do not know exactly why he was displeased. Was he a homosexual whom I had frustrated? But he was not only married, he had made urgent advances to a female friend of mine … I began to dread the arrival of another batch of reproaches. The breaking-point was a letter that accused me of dropping him 'like a red-hot brick': he wrote it while I was on my honeymoon. I wrote back that I could not continue the correspondence.

In March Frederic Warburg was reported as going around London telling everyone that he had the autobiography of the century!

Paris and Bandol in mid-May – sun, sea, good meals, and the company of old friends – somewhat restored Jimmy to a better humour. 'Each time I return to the sea, I realize more & more that it is my home.'

From Jimmy to Nora Sayre on 13 June 1971:

… On Whit Saturday we got a phone call from Louisa Calder on the Loire, saying that Sandy [Alexander] had been taken ill & was being flown to New York (to his surgeon) on Tuesday. The very day we were supposed to arrive to stay with them. Instead, we stayed in Paris. The sun came out, grew warmer & warmer, until at long last I began to purr. We stayed a week. I don't think I have ever met so many people I know (and like) in so brief a time. Some I ran into in the street – Americans from New York and Conn. whom I had not seen in 5 and as many as 16 years. They of course did not recognize me behind the beard, so I had a gorgeous time staring at them until either they fled or flew into a rage: 'What the hell are you staring at me like that for?' And we spent a lovely hour with Sam Beckett in his 7th floor flat in the 14th arr. – only a few yards from where I lived (and wrote!) 40 years ago. Before leaving he gave me a copy of his *Proust* (which he wrote at the age of 24 & which I did not know had been reprinted). I opened the book at random and after a moment's consideration read aloud the following sentence: 'Proust had a bad memory …' It is worth going to Paris to see Sam laugh. Yes, see.

He is not well. In a note a few days earlier he had warned me: 'I am not grand.' Only a Dubliner could write that. I told him I thought he had a mild bout of malaria, but he denied the possibility.

A visit to Florence in September to see Harold Acton at La Pietra put both Sterns in a good mood, as had many of their European excursions. But the following month during a visit to London they suffered a mugging in the darkness of Jermyn Street after a visit to a theatre to see Michael MacLiammóir as W. B. Yeats in a solo performance. Jimmy sent the details to Isabelle Evans:

I was suddenly confronted, out of nowhere, by a huge man, presumably drunk, who threw up my right arm, shouted I don't know what, & hugged me. And in a split second, again shouting (something about a football team being the best in the world) he was gone. During this half minute – no, 10 seconds – T behind me was being confronted (but not hugged or touched) by another man. Assuming that both men were drunk we considered ourselves lucky & went on home. At 9am I put my hand into my inside jacket pocket for my wallet – it was not there. It has been there for at least 15 years, so I still feel as though I am without a limb. What was in it? About £30 in cash, French Frs 150, & every imaginable document of importance, including cheque cards, driver's licences both English & French etc etc.

To add to their suffering, on their thirty-sixth wedding anniversary, earlier in November, there was renewed contention: 'T's coldness grows so frigid as the day sorrowfully passes that I cannot bear to share our bed. Eventually I end up in the attic – with her hotwater bottle ... A 100% sleepless night in the attic, with thoughts moving between extreme melancholia & suicide ... Everything she says is an indirect criticism of me. (Nothing new!) "Well, you are anti-everything." Sure, most things. So, of course, is she!'

10

The Festschrift
1972–1976

For several years Jimmy had been an admirer of the South African novelist and short story writer Nadine Gordimer, who was awarded the Nobel Prize in 1991, the third friend of the Sterns to be thus honoured. She had consistently and forcefully exposed the apartheid regime's iniquitous policies in a series of highly praised novels. It was a case of mutual admiration, for in July 1997 she wrote to me: 'Jimmy was irreplaceable. Not alone a wonderful writer but full of the best kind of contradictions: loving and irascible, loyal and impatient of low values, a patrician with the gusto of an adventurer. I was lucky to be his friend! And do you know, he "discovered" me for American readers – he wrote a glowing review of my first book, splashed in the *New York Times* in the 50s.'

From Hatch Manor he wrote to her on 5 December 1972:

… A couple of days ago I cut out of the Lonmag [*London Magazine*] your excellent review of Carson's [McCullers] sister's book on Carson – sorry, Carson's book edited by her sister. And I sent it to David Garnett in the Lot, to his cottage where he lives alone and where he (now 81) cooked us a delicious dinner just 2 months ago (which does not seem possible). Why I sent the review to him is a long & most improbable story. I will only say that in 1942, when by chance he read *Reflections in a Golden Eye* [1941], his first wife was dying, or perhaps had just died, and this book gave him courage to live. Is not this astonishing? He at once wrote to C. and as soon as it was possible he crossed the Atlantic to meet her. He has some excruciating stories about her. He is a glorious man. I did not know quite how to approach him, so I wandered about the market of his village, and sure enough there he came, snow white hair floating away from large black beret, large basket on one arm. When I told him my name, he gripped my elbow: 'Just the man I want to see,' he said. We have many friends in common

& he knew we knew Carson. It was a lovely evening, but I was tired after having driven so far, so that it was all too brief.

... I refrained (like you) from mentioning grisly details of some times with her, one of which I can't quite bring myself to put on paper. Not that he would have been shocked, but – well, on the contrary: what I did find shocking I feared he might find funny.

... An aunt of mine died, she lived near William P. [Plomer], & as a result we were in touch for a brief time, but did not meet. I can't help wondering how disappointed he was not to be chosen Laureate, or do you think this nonsense?

After quick visits to Paris and London in January 1972, the Sterns were fighting again; this time Tania issued a threat never realised: 'I am not going to do anything melodramatic, but I just want to tell you that I am leaving you', and later: 'I want to apologise for having "taken over" [in a discussion with two other people] this morning. I have analysed my motives: I was starved for conversation.' This 'starvation' of the garrulous Tania, Jimmy's refusal to allow any music at home (a deprivation she felt keenly), his drinking, his 'black dog' moods, as Winston Churchill called them, his withdrawals and silences, all over-shadowed their last decades together.

About his attitude to music, Jimmy wrote on 4 April 1975 to John Byrne: 'I "once said" (paraphrasing Joe Brodsky): "Music is but noise buried in the face of silence." Effect: it either drives me insane, or makes me want to howl like a vixen at night. Or it (an endless opera) can send me to sleep ... I had an enchanting and very eccentric German cousin who "ran" the Frankfurt opera in the 1920s; he once insisted on taking both Brian [Howard] and myself to the "Meistersinger" and to his life-long amazement found Brian on one side, I on the other, at the end of an hour, fast asleep.'

That March Jimmy had been cutting an eleven-foot privet hedge, one of seven in the Manor garden, when he fell from the top of a ladder. 'I did not break the leg,' he told Pauline Wynn, 'but if you saw it right now you would hardly know it is a leg. More like a Francis Bacon Butcher Shop – but more colourful. In fact, *blue* is the only colour I can't find. The foot is the colour of the English sky in winter, or rather just before a tempest, and the overall colour of the leg is pernod shot with puce & scarlet. I pulled up my trouser yesterday and shoved it under the gaze of a lady I don't like very much, and she let out a piercing yell, covered her face with her hands, and burst into sobs.'

In the spring Jimmy acquired another 'bureau', across the railway line in Wardour, a building he could see from the windows of Hatch Manor, and to which he could walk in twenty-five minutes. He rented it from a wealthy chartered accountant married to an opera singer, both of whom were based in London. There 'I am faced with the Great Terror: James Stern,' he told Isabelle Evans. But the arrangement failed.

There were further trips to France in May and September. The Fieldings, the Calders, Desmond Ryan, a friend Jimmy had known since 1927 when Ryan was an undergraduate at Oxford, Nicholas Guppy, the Hugheses and others appeared to restore their spirits.

In late November, while visiting the Sterns with their mutual friend, Kitty West, Frances Partridge recorded this acute impression in her journal: 'I like both Sterns. Jimmy is nicer to be with and talk to, because more relaxed. Tania, intelligent and quick-witted, is tiringly over-excited, waves her hands, fixes one with her boot-button eyes; and like surgical instruments they drain the life out of one. They can't talk without irritating each other (not that they don't love each other – they do).'

That month, too, Wystan Auden wrote to say that he would like to stay for Christmas and would arrive on 22 December and leave on 2 January. 'That would kill us both,' Jimmy wrote to Isabelle Evans. 'I have not dreaded anything so much for a long time.' His fears were to be realised.

With Sonia Orwell and Auden as guests, and a 'shapeless silence' permeating the Manor, the annual festival became a valedictory occasion. Auden's poem 'Thank you, Fog', which became the title of his posthumous book of poems, published in September 1974, was written the following May and sent to the Sterns 'with love and gratitude'. Celebrating the last days of 1972 spent with three friends it contains the lines: 'and four selves, joined in friendship/Jimmy, Tania, Sonia, Me.'

But, alas, he had exasperated his hosts. 'Auden sat in front of the fire all day,' Humphrey Carpenter related in his biography,

doing crosswords and reading a book by Hannah Arendt that he had found in his bedroom. The Sterns also noticed that he kept going to the shelves and looking at copies of his own books. They found it impossible to engage him in real conversation. He spurned the freshly-ground coffee that they had bought specially for him, insisting on the instant variety; he also made them order for him the *Daily Telegraph* rather than their usual *Times*, explaining: 'One gets more right-wing as one gets older.' And, though James Stern dropped hints about the price of drink, he made it clear that he wanted plenty of vodka to be provided for him (he did not offer to pay). He took the vodka upstairs with him at night, and by the morning had often consumed the greater part of a bottle. He would not go further than the front door – 'A *walk*? What on earth *for*?' – and when a planned visit by car to the writer Christopher Sykes, who lived forty miles away, had to be cancelled because a blanket of fog had come down, he was visibly pleased, returning delightedly to the fire and his crossword.

'Never again in this house' was the justified reaction from Tania; and from Jimmy: 'Last night, at around 7pm, I handed him some chapters of the childhood memories which he had not read. But he was too far "gone" to read them "just now". He put them where for ten days he has put all his finished and unfinished crossword puzzles. And he completely forgot all about them.'

Although the Sterns had been heavy smokers, they were now cured of the habit and had come to dread the effects of Auden's addiction. Whereas others were sent out to puff away in the garden, they felt that they couldn't forbid someone of his age. They had read that vinegar – and sand in the ashtrays – reduced the smell of tobacco and its lingering potency, which permeated the house for days afterwards. So they secreted bowls of vinegar under sofas and chairs. But the yellowish-brown sand of Wiltshire closely resembles the colour of brown sugar … with results which were hilarious, in retrospect. Another habit of Auden's was particularly irritating to Jimmy: at the first signs of dusk he would draw the curtains in a proprietary gesture, thus obliterating that last view of the fading countryside before nightfall which Jimmy, with his love of nature, especially valued.

W. H. Auden died on 28 September 1973.

On 3 January that year, Jimmy had written to Sonia Orwell from Hatch to thank her 'for the longest and most appreciative bread-&-butter letter we have ever had anywhere'. He went on:

> You are right in thinking that the O(ther) G(uest) has now departed. 'If he left feeling a bit low and sad …?' I suppose the answer is Yes. We too felt the same. On the whole his state is rather worse than I had anticipated. His refusal to talk of the past, the present, or the future, his addiction to crossword puzzles, his

nightly 12 hours in bed, his consumption of cigarettes & vodka, his return to childhood (almost his only topic), his compulsions – including that of leaping at all the curtains the moment dark descends. But oh dear, why go on when you know it all?

What distresses me, and leaves me unusually deflated, is the thought that we helped him in one respect only: we saw him over the Christmas holidays. As he said: 'I don't know what I would have done without you!' But I doubt very much that he wants to return to Hatch any more than he wanted to return to Oxford.

He occasionally made significant remarks, or rather blurted out thoughts not meant to be uttered & upon which one could not very well pounce: 'I made the wrong choice ...', 'Friendship is where one left off after however many years ...'.

We are still not sure of the significance of the first, but feel almost sure it concerns his coming to England. I expect you will know at once. He saw a number of people, of devoted friends even, but he could not stand anyone for long. In the 9 days he was here (need I tell you) he set foot out of the house only to catch the train – which (my God!) we very nearly missed. Why? Because of the bloody crossword in the *Daily Telegraph*!

Later that month Jimmy sent an Irish chapter of his memoirs to Solveig, the young neighbour married to the typographer and book designer Humphrey Stone. 'I consider you blessed with common sense,' Jimmy wrote to her, 'God knows, rare enough at any age. The opinion of a contemporary of mine is far less important than that of a bright and literate lad or lass under thirty ...'

Solveig's parents, the Atchesons, lived in Donegal, five minutes from Jimmy's grandfather's house outside Derry, and knew Jimmy's relations, the Watts, a fact which, besides her charm and good looks, had initially attracted Jimmy to Solveig. She reacted enthusiastically: 'You must go on ... don't stop,' she wrote to him. But such was his paranoia that he took immediate offence and an extended period of silence ensued between them. Rather than interpreting her reaction as a positive encouragement, he took her words to be a warning that if he did not continue he would die before completing the book! A year or so later the misunderstanding was resolved and Solveig and he remained friends until his death.

From Jimmy to Nora Sayre on 25 March 1973:

... We were supposed to have had dinner with Jennifer (Ross) last week, but I went and tore the muscles in my back & was in bed and in agony for two of the 3 days we were to have been in London. I dragged myself there on Thursday, to meet one Prof. Martin Green (*Cities of Light and Sons of the Morning* [1972]) for a Lecture at the Royal Soc. of Lit. on Wm. Beckford. Green, who has a huge Bostonian wife (by a Greek Oak out of George Eliot), is writing a book on the Dandy in English Men of Letters since 1918. (You will appreciate why he was put on to me!) This breed of American writer is utterly alien to me, and what I have seen of their work so far I find quite unreadable. Last weekend the Olney brothers were here, Richard the famous chef, and James, author of *Metaphors of Self* [1972], subtitled 'The Meaning of Autobiography'. I find it so dry and clumsily written (what I call the 'However-Moreover' school of prose) that I have not begun to discover meaning of any kind. And yet he is a very decent, modest guy, with a quite charming blonde wife from Michigan.

Next day, Friday, I lunched at the Garrick ... I cannot repeat much that was said over lunch, because on entering the Club I ran smack into VSP [V. S. Pritchett], who was lunching with John Gross (of the NS [*New Statesman*]), and for the best part of an hour in that enormous bar packed with MEN MEN MEN I sat on a fender seat (in considerable pain), downing one Guinness after another in an attempt to hear what was said & at the same time trying desperately to inject a few hoarse words of my own. (I *do* dislike *clubs*!)

Jimmy suffered more exasperation when in May two friends who had been asked for drinks overstayed their welcome: 'At 7.50 they suggested leaving (or rather *she* did). I said: "Well, stay 5 minutes." They stayed 45. Nothing I did could make T let them go. Nor would T meet my eye. This is the kind of thing which takes years off one's life and/or gives one a heart attack! – unable to eat, or rather fear to eat.' Years later, Kitty West perpetrated a similar social gaffe. She arrived at the front door of Hatch Manor either early, late or on the wrong day, and was summarily dismissed. The three friends were never to speak again.

The same month the Sterns travelled by boat and train from Southampton to Le Havre, Rouen and Paris, where they saw Samuel Beckett, Mary McCarthy and Patricia Highsmith, whom he had known for many years but not one of whose books he had read. They looked at the Soutines in the Orangerie and at an exhibition of Colette at the Bibliothèque Nationale, a 'stinking airless place whose windows cannot have been opened in this century', Jimmy remarked.

'The notorious "bolt hole" in the S. of F.' was still being discussed in July. 'Too late,' Jimmy remarked, but the subject was fuel for further conflict. 'Lie awake hearing again that anti-British, pro-French tirade.' Earlier he had told Isabelle Evans: 'I say I'm too old to emigrate. She says I don't want you to emigrate. "I want the smallest place you can think of, which is ours to go to, in France."' With their shared love of that country, it is difficult not to agree with Tania's point of view. And on 27 July: 'Wake around dawn. Strike bottom. Up at 9. Nights worse than days. Can't tell anyone: the loneliness. Is it all *my* fault?'

To Pauline Wynn he wrote that they had been unusually social in early August:

… a lunch with one Lady Young, to which Julian and Juliette Huxley came – no, they didn't, they were staying in Lady Y's house. One Christopher Hammersley came from the Isle of Wight. Dinner with Cecil Beaton and Irene Worth. I often wondered what she looks like offstage. Just the same as on. Another, Festival, party at Cecil's: the strangest mixture of people: old friend actress Ruth Ford, from Mississippi, great friend of Faulkner; Stephen Tennant of all people, looking like a fat old Madame; Angus Wilson, holding forth as well as fifth; Ralph Kirkpatrick, the harpsichordist; Simon Blow [author of *No Time to Grow: A Shattered Childhood*, 1999], who is probably going to do a biography of Henry Yorke [Green].

From Jimmy to Sybille Bedford on 25 August 1973:

… People have been coming and going: Walker Evans, weighing 7 stone & looking like a minor Moses, came direct, on same day, from Tom Matthews who, as I guess you know, has finished his bio. of Eliot. He and Walker travelled back from New York on the *France*. Walker is on some drug (T has the name of it), which makes him so benign that I think I must try it – though I am antidrug. – Then came Julian Fane, a comparatively new friend, author of a first & beautiful book, *Morning* [1956], evocation of an upperclass childhood. His most recent, a novel, *Gabriel Young* [1956], I found rather embarrassing. He is one of the few friends of today who has a 'man', an ex-alcoholic, who does *everything* for his Master! Oh, lucky Master – though I don't suppose I could stand it for five minutes.

During the last week in September they were unable to defer a long-anticipated trip to France, in spite of having received a telegram the day before announcing the unexpectedly sudden death of William Plomer. They took their car on a ferry to the Brittany port of Etretat, where it promptly gave up on them. While enjoying their *fruits de mer* and iced Pouilly in the sun, they read in *Le Monde* of the death of their friend Pablo Neruda, the Chilean poet and diplomat. After recrossing the Channel and arriving in Hatch, they read in *The Times* of the death of yet another friend, A. S. Neill. Later, a telephone call from Sonia Orwell told them that W. H. Auden had also died. This devastating roll-call was laconically described by Jimmy as a 'wicked week'.

From Nadine Gordimer in France on 24 October 1973:

... This has been a year of deaths; so thank heaven for a marriage [N.G.'s daughter's], however unlikely. William's [William Plomer's] death was a real shock – I picked up the paper, and there it was. I thought at once, and first of you, and wanted to talk to you. So your letter, which arrived the day I left South Africa, was exactly what I needed. I feel distressed and somehow disloyal because I did not write an obituary for an S.A. paper. There are things to be said about William that only his friends can say. For myself, I loved him with the deepest respect, almost veneration; and the standards of – what can one call it? not modesty, that cringing term – the standards of self-knowledge, of proportion, of knowing one's worth as a writer & never being led into vanity any more than into self-depreciation, that I have tried to learn from him, have been a great influence in my life. William was *there*; an indispensable presence. We'll never fill it.

I am glad he had a quiet death. But of course; William knew how to live and he would know how to die. I treasure his wonderful, witty letters, at once reserved and full of tender friendship. You must have many more than I; and of course live memories, better than letters.

From Jimmy to Nora Sayre on 10 November 1973:

... Just returned from two days in London, chiefly for the Plomer Memorial Service at St Martin-in-the-Fields. Betjeman reading Plomer poems, John Sparrow reading the lesson, and van der Post in the pulpit, delivering a quite marvellous address and Farewell. Church packed. Who should be handing out Words of the Service but Alan Ross! Don't ask me why. We had been invited to lunch chez Ross in advance. Again I don't know why. Other guests: Ted Walker (a somewhat obese young poet with a wife whom I took for his mother) and novelist Susan Hill, who I understand is famous. A very self-assured young lady whose clothes suggested she was about to play tennis. But she was nice and easy to talk to. Alan, it seems, is again about to pop off in your direction! The Wm Plomer number of *Lonmag* has a cover photo of Wm Plomer sitting on a gate in the country, accompanied by Morgan Forster & Isherwood ... Night before the Memorial Service, had dinner at the Ritz with Natasha and Stephen Spender, talked – needless to say – W. H. Auden more or less nonstop. Harold Acton had arrived (at the Ritz) that very day, so I left him a note, telling him we were downstairs & suggesting he come down if he was free and not too tired. Well, he didn't turn up & I have so far not heard a word of him, which seems a little strange. Can only imagine he never got my note.

From Jimmy to Sybille Bedford on 12 November 1973:

I have at last read your *Aldous* [*Aldous Huxley: A Biography*, 1973], every word of it.

In my humble way (no false modesty; I simply could not contemplate such a task) I have little but praise to offer you, above all, I think, for your perseverance, your endurance. '... give a man some kind of shape after his death'. He [Huxley] is but 45 and I feel I could tell how he would react to almost any given situation.

But I do wonder (before I go any further) why Toynbee – and yes, Christopher Sykes, too – sounded so aggressive, even hostile? I do remember, when I was very young, a certain hostility, of a kind that was levelled at the Sitwells at more or less the same time, from the Philistines. But not surely, from intellectuals, from literary people? From CS it may be that he feels hostile towards pacifists, or to those who took no active part in the last War, as I believe Harold Nicolson did. I do think (you will see the connection) it's unfortunate that the biography should appear in two vols.

If I were asked if I agreed with any of the negative criticism in the reviews of the above, I would say – and even then hesitantly – that yes, occasionally the writing itself is not as 'distinguished' as that in other books by the author! There are clichés, now and then, and there are French tags, occasionally, where the English equivalent would suffice. So what! They are surely not worth mentioning. What I consider worth mentioning is the way in which the narrative, covering so much geography, so many characters, has been *sewn together*. Also extremely important is that one can see and hear Maria as vividly as AH.

The last day of the year produced a 'sudden attack from T for not talking enough, or trying to persuade her to make a long story shorter, "we no longer have any conversation." Hard luck (for her) that I no longer "write". As she would say: "You never did." ... And yet only today I discovered that 'The Woman [Who Was Loved]' has been printed at least 13 times in 28 years!'

From Jimmy to Sybille Bedford on 18 January 1974:

... London was not so gloomy as described or anticipated, partly no doubt because one had been warned. We went to the theatre twice. Unheard of! Once to Pinero's *Dandy Dick* (because Charles Lloyd-Pack, Uli's husband, is in it) and to *Equus* at the Old Vic, most recent play by Peter Shaffer, friend of Frank Tait. A most shattering evening for those with a childhood the likes of mine. A boy goes through the whole process of psychoanalysis on stage ... I couldn't eat until the following day, had to cancel a table at a new restaurant off Sloane Square!

... We had a sandwich lunch with Stephen Spender at the Ritz, downstairs. That morning I had found at Sandoe's the current *Encounter* with a memoir of WHA by Golo Mann. Very good, I think. He quotes the lines [from *Fragmente 1* by Holderlin]: '*Ich bin nichts mehr, ich lebe nicht mehr gerne.*' ['I am nothing any more, indifferent to each day.' Translated by Michael Hamburger]

... They express exactly what I felt about W. on his last visit here. S. Spender sent my Memoir straight to the printer, which was not what I meant him to do. I wanted to discuss with him how I could best avoid describing that last visit, but I find SS very difficult to talk to – so 'busy' and self-obsessed. Can't imagine that he can be a good teacher.

... I wish you were here to read a passage from Fred Warburg's autobiography [*An Occupation for Gentlemen*, 1959] in which he has his wife describe how, at a large luncheon party in London to celebrate the publication of *Faustus*, she 'felt (Thomas Mann's) left hand on my bare thigh just above my nylons'. In thanking him for his book I wrote to Warburg that even if this passage were true I was surprised he saw fit to print it. Yesterday came a letter from FW: 'I'm surprised that you should find this offensive. It seems to indicate a prudish temperament, which I hadn't previously associated with you.' It seems to me that the only possible excuse for printing such stuff is if 1) it's true, *and* 2) characteristic. Do you think the latter is possible? If not, is it not libellous?

In mid-April Jimmy described to Pauline Wynn the new cottage they had had converted from an old barn some fifty yards down the lane from the Manor, in which they installed the Cross family.

You ask for details, I am not sure what of, presumably the building. Well, it's nothing to brag about, except that I think it is extremely well built (of the stone of the former ruin) and has a roof of beautiful old tiles, specially picked, at my insistence. It has an L-shaped sitting-cum-dining room, a hall, a WC, and upstairs 3 bedrooms, bath & WC. What is rather special is the view, facing SE, more or less towards Wardour or Cranborne Chase School ... The Crosses ... What do they consist of? Harold, tough son of a local gamekeeper, pretty local wife, very inhibited with a nervous giggle, & a couple of quite darling daughters, aged 9 and 5, usually to be seen hand-in-hand, which makes me want to boo-hoo. Harold will work for us two half days a week, Anne 2 hours four times a week (so T thinks). Harold is in such demand locally that he could work a ten-day week & still be found wanted.

The Crosses worked for the Sterns for the next twenty years. Although Harold would suffer from time to time the sharp edge of Tania's tongue, it is obvious that without their loyalty, patience and hard work, the Sterns could not have survived in the Manor as long as they did. Their reward is that the cottage is theirs for their lifetime.

In July Jimmy and Tania had another of their many car crashes. This time he drove head-on into a large car but escaped with a bang on the head and a swollen knee, while Tania was badly bruised and cut about the face and head, and was an invalid for many weeks. No bones were broken but she sustained a hole in her forehead and wore a collar to keep her chin up when finally emerging from the disaster. 'I am a good Nurse, but was not born to witness daily pain,' he told Isabelle Evans two weeks after the accident. 'T timed her accident badly,' he went on with what may be considered a glaring instance of unselfawareness, given his driving capabilities. 'A month later she might possibly have been able to spend her invalidism in the New Room.' The Sterns were about to start major alterations to the Manor by adding a bedroom and a bathroom to his ground floor study, so that one of them could be ill without the other climbing the notorious stairs.

From Jimmy to Nadine Gordimer on 20 November 1974:

> ... Hard to believe that for a book [*The Conservationist*, 1974] which has had the magnificent reviews that I have seen you will possibly have received 'a dour and miserable one' – but oh, I see – a female novelist [Isabel Quigly, *Financial Times*], she must be. If I were an Editor I would do everything I could to prevent a good novel by a female novelist getting into the hands of another such a dame! I guess that would be difficult.
>
> ... How I should have loved to have dropped in on you and Laurens van der Post. Until I met him (at Wm's funeral) I used to wonder if I would like him, or rather if we would have enough in common: I thought he might be too saintly, a little lacking in humour, I thought, for the likes of me. But the moment I saw him I was struck by the beauty of his face. Did you by chance read the Address he gave at Wm's Memorial Service? If it's in print I should love to have a copy. I remember being profoundly moved. I'd like to meet him again, if that would be possible without effort from him. But I think for this I should talk to Ian and Trekkie Parsons.
>
> In London last week I saw that Grand Homme and old friend Victor Pritchett, for whom I have boundless admiration. The same evening I met for the first time an American woman who is writing a biography of Sam Beckett. Imagine. She has been at it for 3 years and has a contract with Cape for publication next Fall. Her name is Deirdre Bair (39), married with 2 teenage kids. We both found her enchanting. I have known Sam B. for 40 years, but I learned more about him from her in an hour than I could have told her in a year! Not surprising, I suppose.

1974 was the year of Jimmy's seventieth birthday. In an act of rare foresight and generosity, a young acquaintance and admirer, John Byrne, assembled a finely printed and produced twenty-five-page *Festschrift* to mark the occasion. Byrne, who worked for the antiquarian booksellers Bertram Rota, became a close friend of the Sterns in the course of the next twenty years. Jimmy was overwhelmed by this

kindness and attention and (for many other reasons) asked John to be
his literary executor. The *Festschrift* contained letters from twenty-six
friends, with illustrations by Mary Fedden and Julian Trevelyan. Seven
of these follow:

Nadine Gordimer in Johannesburg:

I'm writing to you long before your birthday, and from a long way
off. But that's in the character of our bond. We were names to
each other, and work attached to names, for years before we were
introduced by William Plomer in London – when? – in '61. And
what is certainly for me a very special friendship continues to
flourish while we are mostly in different hemispheres and meet
once a year or so, sometimes in rather curious circumstances.
Friendship itself is our home ground.

   Because I'd like this to be a special letter I'm finding it hard to
write; in fact, I've thought about it on and off for several weeks. I
won't be able to get it right. The nearest I came was while walking
on the farm (the place I've told you about) on one of these beautiful winter mornings we've been having. My mind switched from
the letter simply to the companion, Jimmy Stern and no other, I'd
like to have had walking with me in the veld. I know we'd have
gone far over the rise, leading to a rural shanty-town, that's
usually my point of return; you're such a great walker, and such a
beguiling talker (is it the Irish, Jewish, or English in you?) that I
wouldn't have felt tired. I found I thought of you as belonging
there, in the dry veld, as unthinkingly as myself; indeed, I understood that although you have been gone from Africa for many
years the experience is embedded in you as well as in your writing.
It's there when you're buying white wine in London or whisky in
France … It is a wide ring of growth in the three-score-and-ten of
that still incredibly graceful trunk that is you. When we talk about
Southern Africa I often have the strange feeling that, although I
live there, I am learning from you, you knew it all instinctively, in
advance, long ago – just as I used to feel with William.

   Of course, usually when I write to you the letters are all about
me, grumbling, confessing, gossiping, planning. This one is meant
to be only about you; but the fact is that you have been and are a
man so generous in faith in other writers, so *really* devoted to
encouraging those among them who are lucky enough to have you
believe in them, that it's difficult to keep oneself out of the picture

when writing about knowing you. Twenty years ago you wrote in the *New York Times* a review of an early story collection of mine that put me in seventh heaven; since then you have always found the time and interest to read everything I've written, and your criticism of what you didn't like has been as precious to me as your praise. I'm proud to belong to that small band of writer-friends who must also – alas – feel guilty that the attention and energy you have given us have kept you from writing as much as we would have wished. But – to borrow William's definition of himself – you are no battery-hen among writers; if the books we have from you are few, they are made of the real stuff of your life and thought, not one word has been forced into being by the arc-lamps of any artificial stimulus. You've never 'produced' for the public maw or the private appetite for money; you have written as you wished, in your own fullness of time. That's something not to be calculated by anyone other than oneself.

Jimmy, I celebrate your presence in this world, on your birthday and always. So many of the joys and possibilities of life seem embodied in your personality. I embrace you and Tania and Hatch Manor in a birthday accolade.

Constantine FitzGibbon in Dublin:

Having never before written a public birthday letter to anyone, I am confronted with a new literary form which I shall certainly handle with less skill than would you, the master of the terse, the pointed, and the relevant, with never a trace of overstatement, sentimentality or other false emotions disguising the true ones that are the mark of all your writings and that have made you, in my opinion, the foremost short story writer in the English language now living. The comparative smallness of your output is undoubtedly connected with this clarity and economy. I shall not try to compete, but shall waffle on.

Seventy years old! Quite incredible! I have known you so long and so well, you have repeatedly been present at major points of crisis in my life, that I feel I have known you for twice that number of years at least. But our friendship in fact only started just a quarter of a century ago. And then we did not meet for a few more.

It was in Rome, in 1949, that I received your review of my second novel, *The Iron Hoop*. It was what they used to call a rave review, and the American publisher informed me that you actually

bought several copies of the book, an action he believed unprece-
dented on the part of a critic. I agreed and agree with him in his
astonishment. And because of this I wrote to you – I have never
written to another critic personally unknown to me – and you
wrote me a grave and friendly reply. Now I was utterly miserable
in Rome that hot summer, penniless and in my opinion a failure
both as a man and as a writer. It is no exaggeration to say that
your entry into my life gave me fresh hope and was indeed a sort
of turning point.

A little later my old friend and yours, John Davenport, turned
up in Rome. 'Who', I asked John who always knew everything
and everybody in the literary world, 'is this James Stern?' And he
told me, and he explained that a column of praise from you was
worth a whole *New York Sunday Times* weight of words from
ordinary critics. And since John was a man not only of impeccable
taste but also incapable of telling lies about literature, I was even
more encouraged. I naturally read everything of yours I could lay
my hands on and saw that John was, as usual, right. Since then I
have read everything, I think, that you have published. My opinion has been fortified. Why, you even allowed me to quote a long
passage from your excellent and undeservedly forgotten book
about immediate post-war Germany, *The Hidden Damage*, in a
book of my own.

Then, in Paris a very few years later, I rang my old friend,
Desmond Ryan. He was away and had lent his flat to a friend. I
gave this stranger my name, and it turned out he was you. It seems
to me that you and Tania and my wife and I talked from café to
café for days on end, all interesting and all gay, for one of your
characteristics which is perhaps not immediately visible in your
books is your infectious gaiety, your sheer sense of fun, and your
wittiness. We might disagree – for instance I have always thought
that your beloved Freud was in a large measure a mountebank, his
thoughts riddled with Viennese *Schlamperei* – but we never quar-
relled about anything.

When we were both living in England, we frequently visited
one another, and your houses in Dorset had a warm, one might
say a continental atmosphere that I appreciated immensely. Indeed
it was my visits to you in Dorset that prompted me to move there.
To have you as a near neighbour was a further inducement. And
you and Tania were lunching with me on another, and this time a

very climacteric moment in my life. During that lunch on July 18th, 1961, the hospital telephoned to tell me my wife had given birth to my son, Francis. And you were the first person to raise a glass to his health and happiness.

Since coming to live in Ireland, the land of your birth, I have alas seen little of you. But one day I must tell the story of your intervention at a meeting of the Irish Academy of Letters, of which you are not a member but to which I took you. A pompous and obviously nameless if not actually faceless booby had been given a prize. He took the opportunity to deliver a sort of lecture to us Irish writers on, of all subjects, James Joyce. Faces grew taut, feet began to shuffle, as this man droned on and on. At last you could bear it no longer. With what might have been the first two steps of an Irish jig, you were in the middle of the room and silenced the man, to everyone's immense relief, by announcing loudly and clearly: 'But Joyce knew how to *laugh*!'

And so, my dear Jimmy do you. For your hundredth birthday I shall not write another encomium. Instead I shall drag my own aged carcass to wherever you are, and we shall drink a bottle of champagne together, and we shall *laugh*.

Kay Boyle in San Francisco:

This is to greet you on your birthday. The older I get the more difficult I find it to use the word 'Happy' when you don't want the discomfort of saying something more accurate. So I don't offer you that word now, but wish you instead a birthday of fine weather (which is frequently to be wished for in England), and the love of old friends, and a continuing supply of the wit and varying humours that have always been so remarkably yours. (At this point, although it may be hard to believe, I opened your book of short stories quite at random, and it is page 243, and in the middle of that page you are saying: 'Happy is not a word I use nowadays'. I myself could scarcely believe this coincidence, but there have been a number of coincidences in the more than forty years we have known each other, so I accept this almost without wonder as just one of the shared ideas that have made us friends.)

Once I dedicated a book of mine to you, and you dedicated a story to me; but 'memories' is another vague word that lacks a fine, sharp edge. So I'll just mention two or three specific moments in our lives, and this will be a part of my birthday present to you, a reminder that I have not forgotten certain exact times, and never will forget. [Two of these 'specific moments' have already been quoted on p. 51.]

There were explicit moments in Paris, in Mégève, in New York, and there was a night in Connecticut in 1953. You came to a small, dark house near Danbury – far, far from the bright afternoon and dusk of the *Midi* twenty years before. You drove a car that wasn't functioning well, and didn't know the countryside, but you drove the strange roads to the narrow way miraculously named Star's Plain. By your coming, by your presence there that night, at a time when the Un-American Activities Committee had made it impossible for my beloved Joseph to make a living or for me to place my writings anywhere, you confirmed what Janet Flanner, a character witness for me at our trial, once wrote me. Janet Flanner wrote: 'When I die, it won't be inscribed on my tombstone that I worked fifty years for *The New Yorker Magazine*. It will be said in stone "Once I stood by a friend".' I thank you for your presence. And on this occasion of your birthday, I send you my love.

Sonia Orwell in London:

You have, dear Jimmy, such an elegant gift for friendship, such a lovely perception of where our wounds and pleasures really lie, such a glorious giggle if the problem is on the comical side and such gloriously warm words if it stems from the blacker aspect. I have often thought this quality of yours emerges from your gifts as a writer, from the born writer's feeling for the texture of our existence; and I believe that artists do dig a richer vein than most of us and can sometimes, as you do, give correspondingly richer treasures of friendship, understanding, and just straightforward fun.

I have never enjoyed a Black Velvet so much as with you, and shall never forget the huge pleasure of those late-afternoon walks to Old Wardour Castle looking so bewitching in the red, winter sun. I hope we have many more drinks and many more walks and I wish you all possible good things and joy today.

David Garnett in France:

… you have given me in several stories what I most seek in every form of art and which indeed I think is the *raison d'être* of art: –

that is vicarious experience. I like your stories of children best and 'The Woman Who Was Loved' is my favourite.

But though we have only met at rare intervals, I know you well enough to envy you – not because of your stories since, as a writer, I only want to be myself. And not because of anything I have been told about you. Why then?

Because of the tone of voice in which your friends speak of you – for several women I know are old friends of yours. How shall I describe that tone? It is as though at that moment – that is when your name is mentioned – she had gone to the bedroom window, drawn back the curtains, and seen that it was a beautiful day, the dew sparkling on the grass, or the hoar frost on the dry leaves and the sun shining.

John Lehmann in London:

… Your first contribution to *New Writing* was, I remember, a reportage rather than story, called 'A Stranger among Miners', which nevertheless showed your remarkable powers of vivid description and your painfully acute sense of human suffering. Among the half dozen or so stories which I was later privileged to publish, my favourites have always been 'Next Door to Death' and 'The Woman Who Was Loved': the former more like a poem than a story (and quite perfectly realized), and the latter containing one of your most brilliantly created misfits and eccentrics, Miss Whitmore. You have always excelled in portraying people who, by nature or experience, are despisers of conventional attitudes and codes of behaviour: they, like Miss Whitmore or Major Carter, are the true heroes of your world. Never shall I forget the scene on the road, in 'The Man Who Was Loved', when Major Carter confronts the mamba. And the funeral at the end of that story reminds me of what is perhaps your most exceptional gift of all: the nervous vitality, like a dancing flame, that runs through some of your pieces, and can generate an almost unbearable tension of emotion. What an achievement – for someone who obviously hates the huntin' and shootin' world – to have described the excitement of riding to hounds so overwhelmingly in that splendid story 'The Broken Leg'. Recently I re-read 'Travellers' Tears', another of your unique masterpieces, and the explosion of nostalgia you produce in that story, dissolving so uncannily the inhibitions of all the voyagers, brought tears to *my* eyes. Is that because (thank goodness) I cry more easily as I grow older? Or just your magic?

Patrick White in Sydney:

… Yours is a birthday all your friends can only hope will recur to the end of their lives. We first met in print, you as a generous critic, myself as a humble subject. I did not imagine we might meet eventually in the flesh, or that a friendship would form, and even more, endure over the years. That your friendship inspired jealousy in others increased its value, just as your own stories became a more exciting discovery from lurking behind your modesty. I shall remember you above all in a context of Wiltshire landscapes, a feast of grouse in a Salisbury inn, disagreements on railway platforms, and always look forward to the day when the four of us meet again to enjoy those acerbic shouting matches.

Three weeks after the fortieth anniversary of the Sterns' first meeting, on 26 November 1974, Cyril Connolly died. Although they were never close, he had been an important peripheral presence for over half a century, and they mourned the passing of a colourful if erratic figure in their lives.

Old friends were 'hopping the twig', but Jimmy and Tania were alive, though in frail health, and still together, in spite of their differences.

A feature of the last thirty years of Jimmy's and Tania's lives was the strenuous activity of their daily existence, as meticulously recorded in his journals: their almost fortnightly visits to London to meet friends and to see plays and art exhibitions; their annual train journeys (never by air) to Paris, the south of France and Italy; their short summer stays in a congenial hotel in Sidmouth and Billy Henderson's seaside retreat in north Devon; their shopping forays to Tisbury and Salisbury (where from 1982 to 1984 they would lunch on Tuesdays at the White Hart Hotel with Chantal Stokely), Jimmy always driving, since Tania never 'qualified' in spite of numerous lessons; their repeated invitations to evening drinks to neighbours from far and near; their constant summer invasions of North Americans, many of them Jimmy's long-established correspondents and intimates from their New York days; their invitations to dinner or lunch from those who lived nearby like Cecil Beaton, David and Rachel Cecil, Judge Billy Hughes and his wife Jenny, Raymond Mortimer and Christopher and Camilla Sykes.

Magouche Fielding remembers the Sterns' untiring sociability when she was staying at Hatch. But she also recalls, with some sorrow, the revelation of Jimmy's innate conservatism and reactionary views on how women should dress. For example, he was to show a cruel streak in his character when criticising Magouche's daughter's clothes on a visit to Paris. His uninformed opinion was so violently expressed that the girl's friendship with Jimmy was permanently impaired.

From time to time Tania would take the train to Birmingham, usually from London, to see her elder sister, who was someone kept very much in the background. (Once, this mysterious relation turned up at Hatch uninvited, to Tania's fury.) Anna, who was born in 1897, is described by her nephew, Christian Geissler, as 'unmarried, naïve, loudly singing, very normal, but in the elite, cosmopolitan family of the Kurellas, a bit of a cuckoo'. She had lived until 1947 in the Polish town of Kaliningrad (formerly Konigsberg) in the Gulf of Danzig near Gdansk. Subsequently she returned to West Germany and later settled in Birmingham. Although the Sterns had severed all connections with Tania's German-Polish family – her sister Marie who had married a Nazi, her brother Alfred with his Moscow connections – Tania did try and support Anna, providing her with money and, by her occasional visits, relieving her loneliness. She died in 1967.

They also occupied themselves enthusiastically with the well-being of their friends' children, many of whom attended the school at Wardour nearby. The girls – they were all girls – came to tea, and the Sterns went to concerts and lectures with impressive alacrity.

And then there was the gardening: Tania amongst the flowers and shrubs, Jimmy ('You can't eat flowers') in his vegetable patch, up a steep bank, across the lane from the house. In the corner, well hidden behind brambles and overhead foliage, was a 'bottle grave' whose capacity was difficult to determine, yet not to imagine.

Jimmy also liked to walk. His solitary, bucolic ramblings took him in a four or five mile radius of the village. He had several prescribed routes; one, a favourite, took him by Wardour Castle and to the doorsteps of the houses of his friends, the Hugheses, and the Sampsons, Anthony and Sally. And the pubs along these routes, in which he became a respected and popular 'regular', were a tangible escape from his periodically tormented existence at the Manor.

His love of the country is expressed in this passage in *The Hidden Damage*; he is travelling by train from London to his parents' house in Dorset after the wartime years in America:

The fields, the hedges, the woods of Wiltshire looked even greener than I'd remembered, their silence and quality of peace more intense … everything on the landscape seemed to have acquired a quality of *finished* harmony – the grey stone houses of the occasional villages to have been there always, the ancient oaks and elms to be immortal and never to have been young, the smallest meadow to be cared for as a garden, even the cattle, stretching their necks against a strand of wire, to be chewing the cud of confidence and content. No wonder, I thought, as the train trundled into Templecombe, no wonder the nearest this land came to a revolution was a bloodless general strike!

In January 1975 Jimmy was rushed to Moorfields Hospital in London with a detached retina. He wrote to Maeve Slavin on 22 February 1982:

There, in a ward with a number of non-stop smokers, I derived some considerable relief (the windows couldn't be opened on account of the hideous noise of traffic on City Road) from just this 'Talking Book Service' (of which I had never heard). Permanently tired & blind, I accepted from the overworked guy with the trolley of 'books' anything he felt like leaving by my bed. Well, imagine my – yes, emotions – when one day or night (one never knew which) I lay there & suddenly out of the darkness heard sentences so familiar that I found myself, my body, spring to attention! I was listening to my own old stories [from *The Heartless Land*] of Africa, of Zimbabwe, in 1925 … I eventually lay back exhausted as well as uplifted at the (I suppose) ridiculous thought that certainly he [the author], possibly I, had not lived in vain … !!

Tania was frustrated by the strange Kafka-esque conspiracy of silence from doctors and nurses when she tried to elicit Jimmy's progress. Obviously, it was 'not done' to ask questions.

From Jimmy to Nadine Gordimer on 6 January 1975 in reply to her seventieth birthday letter to him:

'Because I'd like this to be a special letter I'm finding it hard to write.' And because it is to you, in confidence, to you whom I love, I am not going to try. I just want to hug you in gratitude, then go very slowly for a long walk, arm-in-arm, along these lanes.

Can you imagine what it was like to be me, on Boxing Day, at my brother's in London, opening a brown paper parcel, to find a dozen copies of a slim beautifully produced book – with my name in huge letters, & under it 'Some letters for his seventieth birthday'? What the Germans call a *Festschrift*, as you know. Compiled in secret, over some two years or more by a young man whom I have seldom seen, who was brought here once, for an hour, by a friend!

From Jimmy to Nadine Gordimer on 13 March 1975:

D'you know whom I feel like? Like the person who wanted to write 'a special letter', but felt (mistakenly) she wouldn't be 'able to get it right'. Now I *know* I have *no hope* of getting mine right.

I said au revoir to Mehring & Jacobus & Co. [characters in Nadine Gordimer's novel *The Conservationist*] two or three days ago, and have been feeling oh so lonely ever since. Not for want of their company (though of course I shall visit them again), but (since I cannot have yours) for William's [Plomer's]. There is literally no one – in my world, at least – to take his place.

How we would chatter, no doubt by post! for this is his Africa as well. Or was. And I would pester him with questions. What's more, he would answer – the Good Friend he was. Because it's not my Africa. And yet – and what more can one ask of literature? – those 400 acres of veld are already part of my day and my dream landscape.

At sight or sound of the word *Ikona* I am promptly in a valley of rocks and mopani and euphorbia and the distant jabber of Sindabili. But for the past month and for the rest of my days at sight of the word Mehring I shall be transported to the Transvaal, to the close-up of willows and tough, dry reeds, among men some of whom are 'good only for holding things steady', and who buy their 'Epsom from the India' and in crises bless our common tongue with the genius of children: 'We think something is happen.' – Oh, how it makes one long to be able to write!

For his last three or four books, and this includes some long stories, I have been saying to Patrick W. [White] that I know no one's work which demands as much concentration, is so greatly rewarded by two and more readings. I feel just this, only more so, about *The Conservationist* – a word I can neither pronounce nor write without stuttering!

... In this novel I kept losing my way, having to retrace my steps, as I invariably do when I (stupidly) try to read the financial page of a daily paper, or any other paper. Quite often I blamed the author for being over-subtle, for *under*-writing, occasionally for refusing to use quotes, for insisting throughout on the present tense. With little or no justification, I fear.

You know those moments when you see, read, or hear something which you realize simultaneously is indelible? One such moment came while in the midst of your flood. A sheer marvel of descriptive writing.

And yet I guess I have not yet mentioned possibly the most important aspect of all: what I learned about the Mehrings of this, your Africa. Which is pretty well everything! Do you realise (you do of course) that in a very few weeks (May 22) it will be 50 (fifty) years since the 20-year-old youth escaped (there is no other word for it) from Southampton via the Cape to a farm 40 roadless miles N. of Bulawayo? Escaped from his family. And for a long long time kept heaving sighs of relief.

And where is he today, that same youth? 10 miles from where I set out.

During March a Canadian film crew threatened to descend on Hatch to interview Jimmy for their film on the life of Malcolm Lowry, but he diverted them most appropriately to the bar of The Lamb at nearby Hindon, where he obliged with oft-repeated memories of his friend. From Jimmy to Sybille Bedford on Easter Monday (31 March) 1975:

I hear from all sides (if Hatch can be said to have any sides at all) not only that *A Legacy* [1956] is being serially televised with a galaxy of stars as cast, but from all accounts (three at least) much of it is excellently done. Rather than risk Righty (for alas Lefty has not improved since his last ordeal at Moorfields) with the rigours of the box, I have been re-reading The Book of the Film. The first seventy pages since yesterday. Goodness, they are brilliant. I cannot now believe that I read them, what is it? Twenty years ago! The characterization, the prose, both classic and colloquial! And now I hear from another side (closer to you!) that you, the author, knew nothing of this event of which Town and Country are talking. Worse, a thousand times, that you are but a pittance the better off? Is not, was not something very wrong? Should not your agent have seen to it that you were, are, properly rewarded? I remember, some years ago, someone in London predicting that one day, when Television had come of age some story of mine (mine!)

would undoubtedly make a fortune for the writer. Was the man talking nonsense – by which I mean: does it not pay to have one's work televised?

That it sells the book I have no doubt (and thank God for that!) but this is not what I mean.

From Sybille Bedford in London on 1 April 1975:

... *A Legacy*. Oh dear, it is odd what television does to one; I feel rather sardonic and sad about it, believing in the printed word. Delighted that *you* like the printed word.

My dealings with the BBC can be briefly summed up. Apparently they are typical. The BBC pays writers, as distinct from scenario writers, producers etc, badly. ITV pays rather better; but stories of fortunes to be made are surely exaggerated. The BBC 'bought' *A Legacy* in the summer of 1973, van Loewen my (and Coward's, Sartre's) dramatic agent and a very experienced one doing a deal. They offered £600 in all; van L upped it to £700. £350 was paid in 1973. 10% went to Collins, another 10% to van L. Now at the end of the serial there will be another £350 minus the £75 percentages (and minus income tax) and of course counted on beforehand by me. This is quite usual and top pay apparently. What was unusual was not letting me see the script (they were supposed to by contract) ... On Thursday also there was a preview (of the whole thing I assume) laid on by the BBC to which I wasn't asked. And of course I only knew from the *Radio Times* last issue that the play was actually on.

In mid-April, Jimmy wrote in his journal: 'Try to face the facts: 1) We are overhoused; 2) we must realize that we cannot, or should not, *die* here. What would happen to the other?' On this subject, their Tisbury neighbour, Frank Tait, recalls a particularly apt Irishism from Tania: 'If one of us dies first, I am going to London.'

From Malcolm Cowley in Sherman, Connecticut on 19 May 1975:

... I've been reading (for review) Bunny [Edmund] Wilson's notebooks of the 1920s as edited by Leon Edel. Leon did a good job. The notebooks themselves remind me a little of Evelyn Waugh's diary; they're almost as scandalous, though much less entertaining because Wilson hadn't a very strong narrative sense; also he was writing for himself, so he set down purple passages that he might use in books, as well as events in the form of jottings, reminders, almost like strings tied to his fingers. But what a hopping in and out of beds, what an imbibation of raw alcohol, what hard pricks and moist cunts (he's fond of those two words). At first, 1920–25, excitement about everything, then in the second half of the decade the parties turn sour and Wilson himself has a nervous breakdown in '29 (like so many others); also he was more or less in love with a Ukrainian waitress and ten-cents-a-dance girl who gave him a dose of clap. Meanwhile with that vigor and zing of the 1920s, he was working like hell on plays, essays, and a novel. How Edmund survived to 77, outliving his early friends, who kept dying of alcoholic livers or getting killed drunk at level crossings, is more than I can understand.

From Malcolm Cowley on 3 September 1975:

... I'm writing you when I should be writing a review of Lewis Mumford's new book. It's a magnificent display of egotism – Lewis has delved into his files of unpublished articles, unfinished manuscripts, random notes, and letters to lady friends and has put them together as a portrait of LM from 1914 to 1936. Do we need that collage? Actually he emerges as an interesting character, a little solemn and self-reverent, but ambitious for himself and the world, energetic and persistent. Candid, too, about his love affair with Casey Bauer, a lumpy-faced, beautiful-bodied, bright young woman who almost humanized him, then got tired of being just a mistress and dismissed him in 1934. Reconciled with Sophie, Lewis produced a daughter, Alison, who was engaged to my son when they were both at Harvard – but Rob got scared of being taken over by the Mumfords and broke the engagement ...

The one failure of candor in his collection, his 'analects' he calls the book, is that he makes no mention at all of Lewis Mumford, Sr. – what the hell happened to his presumably English father? At 25 he acquired a spiritual father, Sir Patrick Geddes, whom he talks about a great deal. The biological parent is *spurlos versenkt*, dead or gone away. It's a hell of a book for me to review ...

Having acknowledged with, it might be supposed, grim satisfaction that on 23 November they had survived fifteen years at Hatch, three weeks later they welcomed a new and shining presence into their lives – more particularly Jimmy's – in the shape of Diana Petre, who immediately made a profound impression on him. Initially she possessed three features which recommended her: she was a tall, alluringly handsome person of great charm with a melodious voice, she had recently published *The Secret Orchard of Roger Ackerley* (1975), the haunting story of growing up as one of her father's second, hidden and unacknowledged family, which Jimmy much admired, and she had been married for a brief period to an old friend of his, the writer Louis Wilkinson. When they met a spark was kindled, as the following very warm, very affectionate, rather breathless letter from Hatch Manor on 3 January 1976 reveals:

Oh you are an angel to have phoned. I was sure you wouldn't, which made it all the lovelier. I do wish I were able to make sense over the phone – by the way, it's only four minutes since I said goodbye, or whatever we said. I am so stupidly shy, & the phone makes me shyer. – I am now going to talk at random. Your book & you are the Best Thing that's happened to us for years; life, I have kept saying ever since, is worth living again, if *you* are somewhere about. One must love people, but to find someone – oh, it's so rare. Nothing else is worth living for. Do you have regrets? Are you a regretter? I'm not. T is. I regret only one thing: that I cannot *paint*. *That's* what I'd like to have been. – I don't *like* writing. I don't like thinking. I like walking. And Nature – no, not that word: land, and sky, & above all the *sun and sea*. And trees at all seasons. And cats. And Paris. And whisky. Wine. And fresh fish. And all veg, except celery – my father made such a hideous noise eating it. Oh, but what I love best of all – guess? Children. Innocence. I could watch children for ever. The awful thing is, I always want to hug them, eat them. And children don't like to be eaten. Not when they realize you really *mean it*! – Oh, what I wrote in my letter – which I destroyed? It began Darling Beautiful Di – Henceforth DiB. No, DBD. There then followed a 'humble apology' for daring to talk, to dare mention in your presence that I had had an 'unhappy childhood'. Such a cliché, anyway. Who has had a *happy* childhood? T had – at least until the age of 9 or 10 when she hadn't enough to eat (like you, but she didn't have rickets – how do you spell it?) & her father was killed (in the war) & her mother, destitute with 6 children, died of cancer. So that at 16 (when I was trying to pluck up courage to run away from Eton & 'live') T was compelled to 'live' – by earning her living. But one's entire life is governed by one's first years, don't you agree? –

although you're hardly the person to be asked such a question! As a result of those first years, of wonderful free unconventional immensely gifted parents (he a psychiatrist who spoke 14 languages, she a Polish aristocrat who translated from seven), & as the fifth of six (I dare say) happy children, T has immense vitality. I have next to none. Like you, she likes 'people'. I like silence. DBD, perhaps you *shouldn't* come here? When T stops talking, you *may* hear a dog bark, or an owl hoot. But I wouldn't bet on it.

To Pauline Wynn Jimmy enthused about his new friend:

Diana? She is an extraordinary woman ... one of the most balanced human beings I have ever met. Perfectly content to live alone, or rather with an Australian terrier, which does not bark or whine, and over whom she makes no fuss whatever. I have a hunch she knows she would be no good at marriage or living à deux. She is gloriously funny about Louis [Wilkinson, her husband] ... In the middle of their honeymoon they were having lunch at some hotel or restaurant, when he suddenly leaned over towards her (she was sitting opposite) and in his loud uninhibited voice: 'I say, darling, I am in the most awful draught here, would you mind changing places!' After the initial shock, she burst out laughing. 'I really can't see the joke!' said Louis, mystified.

Diana declined to change places.

Three weeks later he again wrote to Pauline:

Good. I thought you couldn't help falling for *The Secret Orchard*. I, too, think Diana is a better writer than Joe [Diana's half-brother J. R. Ackerley]. It's astonishing that this book should be so flawless; I must try to find out if and how much it was edited ... She went away with a copy of *The Hidden Damage* and in a letter this morning says it has given her an inferiority complex! ... she has 'never read anything like it'.

From Jimmy to Diana Petre on Leap Day (29 February) 1976:

Darling Potty [a reference to a self-deprecating remark by Diana Petre in a previous letter of hers]: ... I am the oldest of five. Fifteen months after me came my jockey brother, Reggie. Killed in 1941 in the Blitz. After him, in 1910, came my elder sister Leila, who died of sleeping sickness (as it was then called) [actually polio] in 1928. At this date my younger sister Rosemary was 15 years old.

And this was when her troubles began. The shock of Leila's death arrested Rose's development. Today, at 63, she is not much older than she was then. Over the years I have seen her into several 'homes', last time less than ten years ago. My sadistic mother always treated her abominably, and my unimaginative, from the human point of view, utterly stupid father was not much help. When he died in 1958 Rose was left alone with my mother, who proceeded to torture her in various insidious ways, even locking her out of the house. Soon she had to be 'taken away' once more, and when she was discharged this time she went to live with my mother's sister and her unmarried fifth daughter, two years younger than Rose, but (amazingly) a person of great strength, intelligence, practical sense, and – most important – a trained nurse. And there, to this day, are these two women, together, in a remote thatched cottage in Dorset. They – and the usual number of dogs, large and small.

In 1969 I had the surprise of my life. For years I had been dreading my mother's death: I felt almost certain that Rose would automatically come and live at Hatch Manor. This I could not bring myself to face. 'In the event', my mother was (ha ha!) hardly in her grave when Rose, for the first time in her life, began to 'live'. Well, almost. There was never any question of her leaving, or wanting to leave, her cousin – whose mother, of course, also had died; in fact, she died before my mother. What they did do was to leave my aunt's house, and set themselves up in this remote thatched cottage – where Rose is now dying. The last five years, motherless, have been the happiest of her life. Thank God she was vouchsafed them.

From Jimmy to Diana Petre on 6 March 1976:

... Trouble is: Unlike you, I have never quite outlived my child-hood ... Potty, how can you write such (what my father used to call) tommy-rot! You actually ask if I agree that 'we simply must meet as often as reasonably possible'? Darling, darling, how can you ask such a question? Each day I say: Won't it be lovely to have Di here after all this is over? And T says: Yes, yes, yes. As a one-time wife of LW [Louis Wilkinson], you may (just) be forgiven for such remarks as '... no matter what YOU may tell yourself!' But you may not be forgiven a second time. T says, I say, we both say, it depends who the guest is: You, Potty, are not only not 'exhausting', you are a permanent delight. And a help. We love you, and everything about you. (Hugs, please). The moment we are 'free', you must come at once, and let us pray you will be able to, and not promised to someone else.

... Sunday the 7th March 11am. Rose, my sister, died this morning at 5.30.

In June and again in December there was more animosity: 'T retires to bed c.2.30 and was still there at 5.45. Furious, suicidal. Drank too much before lunch, now dares to say she was 'poisoned' ... *Crise* – retire in misery to new room, entered in misery by T at 1am ... Violent unexpected attack at 11.15 from T ... Such resentment, such hatred, is terrible to see. But to live with!'

From Jimmy to Nora Sayre on 6–7 September 1976:

... Does Arthur Ransome (1884–1967) mean anything to you? Author of famous books for children. Famous in England. In the USA? To me he has always been the man who wrote a book about Oscar Wilde (1912), for which he was sued for libel by Bosie Douglas – AR won! Now that book was written at Hatch Manor Farm. And y'day Ransome's autobiography arrived here (Cape), edited by Rupert Hart-Davis. Fascinating local history, which I am slowly compiling, but really no subject for a letter. Tailpiece: Ransome covered the Russian Revolution for the *NY Times* & married Trotsky's secretary. Ears pricking? His first guests at Hatch: Edward Thomas, Lascelles Abercrombie, Martin Secker!

On 23 October Eda Lord died. With a surprising failure of nerve, neither of the Sterns could endure the emotional strain of attending her funeral.

11
'Fiction, Fact and Friends'
1976–1990

In November 1976 Jimmy had the idea for a book to be entitled *Fiction, Fact & Friends*. He had decided to combine his memoirs with a selection of his best stories and the pen portraits of his friends, which had been published in *Penguin New Writing*, *Winter's Tales*, *Encounter*, *The Listener* and the *London Magazine*. He consulted several people, Malcolm Cowley and Arthur Calder-Marshall among them, about the contents, and also his agent, Elaine Greene.

Three years later, the 'book' was still in gestation. Tom Rosenthal, chief executive at Secker & Warburg, received this letter from Jimmy in March 1979: '… What has been generally expected of me for years is a long gossipy autobiographical book about people I have known in various parts of the world. In other words: NAMES. This I have never had any intention of doing. And never will. So, if by chance this is the kind of thing you too expect from me, I suggest that you save your precious time by returning this package without so much as opening it.'

The package was the collection of 'pieces' and stories upon which he had worked so hard, but which he had never fashioned into a coherent autobiographical narrative. Paradoxically, he wrote to Pauline Wynn in September 1986 that 'I do know that I myself am always interested in reading what others have thought of the famous, and infamous! Of how they have met, when & where!' But he wasn't prepared to compromise his fastidiousness and produce a book which, at one remove, he himself would have enjoyed and one which would have been valued by many. Nor was he prepared to take the word of a professional writer, Arthur Calder-Marshall, to whom he had turned for advice many times before.

From Nora Sayre in New York on 8 January 1977:

I am so excited to learn about that Memoir of Walker [Evans] – do, do let me entreat you to do more on it. Please! Since he admired you so much, who else could do him better? (I remember his telling me how lucky I was about to be meeting you and Tania, just before he introduced us. And I remember that John Dav. was quite annoyed that he hadn't been the one to bring us together.) You knew Walker earlier than most of the others I saw him with: I long to know what he was like before fatigue became a part of his life – as it was by the time I met him. I remember your saying years ago that he was the ideal bachelor: you mentioned how he once said with satisfaction that he was going to have 'a little steak' on his own in a restaurant – rather than dining with others ... I appreciate the difficulty of writing about him; I made some notes last summer, but haven't tackled it yet, and won't for a while. Maybe it's the memory of his own fastidiousness that makes it hard. And yet, one then immediately recalls how unfastidious his life was at moments ... I wasn't quite sure what it was that haunted him: surely something did, it showed in the face ... Well, I would love to understand him more through you ...

From Jimmy to Nora Sayre on 13–14 January 1977:

... On Walker [Evans] I have now done some 5,500 words. I travel at about half a page a day, & occasionally send Alan Ross a post-card to say that the snail is still creeping. Today I added the few words you quoted me as saying about his being the Ideal Bachelor and preferring to eat alone. It fitted in perfectly on that particular page. Thank you.

You say you never knew him well enough to guess what it was that haunted him. [Nora Sayre later came to believe that Walker Evans was haunted by his bisexuality.] Nor did I. That's my main trouble. Not that I (or T for that matter) feel he was 'haunted'. If I didn't feel that it would be misinterpreted, I would like to quote, preferably as a sub-head, a line or two in Leslie's [Katz's] inter-view: 'Writing's a very daring thing to do.' I have a hunch this sentence 'speaks volumes'. Agee dared. And that, you see, is what I have against photography – not just in particular, but in general. Although I say it in a whisper, I cannot believe in it as an Art, only as a compromise. Time will probably prove me wrong, if wrong is the word. Films will no doubt be the Art of the 20th century. I think Agee would agree. Jim compromised only in so far that he worked for Time, Inc. to keep not just his body & soul alive, but those of his family. But he also did much of what he felt born to do, and – God rest his soul – killed himself in the process. I tell you all this in an effort to show – which I am sure is unnecessary, for you know it anyway – how impossible it is (except in the v. rarest of cases, such as Sandy [Calder]) to be fair & just & truthful in a Memoir about any contemporary. Anyway, I always say: Tell me the background & first 3 years of a human being's life – and I can go from there with some sureness of foot. Of Walker I know neither. So it's all rather superficial. Of Auden. Of Lowry, even of Joyce (of all of whom I have done Memoirs) I have known more. Which I suppose is odd to think of.

From Nora Sayre on 30 January 1977:

What glorious news: 5,500 words on Walker. I am so happy that you have kept going. You know, that quote about writing being 'daring' does ring a bell: he certainly implied that he had wanted to be a writer when he was very young; I remember lots of references to that ...

... When I said Walker was haunted: maybe that's the wrong word. I just got a sense of somebody who felt a shadow over his head, something hovering over him. Maybe it was just the kind of quiet depression that a sensitive person carries around, plus the dilemmas of how to earn enough while doing work he really wanted to ...

... Tomorrow I am going to interview Alger Hiss for my book. He's so nice even on the phone; (I've met him once.) I don't want to ask him to repeat the questions that so many have laid on him – it's taking a lot of preparation: to try to think up questions that will interest him. Mainly I want to know about the world that he found after he got out of jail. I know that his many friends rallied, that he had a good deal of moral support for himself. But people were so scared to have any political opinions at all at that time ...

From Nora Sayre in New Hampshire on 28 February 1977:

... I've just written the first draft of the Davenport memoir (2,000 words, space is tight these days), and how I wish I could talk with you ... I do hope to hell I've got the balance right: between the elegant mind and the rowdy nature. Only I simply can't write about John without evoking some of the uproar. But I don't want to give any distress to the family, so I've left out some memorable moments. Oh, the facts are hard to check: I've tried to handle things carefully. Some of the best Dav. stories I heard from Muriel

Spark, Bernard Wall (that terribly nice editor of *The Twentieth Century*) and Roger Lubbock: all far beyond reach.

Well, it was enjoyable to write. I also put in quite a few quotes from C. Connolly, because I do think *Enemies of Promise* [1938] had passages that helped to explain John's work blocks. Now I'd love a bit of help ... What writers – new or old – do you recall as his favourites, including those whom he encouraged? I did say that you introduced him to the work of Patrick White, I also remember his enthusiasm for Isaak Dinesen, Faulkner (of course Malcolm Lowry and D. [Dylan] Thomas), also Melville and Henry Adams – very unEnglish in his liking for the last two.

From Jimmy to Nora Sayre, before leaving for their favourite Sidmouth hotel for a few days, and prior to Paris in mid-April, on 9 March 1977:

... Your JD [John Davenport] memoir. How I wish we could talk. BUT if one has to be inhibited by the 'family', of course that does create difficulties. The Memoirs I have done (Auden, Plomer, Joyce, Lowry, Walker) are all personal – i.e. of friends. And this is where I must admit some embarrassment about Joyce. Not that JJ would give a damn – he called me Bloom, after all! And telephoned Tania in the middle of her work – with half a dozen females next-to-nude lying therapootically on the floor – to tell her at great length that a certain Abbey (Cistercian, c 1200 AD) across the River Boyne on the far side from us at home was spelt and pronounced in such & such a way, and would she please tell her husband (me). T was so paralysed by The Great Man she did not dare to tell him she was working & would he please shut up; she couldn't tell him to ring me, for *I had no phone*!

From Jimmy to Nora Sayre on 15 April 1977:

... I am afraid my Evans effort, four times longer, will look pretty shoddy beside your Dav. So much more professional, yours. But then I am not a pro – at anything. A slothful amateur, who has written a handful of stories which just might outlive the 20th century. Such is my conceited obit.

... I am not quite sure what [Enid] Bagnold meant when she said that [Desmond] MacCarthy 'couldn't invent'. Surely that was the trouble with the whole tribe: they just could not be satisfied with what they could do supremely well. Has there ever been a

novelist, good or bad, who longed to be a Great Critic? It's not
even lack of recognition: a good critic is 'recognized' almost every
week, a novelist or poet maybe once a year. Sainte-Beuve & Gosse
& MacCarthy & CC [Cyril Connolly] will 'live', and JD [John
Davenport] will certainly have his niche, for which he and all his
friends will certainly be grateful to a Certain Very Talented
American who seems to be that very rara avis: one who has no
particular desire to 'invent'. And here's the crunch: I don't think I
have ever known anyone, not even the most inspired Dublin talker
at midnight, with as great a capacity to 'invent' as JD – at our
locals around Hatch or in the bars of Sloane Square, at noon!

On 27 November 1978 they celebrated Fred Warburg's eightieth
birthday in the Banqueting Hall of the London Zoo. Secker and
Warburg had been Jimmy's publishers since 1938.
From Arthur Calder-Marshall, 'About February 12th by the feel'
1980:

> ... At its vulgarest, what they [publishers] want is name-dropping.
> But there is something valuable, which you could say which
> would not be botanising your friends. Imagine someone, aged 20
> to 30, of whom you are fond: and try to explain what life was like
> when you were in South Africa, came back to England, Paris in
> the 30s, New York during the War, going to Germany at the end
> and so on: hazards, humour, questions answered or unanswered.
> That sort of book might, I think, be valuable, to you, a publisher
> and the public. Think it over ...

From Jimmy to Nora Sayre on 18 May 1980:

> ... I met Bunny [David Garnett] many years ago when he was
> married to his first wife, Frances Partridge's sister. That was in the
> 1920s. Then we didn't meet for years, until 1945 when I returned
> to London (for USSBS) en route to or from Germany, to discover
> that in the intervening years he had seduced God-knows-how-
> many females, among them one of my oldest chums, a notorious
> Lesbian. To cut it short, through her we made a pilgrimage to the
> Lot without telling him we were coming ... there followed a
> dinner cooked by him in his French hideout (he lives completely
> alone there), during which I made HIM talk about both D. H. and
> T. E. Lawrence, the only person I've ever met who knew both inti-
> mately. Alas, alas, the dinner was so good, the wine was plentiful,

the night so long, that I remember hardly a word he said. *C'est la vie* ... He is a Great Man ... I've always been madly envious of his early life, his parents, and their friends ... Imagine being taken to Russia by your mother in your teens, being taught how to sail by Joseph Conrad, & bouncing about in haystacks with Lawrence & Frieda in Bavaria! And be alive and writing in 1980 ...! Holy Mother, as they say where I come from!

Whilst close and lesser friends continued to expire (Djuna Barnes in 1982, Constantine FitzGibbon in 1983, Ethel Mannin in 1984, Christopher Isherwood in 1986, and John Lehmann in 1987), some of the former celebrated birthdays, and in style: in 1978 Alec Waugh was 89 and Alan Pryce-Jones was 70; in 1985 V. S. Pritchett was 85. Jimmy's life-long attention to dates and anniversaries, as recorded in diaries and letters, and his nurture of friendships, made him acutely aware of 'the dying of the light' and the retreat of his own talents. But Pryce-Jones, Pritchett and Waugh were still with him ...

Jimmy's 'problem book', the memoirs combined with his stories and pen portraits, was his main preoccupation during 1979 and '80. Also, as part of a 'publishing package', presumably on the advice of Elaine Greene, Jimmy hoped that *The Hidden Damage* might be a paperback proposition. However, it was not until 1990 that this book, so highly praised on its first publication in New York forty-three years earlier, was published in England.

It is a sad fact that no fewer than six publishers – Secker & Warburg, Constable, Faber & Faber, HarperCollins, Compton Press and Harcourt, Brace in America – rejected his admittedly unwieldy and ill-assorted script. Furthermore, although Michael Mann of Element Books offered to publish *The Stories* and *The Hidden Damage* in November 1984, the offer was never realised.

'... Pleasant surprise (and how often does that happen?)' Jimmy exclaimed to Nora Sayre on 25 January 1981.

A few days ago in the mail came an anthology of short stories entitled *Englische Kinder*, published in Zurich in (natch) German. I opened the Contents page to find – and here you must forgive the boast! – the following list of chosen contributors: Oscar Wilde,

Charles Dickens, Hugh Walpole, Rudyard Kipling, Saki, Graham Greene, James Stern, Kenneth Grahame, Katherine Mansfield, Jean Rhys, Robert Louis Stevenson, Lucy Lane Clifford [d.1929].

The JS story is 'The Woman Who Was Loved', and – thank the Lord – quite brilliantly translated. I 'm afraid I shall find myself dining out (as if we ever do!) on this surprise for quite a while.

No, I have never met, and hope I never will meet, that woman (?) Lillian Hellman. Nora, you amaze me when you 'really enjoyed' her! I think it's a hideous story. It reminded me of something I hadn't thought of for years: that I once had a vol. of autobiography of hers. I found it last night, and I can't remember ever having opened it, let alone read it. It's called *An Unfinished Woman* (which surely is an invitation to someone to finish her off?) & was published in 1969 by Macmillan. You've probably read it. In the book, however, I found a cutting from Clive Barnes's *New York Notebook* entitled: 'When literary ladies fall out'. Quote: 'Unquestionably the literary event of the year (1980) has been a pitiably silly squabble between L. Hellman & Mary McCarthy. The latter apparently called the former "a dishonest writer" and "a liar". Whereupon Miss H "took umbrage" and sued "Miss McC, the interviewer and the network" for $1.75 million "for mental pain and anguish" as well as for "being injured in her profession". Now, I ask you, do either of these ladies sound nice?'

From Jimmy to Sybille Bedford on 1–2 July 1981:

… Humphrey Carpenter's *WHA* [*W. H. Auden*, 1981]: T., who has read only a couple of reviews, is horrified. We of course were 'involved' to the extent of having the author here (we liked him very much), & seeing him in London for an hour or two; but all we were shown were those passages in which one or both of us were mentioned. I 'passed' these passages with some critical comments which were all taken. – As you probably saw in the *S. Telegraph*, Nigel [Dennis] called the portrait of W. by Carpenter 'more like that of a monster than a man'. And today's (July 2) *Times*, while saying that 'There can be no doubt that this is a brilliant biography', must leave the reader who didn't know W. with feelings of horror. The trouble must be that the emphasis is all wrong. I can't really judge, since I have only dipped into the book here & there. It strikes me as extraordinarily thorough; an enormous amount of work & research must have gone into it. What I wonder is: did W's brother John read it and 'pass' it ...? If reviews are anything to go by, I'm afraid the book won't do poor W. any good. What a sad end to such a brilliant creature. 'He was not a very pleasant character,' says the *Times* reviewer. That's a damned lie!

In mid-July Jimmy was involved in another car crash. The narrow Wiltshire lanes were always a hazard. He and his car escaped without damage, but the sight of the other vehicle screeching to a halt and turning upside down in front of him gave him 'daymares'. While Jimmy presumed the worst, the young driver crawled to safety through an open window.

I often write you a 'letter' in the bath [Diana Petre told Jimmy on 17 August 1982], but as soon as I'm out of it there is Rosie with her ardent great eyes and wiggling tail begging to be taken for a skitter round the block – and when I get home ... Well, you know how it is. Then, the other day, at a party at Caroline's [Lowell's], there was Jennifer Ross looking so beautiful and sober and un-melancholic asking me at once if I'd seen you recently and saying how much she would love to, and Caroline joining in, and me saying, wildly, Oh, the very next time he comes up and is coming to me you both must come too and we'll have the most lovely time all together – and feeling guilty because I knew we wouldn't. And then, last night, Sybille [Bedford] here for dinner with Bruce Chatwin and Teddy Millington-Drake, and all of us talking about you and S. saying she is going to stay with you soon. Actually I'm feeling a bit frail today because Bruce brought a stunning bottle of champagne and then we drank two bottles of unlabelled claret which have been in my wee cellar for over 20 years – all those years ago Sally said it was Gerald's[22] 'best' claret – and S. spent the greater part of the evening in a frenzy trying to decide what it was and what year and waxing so lyrical about it that it reminded me of Louis [Wilkinson] about wine, but he never talked as well as Sybille did last night. Later we all reeled out into the night, me with Rosie round the block, Bruce on foot home, and S. was swept off in a wonderful black Mercedes by Teddy. It was a lovely evening and I wish you had been with us.

22 Gerald Grosvenor, 4th Duke of Westminster, married Diana Petre's sister Sally in 1945.

So WHEN are you coming? Daphne [Fielding] was here for 3 nights staying in the house recently, and of course, again, we talked a lot about you. She's lost 2 stone in weight and has never looked more beautiful or been more delightful to be with. I drove her down to Glos. on Monday and we lunched with Sal and then went over to Badminton to see The Laundry, which is being converted into a house for her – they say by Christmas, but I doubt that. She's going back to Uzès until it's ready, which is not a very good idea because she has no friends really near and forgets to eat and then has tumbles. But where else could she go? It's such a problem and she's so immensely courageous about it. Caroline [Lowell] came to dinner one night and they both enjoyed each other no end, so did I. They know masses of people in common. It must be unbelievably awful to have to live alone for the first time in your life aged 78. But D. inspires such devotion wherever she goes that I guess things will turn out semi-ok. My maid, who adores D., dropped in one evening for a drink, knocked back about half a pint of whisky without turning a feather, and has been in transports ever since. Servants, above all, dote on her, and don't mind in the least that she miraculously turns a room upside down within five minutes.

From Jimmy to Nora Sayre on 31 January 1983:

... Am most surprised that you make no mention of the [Joan] Givner biog. of K. A. Porter! Sally Sampson (of Cape) lent it to me about 10 days ago, and I must say that though I was glued to it partly because I had known & corresponded with her since 1933, I was very often horrified by the emphasis on her vices, notably her malice. I was amazed by the number of men in her life. She seems to have changed men (almost all 10 to 20 years younger than herself) about as often as she changed addresses! I found myself longing to talk to someone who knew her as well as, if possible better than, I did. Only to conclude that there just ain't no one I can reach even by phone this side of the Atlantic. In the end I wrote a nostalgic postcard to Monroe Wheeler & Glenway Wescott, though by no means sure that they are alive. I know that Glenway will be 82 in April, and I'm sure Monroe is older. What a marriage that is; must surely beat all records. Well, 'in the event', Monroe had written to me on the same day, enclosing the long [Elizabeth] Hardwick review in the NYT Review of Books, which evidently infuriated the author. And now, of course, I have been asked (by a charming-sounding woman who lives in Ontario) for photocopies of my letters from KAP – of which I have kept some 60, going back 50 years. I have just finished re-reading them, and am astonished how interesting (from the writing point of view; it seems that I sometimes had the audacity to be critical of her work) they are. I should be very interested to hear what you think of the biog. – should you ever have time to read it.

David Plante [author of *Difficult Women* (1984), a memoir of Sonia Orwell, Jean Rhys, and Germaine Greer]: by a strange coincidence Jim Storey has sent me the *NY Times* review of the book with a ring round Sonia Orwell; it arrived this morning. And I must say I am amazed. On Wed. the 19th of Jan. we spent a night in London in order to attend a 'Jean Rhys' meeting of the P. E. N. Club. Panel: Diana Athill (André Deutsch), Bill Webb of the *Guardian*, Josephine Hill (jeune-ish fille, who obviously loathed Plante), and David Plante … The result has been described by several members of the audience (packed!) as a 'lively evening'. We happened to be given seats in the front row, so that even I had the audacity to ask D. Athill (the only one who knew how to talk in public) if any member of the panel could tell us anything about JR's years in Paris? 'Paris? Oh no, I'm afraid not … That's before our time … ' Or words to that effect (Those years, of course, coincided with my time!).

Finally, Plante – whom I had seen once, at some kind of meeting of Friends of Sonia Orwell after that Diffy Woman's death. I remember that the meeting was run by Mary McCarthy (very badly), that Natasha Spender read a very sensible straightforward unsentimental speech, & that the awful Plante read from his diary of days – oh, dear, I can't really remember what he said, I only remember that I took an instant and lasting dislike to the creature: I feel almost sure because he was writing & talking all the time about – himself. And this impression at the P. E. N. was reinforced by almost everything he said, the predominant & reiterated words, to a storm of abuse from the audience, which included Antonia Fraser & [Harold] Pinter, sitting beside us in the front row, the latter actually shouting at him each time the Plante repeated: 'Well, I am a writer, you see … I am a writer … !' A day or two later, we listened to him being attacked on the radio by presumably young & not at all Diffy Women, one of whom, at the limit of her patience, shouted: 'This is a personal question: Are you GAY?'

From Jimmy to Nora Sayre on 6–7 March 1983:

This can't be much of a letter because I am going slowly but very surely stark mad from trying to review (for the Please do! of Alan Ross, natch!) that biog. of KAP. This idiotic inability to say no to any kind of literary challenge stems from my first years (no, most of our years) in New York when we did literally have to live 'hand-to-mouth'. You'd think by 1983 at Hatch Manor I might have shed this hangover. The awful thing is that I think I undertook this job at least partly to defend an old & departed friend ... Well, well, I'm saying no more at the moment, I'm that confused by trying so hard to differentiate between one person's 'truth' and another's, but mostly, & worst of all, between the fiction & the truth of the Subject. Oh, I keep saying, if only I had never met the dear, crazy, talented, tempestuous, tubercular female whose most astonishing as well as most tragic feat was to live at least ten years too long!

    ... I of course was fascinated by simply the fact that you had set eyes on Prof. Joan Givner – who I understand from the blurb was born & brought up in, I think, Manchester, Eng. Malcolm Cowley writes that KAP 'chose the wrong biographer' – to which I have replied in effect: 'Just what do you mean by that?' ... Having read every single word of this 500-page book, what distresses me more than the inability to distinguish fact from fiction is the emphasis (the facts are bad enough) on KAP's alleged malice and her anti-Semitism – the latter only too apparent in the character of Lowenthal in that (to my mind) highly over-rated novel *Ship of Fools*. What fascinates me is that only once in 90 years (I had thought never) did she come to England, to the BBC. What for? Need you ask? To talk about herself, natch. And by God, could she do that!

From Nora Sayre in New York on 1 May 1984:

... Last week I had a great treat: snatched a few hours to hear Malcolm Cowley talking about memoirs at P. E. N. It was marvellous – just what a P. E. N. evening should be (and often isn't!). I took notes and can't include all of them here, but he compared memoirs to fiction, adding that the novelist has 'the freedom to recount what never happened'. He said that some 'memoiristic novels' are 'written too soon, when the author has had too little experience', and he spoke of the writer's progress 'from being a mere twerp to being an accomplished oaf'. *Exile's Return* started out as 'a personal memoir', then it changed and became 'a collective novel' of his generation. The memoirist's task is 'to sweep away the rubbish and find the shape of his story'. He quoted Kenneth Burke on looking for 'watershed moments' in memory. He stressed that if the writer has done a good job of portraying his life and period, others will recognize themselves (at least partially) in the portrait. Toward the end: 'Erect in an armchair or sprawled on a couch, I try to read the book of my life. It was set in type long ago, by an amateur ... Whole pages, whole chapters, have been torn from the binding and mislaid ...' Then he continued with the metaphor of memory: 'Turning the imaginary pages' of the book of one's life.

Well, it was stunning. His son Rob also spoke, most touchingly, about being the offspring of a writer of memoirs: he said that sometimes his father's memories seem like his own. (I have felt that about some of my father's memories.)

Afterward, I went up to thank him (thanks to you, I've met him twice – some years ago. As I think you know, I'm one of his gigantic fans, am continually re-reading his books.) I said that I would write to you about the evening. Then a P. E. N. official came up to thank him, and asked if he had any questions. Wide smile: 'Yes. When are you going to pay me?' Reply: 'As soon as you send us your Social Security number.' MC recited it on the spot – which staggered his listeners, since almost no one knows his number by heart.

What a man! What an evening! We all went home elated.

In October, when Jimmy was drinking more than usual and his rage was directed more than ever at Tania, she again told him that life had become impossible and that maybe the time had come to separate. (Her conviction was that Jimmy had been entirely truthful throughout their lives together on every subject except that of alcohol.) The shock of what she had said, she later believed, might have brought on the shingles which in two months was to attack him and painfully remain for many years.

On 15 January 1985, the day on which this affliction struck, Jimmy celebrated his eightieth birthday at a dinner party in Provost Road, north London. The company included Sybille Bedford, John Byrne, Michael Davie and his wife Anne Chisholm, Elizabeth and David Hughes (on the night that he heard his novel, *The Pork Butcher*, had won the W. H. Smith Award), Diana Petre, Alston Purvis, Sally and Anthony Sampson, Nora Sayre, and Frank Tait. A toast to 'the man who was loved', alas, received no response – he was feeling too ill.

In May, while avoiding a taxi near Sloane Square, Jimmy fell flat on his face, crushing his wrist, knee and ribs. Although he was in pain and facing the prospect of lengthy treatment, a beneficial result of this accident was that he gave up drinking spirits. That September, he wrote to 'Dearest Squif ... There are hours of each day when my right eye, & all the flesh surrounding it, feels as though it's on fire. Alas, worse than the pain are the accompanying depressions. I don't remember a year quite as miserable as this. In efforts to take meself out of meself I do the strangest things. Last night, for instance, I attended an Old Etonian Dinner at Sherborne School, where I was the oldest of 75 men!'

Humphrey Stone, an Old Etonian himself and a close neighbour of the Sterns, was dragooned by Jimmy into attending this dinner, at which William Waldegrave, then a Cabinet Minister in Margaret Thatcher's government, gave a speech. Stone maintains that Jimmy, in truth, was proud to have been at Eton and enjoyed the cachet which his old *alma mater* brought him, although for most of his life he had studiously avoided the mantle of any social or educational elitism.

While in the next nine years the arc of Jimmy's life began to descend more rapidly, his sporadic displays of frustration and discontent continued. 'I dare say you suffer a great deal and that's your main occupation,' Tania once remarked, not without justification.

His anger, principally directed at Tania, was the subject of continual concern to his family and friends. Such were its frequent manifestations that one of his nephews refused to visit Hatch. One row over the dinner table in front of neighbours resulted in a bloody dénouement: Jimmy, while on his feet pouring wine, unable to disengage Tania's characteristically intense involvement with the topic of conversation, shouted '*Will* you let me speak?' and attacked her, scratching her hands. Later she returned to the table in bandages.

On another occasion, in the spring of 1986, during a typical outburst, Tania felt obliged to leave the room, near to tears. A friend, who was staying and who had been a witness of the Sterns' countless rows over more than three decades, stood up and, extemporarily, let rip with what obviously seemed to Jimmy a prepared speech of remonstrance. 'How dared he!' he later exclaimed to Tania. But after a few weeks' reflection, he sent this amiable reaction:

> ... ever since your astonishing speech (to put it mildly) in our dining room, I have been very slowly recovering from the shock! ... I can't help feeling that you may have missed your true vocation! ... I can hardly believe that this 'speech', so fast & faultlessly delivered, was 'off the cuff'. That it wasn't composed & learned by heart – perhaps, as its content suggested, over the years! Whether yes or no, rest assured that it will not be forgotten. Indeed, I congratulate you, appreciate your friendly interest ...

It was obvious to all that with his failing health and loss of memory Jimmy became more and more acquiescent and dependent on Tania, until near the end of his life he had retreated into a quiet world of his own, free from the rages which had engulfed him, a state which induced great loneliness in Tania, for his anger had long been an essential part of his character. His frustration may have had its origins in the fact that after his return to England in 1956 he went unrecognised as the eminent critic he had become in America, a theory suggested earlier. The reviews he was writing for the *New York Times* were as distinguished as those by his friends and contemporaries – Nigel Dennis, Cyril Connolly – who were the big 'literary guns' on the English 'heavies'.

Memories of his New York heyday were provided during Easter 1986 when he attended PEN's Annual Writers' Day in London. The chief speaker was Saul Bellow, a colleague from Jimmy's days on *Time*, whom he had not seen for forty-three years. Rather to Jimmy's surprise, in front of a large audience, they took one look and fell into each other's arms.

As far as his writing was concerned, people were active on his behalf. His young friend Alston Purvis, a protégé of Walker Evans from Boston, tried to interest two American publishers, Houghton Mifflin and David Godine in Jimmy's memoirs. Nora Sayre, John Byrne and I all took part in shaping the refractory 'knitting' – to no avail.

Alston Purvis, since 1997 Director of the Visual Arts Divison of the Boston University School for the Arts, first met the Sterns in 1971 through Isabelle Evans when she was married to Walker. He recalls the repeated seasonal vists to Hatch Manor, which began in 1972 and ended twenty-two years later. In the Sterns' visitors' book he was the most frequent visitor to Hatch of all their friends.

> I remember vividly the afternoon when I arrived for the first time at Tisbury [the nearest railway station]. I was with Isabelle, and Jimmy met us on the platform. At first he seemed to regard me with suspicion, and then with a twinkle in his eyes he seized me by my beard, which was his way of showing approval. This was the first of many visits to Hatch Manor, a house I would come to know almost as well as my own. Seeing in the New Year there became a ritual.
>
> They were both attached to ritual, and any variation, even when it involved the time of a train arrival, was something to be avoided. Once I suggested that I should come for Christmas instead of the New Year. 'Well, if you must,' was Jimmy's icy reply, and I never mentioned the subject again.
>
> On New Year's eve, according to custom, I would have lunch with an old friend in London and afterwards trudge across Waterloo Bridge, heavy suitcase in hand, just in time to catch the Exeter train at 3.10. Both Jimmy and Tania would meet me around 5 at Tisbury station. I can see Jimmy now anxiously pacing the platform; on one occasion I had forgotten to get off the train in time.
>
> Dinner was served in the kitchen, and on New Year's eve the fare was always pheasant and red cabbage. Tania would be cooking below, while Jimmy and I would sit with our drinks before the fire in the living room. Convinced that Southerners preferred only Bourbon, he kept a special supply for me and insisted upon that being my drink. I never had the heart to tell him how much I envied his Scotch. I would probe him about his past, and often the names of their friends would form the core of the conversation: W. H. Auden, Cyril Connolly, Berenice Abbott, Harold Acton, Walker Evans and Alexander Calder. He would also reminisce about such subjects as his Irish upbringing, his Jewish heritage and Ernest Hemingway's brutality towards one of their friends in a Paris bar. Eventually Tania would send a summons for dinner, which, to her annoyance, neither of us would ever seem to hear. After dinner, Jimmy would inspect my plate for any remaining food and, should a morsel be discovered, he would proclaim that I had obviously 'never lived through a war'. Tania would then

whisper to me: 'Neither has Jimmy.' He and I would then proceed to that rarely used dining room next to the kitchen to pay homage to the portrait of his sensuous, long-deceased ancestor. Jimmy would usually kiss her on the lips. [The portrait was of his great-great-great-grandmother, Charlotte Pfeiffer (1786–1812).]

After dinner, there would still be three hours until midnight, and it would be announced that we should retire early and sleep in the New Year. Without fail though, they would keep me up until the end. Once, Jimmy, after having imbibed heavily, danced a furious Irish jig until he collapsed. That was the night I carried him up to bed; I was surprised how light he was. The next morning he spent sequestered in his study avoiding Tania's wrath.

In the afternoon of New Year's Day, sometimes even in raw weather, Jimmy and I would take a long walk, always following a circular path that would eventually bring us back to the house. Often he would gather wild mushrooms and, although he tried to persuade me that he could distinguish between ones which were edible and those which were lethal, I remained convinced that he would find the 'fool's mushroom' and that my life would end at Hatch. During the part of the afternoon when the Sterns were napping, I would explore the bookcases, where I would inevitably discover previously unknown volumes. Jimmy would have prepared a stack of books in advance for me to examine, and upon my return to London I would usually buy them.

I relished the smells of Hatch, especially those of the hearth; I seemed to be forever fixing the fire screen, a ritual I anticipated with pleasure, along with bringing in the firewood from the garage and preparing the fire, a practice which without fail Jimmy would correct. Also, I loved the silence of the place – there was ample room for everyone to have their own corner. And never have I slept so soundly as during those nights in the cold top bedroom with the crackling old heater.

I would depart for London after lunch on 2 January. Jimmy would have the car waiting in advance at the front door. Usually we had enjoyed a long lunch and had to rush to the station. As Jimmy would roar along the narrow lanes, Tania and I would sit on the back seat clasping each other's hands in terror. Once, a neighbour's herd of cows was blocking the road. With protruding chin, he drove right through them, prompting one to leap and hoof its way over the bonnet of the car. Chuckling, Jimmy commented as he drove on: 'Shook that milk up, didn't I?' He later confessed that the farmer was less than amused.

I have been fortunate in my life to have had great individuals to inspire me and believe in me. Jimmy and Tania were among the most important and provide so many memories that it would take volumes to relate them. How far away those days at Hatch now seem, those golden times that helped to form the core of my artistic and spiritual existence! Early on, Jimmy gave me a book of his short stories in which he wrote: 'With Great Expectations for a Dickens of a Good Life.' With each visit my life was indeed enriched beyond any expectations.

Another instance of Jimmy's atrocious driving is provided by John Byrne in a letter of 31 January 1986 to Anthony and Tanya Hobson:

The journey back to Hatch Manor was terrifying, rather like being Jehu's passenger. Jimmy can't see too well at the best of times and I'm sure he shouldn't be allowed to drive. Driving directly into a low sun, he simply yells with anger and puts his foot down. Wouldn't stop and let me take over (people never believe that you can drive if you don't have a car), wouldn't stop and let me get out and walk, however many miles it might take ... Tania sat blithely confident throughout, and we survived.

In fact, his driving days, feared by many, finally came to a close in June 1989 when he and Tania careered into the back of a lorry on a roundabout entering Salisbury. Nobody was hurt but the police waived any prosecution on the condition he drove no longer. They both felt the deprivation severely, and for the rest of their lives were dependent on friends and neighbours and – much resented – taxis for transportation of any kind.

John Byrne remembers that

in the latter 1980s Hatch Manor became less fraught. Some of Jimmy's angry fire had gone out – which was sad in a way, but meant that the dining-table was less like the battlefield of Culloden. Now T could rattle on without J's furious interruptions. I was allowed to do the washing-up on my own and, with T taking a rest after lunch, to enjoy solitary walks. (They remained solitary. I still felt quite jealously guarded and would not drop in upon the

Sampsons or the Stones.) For J the high points of my visits, almost the reason I was asked, were our grand games of six-pack bezique, which I'd learned by sitting at T's shoulder. For 50 years or more she'd been an infuriating opponent, because she would feel sorry for J when she was leading and not try to win. She was happy to be relieved of playing, I to join battle; it was not through my sympathy that he achieved one evening his highest ever score, only wishing that his beloved Prince's Gate grandmother could see it.

For years J had indicated, not over-subtly, that I was his discovery, his friend. But now I spent much more time with T. She was the one who felt isolated, who craved dialogue, whose curiosity knew no bounds – rather like the jealously guarded and ever growing mountains of newspapers that she intended eventually to read. We would laugh as I tried to follow, or escape from, the labyrinthine twists of her conversation, and if sometimes she probed a little harshly, I think she probed with love.

Despite six years of disappointment, 1990 was the year that the British reading public could at last appreciate *The Hidden Damage*. Sean Wyse Jackson, of John Sandoe's Chelsea bookshop, published Jimmy's long-neglected book, with an introduction by Stephen Spender, under the imprint of The Chelsea Press. Jimmy dedicated the book 'To the memory of "Reggie" Stern, killed in action Swansea. Feb.21, 1941'. On the same date forty-nine years later the Sterns held a small party to celebrate publication in Durley House, Sloane Street, in one of the apartments they habitually rented on their London visits. Stephen Spender, Diana Petre, Anne Chisholm, Michael Davie, John Byrne, and Sean Wyse Jackson and his partner at the Chelsea Press, Bernard McGinley, were among those present. It was noticed that Stephen Spender was in an uncommunicative mood. When he had sent his introduction to Jimmy, it was found to be somewhat slapdash and ungrammatical. 'I'm afraid SS will get a bit of a shock when he sees the amount of "editing" that's been done to those few pages!' Jimmy wrote to Jackson.

By chance the book appeared within months of the fall of the Berlin Wall (9 November 1989), which no doubt accounted for some of the publicity it received. As the reissue of a book first published in 1947, albeit in the USA, it was widely reviewed. David Pryce-Jones in the London *Evening Standard* declared that its 'impact here is all the stronger for the delay'. Stern, he wrote, was 'a writer of unusual power with a magically simple style'. Julian Symons in the *Sunday Times* wrote that it 'must be called a period piece, but one that has gained poignancy and depth with the years'. Anthony Curtis in the *Financial Times* rightly reported that 'Stern, now in his eighties, is the least famous of the writers in the Auden circle, but one of the most highly regarded in that circle ... Stern's skill at a kind of reflective reportage really comes into its own ... Its impact now in Britain is likely to be as great as when it first appeared in 1947.' Paul Binding in the *Listener* found 'James Stern's account ... extraordinarily powerful. Though cast in the form of a travelogue, the book depends for its success less on the appeal to the eye than to the ear. There is a kind of *montage* of dialogue, his remarkable sense for which shows that James Stern's is essentially a novelist's mind, fascinated by the discrepancies between appearances and what lies below them.'

Jimmy's own judgement on *The Hidden Damage* was characteristically terse and self-critical: 'A self-indulgent hotch-potch ... But the personal technique was my only hope. I'm not a journalist.'

Jackson's enthusiasm and his belief in Jimmy's writing encouraged him to think of publishing a selection of the stories and the problematical memoirs. He even commissioned William Boyd to write an introduction to the former, quoted on p. 237. For the next four years he attempted to persuade publishers that a selection of Jimmy's stories was a desirable and viable proposition. But Tom Rosenthal's letter, an exemplary publisher's rejection, from André Deutsch in January 1994, after Jimmy's death, finally persuaded him to abandon his quest:

> ... four of us have read or in two cases, re-read the collection, and we are, alas, unanimous in our view. It is a classic and well-chosen collection, of that there is no doubt. It shows this lovely writer at his best, and we all thoroughly enjoyed ourselves, but what we absolutely cannot see in this horrendous time for fiction publishing is a half way decent market for any book which does not instantly strike the correct note of high fashion (eg Will Self etc) ... I find this heartbreaking, but I can't single-handedly turn the tide ...

The sales of *The Hidden Damage* were modest and The Chelsea Press barely broke even on their investment. Jimmy, who throughout his life had armoured himself against disappointment, was resigned to the failure of these prolonged and persistent attempts to publish his memoirs, the intractable task he had worked on for so long.

Anne Chisholm, the biographer of Nancy Cunard, Rumer Godden, and, with her husband Michael Davie, Lord Beaverbrook, remembers her first meeting with the Sterns and in the following pages describes the course of her close friendship with them:

When I first met Jimmy and Tania, through Nora Sayre, in the early seventies, they were still quite dazzling and remained so, to me, for about ten years. My strongest recollection is of that first impact, when the falling-in-love-stage of a friendship happens. I think that even then I loved them equally, as I continued to do, although Jimmy of course made all the running, wrote the letters, initiated dates and weekends and meetings and was always subtly flirtatious, even amorous, though nothing more than a lingering hug or gentle kiss ever took place. He would talk freely about his 'queer period' and I certainly felt sure he had had affairs with men, notably Brian Howard, and also with other women – always long in the past, like Ethel Mannin.

The Sterns both looked wonderful: Jimmy in his tweeds, never a dark suit, as I recall, but good tweeds in soft country colours, with shirts and ties to match and always very well barbered, and Tania very trim in navy blue with touches of red and green, never the county lady, always a hint of Berlin or Paris there somewhere. Delicious food and drink were invariably produced, and I recall the sense of endless conversations waiting to be enjoyed, with both of them instinctively generous about who they knew and marvelling at how much *one* knew, and who, which was no one by comparison. Jimmy and I would meet at the Ritz Bar, or have lunch at Wheelers in Soho or Bentleys off Piccadilly. They made me feel part of their magic circle, as if I'd known Wystan Auden and Brian Howard and Patrick White. He actually introduced me to Beckett, who had known Nancy Cunard well.

Even early on I knew – or sensed – as with most sudden loves there would be a falling away or a change of cast in due course, but it happened gradually and the first glow never altogether faded. Because I lived in Australia from 1977 to '82 there was a natural break, though I recall staying at Hatch soon after my Nancy Cunard book was published in 1979 and very little had changed. We sat in the garden among the roses and read my reviews. Even though they liked Michael a lot, it was always somehow easier to be there on my own, trotting between the two of them, drinking a bottle of wine with Jimmy upstairs and then going down to help Tania in the kitchen. I don't remember the rows being so bad then, though there was always a slightly competitive feeling ...

The scene had darkened somewhat by the mid-eighties. Their trips to London seemed more anxious, arrangements trickier, the need to make sure that Jimmy didn't drink too much at lunch more urgent. While Sunday night drinks at their rented Durley House apartment in Sloane Street became a regular event, visits to Hatch continued, but were not quite so much of a treat, as the rows grew angrier. Jimmy would complain upstairs about how Tania made his life difficult and poor Tania would grumble downstairs – usually about lack of communication and understanding – and I would try not to betray either of them, in the hope that matters weren't as bad as they seemed and that the rows were a performance put on in response to a visitor, and that peace would eventually reign when they were alone again ... but maybe not. I certainly assumed that they were *au fond* deeply devoted, that the mystery of all long marriages was just a bit odder than usual with them.

It became really sad when Jimmy started to be seriously withdrawn, wanting not to talk but to watch television, and could only be roused or cheered rather briefly, and to drink a bottle of wine together was no longer a good idea, and watching either of them negotiate the stairs to the kitchen was nerve-racking ... which reminds me of the most nerve-racking aspect of all, the driving ...

Once, at Jimmy's suggestion, I met them for lunch in an Italian restaurant in Salisbury. He drove us home after at least two bottles of wine between us. It was horrific! Swinging around blind corners with a mad cackle, and the more Tania and I tried to slow him down the faster and wilder he became – a real torture or tease or even deathwish performance, which made me quite angry. After that, Tania and I used to have regular driving conversations; I hadn't yet passed my test, which I only did when I was over forty, and she used to urge me to do so and to say she wished she had, and I would say well you still can, and she would insist that Jimmy would never let her, that he had to be in the driving seat in every sense and couldn't imagine that she would ever be competent enough to drive, and I recall feeling cross on her behalf. When I did pass my test, she was really pleased for me.

With Tania, I realise looking back, talk was at least as much about oneself as about her. With Jimmy, it was much more a matter of triggering his memory and enjoying him talking about himself, writing, and his friendships with writers. As a biographer myself, I used occasionally to feel uneasy about his tirades against 'brainpickers', until I came to see that actually he enjoyed being consulted, that being a source had become, like letter-writing, a substitute for writing, so that he was a part of other people's books instead of getting on with his own. I do remember thinking even then how hard it was for Tania to have the theory, which she certainly did, that by making him happy she had undermined his need to write. But now we know that they were often exceedingly unhappy, and still no great works appeared, so ... He was incredibly dependent on her, for good or ill – I remember his habitual call to her: *Bist du da*? Are you there? – and I guess vice versa, although some part of her continued to struggle to assert herself.

When I think of Hatch I remember the greenish golden light inside the house, the punctiliously arranged books each with their enclosure of a letter or review, the garden in its heyday, especially the roses and Tania's herb patch, and Jimmy across the lane tending his artichokes and asparagus. I remember once saying to Jimmy, to please him, that 'of course Hatch is the centre of the universe', and in a way it was not just for them, but for their friends, almost till the end.

12
Dying Fall
1990–1995

Tania was to pass her last five years on the planet in better shape than her husband. 'J seemed to be retreating into memories of earlier times, pre-Tania times,' John Byrne has written. 'This was surely frustrating for her – there was unfinished business in the air – but not painful or unhappy for him.'

To many who visited them, he appeared petulant and often mute; 'Jimmy was very selfish and self-absorbed and, unlike Tania, not interested in the lives of others' was the judgement of Anthony Sampson, who had known him since the early '6os. This contrasts poignantly with the way Nora Sayre remembers Jimmy in the late '5os, when he would enjoy 'sitting in a glitzy pub in Sloane Square, keenly watching the youngish people there. What a tremendous interest he took in others, including strangers! I remember a real thrill when I first met him at dinner. Maybe it – Jimmy's magic – was partly the way he listened: intense, totally focused on the other person.'

He still liked to gossip, especially about his closest neighbours, Charles Wintour and Audrey Slaughter, in the 'Slaughterhouse' next door, to discuss the relative merits of Freud, Jung and Adler (the Sterns favoured the latter), to reminisce about J. C. Squire and *The London Mercury* (how he'd had to look after Mrs Thomas Hardy and Ezra Pound while Squire was drinking), to speak fondly of Wystan Auden who, he said, was the loneliest man he'd ever known (Auden used to hug himself in bed, for the lack of another to do so; Chester Kallman provided physical love but never real understanding), to converse about writers and drink and whether alcohol engendered creativity.

On the other hand, full of insights, Tania, who relished Sampson's company, would talk vigorously about hoarding newspapers, the fear of death, Christianity, humility and her own indecisiveness, and about life and politics. ('Jimmy couldn't bear Tania talking about politics and world affairs; each was uninterested in the other's subjects,' Sybille Bedford has remarked). Although Tania claimed that she still did not know who she was, she didn't worry about not fitting in; what she was really frightened of was the chaos inside herself, an echo of a remark in her letter to Jimmy's lover, Joan Lewisohn, in 1944: 'I seem to need the clarity about some essential things in my life – a clarity which I have to pursue and protect at all costs.'

She and Sampson would talk about Kafka's masochism and his need to write, and about psychoanalysis, which, she said, would have stopped him writing. She said that she once tried to have Jimmy psychoanalysed but the analyst assured her that he wouldn't be able to take it, his child-hood was so unloved, so fragile. And they agreed about the importance of friendship, which Sampson told her was their genius. Her humour, too, proved itself as sharp as ever: when the Sterns visited the Wintours for dinner one night, Audrey opened the door in a flowing white gown. 'How brave of you to wear your nightdress' was Tania's opening remark.

By the end of 1990 the Sterns' memories were fast disappearing, a state which made for a certain serenity, especially in Jimmy. In January 1991 he wrote to his 'Dearest Squif': 'Life here has changed completely since our car accident, & the loss of a car. Ever since then I have been a prisoner in my own home! For one in his 87th year I suppose I am as well as can be expected! Apart, perhaps I should add, from the perma-nent pain above my shingled eye. Reading and writing grow increas-ingly difficult. But I really shouldn't complain: at least I am not alone! Life without T wouldn't be worth living.' It was a sincere tribute to 'the woman who was loved' – alas, probably unaddressed to her – and to their long years together.

'Great age was treating him quite kindly'(John Byrne again) 'until he broke a hip and was confined to a grim hospital outside Salisbury. Visiting with T was complicated and a miserable experience, but his need of her was very palpable and his incomprehension at being told he must stay wrung the heart.'

In April 1993 Jimmy's final decline began with three falls at Hatch, one on those perfidious stairs, the second on the path to the garage and, within days of the latter, another in his wood-panelled study. For weeks he was confined to the hospital at Odstock where he was visited almost daily by Tania, driven there by generous friends. Often his bed in a public ward could be found surrounded by well-wishers, usually a loquacious group, while Jimmy lay back invariably silent.

By August he was attending the outpatients department, while at home he took to his bed in the room next to his study where he lay for three months until his death. John Byrne last saw him when I responded (too slowly she thought) to an impatient summons from T: some books had met with a watery mishap. No sign of T, doubtless shopping. I let myself in and found J in his study, gently beaming. There was something in the paper about Lucian Freud and he knew that he knew Freud, in small verbal circles. Then I asked him about the cat. No, it wasn't still visiting, it had moved in, and often sat just there on that table. He was tired and this was enough. When T appeared with her reproaches I said I'd seen J and enjoyed a little chat. 'He spoke to you?' she asked. Yes, I said blithely, describing Freud and Pussy, not knowing that he had already stopped speaking to her.

Anne and Harold Cross attended Jimmy and Tania devotedly during their decrepitude. Eventually, the situation required round-the-clock nursing, a service provided by the Leonard Cheshire Foundation. Tender, loving care is a cliché which they personified.

Jimmy breathed his last during the night of 22 November 1993. His cremation took place at Salisbury's London Road Cemetery. Gill Stern, Peter's wife, and Wenzel Geissler, Tania's great-nephew, sat either side of the grieving widow, holding her hands. The grim occasion, accentuated by Tania's insistence on no pomp, circumstance, flowers or music – described by Humphrey Stone as 'an apology for a service' – was attended by Sally and Anthony Sampson, Michael and Anne Davie, Lila Duckworth, Chantal and Michael Stokely, and Jimmy's surviving brother, Peter, whose son, Simon, read W. H. Auden's poem, 'Thank you, Fog.'

At J's cremation, which some callous coincidence caused to fall on my birthday [John Byrne recalls], T looked like a tiny broken bird. I could feel her misery and confusion, her bitterness. But through the good sense and warmth of Chantal Stokely [who lived in Salisbury] and Gill Stern my duties as executor – physically removing bequeathed papers from the house – were made smoothly possible. Several letters were exchanged (although T was justly famed for never writing), warmth and understanding were renewed. It is still rather shattering to find in her last letter, 16 December 1994: 'I will be always at your service.'

Perhaps I should not have been so surprised when I visited her four months later, alerted by Gill that the end was near. T was 91 and she was worn out by trying to make sense of everything; she had taken to her bed and stopped eating. She looked magnificent, the skin drawn tight over the beautiful cheekbones, like some medieval effigy, flat and straight and proud. There were nurses in the room and there was nothing to say, so I took her hand in mine and hummed something under my breath a little like purring, I was sure she could feel the rhythm. After a few minutes of this I bent forward, kissed her forehead and made as if to leave, when her other little hand sought my other hand and she briefly pressed both of them to her shrunken chest. Her blessing. She died two days later.

Tania died in the evening of 17 April 1995. Chantal Stokely and Sue Millard, from Family Support, were with her. Her cremation, also in Salisbury's cemetery, was attended by many of the Sterns' friends. Wenzel Geissler, who was accompanied by his wife, Ingaborg, read a poem of Rilke's, and Jimmy's niece, Ginny Green, Tania's god-daughter, read from T. S. Eliot's 'East Coker': 'Home is where one starts from. As we grow older/ The world becomes stranger, the pattern more complicated ... ' concluding with 'In my end is my beginning.' It was certainly an event with a more positive air than was apparent at Jimmy's departure. The feeling that with Tania's going an epoch had been reached, an extraordinary chapter – indeed a whole volume – of unique quality had closed forever, was all-pervasive.

Two occasions marked the finale of the Sterns' existence: the burial of their ashes on 12 May 1995 alongside Harry, Connie, Reggie and Rose in Henstridge Church and, a day later, a wake on the lawn at Hatch Manor, hosted by Gill and Peter Stern, at which twenty-five or so family and friends enjoyed a celebration of Jimmy's and Tania's lives. At the former private ceremony, accompanied by Gill and Peter, Chantal Stokely at the graveside read this poem by William Penn (1644–1718):

> They that love beyond the world,
> Cannot be separated by it.
> Nor can spirits ever be divided,
> That love and live in the same divine principle,
> The root and record of their friendship.
> If absence be not death, neither is theirs.
> As friends do, crossing the sea,
> They live in one another still.

In this divine glass they see face to face,
And their converse is free.
This is the comfort of friends,
That though they may be said to die,
Yet their friendships and society are ever present
Because immortal.

Jimmy must be allowed the last word. The following is a draft of an obituary written by himself in 1960:

James Stern was an Irish short-story writer who suffered that ultimate failure of nerves which many writers experience and which sometimes leads to suicide. Fortunately Mr Stern married a woman (Tania Kurella, with whom he translated many books from the German into English) who saved him from himself.

The Man Who Was Loved, his third and last collection of stories, reveals him as an uneven but meticulous anatomist of suffering, the suffering of both children and adults and of failure in a world of wealth, vanity, insensitivity and, above all, lack of affection and love.

On the evidence of this book, Stern was a considerable writer of wide, intense, and true perceptions, but who seldom fictionalized a situation. He is to be judged by the highest standards; but his art remains a probing of wounds and somehow, lacking as it is in power of invention and ultimate detachment, fails to achieve its own release from pain.

Publications

FICTION (SHORT STORIES)

The Heartless Land, London, Macmillan; New York, Macmillan, 1932
Something Wrong, London, Secker & Warburg, 1938
The Man Who Was Loved, London, Secker & Warburg, 1952; New York, Harcourt Brace, 1951
The Stories of James Stern, London, Secker & Warburg, 1968; New York, Harcourt Brace, 1969

UNCOLLECTED SHORT STORIES

'The Dunce', *The London Mercury*, July 1931
'Stranger Defeated', *The London Mercury*, August 1933
'The Man from Montparnasse', *Penguin Parade 1*, London, Penguin, 1937
'The Thief', New *Statesman and Nation*, (London), September 1940
'The Young Lady', *Penguin Parade 7*, London, Penguin, 1940
'The Ebbing Tide', *Penguin New Writing*, London, Penguin, 1942
'The Pauper's Grave', *Harper's Bazaar 9*, (New York), 1946
'A Day at the Races', *Dublin Magazine*, Winter 1970–71
'Allergies', *London Magazine*, June 1970
'Bloody Monday', *London Magazine*, June–July 1972
'The Facts of Life', *Winter's Tales 23*, London, Macmillan, 1977; New York, St Martin's Press, 1978
'The Terrier's Treat', *Irish Press* (Dublin), February 1979

PLAYS

The Caucasian Chalk Circle, with W. H. Auden and Tania Stern, adaptation of the play by Bertolt Brecht (produced London, 1962); *Plays*, London, Methuen, 1960
Sons of England, a play for radio broadcast by BBC, 9 January 1970

NON-FICTION

The Hidden Damage, London, Chelsea Press, 1990; New York, Harcourt Brace, 1947

TRANSLATIONS

Grimm's Fairy Tales (also editor), London, Routledge, 1948; New York, Pantheon, 1944

The Complete Grimm's Fairy Tales (also editor), London, Routledge, 1975; New York, Pantheon, 1974

Over a period of thirty-two years, alone or with E. B. Ashton, Tania Stern or Elisabeth Duckworth, James Stern translated the following:

Brazil: Land of the Future by Stefan Zweig

Amerigo: A Comedy of Errors in History by Stefan Zweig

The Rise and Fall of the House of Ullstein by Herman Ullstein

The Twins of Nuremberg by Hermann Kesten

Spark of Life by Erich Maria Remarque

Selected Writings by Hugo von Hofmannsthal

Letters to Milena by Franz Kafka

Letters to Felice by Franz Kafka

Description of a Struggle and Other Stories by Franz Kafka

A Woman in Berlin by Anonymous

Casanova's Memoirs by Jacques Casanova de Seingalt

The Foreign Minister by Leo Lania

Letters of Sigmund Freud 1873–1939

Index

'A great joy to get one of your famous letters . . . If I survive you,
I'm going to edit your letters.'
W. H. AUDEN

'You are entirely the best letter writer living, and if you had lived in
the nineteenth century you would be collected in two volumes –
perhaps you will anyway.'
VAN WYCK BROOKS

'If you had never written anything else, your letters would
reveal you as the artist that you are.'
JOHN HALL WHEELOCK

'Stern's wealth of subject matter is astonishing. He can write
with equal power about horses, old ladies, poisonous snakes,
English drawing-rooms, South Sea islands, fishermen, governesses,
little girls. He is equally at home when describing complicated
mental processes and scenes of violent action. He seems to have
no formula, no pattern; each story is a fresh surprise. If the
English could recognize genuine, solid talent, undecorated by the
tricks which make for notoriety, Stern's name would be
famous in England today.'
W. H. AUDEN AND CHRISTOPHER ISHERWOOD

'Like Somerset Maugham he [James Stern] could make you see
persons and places in primitive isolation, but he penetrated the
loneliness and frustration of individuals more deeply than Maugham,
without that slick artifice which makes you exclaim
"How clever" and forget them.'
HAROLD ACTON

'"The Broken Leg" is one of the best stories of its kind
since Lawrence. In any collection of English stories in the
last twenty years it would have a high place.'
V. S. PRITCHETT